Dana Facaros and
Michael Pauls

ROME VENICE FLORENCE

'The prima donna, dripping splendour,
the agate-eyed goddess of the sea and
the proud, clear-eyed genius...if this is
your first visit, we can only envy you.'

CADOGANguides

Contents

Reference

About the authors

Dana Facaros and **Michael Pauls** have written over 30 books for Cadogan Guides, including all the Italy series. For three years they lived in a tiny Umbrian hilltop village, where they suffered massive overdoses of food, art and wine, and enjoyed every minute of it. They have since lived all over Europe, but have recently moved to a farmhouse surrounded by vineyards in the Lot Valley.

About the updaters

Trained as a professional musician, **Nicky Swallow** (Florence and Venice) has lived in Italy for 20 years. During that time, her enthusiasm for all things Italian has led to an in-depth knowledge of the country.

Mary-Ann Gallagher (Rome) has written and updated more than a dozen titles for Cadogan guides, and writes regularly for other travel publishers and magazines.

Cadogan Guides
Highlands House, 165 The Broadway,
London SW19 1NE
info.cadogan@virgin.net
www.cadoganguides.com

The Globe Pequot Press
246 Goose Lane, PO Box 480, Guilford,
Connecticut 06437–0480

Copyright © Dana Facaros and Michael Pauls
  1997, 1999, 2001, 2003

Cover and photo essay design by Kicca Tommasi
Book design by Andrew Barker
Cover photographs: Kicca Tommasi, OLIVIA and
  John Ferro Sims (front); John Ferro Sims (back)
Maps © Cadogan Guides,
  drawn by Map Creation Ltd
Managing Editor: Christine Stroyan
Editor: Linda McQueen
Art Direction: Sarah Rianhard-Gardner
Indexing: Isobel McLean
Production: Navigator Guides Ltd

Printed in Spain by Mateu Cromo
A catalogue record for this book is available
  from the British Library
ISBN 1-86011-899-2

Sulla (the Senate's darling in the army), and by an offer to extend Roman citizenship to all Italians. A military coup by Sulla followed, with the backing of the Senate. An effective dictatorship was created, and all opponents either murdered or exiled. Italy careened into anarchy, with many rural districts reverting to bandit-ridden wastelands, a setting for the remarkable revolt in 73 BC of **Spartacus**, an escaped gladiator who led a motley army of dispossessed farmers and runaway slaves – some 70,000 of them – back and forth across the south until the legions finally defeated him in 71 BC.

All this had exhausted both sides, and finally discredited senatorial rule. After Sulla's death, no one minded when the consulship and real power passed to **Pompey**, another successful general but one who cared little for politics. Like Sulla before him, Pompey soon set out for the east, where the most glory and booty were to be gained, and his departure left the stage in Rome open to 33-year-old **Julius Caesar**, a tremendously clever soldier-politician, but a good man anyhow. With his two surpassing talents, one for rhetoric and the other for attracting money, he took up the popular cause in better style than anyone had done it before. A taint of connection to the **Catiline conspiracy** of 68 BC (a revolt of adventurers, disaffected nobles and other loose ends) proved a temporary setback, just as it advanced the fortunes of **Marcus Tullius Cicero**, the great orator, writer and statesman who still dreamed of founding a real republic with a real constitution, opposing both extreme parties and pinning his hopes on the still-surviving Italian middle class. Few people in Rome cared for such principles, however, and after Pompey returned from bashing the Pontic Kingdom and the Cilician pirates, he, Caesar, and a wealthy building contractor named Licinius Crassus sliced up the republic between them, forming the **First Triumvirate** in 59 BC.

What Caesar really wanted, of course, was a military command. Following the accepted practice, he managed to buy himself one in the north, and undertook the conquest of most of Gaul, with well-known results. In his four years as ruler of Rome, Caesar surprised everyone, even his enemies; everything received a good dose of reform, even the calendar, and a beginning was made towards sorting out the economic mess and getting Italy back on its feet. His assassination by a clique of Republican bitter-enders in 44 BC plunged Italy into civil war again, and left historians to ponder the grand question of whether Caesar had really intended to make himself a king and finally put the now senile Republic to sleep. A **Second Triumvirate** was formed, of Caesar's adopted son Octavian, a senatorial figurehead named Lepidus, and Caesar's old friend and right-hand man, a talented, dissipated fellow named Marcus Antonius (Mark Antony), who according to one historian spent the equivalent of $3 billion (of other people's money) in his brief lifetime. While he dallied in the east with Cleopatra, Octavian was consolidating his power in Italy. The inevitable battle came in 31 BC, at Actium in Greece, and it was a complete victory for Octavian.

31 BC–AD 251: The Empire

With unchallenged authority through all the Roman lands, Octavian (soon to rename himself **Augustus**) was free to complete the reforms initiated by Caesar. For his career, and those of his successors, you may read the gossipy, shocking, and wonderfully unreliable *Lives of the Caesars* of Suetonius. All Rome tittered at the scandals of the later Julian emperors, but reality was usually much more prosaic. **Tiberius** (AD 14–37) may have been a monster to his girlfriends and boyfriends, but he proved an intelligent and just ruler otherwise; his criminally insane successor **Caligula**, or 'Bootkin', lasted only four years (37–41) while the bureaucracy kept things going. **Claudius** (41–54) governed well and conquered southern Britain, while his stepson **Nero** (54–68) generally made a nuisance of himself in Rome but did little to disturb the system. Nevertheless, a commmander in Spain (Galba) declared him unfit to be emperor and marched on Rome to take his place; Nero just managed to commit suicide before they caught him. Now the genie was out of the bottle again, as the soldiers once more realized that the real power lay with them. Another general, Otho, commander of the emperor's Praetorian Guard, toppled Galba, and soon lost out in turn to Vitellius, commander on the Rhine. The fourth emperor of the fateful years AD 68–69 was **Vespasian**, leader of the eastern armies. He had the strongest legions and so got to keep the job; his reign (69–79) and those of his sons **Titus** (79–81) and **Domitian** (81–96), the three Flavian emperors, were remembered as a period of prosperity. Vespasian began the Colosseum; whether intentionally or not, this incomparable new charnel house made a perfect symbol for the renewed decadence and militarization of the state.

For the moment, however, things looked rosy. After the assassination of Domitian, another bad boy but not an especially calamitous ruler, Rome had the good fortune to be ruled by a series of high-minded and intelligent military men, who carefully chose their successors in advance to avoid civil war. The so-called **Antonine emperors** presided over the greatest age of prosperity the Mediterranean world ever knew; in Italy they ran a surprisingly modern state (though one still based on slave labour) that would seem familiar to us today: public libraries, water boards to maintain the aqueducts, rent control, agricultural price supports, low-cost loans for starting new businesses and many other such innovations. The first of the Antonines was **Nerva** (96–98), followed by **Trajan** (98–117) and **Hadrian** (117–138), both great soldiers and builders on a monumental scale, especially in Rome; after them came **Antoninus Pius** (138–61), little known only because his reign was so peaceful, and **Marcus Aurelius** (161–80), soldier, statesman, and Stoic philosopher. His choice for successor was his useless son **Commodus** (180–93) and the string of good emperors was broken.

The 2nd-century prosperity was not without its darker side. The arts were in serious decline, as if the imagination of the Greco-Roman Mediterranean was somehow failing. Education was in poor shape, and every sort of fatuous mysticism imported from the East permeated the minds of the people. Economically, this period saw the emergence of the well-known north–south split in Italy.

251–475: Decline and Fall

For all it cost to maintain them, the legions were no longer the formidable military machine of Augustus' day. They were bureaucratic and a little tired, and their tactics and equipment were also falling behind those of the Persians and even some of the more clever German barbarians. The Goths were the first to demonstrate this, in 251, when they overran the Balkans, Greece, and Asia Minor. Five years later Franks and

Alemanni invaded Gaul, and in 268 much of the east detached itself from the empire under the leadership of Odenathus of Palmyra. Somehow the empire recovered and prevailed, under dour soldier-emperors like **Aurelian** (270–5), who built Rome's walls, and **Diocletian** (284–305), who completely revamped the structure of the state and economy. His fiscal reforms, such as the fixing of prices and a decree that every son had to follow the trade of his father, ossified the economy and made the creeping decline of Italy and all western Europe harder to arrest.

More than ever, the Empire had become an outright military dictatorship, in a society whose waning energies were entirely devoted to supporting a bloated, all-devouring army and bureaucracy. The confused politics of the 4th century are dominated by **Constantine** (306–37), who ruled both halves of the Empire, defeated various other contenders (Battle of the Milvian Bridge, outside Rome, in 312), and founded the new eastern capital of Constantinople. He adroitly moved to increase his and the Empire's political support by favouring Christianity. Though still a small minority in most of the Empire, the Christians' strong organization and determination made them a good bet for the future.

The military disasters began in 406, with Visigoths, Franks, Vandals, Alans and Suevi overrunning Gaul and Spain. Italy's turn came in 408, when Western Emperor Honorius, ruling from the new capital of Ravenna, had his brilliant general Stilicho (who himself happened to be a Vandal) murdered. A Visigothic invasion followed, leading to Alaric's sack of Rome in 410. St Augustine, probably echoing the thoughts of most Romans, wrote that it seemed the end of the world must be near. Rome should have been so lucky; judgement was postponed long enough for **Attila the Hun** to pass through Italy in 451. Then Gaiseric the Vandal, who had set up a pirate kingdom in Africa, raided Italy and sacked Rome again in 455. So completely had things changed, it was scarcely possible to tell the Romans from the barbarians. By the 470s, the real ruler in Italy was a Gothic general named **Odoacer**, who led a half-Romanized Germanic army and probably thought of himself as the genuine heir of the Caesars. In 476, he decided to dispense with the lingering charade of the Western Empire. The last emperor, young, silly Romulus Augustulus, was packed off to premature retirement in Naples, and Odoacer had himself crowned King of Italy at Pavia.

475–1000: The Dark Ages

At the beginning, the new Gothic-Latin state showed some promise. Certainly the average man was no worse off than he had been under the last emperors; trade and cities even revived a bit. In 493, Odoacer was replaced (and murdered) by a rival Ostrogoth, **Theodoric**, working on behalf of the Eastern emperor at Byzantium.

A disaster as serious as those of the 5th century began in 536, with the invasion of Italy by the Eastern Empire, part of the relentlessly expansionist policy of the great **Justinian**. The historical irony was profound; in the ancient homeland of the Roman Empire, Roman troops now came not as liberators, but foreign, largely Greek-speaking conquerors. Justinian's brilliant generals, Belisarius and Narses, ultimately prevailed over the Goths in a series of terrible wars that lasted until 563, but the damage to an already stricken society and economy was incalculable. Italy's total exhaustion was exposed only five years later, when the **Lombards**, a Germanic tribe who worked hard to earn the title of barbarian, overran northern Italy and parts of the south, establishing a kingdom at Pavia and separate duchies in Benevento and Spoleto. A new pattern of power appeared, with semi-independent Byzantine dukes defending many coastal areas, the Byzantine Exarchs of Ravenna controlling considerable territory on the Adriatic and in Calabria, and Lombard chiefs ruling most of the interior. The popes in Rome became a force during this period, especially after the papacy of the clever, determined **Gregory the Great** (590–604). Scion of the richest family in Italy, Gregory took political control in Rome during desperate times, and laid the foundations for the papacy's claims to temporal power.

With trade and culture at their lowest ebb, the 7th century marks the rock bottom of Italian history. The 8th showed some improvement; while most of the peninsula lay in feudal darkness, **Venice** was beginning its remarkable career as a trading city, and independent Amalfi and Naples emulated its success on the Tyrrhenian coast. The popes, along with other bishops who had taken advantage of the confused times to become temporal powers, intrigued everywhere to increase their influence; they finally cashed in with a Frankish alliance in the 750s. At the time the Lombard kings were doing well, finally conquering Ravenna (751) and considerable territories formerly under the popes, who invited in **Charlemagne** to protect them.

When Charlemagne's empire disintegrated following his death in 814, Italy reverted to a finely balanced anarchy. Altogether the 9th century was a bad time, with Italy caught between the Arab raiders and the endless wars of petty nobles and battling bishops in the north. The 10th century proved somewhat better – perhaps much better than the scanty chronicles of the time attest. Even in the worst times, Italy's cities never entirely disappeared. A big break for them, and for Italy, came in 961 with the invasion of the German **Otto the Great**, heir to the imperial pretensions of the Carolingians. He deposed the last feeble King of Italy, Berengar II of Ivrea, and was crowned Holy Roman Emperor in Rome the following year. Not that any of the Italians were happy to see him, but the strong government of Otto and his successors beat down the great nobles and allowed the growing cities to expand their power and influence. A new pattern was established; Germanic emperors would be meddling in Italian affairs for centuries, not powerful enough to establish total control, but at least usually able to keep out important rivals.

1000–1154: The Rise of the *Comuni*

On the eve of the new millennium, most Christians were convinced that the turn of the calendar would bring with it the end of the world. On the other hand, if there had been economists and social scientists around, they would have had ample evidence to reassure everyone that things were looking up. Especially in the towns, business was very good, and the political prospects even brighter. The first mention of a truly independent *comune* (plural: *comuni*, meaning a free city-state; the best translation might be 'commonwealth') was in Milan, where in 1024 a popular assembly is recorded, deciding which side the city would take in the Imperial Wars.

Throughout this period the papacy had declined greatly in power and prestige, a political football kicked between the emperors and the piratical Roman nobles. Beginning in the 1050s, a remarkable Tuscan monk named Hildebrand controlled papal policy, working behind the scenes to reassert the influence of the Church. When he became pope himself, in 1073, **Gregory VII** immediately set himself in conflict with the emperors over the issue of investiture – whether the Church or secular powers could name Church officials. The various Italian (and European) powers took sides on the issue, and 50 years of intermittent war followed.

Southern Italy knew a different fate. The first **Normans** arrived about 1020, on pilgrimages to Monte Sant'Angelo in the Gargano. They liked the opportunities they saw for conquest, and soon younger sons of Norman feudal families were moving into the south, first as mercenaries but gradually gaining large tracts of land for themselves in exchange for their services. Usually allied to the popes, they soon controlled most of Puglia and Calabria.

1154–1300: Guelphs and Ghibellines

While all this was happening, of course, the **First Crusade** (1097–1130) occupied the headlines. It was, in part, a result of the new militancy of the papacy begun by Gregory VII. For Italy, especially Pisa and Venice, the two states with plenty of boats to help ship Crusaders, the affair meant nothing but pure profit. Trade was booming everywhere, and the accumulation of money helped the Italians to create modern Europe's first banking system. It also financed the continued independence of the *comuni*, which flourished everywhere, with a big enough surplus for building projects like Pisa's cathedral complex. Culture and science were flourishing, too, with a big boost from contact with the Byzantines and the Muslims of Spain and Africa. By the 12th century, far in advance of most of Europe, Italy had attained a prosperity unknown since Roman times. Even Italian names were changing, an interesting sign of the beginnings of national consciousness; quite suddenly the public records (such as they were) show a marked shift from Germanic to classical and Biblical surnames – fewer Ugos, Othos, and Astolfos, more Giuseppes, Giovannis, Giulios, and Flavios.

Emperors and popes were still embroiled in the north. **Frederick I Barbarossa** of the Hohenstaufen – or Swabian – dynasty was strong enough in Germany, and he made it the cornerstone of his policy to reassert imperial power in Italy. Beginning in 1154, he crossed the Alps five times, molesting free cities that asked nothing more than the right to continually fight one another. He spread terror, utterly destroying Milan in 1161, but a united front of cities called the Lombard League defeated him in 1176. Frederick's greatest triumph in Italy came by arranging a marriage with the Normans, leaving his grandson **Frederick II** not only emperor but king of Sicily, giving him a strong power base in Italy itself.

The second Frederick's career dominated Italian politics for 30 years (1220–50). With his brilliant court, in which Italian was used for the first time (alongside Arabic and Latin), his half-Muslim army and his incredible processions of dancing girls, eunuchs and elephants, he provided Europe with a spectacle the like of which it had never seen. Frederick founded universities (as at Naples), gave Sicily a written constitution (perhaps the world's first), and built geometrically arcane castles and towers all over the south. The popes excommunicated him at least twice.

The battle of pope and emperor had become serious. All Italy divided into factions: the **Guelphs**, under the leadership of the popes, supported religious orthodoxy, the liberty of the *comuni*, and the interests of their emerging merchant class. The **Ghibellines** stood for the emperor, statist economic control, the interests of the rural nobles, and religious and intellectual tolerance. Frederick's campaigns and diplomacy in the north met with very limited success, and his death in 1250 left the outcome very much in doubt.

His son **Manfred**, not emperor but merely king of Sicily, took up the battle with better luck; Siena's defeat of Florence in 1260 gained that city and most of Tuscany for the Ghibellines. The next year, however, Pope Urban IV began an ultimately disastrous precedent by inviting in **Charles of Anjou**, a powerful, ambitious leader and brother of the King of France. As protector of the Guelphs, Charles defeated Manfred (1266) and murdered the last of the Hohenstaufens, Conradin (1268). He held unchallenged sway over Italy until 1282, when the famous revolt of the Sicilian Vespers started the party wars up again. By now, however, the terms *Guelph* and *Ghibelline* had ceased to have much meaning; men and cities changed sides as they found expedient.

Some real changes did occur out of all this sound and fury. In 1204 Venice hit its all-time biggest jackpot when it diverted the Fourth Crusade to the sack of Constantinople, winning for itself a small empire of islands in the Adriatic and Levant. Genoa emerged as its greatest rival in 1284, when its fleet put an end to Pisa's prominence at the Battle of Meloria. And elsewhere around the peninsula, some cities were falling under the rule of military *signori* whose descendants would be styling themselves counts and dukes – the Visconti of Milan, the della Scala of Verona, the Malatesta of Rimini. Everywhere the freedom of the *comuni* was in jeopardy; after so much useless strife the temptation to submit to a strong leader often proved overwhelming. During Charles of Anjou's reign the popes extracted the price for their invitation. The Papal State, including much of central Italy, was established in 1278. But most importantly, the Italian economy never seemed to mind the trouble. Trade and money flowed as never before; cities built new cathedrals and created themselves incredible skyscraper skylines, with the tall tower-fortresses of the now urbanized nobles. And it was, in spite of everything, a great age for culture – the era of Guelphs and Ghibellines was also the time of Dante (b. 1265) and Giotto (b. 1266).

1300–1494: Renaissance Italy

This paradoxical Italy continued into the 14th century, with a golden age of culture and an opulent economy side by side with almost continuous war and turmoil. With no serious threats from the emperors or any other foreign power, the myriad Italian states were able to menace each other joyfully without outside interference. One of the secrets to this state of affairs was that war had become a sort of game, conducted on behalf of cities by bands of paid mercenaries led by *condottieri*, who were never allowed to enter the cities themselves. The arrangement suited everyone pretty well.

By far the biggest event of the 14th century was the **Black Death** of 1347–8, in which it is estimated Italy lost one-third of its population. The shock brought a rude halt to what had been 400 years of almost continuous growth and prosperity, though its effects did not prove a permanent setback for the economy. In fact, the plague's grim joke was that it actually made life better for most of the Italians who survived; working people in the cities, no longer overcrowded, found their rents lower and their labour worth more, while in the country farmers were able to increase their profits by tilling only the best land.

It is impossible to speak of 'Italian history' in this period, with the peninsula split up into long-established, cohesive states pursuing different ends and warring against one another. Italian statesmen understood the idea of a balance of power long before political theorists invented the term, and, despite all the clatter and noise, most probably believed Italy was enjoying the best of all possible worlds. Four major states, each a European power in its own right, dominated the region's politics: first **Venice**, the oldest and most glorious, with its oligarchic but singularly effective constitution, and its exotic career of trade with the East. The Venetians waged a series of wars against arch-rival Genoa, finally exhausting her after the War of Chioggia in 1379. After that, they felt strong enough to make a major change in policy. Once serenely aloof from Italian politics, Venice now carved out a small land empire for itself, by 1428 including Verona, Padua, Vicenza, Brescia and Bergamo.

Florence, the richest city-state thanks to its banking and wool trade, also enjoyed good fortune, extending its control over most of Tuscany, and gaining a sea port with its conquest of now decadent Pisa in 1406. In 1434, **Cosimo de' Medici**, head of the largest banking house, succeeded in establishing a *de facto* dictatorship. Even though the forms of the old republic were maintained, Florence was well on its way to becoming a signorial state like its greatest rival, **Milan**. Under the Visconti, Milan had become rich and powerful, basing its success on the manufactures of the city (arms and textiles) and the bountiful, progressively managed agriculture of southern Lombardy. Its greatest glory came during the reign of **Gian Galeazzo Visconti** (1385–1402), who bought himself a ducal title from the emperor and nearly conquered all north Italy, before his untimely death caused his plans to unravel.

In the south, the huge **Kingdom of Naples** suffered from the heritage of the Normans, who had made it the only part of Italy where north-European-style feudalism had taken root. When times changed, the backward rural barons who dominated the south retarded its commerce and its culture. Despite such promising periods as the reign of the King of Aragon, **Alfonso the Magnanimous** (1442–58), a prototypical Renaissance prince and patron of the arts who seized Naples and added it to his domains, the south was falling far behind the rest of Italy.

And what of the Renaissance? No word has ever caused more mischief for the understanding of history and culture – as if Italy had been Sleeping Beauty, waiting for some Prince Charming of classical culture to come and awaken it from a thousand-year nap. On the contrary, Italy even in the 1200s was richer, more technologically advanced, and far more artistically creative than it had ever been in the days of the Caesars. The new art and scholarship that began in Florence in the

1400s and spread across the nation grew from a solid foundation of medieval accomplishment. The gilded, opulent Italy of the 15th century felt complacently secure in its long-established cultural and economic pre-eminence. A long spell of freedom from outside interference lulled the nation into believing that its political disunity could continue safely forever; except perhaps for the sanguinely realistic Florentine Niccolò Machiavelli, no one realized that Italy in fact was a plum waiting to be picked.

1494–1529: The Wars of Italy

The Italians brought the trouble down on themselves, when Duke Ludovico of Milan invited the French King Charles VIII to cross the Alps and assert his claim to the throne of Milan's enemy, Naples. Charles did just that, and the failure of the combined Italian states to stop him (at the inconclusive Battle of Fornovo, 1494) showed just how helpless Italy was at the hands of emerging monarchies like France or Spain. When the Spaniards saw how easy it was, they too marched in, and restored Naples to its Spanish king the following year (an Aragonese dynasty, cousins to Ferdinand and Isabella, had ruled Naples since 1442). Before long the German emperor and even the Swiss entered this new market for Italian real estate. The popes did as much as anyone to keep the pot boiling. Alexander VI and his son Cesare Borgia carried the war across central Italy in an attempt to found a new state for the Borgia family, and Julius II's madcap policy led him to egg on the Swiss, French and Spaniards in turn, before finally crying, 'Out with the barbarians!' when it was already too late.

By 1516, with the French ruling Milan and the Spanish in control of the south, it seemed as if a settlement would be possible. The worst possible luck for Italy, however, came with the accession of the insatiable megalomaniac **Charles V** to the throne of Spain in that year; in 1519 he bought himself the crown of the Holy Roman Empire, making him the most powerful ruler in Europe since Charlemagne. Charles felt he needed Milan as a base for communications between his Spanish, German and Flemish possessions, and, as soon as he had emptied Spain's treasury, driven her to revolt and plunged Germany into civil war, he turned his attentions to Italy. The wars began anew, bloodier than anything Italy had seen for centuries, climaxing with the defeat of the French at Pavia in 1525, and the sack of Rome by an out-of-control imperial army in 1527. The French invaded once more, in 1529, and were defeated this time at Naples by the treachery of their Genoese allies. All Italy, save only Venice, was now at the mercy of Charles and the Spaniards.

1529–1600: Italy in Chains

The final treaties left Spanish viceroys in Milan and Naples, and dukes and counts toeing the Spanish line almost everywhere else. Besides Venice and the very careful Republic of Lucca, the last bastions of Italian liberty were Siena and Florence, where the Medici had been thrown out and the republic re-established. Charles' army besieged and took the city in 1530, giving it back to the Medici, who gained the title of Grand Dukes of Tuscany. They collaborated with Spain in extinguishing Siena's independence, despite a desperate seven-year resistance (1552–9), and the new Medici state assumed roughly the borders of Tuscany today.

The broader context of these events, of course, was the bitter struggles of the Reformation and Counter-Reformation. In Italy, the new religious angle made the Spaniards and the popes natural allies. With the majority of the peninsula still nominally controlled by local rulers, and an economy that continued to be sound, both the Spanish and the popes realized that the only real threat would come not from men, but from ideas. Under the banner of combating Protestantism, they commenced a reign of terror across Italy. In the 1550s, the revived Inquisition began its manhunt for free-thinkers of every variety. A long line of Italian intellectuals trudged to the stake, while many more buried their convictions or left for exile in Germany or England.

Despite the oppression, the average Italian at first had little to complain about. Spanish domination brought peace and order to a country that had long been a madhouse of conflicting ambitions. Renaissance artists attained a virtuosity never seen before, just in time to embellish the scores of new churches, palaces and villas of the mid-16th-century building boom. The combined Christian forces had turned back the Turkish threat at Malta (1566) and Lepanto (1571), and some Italians were benefiting greatly from Spanish imperialism in the New World – especially the Genoese, who rented ships, floated loans, and snatched up a surprising amount of the gold and silver arriving from America.

1600–1796: The Age of Baroque

Nevertheless, the first signs of decay were already apparent. Palladio's country villas for the Venetian magnates, and Michelozzo's outside Florence, are landmarks in architecture but also one of the earliest symptoms. In both cities, the old mercantile economies were failing, and the wealthy began to invest their money unproductively in land instead of risking it in business or finance. Venice, between its wars with the Turks and its loss of the spice trade when the Portuguese discovered the route to the Indies, suffered the most. By 1650 it no longer had an important role to play in European affairs, though the Venetians kept their heads and made their inevitable descent into decadence a serene and enjoyable one.

The troubles were not limited to these two cities. After 1600 nearly everything started to go wrong for the Italians. The textiles and banking of the north, long the engines of the economy, both withered in the face of foreign competition, and the old port towns (with the exceptions of Genoa and the new city of Livorno) began to look half-empty as the English and Dutch muscled them out of the declining Mediterranean trade. Worst off of all was the south, under direct Spanish or papal rule. Combining incompetence and brutality with outrageously high taxes (the Spaniards' to finance foreign wars, the popes' to build up Rome), they rapidly turned the already poor south into a nightmare of anarchic depravity, haunted by legions of bandits and beggars, and controlled more tightly than ever by its violent feudal barons. To everyone's surprise, the south rose up and staged an epic rebellion. Beginning in Naples (Masaniello's Revolt, 1647), the disturbances soon spread all over the south and Sicily. For over a year peasant militias ruled some areas, and makeshift revolutionary councils defended the cities. When the Spanish finally defeated them, however, they massacred some 18,000, and tightened the screws more than ever.

Bullied, humiliated and increasingly impoverished, 17th-century Italy at least tried hard to keep up its ancient prominence in the arts and sciences. Galileo looked through telescopes, Monteverdi wrote the first operas, and hundreds of talented though uninspired artists cranked out pretty pictures to meet the continuing high demand. Bernini and Borromini turned Rome into the capital of Baroque – the florid, expensive coloratura style that serves as a perfect symbol for the age itself, an age of political repression and thought control where art itself became a political tool. Baroque's heavenly grandeur and symmetry helped to impress everyone with the majesty of Church and state. At the same time, Baroque scholars wrote books that went on for hundreds of pages without saying anything, but avoided offending the government and the Inquisition.

By the 18th century, there were very few painters, or scholars, or scientists. There were no more heroic revolts either. Italy in this period hardly has any history at all; with Spain's increasing decadence, the great powers decided the futures of Italy's major states, and used the minor ones as a kind of overflow tank to hold surplus princes and those dispossessed by wars elsewhere (Napoleon on Elba was the last and most famous of these). In 1713, after the War of the Spanish Succession, the Habsburgs of **Austria** came into control of Milan and Lombardy, Mantua and the Kingdom of Naples. The House of Lorraine, related to the Austrians, won Tuscany upon the extinction of the Medici in 1737. These new rulers improved conditions.

1796–1830: Napoleon, Restoration, and Reaction

Napoleon, that greatest of Italian generals, arrived in the country in 1796 on behalf of the French revolutionary Directorate, sweeping away the Piedmontese and Austrians and setting up republics in Lombardy (the 'Cisalpine Republic'), Liguria, and Naples (the 'Parthenopean Republic'). Italy woke with a start from its Baroque slumbers, and local patriots gaily joined the French cause. In 1799, however, while Napoleon was off in Egypt, the advance through Italy by an Austro-Russian army, aided by Nelson's fleet, restored the status quo. This was often accompanied by bloody reprisals, as peasant mobs led by clerics like the 'Army of the Holy Faith' marched across the south massacring liberals and French sympathizers.

In 1800 Napoleon returned in a campaign that saw the great victory at Marengo, giving him the opportunity once more to reorganize Italian affairs. Napoleon crowned himself King of Italy; Joseph Bonaparte and later Joachim Murat ruled at Naples. Elisa Bonaparte and her husband got Tuscany. Rome was annexed to France, and the pope was carted off to Fontainebleau. Napoleonic rule lasted only until 1814, but in that time important public works were begun and laws, education and everything else reformed after the French model; immense Church properties were expropriated, and medieval relics everywhere put to rest – including the Venetian Republic, which Napoleon for some reason took a special delight in liquidating. The French, however, soon wore out their welcome. Besides hauling much of Italy's artistic heritage off to the Louvre, implementing high war taxes and conscription (some 25,000 Italians died in the invasion of Russia), and brutally repressing a number of local revolts, they systematically exploited Italy for the benefit of the Napoleonic élite and the crowds of speculators flocking over the Alps. When the Austrians and English came to chase all the little Napoleons out, no one was sad to see them go.

Almost immediately, revolutionary agitators and secret societies like the famous *Carbonari* emerged that would keep Italy convulsed in plots and intrigues. A large-scale revolt in Naples forced the reactionary King Ferdinand to grant a constitution (1821), but when Austrian troops came down to crush the rebels he revoked it. The French July Revolution of 1830 also spread to Italy, encouraged by the liberal King **Carlo Alberto** in Piedmont-Savoy, but once more the by now universally hated Austrians intervened.

1848–1915: The Risorgimento and United Italy

Conspirators of every colour and shape, including the legendary **Giuseppe Mazzini**, had to wait another 18 years for their next chance. Mazzini, a sincere patriot and democrat, agitated frenetically all through the years 1830–70, beginning by founding the *Young Italy* movement, all with little practical effect.

The big change came in the revolutionary year of 1848, when risings in Palermo and Naples (in January) anticipated even those in Paris itself. Soon all Italy was in the streets. Piedmont and Tuscany won constitutions from their rulers, and the people of Milan chased out the Austrians after a month of extremely bloody fighting; at the same time the Venetian Republic was restored. Carlo Alberto, the hope of most Italians for a war of liberation, marched against the Austrians, but his two badly bungled campaigns allowed the enemy to re-establish control over the peninsula. By June 1849, only Venice, under Austrian blockade, and the recently declared Roman Republic were left. Rome, led by Mazzini, and with a small army under **Giuseppe Garibaldi**, a former sailor who had fought in the wars of independence in Latin America, beat off several attacks from foreign troops invited in by the pope. The Republic finally succumbed to a large force sent by, of all people, the Republic of President Louis Napoléon (soon to declare himself Napoléon III) in France. Garibaldi's dramatic escape to safety in San Marino (he was trying to reach Venice, itself soon to surrender) gave the Risorgimento one of its great heroic myths.

Despite failure on a grand scale, at least the Italians knew they would get another chance. Unification was inevitable, but there were two irreconcilable contenders for the honour of accomplishing it. On one side, the democrats and radicals dreamed of a truly reborn, revolutionary Italy, and looked to the popular hero Garibaldi to deliver it; on the other, moderates wanted the Piedmontese to do the job, ensuring a stable future by making **Vittorio Emanuele II** King of Italy. Vittorio Emanuele's minister, the polished, clever **Count Camillo Cavour**, spent the 1850s getting Piedmont in shape for the struggle, building its economy and army, participating in the Crimean War to earn diplomatic support, and plotting with the French for an alliance against Austria.

War came in 1859, and French armies did most of the work in conquering Lombardy. Tuscany and Emilia revolted, and Piedmont was able to annexe all three. In May 1860, Garibaldi and his red-shirted 'Thousand' sailed from Genoa – Cavour almost stopped them at the last minute – and landed in Sicily, electrifying Europe by repeatedly beating the Bourbon forces in a quick march across the island. The Thousand had become 20,000, and when they crossed the straits bound for Naples it was clear that the affair was reaching its climax. On 7 September, Garibaldi entered Naples, and though he proclaimed himself temporary dictator on Vittorio Emanuele's behalf, the Piedmontese were alarmed enough to occupy Umbria and the Marches. The king met Garibaldi on 27 October, near Teano, and, after finding out what little regard the Piedmontese had for him, the greatest and least self-interested leader modern Italy has known went off to retirement on the island of Caprara. Just as the French made all this possible, some more unexpected help from outside allowed the new Italy to add two missing pieces and complete its unification. When the Prussians defeated Austria in the war of 1866, Italy was able to seize the Veneto. Only Rome was left, defended by a French garrison, and when the Prussians beat France at Sedan in 1870, the Italian army marched into Rome almost without opposition.

The first decades of the Italian Kingdom were just as unimpressive as its wars of independence. A liberal constitutional monarchy was established, but the parliament almost immediately decomposed into cliques and political cartels representing various interests. Finances started in disorder and stayed that way, and corruption became widespread. Peasant revolts occurred in the south, as people felt cheated by inaction after the promises of the Risorgimento, and organized brigandage became a problem, partially instigated by the Vatican as part of an all-out attempt to discredit the new regime. The outlines of foreign policy often seemed to change monthly, though like the other European powers Italy felt it necessary to snatch up some colonies. The attempt revealed the new state's limited capabilities, with embarrassing military disasters at the hands of the Ethiopians at Dogali in 1887, and again at Adowa in 1896.

After 1900, with the rise of a strong socialist movement, strikes, riots, and police repression often occupied centre stage in Italian politics. Even so, important signs of progress, such as the big new industries in Turin and Milan, showed that at least the northern half of Italy was becoming a fully integral part of the European economy. The 15 years before the war, prosperous and contented ones for many, came to be known by the slightly derogatory term *Italietta*, the 'little Italy' of modest bourgeois happiness, an age of sweet Puccini operas, the first motorcars, blooming 'Liberty'-style architecture, and Sunday afternoons at the beach.

1915–45: War, Fascism, and War

Italy could have stayed out of the First World War, but let the chance to do so go by for the usual reasons – a hope of gaining some new territory, especially Trieste. Also, a certain segment of the intelligentsia found the *Italietta* boring and disgraceful: irredentists of all stripes, some of the artistic Futurists, and the perverse, idolized poet **Gabriele D'Annunzio**. The groups helped Italy leap blindly into the conflict in 1915, with a big promise of boundary adjustments dangled by the beleaguered Allies. Italian armies fought with their accustomed flair, masterminding an utter catastrophe at Caporetto (October 1917) that any other nation but Austria would have parleyed into a total victory. No thanks to their incompetent generals, the poorly armed and equipped Italians somehow held firm for another year, until the total exhaustion of Austria allowed them to prevail (at the Battle of Vittorio Veneto you see so many streets named after), capturing some 600,000 prisoners in November 1918.

In return for 650,000 dead, a million casualties, severe privation on the home front, and a war debt higher than anyone could count, Italy received Trieste, Gorizia, the South Tyrol, and a few other scraps. Italians felt they had been cheated, and nationalist sentiment increased, especially when D'Annunzio led a band of freebooters to seize the half-Italian city of Fiume in September 1919, after the peace conferences had promised it to Yugoslavia. The Italian economy was in a shambles, and, at least in the north, revolution was in the air; workers in Turin raised the Red Flag over the Fiat plants and organized themselves into soviets. The troubles had encouraged extremists of both right and left, and many Italians became convinced that the liberal state was finished.

Enter **Benito Mussolini**, a professional intriguer in the Mazzini tradition with bad manners and no fixed principles. Before the War he had found his real talent as editor of the Socialist Party paper *Avanti* – the best it ever had, tripling the circulation in a year. When he decided that what Italy really needed was war, he left to found a new paper, and contributed mightily to the jingoist agitation of 1915. In the post-War confusion, he found his opportunity. A little bit at a time, he developed the idea of **Fascism**, at first less a philosophy than an astute use of mass propaganda and a sense for design. (The *fasces*, from which the name comes, were bundles of rods carried before ancient Roman officials, a symbol of authority. *Fascii* also referred to organized bands of rebellious peasants in 19th-century Sicily.) With a little discreet money supplied by frightened industrialists, Mussolini had no trouble in finding recruits for his black-shirted gangs, who found their first success beating up Slavs in Trieste and working as a sort of private police for landowners in stoutly socialist Emilia-Romagna.

Mussolini's accession to power came on an improbable gamble. In the particularly anarchic month of October 1922, he announced that his followers would march on Rome. King Vittorio Emanuele III refused to sign a decree of martial law to disperse them, and there was nothing to do but offer Mussolini the post of prime minister. At first, he governed Italy with undeniable competence. Order was restored, and the economy and foreign policy handled intelligently by non-Fascist professionals. In the 1924 elections, despite the flagrant rigging and intimidation, the Fascists only won a slight majority.

One politician who was not intimidated was Giacomo Matteotti, and when some of Mussolini's close associates took him for a ride and murdered him, a major scandal erupted. Mussolini survived it, and during 1925 and 1926 the Fascists used parliamentary methods to convert Italy into a permanent Fascist dictatorship.

Compared to the governments that preceded him, Mussolini looked quite impressive. Industry advanced, great public works were undertaken, with special care towards the backward south, and the Mafia took some heavy blows at the hands of a determined Sicilian prefect named Mori. In the words of one of Mussolini's favourite slogans, painted on walls all over Italy, 'Whoever stops is lost.'

Mussolini couldn't stop, and the only possibility for new diversions lay with the chance of conquest and empire. His invasion of Ethiopia and his meddling in the

Spanish Civil War, both in 1936, compromised Italy into a close alliance with Nazi Germany. Mussolini's confidence and rhetoric never faltered as he led an entirely unprepared nation into the biggest war ever. Once more, Italian ineptitude at warfare produced embarrassing defeats on all fronts, and only German intervention in Greece and North Africa saved Italy from being knocked out of the War as early as 1941. The Allies invaded Sicily in July 1943, and the Italians began to look for a clever way out. They seized Mussolini during a meeting of the Grand Council, packed him into an ambulance and sent him off first to Ponza, then to a little ski hotel up in the Apennines. The new government under Marshal Badoglio didn't know what to do, and confusion reigned supreme.

While British and American forces slogged northwards, in this ghetto of the European theatre, with the help of the Free French, Brazilians, Costa Ricans, Poles, Czechs, New Zealanders and Norwegians, the Germans poured in divisions to defend the peninsula. They rescued Mussolini, and set him up in a puppet state called the Italian Social Republic in the north. In September 1943, the Badoglio government signed an armistice with the Allies, too late to keep the War from dragging on another year and a half, as the Germans made good use of Italy's difficult terrain to slow the Allied advance. Meanwhile Italy finally gave itself something to be proud of, a determined, resourceful Resistance that established free zones in many areas, and harassed the Germans with sabotage and strikes. The *partigiani* caught Mussolini in April 1945, while he was trying to escape to Switzerland; after shooting him and his mistress, they hung him by his feet from the roof of a petrol station in Milan.

1945–the Present

Post-war Italian *cinema verità* – Rossellini's *Rome, Open City*, or de Sica's *Bicycle Thieves* – captures the atmosphere better than words ever could. In a period of serious hardships that older Italians still remember, the nation slowly picked itself up and returned things to normal. A referendum in June 1946 made Italy a republic, but only by a narrow margin. The first governments fell to the new Christian Democrat Party under Alcide de Gasperi, which has run the show ever since in coalitions with a preposterous band of smaller parties. The main opposition has been provided by the Communists, surely one of the most remarkable parties of modern European history. With the heritage of the only important socialist philosopher since Marx, Antonio Gramsci, and the democratic and broad-minded leader Enrico Berlinguer, Italian communism is something unique in the world, with its stronghold and showcase in the well-run, prosperous cities of the Emilia-Romagna.

The fifties was Rome's decade, when Italian style and Italian cinema caught the imagination of the world. Gradually, slowly, a little economic miracle was happening; *Signor Rossi*, the average Italian, started buzzing around in his first classic Fiat *cinquecento*, northern industries boomed, and life cruised slowly back to normal. The south continued to lag behind, despite the sincere efforts of the government and its special planning fund, the *Cassa per il Mezzogiorno*. Though the extreme poverty and despair of the post-war years gradually disappeared, even today there is little evidence that the region is catching up with the rest of the country. Nationally, the *Democristiani-*

controlled government soon evolved a Byzantine style of politics that only an Italian could understand. Through the constant parade of collapsing and reforming cabinets, nothing changed; all deals were made in the back rooms and everyone, from the pope to the Communists, had a share in the decision-making. One wouldn't call it democracy with a straight face, but for four decades it worked well enough to keep Italy on its wheels. The dark side of the arrangement was the all-pervasive corruption that the system fostered. It is fascinating to read the work of journalists only a few years ago, seeing how almost without exception they would politely sidestep the facts; Italy was run by an unprincipled political machine, whose members were raking in as much for themselves as they could grab, and everyone knew it, only it couldn't be said openly, for lack of proof. Even more sinister was the extent to which the machine would go to keep on top.

The seventies – Italy's 'years of lead' – witnessed the worst of the political sleaze, along with a grim reign of terrorism, culminating in the kidnapping and murder in 1978 of honourable Christian Democrat prime minister, Aldo Moro. All along, the attacks were attributed to 'leftist groups', though even at the time many suspected that some of the highest circles in the government and army were controlling or manipulating them, with the possible collusion of the CIA. They were indeed, and only recently has some of the truth begun to seep out. On another front, Italians woke up one morning in 1992 to find that the government had magically vacuumed 7 per cent of the money out of all their savings accounts, an 'emergency measure' to meet the nation's colossal budget deficit – a deficit caused largely by the thievery of the political class and its allies in organized crime.

Italians are a patient lot but eventually the lid blew off, leading to an incomplete and very Italian sort of revolution. The business started in the judiciary, the one independent and relatively uncorrupt part of the government. In the early nineties, heroic prosecutors Giovanni Falcone and Paolo Borsellino went after the Sicilian Mafia with some success, and were spectacularly assassinated for it, causing national outrage. Meanwhile, in Milan, a small group of prosecutors and judges found a minor political kickback scandal that led them, through years of quiet and painstaking work, to the golden string that unravelled the whole rotten tangle of Italian political depravity – what Italians call the *tangentopoli*, or 'bribe city'. For over a year, the televised hearings of Judge Antonio di Pietro and his Operation *Mani Pulite* ('clean hands') team from Milan were the nation's favourite and most fascinating serial.

All the old kingpins fell, and the parties at the centre of the corruption and the alliance with southern organized crime, the Christian Democrats and the Socialists, were destroyed. The old guard, however seemed to have prepared for this. They had already helped a shadowy crony, Silvio Berlusconi, gain control of all Italy's private television networks, and now Berlusconi used his money and influence to create an entirely synthetic party (potential candidates were 'auditioned') called Forza Italia. It all worked brilliantly, and Berlusconi gained power in the elections of 1994. Berlusconi had his own problems with political corruption, but, while he managed to avoid conviction, the damage done by the constant revelations and his attempts to cripple the *Mani Pulite* investigations forced him out of office after only a year.

After a brief period under banker Lamberto Dini, who started a strong push for financial reform, a new leftist government was voted in; the 'Olive Tree' coalition under Romano Prodi and Massimo D'Alema managed to stay in the driver's seat longer than anyone predicted. The Italians, who understandably place more hope in Europe than in their national leaders, bit the bullet and supported Dini and Prodi's stringent economic measures, allowing them to squeak into Euroland in January 1999. Prodi had little time to bask in the glory: the same strict measures led to the Communists withdrawing their support of his government in late 1998 and giving it to Massimo D'Alema of the DS (Democratici di Sinistra) party, forming Italy's 60th government since the Second World War.

The D'Alema government did not last long either, and was replaced by yet another coalition of the left, headed, in the excruciating old Italian tradition, by a caretaker, former Socialist minister Giuseppe Amato. Dissatisfaction with the economy helped the coalition of Forza Italia and the neo-Fascist parties win a big victory in the 2001 elections, returning Berlusconi to the Palazzo Chigi. Europe worries about the implications of Berlusconi's synthetic political party, controlled by PR advisors, and about his now-total control over television, both public and private, coupled with his vast publishing empire. That, along with the government's alleged attempts to intimidate the courts investigating the myriad cases of corruption and influence-peddling, have convinced many people that democracy in Italy is under serious threat. Rome itself has been heading in the opposite direction. Following the departure of its young, charismatic mayor, Francesco Rutelli, who led the national 2001 campaign against Berlusconi, Michelangelo's city hall on the Campidoglio is in the hands of another rising star of Italian politics, the former culture minister Walter Veltroni.

Art and Architecture

You'd have to spend your holiday in a baggage compartment to miss Italy's vast piles of architecture and art. The Italians estimate there is one work of art per capita in their country, which is more than anyone could see in a lifetime – especially since so much of it is locked away in museums that are in semi-permanent 'restoration'. Although you may occasionally chafe at not being able to see certain frescoes, or at finding a famous palace completely wrapped up in the ubiquitous green netting of the restorers, the Italians on the whole bear the burden of keeping their awesome heritage dusted off and open for visitors very well. Some Italians find it insupportable living with the stuff all around them; the Futurists, for instance, were worried that St Mark's might be blown up by foreign enemies in the First World War – but only because they wanted to do it themselves, as was their right as Italian citizens.

Pre-Etruscan

To give a chronological account of the first Italian artists is an uncomfortable task. The peninsula's mountainous terrain saw many isolated developments and many survivals of ancient cultures even during the days of the sophisticated Etruscans and

Romans. Most ancient of all, however, is the palaeolithic troglodyte culture on the Riviera, credited with creating some of the first artworks in Europe – chubby images of fertility goddesses. The most remarkable works from the Neolithic period up until the Iron Age are the thousands of graffiti rock incisions in several isolated alpine valleys north of Lake Iseo.

After 1000 BC Italic peoples all over the peninsula were making geometrically painted pots, weapons, tools and bronze statuettes. The most impressive culture, however, was the tower-building, bronze-working Nuraghe civilization on **Sardinia**, of which echoes are seen in many cultures on the mainland. Among the most intriguing and beautiful artefacts to have survived are those of the Villanova culture; the statues and inscriptions of the little-known Middle Adriatic culture, and the statue-steles of an unknown people north of Viareggio.

Etruscans and Greeks (8th–2nd Centuries BC)

With the refined, art-loving Etruscans we begin to have architecture as well as art. Not much has survived, thanks to the Etruscans' habit of building in wood and decorating with terracotta, but we do have plenty of distinctive rock-cut tombs, many of which contain exceptional frescoes that reflect Aegean Greek styles. The best of their lovely sculptures, jewellery, vases, and much more are in the Villa Giulia in **Rome** – where you can also see a reconstructed temple façade. There are also fine Etruscan holdings in the archaeology museum in **Florence**.

The Etruscans imported and copied many of their vases from their ancient Greek contemporaries, from Greece proper and the colonies of Magna Graecia in southern Italy; there are many other excavated Greek cities, but usually only foundations remain. The Archaeological Museum in the **Vatican** contains an impressive collection of ancient Greek vases, statues and other types of art.

Roman (3rd century BC–5th Century AD)

Italian art during the Roman hegemony is mostly derivative of the Etruscan and Greek, with a special talent for mosaics, wall paintings, glasswork and portraiture; architecturally, the Romans were brilliant engineers, the inventors of concrete and grand exponents of the arch. Even today their constructions, such as aqueducts, amphitheatres, bridges, baths, and of course the Pantheon, are most impressive.

Of course **Rome** itself has no end of ancient monuments; also in the vicinity there is **Ostia Antica**, Rome's ancient port, and **Tivoli**, site of Hadrian's great villa. Rome also has a stellar set of museums filled with Roman antiquities – the National Museum in Diocletian's Baths, the Vatican Museum, the Capitoline Museums, and the Museum of Roman Civilization at EUR.

Early Middle Ages (5th–10th Centuries)

After the fall of the Roman Empire, civilization's lamp flickered most brightly in Ravenna, where Byzantine mosaicists adorned the glittering churches of the Eastern Exarchate. Theirs was to be the prominent style in pictorial art and architecture until the 13th century. Apart from Ravenna, there are fine mosaics and paintings of the period in **Rome**, in a score of churches such as Sant'Agnese, San Clemente and Santa Prassede; in Rome the Italian preference for basilican churches and octagonal baptistries began in Constantine's day, and the development of Christian art and architecture through the Dark Ages can be traced there better than anywhere else. There are also many paintings in the catacombs. Other good Ravenna-style mosaics may be seen in Torcello Cathedral in **Venice**, where the fashion lingered long enough to create St Mark's.

'Lombard' art, really the work of the native population under Lombard rule, revealed an original talent in the 7th–9th centuries, as well as a new style, presaging the Romanesque.

Romanesque (11th–12th Centuries)

At this point, when an expansive society made new advances in art possible, north and south Italy went their separate ways, each contributing distinctive styles in sculpture and architecture. We also begin to learn the identities of some of their makers. The great Lombard cathedrals are masterworks of brick art and adorned with blind arcading, bas-reliefs and lofty campaniles. **Florence** developed its own particularist black and white style, exemplified in truly amazing buildings like the Baptistry and San Miniato.

The outstanding architectural advance of this period is the Puglian Romanesque, a style closely related to contemporary Norman and Pisan work – it is impossible to say which came first. This period also saw the erection of urban skyscrapers by the nobility – family fortress-towers built when the *comuni* forced local barons to move into the towns. Larger cities once had literally hundreds of them, before the townspeople succeeded in getting them demolished. In many cases extremely tall towers were built simply for decoration and prestige.

Late Medieval–Early Renaissance (13th–14th Centuries)

In many ways this was the most exciting and vigorous phase in Italian art history, an age of discovery when the power of the artist was almost like that of a magician. Great imaginative leaps occurred in architecture, painting, and sculpture, especially in Tuscany. From Milan to Assisi, a group of masons and sculptors known as the Campionese Masters built magnificent brick cathedrals and basilicas. Some of their buildings reflect the Gothic style of the north while in others you can see the transition from that same Gothic to Renaissance. In **Venice**, an ornate, half-oriental style called Venetian-Gothic still sets the city's palaces and public buildings apart, and influenced the exotic Basilica di Sant'Antonio in **Padua**. This was also an era of transition in sculpture, from stiff Romanesque stylization to the more realistic, classically inspired works of the great Nicola Pisano and his son Giovanni, and his pupil Arnolfo di Cambio (in **Florence**).

Painters, especially in **Rome** and Siena, learned from the new spatial and expressive sculpture. Most celebrated of the masters in the dawn of the Italian Renaissance is, of course, the solemn Giotto. Sienese artists Duccio di Buoninsegna, Simone Martini and Pietro and Ambrogio Lorenzetti gave Italy its most brilliant exponents of the

International Gothic style – though they were also important precursors of the Renaissance. Their brightly coloured scenes, embellished with a thousand details, helped make Siena into the medieval dream-city it is today. In **Florence**, the works of Orcagna, Gentile da Fabriano and Lorenzo Monaco continued that city's unique approach, laying a foundation for Florence's launching of the Renaissance.

Rome, for one of the few times in its history, achieved artistic prominence with home-grown talent. The city's architecture from this period (as seen in the campaniles of Santa Maria in Cosmedin and Santa Maria Maggiore) has largely been lost under Baroque remodellings, but the paintings and mosaics of Pietro Cavallini and his school, and the intricate, inlaid stone pavements and architectural trim of the Cosmati family and their followers (derived from the Amalfi coast style) can be seen all over the city; both had an influence that extended far beyond Rome itself.

The Renaissance (15th–early 16th Centuries)

The origins of this high noon of art are very much the accomplishment of quattrocento **Florence**, where sculpture and painting embarked on a totally new way of educating the eye (*see* **Florence**, p.244). The idea of a supposed 'rediscovery of antiquity' has confused the understanding of the time. In general, artists broke new ground when they expanded from the traditions of medieval art; when they sought merely to copy the forms of ancient Greece and Rome the imagination often faltered.

Florentine art soon became recognized as the standard of the age. By 1450 Florentine artists were spreading the new style to the north, where Leonardo da Vinci and Bramante spent several years. Michelangelo and Bramante, among others, carried the Renaissance to **Rome**, where it thrived under the patronage of enlightened popes. The most significant art in the north came out of **Venice**, which had its own distinct school led by Mantegna and Giovanni Bellini (*see* 'Venetian Art', p.187).

Despite the brilliant triumphs in painting and sculpture, the story of Renaissance architecture is partially one of confusion and retreat. **Florence**, with Brunelleschi, Alberti and Michelozzo, achieved its own special mode of expression, a dignified austerity that proved difficult to transplant elsewhere. In most of Italy the rediscovery of the works of Vitruvius, representing the authority of antiquity, killed off Italians' appreciation of their own architectural heritage; with surprising speed the dazzling imaginative freedom of medieval architecture was lost forever. Some work still appeared, however, notably Codussi's palaces and churches in **Venice**.

High Renaissance and Mannerism (16th Century)

At the beginning of the cinquecento an Olympian triumvirate of Michelangelo, Raphael and Leonardo da Vinci held court at the summit of European art. But in this time when Italy was losing her self-confidence, and was soon to lose her essential liberty, artistic currents tended towards the dark and subversive. More than anyone, it was Michelangelo who tipped the balance from the cool, classical Renaissance into the turgid, stormy, emotionally fraught movement the critics have labelled Mannerism. Among the few painters left in exhausted Florence, he had the brilliant, deranged Jacopo Pontormo and Rosso Fiorentino to help. Other painters lumped in with the Mannerists, such as Giuliano Romano in Mantua and Il Sodoma around Siena, broke new ground while maintaining the discipline and intellectual rigour of the early Renaissance. Elsewhere, and especially among the fashionable Florentine painters and sculptors, art was decaying into mere interior decoration.

For **Venice**, however, it was a golden age, with the careers of Titian, Veronese, Tintoretto, Sansovino and Palladio.

In architecture, attempts to recreate ancient styles and the classical orders won the day. In Milan, and later in Rome, Bramante was one of the few architects able to do anything interesting with it, while Michelangelo's great dome of St Peter's put a cap on the accomplishments of the Renaissance. Other talented architects found most of their patronage in **Rome**, which after the 1520s became Italy's centre of artistic activity: Ligorio, Peruzzi, Vignola and the Sangallo family among them.

Baroque (17th–18th Centuries)

Rome continued its artistic dominance to become the capital of Baroque, where the socially irresponsible genius of artists like Bernini and Borromini was approved by the Jesuits and indulged by the tainted ducats of the popes. As an art designed to induce temporal obedience and psychical oblivion, its effects are difficult to describe, but you can see for yourself in the three great churches along Corso Vittorio Emanuele in Rome and a host of other works (Bernini's Piazza Navona fountains and St Peter's colonnades). More honest cities, such as Florence and Venice, chose to sit out the Baroque era, though **Florence** at first enthusiastically approved the works of 16th-century proto-Baroque sculptors like Ammannati, Giambologna and Cellini. Not all artists fitted the Baroque mould; genius could survive in a dangerous, picaresque age, most notably in the person of Caravaggio.

Neoclassicism and Romanticism (late 18th–19th Centuries)

Baroque proved to be a hard act to follow, and in these centuries Italian art and architecture almost ceased to exist. Two centuries of stifling oppression had taken their toll on the national imagination, and for the first time Italy not only ceased to be a leader in art, but failed even to make significant contributions.

The one bright spot in 18th-century Italian painting was **Venice**, where Giambattista Tiepolo and son adorned the churches and palaces of the last days of the Serenissima. Other Venetians, such as Antonio Canaletto and Francesco Guardi, painted their famous canal scenes for Grand Tourists. In the 19th century, the Italian Impressionist movement, the *Macchiaioli*, led by Giovanni Fattori, was centred in the city of **Florence**. In sculpture, the neoclassical master Antonio Canova stands almost alone, a favourite in the days of Napoleon. Some of his best works may be seen in **Rome**'s Villa Borghese. In architecture, it was the age of grand opera houses and the late 19th-century Gallerias in Milan and Naples.

20th Century

The turn-of-the-century Liberty Style (Italian Art Nouveau) failed to spread as widely as its counterparts in France and central Europe, but the age saw the construction of new Grand Hotels, casinos and villas in nearly every resort, for example in **Venice**. In the 20th century two Italian art movements attracted international attention: Futurism, a response to Cubism, concerned with the relevancy to the present ('the art that achieves speed, achieves success'), a movement led by Boccioni, Gino Severini and Giacomo Balla (well-represented in the National Gallery of Modern Art, **Rome**); and the mysterious, introspective metaphysical world of Giorgio De Chirico, whose brethren – Modigliani, Giorgio Morandi and Carlo Carrà – were masters of silences. Their works, and others by modern Italian and foreign artists, are displayed in the museums of **Rome** and **Venice**.

Architecture in this century reached its (admittedly low) summit in the Fascist period (the EUR suburb in **Rome**, and public buildings everywhere in the south). Mussolinian architecture often makes us smile but, as the only Italian school in the last 200 years to have achieved a consistent sense of design, it presents a challenge to all modern Italian architects – one they have so far been unable to meet. In **Rome** you can see the works of the most acclaimed Italian architect of this century, Pier Luigi Nervi; good post-war buildings are very difficult to find, and the other arts have never yet risen above the level of dreary, saleable postmodernism. Much of the Italians' artistic urge has been sublimated into the shibboleth of Italian design – clothes, sports cars, suitcases, kitchen utensils, etc. At present, though business is good, Italy is generating little excitement in these fields. Europe expects more from its most artistically talented nation; after the bad centuries of shame and slumber a free and prosperous Italy may well find its own voice and its own style to help interpret the events of the day. If Italy ever does begin to speak with a single voice, whatever it has to say will be worth hearing.

Literature, Music and Cinema

Literature

Few countries have as grand a literary tradition – even Shakespeare made extensive use of Italian stories for his plots. Besides all the great Latin authors and poets of ancient Rome, the peninsula has produced a small shelf of world classics in the Italian language; try to read a few before you come to Italy, or bring them along to read on the train. (All the books mentioned below are available in English translations, and may often be found in the English sections of Italian bookstores.) Once you've visited some of the settings of Dante's *Divine Comedy*, and come to know at least historically some of the inhabitants of the Inferno, Purgatorio and Paradiso, the old classic becomes even more fascinating.

Dante (1265–1321) was one of the first poets in Europe to write in the vernacular, and in doing so incorporated a good deal of topographical material from his 13th-century world. His literary successor, **Petrarch** (1304–74), has been called by many 'the first modern man'; in his poetry the first buds of humanism were born, deeply felt, complex, subtle, and fascinating today as ever (his *Canzoniere* is widely available in English). The third literary deity in Italy's late-medieval/early-Renaissance trinity is

Non è questo 'l terren, ch' i' toccai pria?
Non è questo il mio nido,
Ove nudrito fui sí dolcemente?
Non è questa la patria in ch' io mi fido,
Madre benigna e pia,
Che copre l'un e l'altro mio parente?
Per Dio, questo la mente
Talor vi mova; e con pietà guardate
Le lagrime del popol doloroso,
Che sol da voi riposo,
Dopo Dio, spera: e, pur che voi mostriate
Segno, alcun di pietate,
Vertú contra furore
Prenderà l'arme; e fia 'l combatter corto;
Ché l'antiquo valore
Ne l' italici cor non è ancor morto.

Petrarch (1304–74)

Is not this precious earth my native land?
And is not this the nest
From which my tender wings were taught to fly?
And is not this soil upon whose breast,
Loving and soft, faithful and true and fond,
My father and my gentle mother lie?
'For love of God,' I cry,
Some time take thought of your humanity
And spare your people all their tears and grief!
From you they seek relief
Next after God. If in your eyes they see
Some marks of sympathy,
Against this mad disgrace
They will arise, the combat will be short;
For the stern valour of our ancient race
Is not yet dead in the Italian heart.

trans. William Dudley Foulke LL D (1915)

Boccaccio (1313–75), whose imagination, humour and realism is most apparent in his 'Human Comedy' the *Decameron*, a hundred stories 'told' by a group of young aristocrats who fled into the countryside from Florence to escape the plague of 1348. Boccaccio's detached point of view had the effect of disenchanting Dante's ordered medieval cosmos, clearing the way for the renaissance of the secular novel.

Dante, Petrarch and Boccaccio exerted a tremendous influence over literary Europe, and in the 15th and 16th centuries a new crop of Italian writers continued in the vanguard – **Machiavelli** in political thought (*The Prince*), though he also wrote two of the finest plays of the Renaissance (*Mandragola* and *Clizia*); **Ariosto** in the genre of knightly romance (*Orlando Furioso*, the antecedent of Spenser's *Faerie Queene*, among many others); **Benvenuto Cellini** in autobiography; **Vasari** in art criticism and history (*The Lives of the Artists*); **Castiglione** in etiquette, gentlemanly arts and behaviour (*The Courtier*); **Alberti** in architecture and art theory (*Della Pintura*); **Leonardo da Vinci** in a hundred different subjects (the *Notebook*, etc.); even Michelangelo had time to write a book's worth of sonnets, now translated into English.

Other works from the period include the writings and intriguing play (*The Candlemaker*) of the great philosopher and heretic **Giordano Bruno** (perhaps the only person to be excommunicated from three different churches); the risqué, scathing writings of **Aretino**, the 'Scourge of Princes'; the poetry and songs of **Lorenzo de' Medici**; and the *Commentaries* by **Pope Pius II** (Enea Silvio), a rare view into the life, opinions, and times of one of the most accomplished Renaissance men, not to mention the only autobiography ever written by a pope.

Baroque Italy was a quieter place, dampened by the censorship of the Inquisition. The Venetians kept the flame alight: **Casanova**'s picaresque *Life*, the tales of **Carlo Gozzi** and the plays of **Goldoni**. Modern Italian literature, unlike many, has an official birthdate – the publication in 1827 of **Alessandro Manzoni**'s *I Promessi Sposi* ('The Betrothed'), which not only spoke with sweeping humanity to the concerns of pre-Risorgimento Italy, but also spoke in its own language – a new everyday Italian that nearly everyone was able to understand, no matter what their regional dialect; the novel went on to become a symbol of the aspiration of national unity.

The next writer with the power to capture the turbulent emotions of his time was **Gabriele D'Annunzio**, whose life of daredevil, personally tailored patriotism and superman cult strongly contrast with the lyricism of his poetry and some of his novels – still widely read in Italy. Meanwhile, and much more influentially, **Pirandello**, the philosophical Sicilian playwright and novelist obsessed with absurdity, changed the international vocabulary of drama before the Second World War.

The post-war era saw the appearance of neorealism in fiction as well as cinema, and the classics, though available in English, are among the easiest books to read in Italian – **Cesare Pavese**'s *La luna e i falò* (The Moon and the Bonfires), **Carlo Levi**'s tragic *Cristo si è fermato a Eboli* (Christ Stopped at Eboli) or **Vittorini**'s *Conversazione in Sicilia*. Other acclaimed works of the post-war era include *The Garden of the Finzi-Contini* (about a Jewish family in Fascist Italy) by **Giorgio Bassani**, and another book set during the Fascist era, *That Awful Mess on Via Merulana* by **Carlo Emilio Gadda**; then there's the Sicilian classic that became famous around the world – *The Leopard* by **Giuseppe di Lampedusa**.

The late **Italo Calvino**, perhaps more than any other Italian writer in the past two decades, enjoyed a large international following – his *Italian Folktales*, *Marcovaldo*, *The Baron in the Trees*, and *If on a Winter's Night a Traveller* (which includes the first chapters of about 10 novels) were all immediately translated into English; perhaps the best of them is *Invisible Cities*, an imaginary dialogue between Marco Polo and Kublai Khan. Much maligned Sicily continued to produce some of Italy's best works of literature, from the pens of **Leonardo Sciascia** and **Gesualdo Bufalino**. The current celebrity of Italian literature is of course **Umberto Eco**, Professor of Semiotics at Bologna University, whose *The Name of the Rose* kept readers all over the world on the edge of their seats over the murders of a handful of 14th-century monks in a remote Italian monastery, while magically evoking, better than many historians, all the political and ecclesiastical turmoil of the period.

Italy has also inspired countless of her visitors, appearing as a setting in more novels, poems and plays than tongue can tell. There is also a long list of non-fiction classics, some of which make fascinating reading and are readily available in most bookshops: Goethe's *Italian Journey*, Ruskin's *The Stones of Venice*, D. H. Lawrence's *Etruscan Places* and *Twilight in Italy*, Hilaire Belloc's *The Path to Rome*, Norman Douglas's *Old Calabria*, Jan Morris's *Venice*, Mary McCarthy's *The Stones of Florence* and *Venice Observed*, and many others, including the famously over-the-top travellers' accounts of Edward Hutton and the ever-entertaining H. V. Morton. For the Italian point of view from the outside looking in, read the classic *The Italians* by the late Luigi Barzini, former correspondent for the *Corriere della Sera* in London.

Music and Opera

Italy has contributed as much to Western music as any country – and perhaps a little more. It was an Italian monk, Guido d'Arezzo, who devised the musical scale; it was a Venetian printer, Ottaviano Petrucci, who invented a method of printing music with movable type in 1501 – an industry Italian printers monopolized for years (which is why we play *allegro* and not *schnell*). Italy also gave us the *pianoforte*, because unlike the harpsichord you could play both soft and loud, and the accordion, invented in the Marches, and the violins of the Guarneri and Stradivarius of Cremona, setting a standard for the instrument that has never been equalled. But Italy is most famous as the mother of opera, the most Italian of arts.

Italian composers first came into their own in the 14th century, led by the half-legendary, blind Florentine **Landini**, whose *Ecco la Primavera* is one of the first Italian compositions to come down to us. Although following international trends introduced by musicians from France and the Low Countries, musicologists note from the start a special love of melody, even in earlier Italian works, as well as a preference for vocal music over the purely instrumental.

Landini was followed by the age of the ***frottolas*** (secular verses accompanied by lutes), especially prominent in the court of Mantua. The *frottolas* were forerunners of the **madrigal**, the greatest Italian musical invention during the Renaissance. Although sung in three or six parts, the text of the madrigals was given serious consideration, and was sung to be understood; at the same time church music had become so polyphonically rich and sumptuous (most notoriously at St Mark's in Venice) that it drowned out the words of the Mass. Many melodies used were from secular and often bawdy songs, and the bishops at the Council of Trent (1545–63) seriously considered banning music from the liturgy. The day was saved by the Roman composers, led by **Palestrina**, whose solemn, simple, but beautiful melodies set a standard for all subsequent composers.

Two contrasting strains near the end of the 16th century led to the birth of opera: the Baroque love of spectacle and the urge to make everything, at least on the surface, more beautiful, more elaborate, more showy. Musically there were the lavish Florentine *intermedii*, performed on special occasions between the acts of plays; the *intermedii* used elaborate sets and costumes, songs, choruses and dances to set a mythological scene.

At the same time, in Florence, a group of humanist intellectuals who called themselves the *Camerata* came to the conclusion from their classical studies that ancient Greek drama was not spoken, but sung, and took it upon themselves to try to recreate this pure and classical form. One of their chief theorists was Galileo's father Vincenzo, who studied Greek, Turkish and Moorish music and advocated the clear enunciation of the words, as opposed to the Venetian tendency to merge words and music as a single rich unit of sound.

One of the first results of the Camerata's debates was court musician **Jacopo Peri**'s *L'Euridice*, performed in Florence in 1600. Peri used a kind of singing speech (recitative) to tell the story, interspersed with a few melodic songs. No one, it seems, asked for an encore; opera had to wait a few years, until the Duchess of Mantua asked her court composer, **Claudio Monteverdi** (1567–1643), to compose something like the work she had heard in Florence. Monteverdi went far beyond Peri, bringing in a large orchestra, designing elegant sets, adding dances and many more melodic songs (*arias*). His classic *L'Orfeo* (1607), still heard today, and *L'Arianna* (unfortunately lost but for fragments) were the first operatic 'hits'. Monteverdi moved on to bigger audiences in Venice, which soon had 11 opera houses. After he died, though, Naples took over top opera honours, gaining special renown for its clear-toned *castrati*.

Other advances were developing in the more pious atmosphere of Rome, where **Corelli** was perfecting the concerto and composing his famous *Christmas Concerto*. In Venice, **Vivaldi** greatly expanded the genre by composing some four hundred *concerti* for whatever instruments happened to be played in the orchestra of orphaned girls where he was concert-master.

The 18th century saw the sonata form perfected by harpsichord master **Domenico Scarlatti**. Opera was rid of some of its Baroque excesses and a division was set between serious works and the comic *opera buffa*; **Pergolesi** (1710–36 – his *Il Flaminio* was the basis for Stravinsky's *Pulcinella*) and **Cimarosa** (1749–1801) were the most sought-after composers, while the now infamous **Salieri**, antagonist of Mozart, charmed the court of Vienna. Italian composers held sway throughout Europe; they contributed more than is generally acknowledged today towards the founding of modern music.

Italy innovated less in the 19th century; at this time most of its musical energies were devoted to opera, becoming the reviving nation's clearest and most widely appreciated medium of self-expression. All of the most popular Italian operas were written in the 19th and early 20th centuries, most of them by the 'Big Five' – Bellini, Donizetti, Rossini, Verdi and Puccini. For Italians, **Verdi** (1813–1901) is supreme, the national idol even in his lifetime, whose rousing operas were practically the battle hymns of the Risorgimento. Verdi, more than anyone else, re-established Italy on the musical map; his works provided Italy's melodic answer to the ponderous turbulence of Richard Wagner. After Verdi, **Puccini** held the operatic stage, though not entirely singlehandedly; the later 19th century gave us a number of composers best remembered for only one opera: Leoncavallo's *Pagliacci*, Mascagni's *Cavalleria Rusticana*, Cilea's *Adriana Lecouvreur*, and many others down to obscure composers like Giordano, whose *Fedora*, famous for being the only opera with bicycles on stage, is revived frequently in his hometown of Foggia.

Of more recent Italian, and Italian-American, composers there's *The Pines of Rome* of **Respighi** (whose works were among the few 20th-century productions that the great Toscanini deigned to direct) and **Gian Carlo Menotti**, surely the best loved, not only for his operas but for founding the Spoleto Festival. Lately there are the innovative post-war composers **Luigi Nono** and **Luciano Berio**, two respected names in contemporary academic music.

Next to all of this big-league culture, however, there survive remnants of Italy's traditional music – the pungent tunes of Italian bagpipes (*zampogna*), the ancient instrument of the Apennine shepherds, often heard in the big cities (especially in the south) at Christmas time; the lively *tarantellas* of Puglia; country accordion music, the fare of many a rural *festa*; and the great song tradition of the country's music capital, Naples, the cradle of everyone's favourite cornball classics, but also of many haunting, passionate melodies of tragedy and romance that are rarely heard abroad – or, to be honest, in Italy itself these days.

Opera season in Italy runs roughly from November to May. The Teatro dell'Opera in **Rome** and the Teatro Comunale in **Florence** can both put on innovative productions; and hopefully La Fenice in Venice will reopen before too long. Summer festivals are an excellent place to hear music; check through the list of festivals on p.89.

Cinema

After the Second World War, when Italy was at its lowest ebb, when it was finan-cially and culturally bankrupt, when its traditional creativity in painting, architecture and music seemed to have dried up, along came a handful of Italian directors who invented a whole new language of cinema. Neorealism was a response to the fictions propagated by years of Fascism; it was also a response to the lack of movie-making equipment after the Romans – their eyes suddenly opened after a decade of decep-tion and mindless 'White Telephone' comedies – pillaged and sacked Cinecittà in 1943. Stark, unsentimental, often shot in bleak locations with unprofessional actors, the genre took shape with directors like Roberto Rossellini (*Roma, Open City*, 1945), Vittorio de Sica (*Bicycle Thieves*, 1948) and Luchino Visconti (*The Earth Trembles*, 1948).

Although neorealism continued to influence Italian cinema (Rossellini's films with Ingrid Bergman, like *Europa 51* and *Stromboli*, Fellini's classic *La Strada* with Giulietta Masina and Anthony Quinn, Antonioni's *The Scream*), Italian directors began to go off in their own directions. The post-war period was the golden age of Italian cinema, when Italy's Hollywood, Cinecittà, produced scores of films every year. Like the artists of the Age of Mannerism, a new generation of individualistic (or egoistic) directors created works that needed no signature, ranging from Sergio Leone's ultra-popular kitsch westerns to the often jarring films of the Marxist poet Pasolini (*Accattone*, *The Decameron*). This was the period of Visconti's *The Damned*, Antonioni's *Blow Up*, Lina Wertmuller's *Seven Beauties*, De Sica's *Neapolitan Gold*, Bertolucci's *The Conformist*, and the classics of the indefatigable maestro Federico Fellini – *I Vitelloni*, *La Dolce Vita*, *Juliet of the Spirits*, *The Clowns*, *Satyricon*.

In the seventies the cost of making films soared and the industry went into recession. Increasingly, directors went abroad or sought out actors with international appeal in order to reach a larger audience, to help finance their films (Bertolucci's *Last Tango in Paris* with Marlon Brando and *1900* with Donald Sutherland, the overripe Franco Zeffirelli's *Taming of the Shrew* with Taylor and Burton, Visconti's *Death in Venice*). Fellini was one of the few who managed to stay home (*Roma*, *Amarcord*, and later *Casanova* (although admittedly with Donald Sutherland in the lead role), *City of Women*, *The Ship Sails On*, *Orchestra Rehearsal* and *Intervista*, a film about Cinecittà itself).

Although funding became even scarcer in the eighties, new directors appeared to recharge Italian cinema, often with a fresh lyrical realism and sensitivity. Bright stars of the decade included Ermanno Olmi (the beautiful *Tree of the Wooden Clogs* and *Cammina, Cammina*), Giuseppe Tornatore's sentimental and nostalgic *Cinema Paradiso* (1988), Paolo and Vittorio Taviani (*Padre Padrone*, *Night of the Shooting Stars*, *Kaos* and *Good Morning Babilonia*), Francesco Rosi (*Christ Stopped at Eboli*, *Three Brothers*, *Carmen* and *Cronaca d'una morte annunciata*), and Nanni Moretti (*La Messa é finita*), unfortunately rarely seen outside of festivals and film clubs abroad, while Zeffirelli (*La Traviata*) and Bertolucci (*1900*, *The Last Emperor*) continued to represent Italy in the world's movie-houses. Comedy found new life in Mario Monticelli's hilarious *Speriamo che sia femina* and in Bruno Bozzetto, whose animation features (especially *Allegro Non Troppo*, a satire of Disney's *Fantasia*) are a scream.

The 1990s served up fairly thin gruel, a recession of inspiration to go with the economy. Worthy exceptions have been *Il Ladro dei bambini* (1992) by Gianni Amelio, *Mediterraneo* (1991) by Gabriele Salvatores, about Italian soldiers marooned on a Greek island, Nanni Moretti's travelogue to the Ionian islands, *Caro Diario* (1994), Franco Zeffirelli's *Hamlet* (1990), a surprise both for casting Mel Gibson in the leading role and actually setting the film in 12th-century Denmark, and *Il Postino* (1995), directed by Michael Radford, a very Italian story about the relationship of a local postman with the poet Pablo Neruda, exiled on an Italian island.

This was also the decade that Fellini spun his final reel. Although critics at home and abroad sometimes complained that he repeated himself in his last films (*Ginger and Fred* and *La Voce della Luna*, 1990), his loyal fans eagerly awaited each new instalment of his personal fantasy, his alternative hyper-Italy that exists on the other side of the looking glass in the gossamer warp of the silver screen. The last director regularly to use Cinecittà ('Cinecittà is not my home; I just live there,' he once said), his demise may well bring about the end of Rome's pretensions as Hollywood on the Mediterranean.

In the past few years, Bernardo Bertolucci has returned to the scene with *Stealing Beauty* (1996), a lush Tuscan coming-of-age drama, and *Besieged* (1998), the story of the romance between an Italian composer and an African political refugee, filmed in Rome. But all in all the most acclaimed recent Italian film has been Roberto Benigni's unlikely comedy on the Holocaust, *La Vita e Bella* (1999),

Italian films are windows of the nation's soul, but if you don't understand Italian you may want to see them at home, where you have the advantage of subtitles. English-language films in Italy rarely receive the same courtesy, however – Italians like their movies dubbed. Check listings for films labelled '*versione originale*' – you're bound to find a few in Rome (*see* p.108), and often in other big cities as well. There are also Italy's film festivals (where films tend to be subtitled); the most important one is in Venice (last week of August to first week of September); Florence hosts a documentary festival in December.

Snapshots of Italy

Bella Figura

The longer you stay in Italy, the more inscrutable it becomes. Nothing is ever quite as it seems, and you'll find yourself changing your ideas about things with disconcerting frequency. Part of the reason is the obsession to *fare una bella figura*, 'to make a good impression or appearance', one of the most singular traits of the Italian people. You notice it almost immediately upon arrival. Not only is every Italian an immaculately smart fashion victim, but they always seem to be modelling their spiffy threads – posing, gesturing, playing to an audience when they have one, which is nearly always, because Italians rarely move about except in small herds. Their cities are their stage. Long-time observers of the phenomenon have even noted that each city's women tend to dress in colours that complement the local brick or stone.

The Italians' natural grace and elegance may be partly instinctive; even back in the 14th century, foreigners invariably noted their charming manners and taste for exquisite clothes. Many a painting of the Madonna served not only piety's sake, but also advertised the latest Milanese silks or Venetian brocades. Appearance supplanted reality in a thousand ways in the Renaissance, especially after the discovery of artificial perspective, which made artistic representations seem much more clever and interesting than the real thing. Fake, painted marble supplanted real marble, even if the fake cost more; Palladio built marble palaces out of stucco; *trompe l'œil* frescoes embellished a hundred churches; glorious façades on cathedrals and palaces disguise the fact that the rest is shabby, unfinished brick. The gentleman's bible of the day, Castiglione's *The Courtier*, advises that it is no use doing a brave and noble deed unless someone is watching.

Bella figura pleases the eye but irritates just about everything else. Fashionable conformity has a way of spreading from mere clothing and gestures to opinions, especially in the provinces; the Italians remain the masters of empty flattery and compliments, and will say anything to please: 'Yes, straight ahead!' they'll often reply when you need directions, hoping it will make you happy even if they've never heard of your destination.

Nor does fashion slavery show any sign of abating; now that more Italians have more money than ever before, they are using it for fur coats, rarely necessary in most of the country's winters, and for designer clothes for the whole family. Even little children go to bed with visions of fashion dancing in their heads.

Brick Italy, Marble Italy

'Italy', begins the 1948 Constitution, 'is a republic based on labour' – an unusual turn of phrase, perhaps, but one entirely in keeping with a time when a thoroughly humbled Italy was beginning to get back on its feet after the War. The sorrows of the common man occupied the plots of post-war *cinema verità*, and artists and writers began to celebrate themes of Faith, Bread and Work as if they were in the employ of the Church's *Famiglia Cristiana* magazine. To outsiders it must have seemed that Italy was undergoing a serious change, but careful observers would have noted only another oscillation in the grandest, oldest dichotomy in Italian history. Brick Italy was once more in the driver's seat.

Brick Italy is a nation of hard work, humility and piety that knows it must be diligent and clever to wrest a comfortable living from the thin soil of this rocky, resource-poor peninsula. Marble Italy knows its citizens are perfectly capable of doing just that, just as they always have, and seeks to celebrate that diligence and cleverness by turning it into opulence, excess and foreign conquest. The two have been contending for Italy's soul ever since Roman quarrymen discovered the great veins of Carrara marble during the Republican era. Brick Italy's capital in former times was brilliant, republican Siena; right now it is virtuous, hard-working socialist Bologna, a city with more bricks that Woolworth's has nickels. Its triumphs came with the Age of the *Comuni*, with the modest genius of the Early Renaissance, and with the hard-won successes of the last 40 years. Marble Italy reached its height in the days of Imperial Rome; its capital is Rome, always and forever. After the medieval interlude, marble made its great come-back with the High Renaissance, Spaniardism and Michelangelo, the high priest of marble. The Age of Baroque belonged to it completely, as did the brief era of Mussolini. Some confirmed Marble cities are Naples, Genoa, Turin, Pisa, Parma, Trieste, Perugia and Verona. Brick partisans include Pavia, Livorno, Lucca, Arezzo, Cremona and Mantua. Florence and Venice, the two medieval city-republics that eventually became important states on their own, are the two cities that most successfully straddle the fence. Look carefully at their old churches and palaces: you will often find marble veneer outside and solid brick underneath.

Keep all this in mind when you ponder the infinite subtleties of Italian history. It isn't always a perfect fit; medieval Guelphs and Ghibellines each had a little brick and a little marble in them, and the contemporary papacy changes from one to the other with every shift of the wind. Mussolini would have paved Italy over in marble if he had been able – but look at the monuments he could afford, and you'll see more inexpensive travertine and brick than anything else. For a while in the eighties, with Italy's economic successes and the glitz of Milanese fashion and design, it looked as if Marble Italy was about to make another comeback. But today, with Italy in the midst of its long and tortuous revolution, the situation is unclear. If and when a new regime emerges, will its monument to itself be a beautiful symbol of republican aspirations, like Siena's brick Palazzo del Pubblico, or a florid marble pile like Rome's Altar of the Nation, the monument to Italian unification (and one of the biggest hunks of kitsch on this planet)?

Commedia dell'Arte

The first recorded mention of Arlecchino, or Harlequin, came when the part was played by a celebrated actor named Tristano Martinelli in 1601 – the year that also saw the début of *Hamlet*. Theatre as we know it was blooming all over Europe in those times: Shakespeare and Marlowe, Calderón and Lope de Vega in Spain, the predecessors of Molière in France. All of these had learned their craft from late-Renaissance Italy, where the *commedia dell'arte* had created a fashion that spread across the continent. The great companies, such as the Gelosi, the Confidenti and the Accesi, toured the capitals, while others shared out the provinces. Groups of ten or twelve actors, run as co-operatives, they could do comedies, tragedies or pastorals, to their own texts, and provide music, dance, magic and juggling between acts.

The audiences liked the comedies best of all, with a set of masked stock characters, playing off scenes between the *magnificos*, the great lords, and the *zanni*, or servants, who provide the slapstick, half-improvised comic relief. These represented every corner of Italy: Arlecchino is a Bergamese; Balanzone, the wise doctor who 'cures with Latin', is from Bologna; white-clad, warbling Pulcinello a true Neapolitan; Meneghino, the piratical warrior, a Milanese; the drunkard Rugantino is a Roman; and the nervous rich merchant Pantalone is a Venetian; while the maid Colombina apparently belongs to all. To spring the plot there would be a pair of *inamorati*, or lovers – unmasked, to remind us that only those who are in love are really alive.

It had nothing to do with 'art'. *Arte* means a guild, to emphasize that these companies were made up of professional players. The term was invented in 1745 by Goldoni (who wrote one of the last plays of the genre, *Arlecchino, servitore di due padroni*); in the 1500s the companies were often referred to as the *commedia mercenaria* – they would hit town, set up a stage on trestles, and start their show within the hour.

Cultured Italians of the day often deplored the way the 'mercenary' shows were driving out serious drama, traditionally written by scholarly amateurs in the princely courts. In the repressive climate of the day, caught between the Inquisition and the Spanish bosses, a culture of ideas survived only in free Venice. Theatre retreated into humorous popular entertainment, but the Italians still found a way to say what was on their minds. A new character appeared, the menacing but slow-witted Capitano, who always spoke with a Spanish accent, and Italians learned from the French how to use Arlecchino to satirize the hated emperor Charles V himself – playing on the French pronunciation of the names *harlequin* and *Charles Quint*.

Arlecchino may have been born in Oneta, a village north of Bergamo, but he carries a proud lineage that goes back to the ancient Greeks and Romans. From his character and appearance, historians of the theatre trace him back to the antique planipedes, comic mimes with shaved heads (everyone knew Arlecchino wore his silly nightcap to cover his baldness). Other scholars note his relationship to the 'tricksters' of German and Scandinavian mythology, and it has even been claimed that his costume of patches is that of a Sufi dervish. No doubt he had a brilliant career all through the Middle Ages, though it was probably only in the 1500s that he took the form of the Arlecchino we know. At that time, young rustics from the Bergamese valleys would go to Venice, Milan and other cities to get work as *facchini*, porters. They all seemed to be named Johnny – *Zanni* in dialect – which became the common term for any of the clownish roles in the plays; it's the origin of our word 'zany'.

The name 'Arlecchino' seems actually to have been a French contribution. At the court of Henri III, a certain Italian actor who played the role became a protégé of a Monsieur de Harlay, and people started calling him 'little Harlay', or Harlequin. The character developed into a stock role, the most beloved of all the *commedia dell'arte* clown masks: simple-minded and easily frightened, yet an incorrigible prankster, a fellow as unstable as his motley dress. His foil was usually another servant, the Neapolitan Puricinella, or Punchinella – Punch – more serious and sometimes boastful, but still just as much of a buffoon. Try to imagine them together on stage, and you'll get something that looks very much like Stan Laurel and Oliver Hardy. No doubt these two have always gone through the world together, and we can hope they always will.

Pasta

Croton and Sybaris, among other Greek cities of the Ionian Sea, take the credit for introducing the Italians to their future hearts' delight. A small, cylindrical form of pasta called *makaria* – perhaps the original *macaroni* – was a ritual food eaten at funeral banquets; by 600 BC, the Sybarites, always on the hunt for new culinary experiences, had invented the rolling pin and were turning out *tagliatelle* and maybe even *lasagne*. Not yet having tomatoes, they were unable to perfect the concept, but, in a nation that often has trouble baking a decent loaf of bread, this delicious, aesthetically stimulating and eminently practical new staple found a warm welcome everywhere. Pasta's triumphal march northwards finally slowed to a halt in the rice paddies and treacherous *polenta* morasses of Lombardy, but everywhere else it remains in firm control.

Pasta does have its cultural ramifications. The artists of the Futurist movement wanted to declare war on spaghetti, and many of today's Italian *nouveaux riches* wouldn't be caught dead ordering any form of pasta in a restaurant (this, ironically, at a time when their counterparts in northern Europe and America wax ever more enthusiastic about it). Do you think that pasta is all the same? Well, so do millions of Italians, though an equal number revel in the incredible variety of pasta forms and fashions; in your travels you'll find the same flour and water turned into broad *pappardelle* and narrow *linguini* ('tiny tongues'), stuffed delights like *ravioli* and *tortellini*, regional specialities like Puglian *orecchietti* ('little ears') and Sardinia's *malorreddus*, that resemble miniature trilobites. Other inviting forms, among the 400 or so known shapes, include *vermicelli* ('little worms'), *lumacconi* ('slugs'), *bavette* ('dribbles') and *strangolopreti* ('priest chokers'). But even these fail to satisfy the nation's culinary whims, and every so often one of the big pasta companies will commission a big-name fashion designer to come up with a new form.

The Pinocchio Complex

The Italians, as much as they adore their *bambini*, have produced but one recognized classic of children's literature, the story of a naughty wooden puppet who must pass through trials and tribulations before he can become a real boy – a stable, responsible child, a blessing to his father in his old age.

Since the Risorgimento, the Italian government has been a bit of a Pinocchio to the old country that painfully carved it out of wood, admittedly half petrified and half rotted from the start. Each ring of the thick trunk told a dire tale of defeat and tyranny, corruption, papal misgovernment, foreign rule and betrayal. From this piece of flotsam the Italians created a new creature, a national state that sits in the class of real governments like a mischievous, exasperating puppet. This Pinocchio is the bad boy of the EU, with more violations of its trade rules than any other nation. Every day its parliament is in session, its nose grows a little bit longer. With its creaky wooden bureaucracy, unpredictable and not blessed with the soundest of judgements, it is constantly led astray by scheming foxes and cats – like the Mafia, power-hungry cabals of 'freemasons', southern landowners, Mussolinis, popes, Jesuits and whale-sized special interests that threaten to gobble it down whole. The parties that make up its *commedia dell'arte* coalitions, like flimsy wooden limbs and joints, are liable to trip up or fly off at any moment, making the poor marionette collapse (something that since 1946 has occurred an average of once every 11 months).

Just as Pinocchio, by some unexplained power, is able to walk without strings, so Italy, without a real government, functions with remarkable smoothness, and even prospers. Understandably, as Europe grows ever closer together, having a wooden-headed political system becomes more and more embarrassing. Constitutional reform, with the 1993 referendum that changed the electoral system, may prove a threat to this puppet's career. And, with the revelations of the last few years, Italians are beginning to interest themselves in the all-important question of who, all this time, has been pulling the strings.

Food and Drink

04

*In Rome people spend most of their time having lunch. And they do it very well –
Rome is unquestionably the lunch capital of the world.*

Fran Lebowitz, *Metropolitan Life*, 1978

There are those who eat to live and those who live to eat, and then there are the
Italians, for whom food has an almost religious significance, unfathomably linked
with love, La Mamma, and tradition. In this singular country, where millions of
otherwise sane people spend much of their waking hours worrying about their
digestion, standards both at home and in restaurants are understandably high. Few
Italians are gluttons, but all are experts on what is what in the kitchen. For the visitor
this national culinary obsession comes as an extra bonus to the senses – along with
Italy's remarkable sights, music and the warm sun on your back, you can enjoy some
of the best tastes and smells the world can offer, prepared daily in Italy's kitchens and
fermented in its wine cellars. Eating *all'Italiana* is not only delicious and wholesome,
but now undeniably trendy. Foreigners flock here to learn the secrets of Italian
cuisine and the even more elusive secret of how the Italians can live surrounded by
such delights and still fit into their sleek Armani trousers.

The pace of modern urban life militates against traditional lengthy home-cooked
repasts with the family; many office workers in northern cities behave much as their
counterparts elsewhere in Europe and consume a rapid slimline snack at lunchtime,
returning home after a busy day to throw together some pasta and salad. But those
with more leisure can still eat extremely well. Many Italian dishes need no introduction – pizza, spaghetti, lasagne and minestrone are now familiar well beyond
national boundaries. What is perhaps less well known is the tremendous regional
diversity at the table. Each corner of Italy prides itself on its own specialities, the
shape of its pasta, its soups and sauces, its wines and desserts. Tuscan and Umbrian
cooking uses fresh, simple, high-quality ingredients flavoured with herbs and olive
oil, and the local *porcini* mushrooms or truffles. The further south you go, the spicier
and oilier things get, and the richer the puddings and cakes. Modern Romans are as
adventurous at the table as their classical ancestors, and include some stomach-
churning offal in their diets. But the capital is an excellent place to delve into any
style of regional cooking.

Restaurant Generalities

Breakfast (*colazione*) in Italy is no lingering affair, but an early-morning wake-up
shot to the brain: a *cappuccino* (incidentally, first thing in the morning is the only time
of day at which any self-respecting Italian will touch the stuff), a *caffè latte* (white
coffee) or a *caffè lungo* (a generous portion of espresso), accompanied by a croissant-
type roll, called a *cornetto* or *briosce*, or a fancy pastry. This repast can be consumed in
any bar and repeated during the morning as often as necessary. Breakfast in most
Italian hotels seldom represents great value.

Lunch (*pranzo*), generally served around 1pm, is the most important meal of the day
for the Italians, with a minimum of a first course (*primo piatto* – any kind of pasta

dish, broth or soup, or rice dish or pizza), a second course (*secondo piatto* – a meat dish, accompanied by a *contorno* or side dish – a vegetable, salad or potatoes), followed by fruit or dessert and coffee. You can, however, begin with a platter of *antipasti* – the appetizers Italians do so brilliantly – ranging from warm seafood delicacies to raw ham (*prosciutto crudo*), salami in a hundred varieties, lovely vegetables, savoury toasts, olives, pâté and many many more. There are restaurants that specialize in *antipasti*, and they usually don't take it amiss if you decide to forget the pasta and meat and just nibble on these scrumptious hors-d'œuvres (though in the end it will probably cost more than a full meal). Most Italians accompany their meal with wine and mineral water – *acqua minerale*, with or without bubbles (*con* or *senza gas*), which supposedly aids digestion – concluding their meals with a *digestivo*.

Cena, the evening meal, is usually eaten around 8pm. This is much the same as *pranzo* although lighter, without the pasta; a pizza and beer, eggs or a fish dish. In restaurants, however, they offer all the courses, so if you have only a sandwich for lunch you can have a full meal in the evening.

In Italy the various terms for types of **restaurants** – *ristorante*, *trattoria* or *osteria* – have been confused. Although traditionally a *trattoria* is a cheaper, simpler place than a *ristorante*, in reality they are often exactly the same, both in quality and price, the only difference being, presumably, that a *ristorante* has more pretensions. Be careful with *trattorie*, though: the name is beginning to define something more rustic and authentic than your average restaurant (a form of inverted snobbery that classes some *trattorie* as 'chic'). Invariably the least expensive eating place is the *vino e cucina*, a simple establishment serving simple cuisine at simple everyday prices. It is essential to remember that the fancier the fittings, the fancier the bill. If you're uncertain, do as you would at home – look for lots of locals.

People who haven't visited Italy for years and have fond memories of eating full meals for under £1 will be amazed at how much **prices** have risen, though in some respects eating out is still a bargain, especially when you figure out how much all that wine would have cost you at home. You'll often find restaurants offering a *menu turistico* – full, set meals of usually meagre inspiration for €10–20. More imaginative chefs often offer a *menu degustazione* – a set-price gourmet meal that allows you to taste their daily specialities and seasonal dishes. Both of these are cheaper than if you had ordered the same food *alla carta*. In this book we have divided restaurants into price categories (*see* **Practical A–Z**, p.88).

There are several alternatives to sit-down meals. The 'hot table' (*tavola calda*) is a stand-up buffet where you can choose a simple prepared dish or a whole meal, depending on your appetite. The food in these can be truly impressive; many offer only a few hot dishes, pizza and sandwiches, though in every fair-sized town there will be at least one *tavola calda* with seats where you can contrive a complete dinner outside the usual hours. Little shops that sell pizza by the slice are common in city centres. At any grocer's (*alimentari*) or market (*mercato*) you can buy the materials for countryside or hotel-room picnics. For really elegant picnics, have a *tavola calda* pack up something nice for you. And if everywhere else is closed, there's always the railway station – bars will at least have sandwiches and drinks, and perhaps some

Italian Menu Reader

Antipasti
These before-meal treats can include almost anything; among the most common are:

antipasto misto mixed antipasti
bruschetta garlic toast (sometimes with tomatoes)
carciofi (sott'olio) artichokes (in oil)
frutti di mare seafood
funghi (trifolati) mushrooms (with anchovies, garlic, lemon)
gamberi ai fagioli prawns (shrimps) with white beans
mozzarella (in carrozza) cow/buffalo cheese (fried with bread in batter)
prosciutto (con melone) raw ham (with melon)
salsicce sausages

Minestre (Soups) and Pasta
agnolotti ravioli with meat
cappelletti small ravioli, often in broth
crespelle crêpes
frittata omelette
orecchiette ear-shaped pasta, served with turnip greens
panzerotti ravioli with mozzarella, anchovies, and egg

pasta e fagioli soup with beans, bacon, and tomatoes
pastina in brodo tiny pasta in broth
polenta cake or pudding of corn semolina
spaghetti all'Amatriciana with spicy pork, tomato, onion and chilli sauce
spaghetti alle vongole with clam sauce
stracciatella broth with eggs and cheese

Carne (Meat)
agnello lamb
anatra duck
arrosto misto mixed roast meats
bollito misto stew of boiled meats
braciola chop
brasato di manzo braised beef with veg
bresaola dried raw meat
carpaccio thinly sliced raw beef
cassoeula pork stew with cabbage
cervello brains
cervo venison
coniglio rabbit
lumache snails
manzo beef
osso buco braised veal knuckle
pancetta rolled pork
piccione pigeon
pizzaiola beef in tomato and oregano sauce
pollo chicken

surprisingly good snacks you've never heard of before. Some of the station bars also prepare *cestini di viaggio*, full-course meals in a basket to help you through long train trips. Common snacks you'll encounter include *panini* of prosciutto, cheese and tomatoes, or other meats; *tramezzini*, little sandwiches on plain, square white bread (much better than they look); and pizza, of course.

Wine and Spirits

Italy is a country where everyday wine is cheaper than Coca-Cola or milk, and where nearly every family owns some vineyards or has some relatives who supply most of their daily needs – which are not great. Even though they live in one of the world's largest wine-growing countries, Italians imbibe relatively little, and only at meals.

If Italy has an infinite variety of regional dishes, there is an equally bewildering array of **regional wines**, many of which are rarely exported because they are best drunk young. Even wines that are well known and often derided clichés abroad, like Chianti or Lambrusco, can be wonderful new experiences when tasted on their home turf. Unless you're dining at a restaurant with an exceptional cellar, do as the Italians do and order a carafe of the local wine (*vino locale* or *vino della casa*). You won't often be

polpette meatballs
rognoni kidneys
saltimbocca veal, prosciutto and sage, in wine
scaloppine thin slices of veal sautéed in butter
stufato beef and vegetables braised in wine
tacchino turkey
vitello veal

Pesce (Fish)

acciughe or *alici* anchovies
anguilla eel
aragosta lobster
baccalà dried salt cod
bonito small tuna
calamari squid
cappe sante scallops
cozze mussels
fritto misto mixed firied fish
gamberetto shrimp
gamberi prawns
granchio crab
insalata di mare seafood salad
merluzzo cod
ostriche oysters
pesce spada swordfish
polipi/polpi octopus
sarde sardines
sogliola sole
squadro monkfish

stoccafisso wind-dried cod
tonno tuna
vongole small clams
zuppa di pesce fish in sauce or stew

Contorni (Side Dishes, Vegetables)

asparagi asparagus
carciofi artichokes
cavolo cabbage
ceci chickpeas
cetriolo cucumber
cipolla onion
fagiolini French (green) beans
fave broad beans
funghi (porcini) mushrooms (boletus)
insalata salad
lenticchie lentils
melanzane aubergine
patate (fritte) potatoes (fried)
peperoni sweet peppers
peperonata stewed peppers
piselli (al prosciutto) peas (with ham)
pomodoro(i) tomato(es)
porri leeks
rucola rocket
verdure greens
zucca pumpkin
zucchini courgettes

wrong. Most Italian wines are named after the grape and the district they come from. If the label says DOC (*Denominazione di Origine Controllata*) it means that the wine comes from a specially defined area and was produced according to a certain traditional method. DOCG (*Denominazione d'Origine Controllata e Garantia*) is allegedly a more rigorous classification, indicating that the wines not only conform to DOC standards, but are tested by government-appointed inspectors (who are now more in evidence since a hideous methanol scandal claimed 20 lives in 1986). At present few wines have been granted this status, but the number is planned to increase steadily. *Classico* means that a wine comes from the oldest part of the zone of production, though is not necessarily better than a non-Classico. *Riserva*, *superiore* or *speciale* denotes a wine that has been aged longer and is more alcoholic; *Recioto* is a wine made from the outer clusters of grapes, with a higher sugar and therefore alcohol content. Other Italian wine words are *spumante* (sparkling), *frizzante* (pétillant), *amabile* (semi-sweet), *abboccato* (medium dry), *passito* (strong sweet wine made from raisins). *Rosso* is red, *bianco* white; between the two extremes lie *rubiato* (ruby), *rosato*, *chiaretto* or *cerasuolo* (rosé). *Secco* is dry, *dolce* sweet, *liquoroso* fortified and sweet. *Vendemmia* means vintage, a *cantina* is a cellar, and an *enoteca* is a wine shop or museum where you can taste and buy wines. The regions of Piedmont, Tuscany and

Formaggio (Cheese)

bel paese soft white cow's cheese
cacio/caciocavallo pale yellow, sharp cheese
caprino goat's cheese
parmigiano parmesan cheese
pecorino sharp sheep's cheese
provolone sharp, tangy cheese;
   dolce is less strong
stracchino soft white cheese

Frutta (Fruit, Nuts)

albicocche apricots
ananas pineapple
arance oranges
banane bananas
ciliege cherries
cocomero watermelon
fragole strawberries
frutta di stagione fruit in season
lamponi raspberries
limone lemon
macedonia di frutta fruit salad
mandorle almonds
mele apples
more blackberries
nocciole hazelnuts
noci walnuts
pesca peach
pesca noce nectarine

pompelmo grapefruit
prugna/susina prune/plum
uva grapes

Dolci (Desserts)

amaretti macaroons
crostata fruit flan
gelato (produzione propria) ice cream (home-made)
granita flavoured ice, usually lemon or coffee
panettone cake with candied fruit and raisins
semifreddo refrigerated cake
spumone a soft ice cream
torta cake, tart
zabaglione eggs and Marsala wine, served hot
zuppa inglese trifle

Bevande (Beverages)

acqua minerale mineral water
   con/senza gas with/without fizz
aranciata orange soda
birra (alla spina) beer (draught)
caffè (freddo) coffee (iced)
cioccolata (con panna) chocolate (with cream)
latte (interno/scremato) milk (whole/skimmed)
succo di frutta fruit juice
tè tea
vino (rosso, bianco, rosato) wine
   (red, white, rosé)

Veneto produce Italy's most prestigious red wines, while Friuli-Venezia Giulia and Trentino-Alto Adige are the greatest regions for white wines. King of the Tuscans is the mighty Brunello di Montalcino (DOCG), an expensive blockbuster. Pinot Grigio and the unusual Tocai make some of the best whites.

Italy turns its grape harvest to other uses too, producing Sicilian **Marsala**, a famous fortified wine fermented in wooden casks, ranging from very dry to flavoured and sweet and **vin santo**, a sweet Tuscan speciality often served with almond biscuits. **Vermouth** is an idea from Turin made of wine flavoured with Alpine herbs and spices. Italians are fond of post-prandial brandies (to aid digestion) – **Stock** or **Vecchia Romagna** appear on the best-known Italian brandy bottles. **Grappa** is a rough, Schnapps-like spirit drunk in black coffee after a meal (a *caffè corretto*). Other drinks you'll see in any Italian bar include **Campari**, a red bitter drunk on its own or in cocktails; **Fernet Branca**, **Cynar** and **Averno** (popular *apéritif/digestifs*); and a host of liqueurs like **Strega**, the witch potion from Benevento, apricot-flavoured **Amaretto**, cherry **Maraschino**, aniseed **Sambuca** or the herby **Millefiori**.

Travel

05

Getting There

By Air from the UK and Ireland

Rome and Venice have an excellent choice of year-round scheduled flights; Florence has fewer direct flights, but you can travel from Gatwick to Florence with Meridiana Italia and the city is well connected by rail to Pisa.

Over the last few years the airline industry has undergone a revolution. Inspired by the success of the easyJet company, many smaller airlines – Ryanair, Virgin – flocked to join it in breaking all the conventions of air travel in a remarkable attempt to offer fares at rock-bottom prices. Fares are one-way – dispensing with the traditional need to stay over on a Saturday night to qualify for a low fare. You will not be issued with a ticket when you book, and you will be encouraged, sometimes even by a price discount, to book on-line. When you check in, you will be issued with a boarding card, but you may not have an assigned seat. There are no 'air miles', no discounts on top of the low ticket price and no meal will be served, though there will usually be snacks for sale. There are no refunds, and there are charges for excess baggage. Currently Ryanair, easyJet and Now fly to Rome, easyJet to Venice, Ryanair to Treviso for Venice, and Ryanair to Pisa for Florence.

The success of this method of travel has been such that scheduled airlines like BA and Alitalia have begun to copy the tactics, to the advantage of the traveller. The key is, always shop around, and book online of you can.

By Air from the USA and Canada

The main Italian air gateways for direct flights from North America are Rome and Milan, though, if you're doing a grand tour, check fares to other European destinations (Paris or Amsterdam, for example) which may well be cheaper.

It may be worth catching a cheap flight to London (New York–London fares are always very competitive) and then flying on from

there. Prices are rather more from Canada, so you may prefer to fly from the States.

For **discounted flights**, try the small ads in newspaper travel pages (e.g. *New York Times, Chicago Tribune, Toronto Globe & Mail*). Numerous travel clubs and agencies also specialize in discount fares, but may require an annual membership fee.

Travelling to and from the Airport

Rome: The main airport, **Leonardo da Vinci**, is usually referred to as **Fiumicino** (t 06 65951). Taking a taxi from there into Rome should cost about €40, including airport and luggage supplements. There are two rail links from the airport to the city: to Stazioni Trastevere, Ostiense, Tuscolana and Tiburtina (every 20mins; €5) and a direct service to Stazione Termini, Rome's main rail station (every 30mins; €10). Between 1.15 and 5am, COTRAL buses run from outside the Arrivals hall to Stazioni Tiburtini and Termini. The train takes about 30mins from Fiumicino to Tiburtina; the bus at least 50mins. A secondary airport, **Ciampino** (t 06 794 941) is the base for a few flights. A COTRAL bus runs from here to the Anagnina stop at the southern end of the Metro A line, from where it's about 20mins to Stazione Termini, or you can continue to Piazza di Spagna (daily 6.50am–11.40pm, €1).

Venice: Venice's **Marco Polo** airport is 12km north of the city near the Lagoon. It is linked with Venice by water-taxi (t 041 966 170 or t 041 523 5775), the most expensive option (€45); or by *motoscafi* to Piazza San Marco roughly every hour (€10), connecting with most flights from March to October. The journey time is 1 hour 10 mins to or from San Marco. There is also an ATVO bus to Piazzale Roma (€2.70) or, cheapest of all, the ACTV city bus no.5 (€0.77), which passes by twice an hour. Some flights arrive at **Treviso**, 35km to the north. There are trains every 15mins to Venice's Santa Lucia station (€1.80), and ATVO buses (t 041 520 5530, €4.30) run between Piazzale Roma and Treviso airport.

Florence: Florence's **Vespucci** airport was lengthened in 1996, and it now bustles with more international traffic than Pisa. It is 6km out at Peretola, t 055 373 498, flight information t 055 306 1700 (recorded message), and is connected to the city by an airport bus, which stops at the SITA bus

Major Carriers

From the UK
Aer Lingus, Ireland t 0818 365000; UK t 0845 084 4444, www.aerlingus.ie.
Alitalia, London, t 0870 544 8259; Dublin, t (01) 677 5171, www.alitalia.co.uk.
British Airways, t 0845 779 9977, www.ba.com.
easyJet, t 0870 6000 000, www.easyJet.com.
Meridiana, t (020) 7839 2222, www.meridiana.it.
Now, t 0845 458 9737, www.fly-now.com.
Ryanair, t 0871 246 0000, www.ryanair.com.

From the USA and Canada
Air Canada: t 1 888 247 2262, www.aircanada.ca.
Alitalia, t 800 223 5730, www.alitaliausa.com.
British Airways, t 800 AIRWAYS; TTY t (877) 993 9997, www.ba.com.
Continental, t 800 231 0856, Canada t (800) 525 0280, www.continental.com.
Delta, t 800 241 4141, www.delta.com.
Northwest Airlines, t 800 225 2525, www.nwa.com.
United Airlines, t 800 241 6522, www.ual.com.

Discount Agencies and Youth Fares

From the UK and Ireland
Italy Sky Shuttle, 227 Shepherd's Bush Rd, London W6 7AS, t (020) 8748 1333.
Italflights, 125 High Holborn, London WC1V 6QA, t (020) 7405 6771.
Italia nel Mondo, 6 Palace Street, London SW1E 5HY, t (020) 7828 9171.
Trailfinders, 215 Kensington High Street, London W8, t (020) 7937 1234; 415 Dawson St, Dublin 2, t (01) 677 7888, www.trailfinders.co.uk. Branches also in other major cities.
Budget Travel, 134 Lower Baggot Street, Dublin 2, t (01) 661 1866, www.budgettravel.ie.
United Travel, Stillorgan Bowl, Stillorgan, County Dublin, t (01) 288 4346/7.

Besides saving 25 per cent on regular flights, young people under 26 have the choice of flying on special discount charters:
STA, 6 Wright's Lane, London W8 6TA, t (020) 7361 6161, 74 and 86 Old Brompton Rd, London SW7, or 85 Shaftesbury Avenue, London W1V 7AD, Bristol, Leeds, Manchester, Oxford, Cambridge, and branches, t 0870 160 6070. www.statravel.co.uk.
USIT Now, 19–21 Aston Quay, Dublin 2, t (01) 679 8833, and other branches in Ireland, www.usitnow.ie.

Websites
www.airtickets.co.uk
www.cheapflights.com
www.ebookers.com
www.expedia.co.uk
www.flights4less.co.uk
www.lastminute.com

From the USA and Canada
Airhitch, 481 8th Avenue, Suite 1771, New York, NY 10061-1820, t 877 247 4482 or t (212) 736 0505, www.airhitch.org.
Council Travel, 205 E 42nd Street, New York, NY 10017, t 800 2COUNCIL, www.counciltravel.com. Major specialists in student and charter flights; branches from Arizona to Wisconsin. Can also provide Eurail and Britrail passes.
Last Minute Travel Club, 132 Brookline Avenue, Boston, MA 02215, t (800) 527 8646.
Now Voyager, 74 Varick St, Suite 307, New York, NY 10013, t (212) 431 1616. For courier flights.
STA, toll free t (800) 781 4040, www.statravel.com. Has branches at most universities and also at 10 Downing Street, New York, NY 10014, t (212) 627 3111, and ASUC Building, 2nd Floor, University of California, Berkeley, CA 94720, t (510) 642 3000.
TFI Tours, 34 West 32nd Street, NY, NY 10001, t (212) 736 1140, toll-free t (800) 745 8000, www.lowestairprice.com.
Travel Cuts, 187 College St, Toronto, Ontario M5T 1P7, t (866) 246 9762, www.travelcuts.com. Canada's largest student travel specialists; branches in most provinces.

Websites
www.airhitch.org
www.expedia.com
www.flights.com
www.orbitz.com
www.smarterliving.com
www.travelocity.com

station and in Via Santa Caterina da Siena. It runs every 30mins from 6am to 8.30pm and takes 30mins (€4.13). A taxi ride to the centre will cost about €15.50 plus any relevant surcharges.

By Rail

You can still travel by train and ferry from London to Rome; it takes the best part of 20 hours and costs around £176 second-class return (including the couchette). Or you can take a Eurostar to Paris and a high-speed train to Italy, which cuts the journey time to 12 hours (Rome) or 17 hours (Florence or Venice), but costs around £220.

The **Venice-Simplon Orient Express** deserves a special mention: it whirls you from London through Paris, Innsbruck and Verona to Venice in a cocoon of traditional twenties and thirties glamour, with beautifully restored Pullman/ wagon-lits. It's fiendishly expensive but quite unforgettable for a once-in-a-lifetime treat. Prices (including meals) are around £1,270 (US $2,050) per person one-way. The Orient Express runs most Sundays and Thursdays, from March to November.

Rail Contacts

CIT, (UK) Marco Polo House, 3–5 Lansdowne Road, Croydon, Surrey CR9 1LL, **t** (020) 8686 0677, *www.citalia.com*.
(USA) 15 West 44th Street, 10th Floor, New York, NY 10036, **t** (212) 730 2121.
(Canada) 80 Tiverton Court, Suite 401, Markham, Toronto L3R 0Q4, **t** (905) 415 1060.
Eurostar, EPS House, Waterloo Station, London SE1, **t** 08705 186186, *www.eurostar.com*.
Rail Choice, 15 Colman House, Empire Square, High Street, Penge, London SE20 7EX, **t** (020) 8659 7300, *www.railchoice.com* and *www.railchoice.co.uk*. For youth fares and rail passes.
Rail Europe Travel Centre, (UK) 178 Piccadilly, London W1V 0BA, **t** 08705 848848, *www.raileurope.co.uk*. (USA) 226 Westchester Ave, White Plains, NY 10064, **t** (914) 682 2999, or **t** (800) 438 7245, *www.raileurope.com*.
Venice-Simplon Orient Express, Sea Containers House, 20 Upper Ground, London SE1 9PF, **t** (020) 7928 6000 for more information, *www.orient-express.com*.

In an age of low-cost airlines rail travel is not much of an economy unless you're able to take advantage of student, youth, families and young children and senior citizen discounts. **Interail** (UK) or **Eurail** (USA/Canada) passes give unlimited travel for all ages throughout Europe for one or two months. A month's full Interail pass covering France, Switzerland and Italy costs £269, or £195 for the under-26s; for France and Italy only it costs £230, or £169 for the under-26s.

Various youth fares and inclusive rail passes are also available within Italy, and if you're planning on doing a lot of train travel solely in Italy you can organize these before leaving home at Rail Choice (*see above*). They can even send rail passes and Motorail tickets from the UK to the USA by Fedex. CIT offices, which act as agents for Italian State Railways, also offer various deals.

By Road

By Bus and Coach

Eurolines is the main international bus operator in Europe, with representatives in Italy and many other countries. Regular services terminate in Rome, Venice or Florence. Needless to say, the journey is long (36hrs/ 28hrs/32hrs) and the relatively small savings on price (a return ticket from London to Rome costs £115; single £75) make it a masochistic choice in comparison with a discounted air fare, or even rail travel. Within Italy, you can obtain more information on long-distance bus services from any CIT office.
Eurolines, Victoria Coach Station, London SW1, **t** 08705 143 219, *www.gobycoach.com*.

By Car

Driving to Italy from the UK is a rather lengthy and expensive proposition, and, if you're only staying for a short time, compare your costs against Alitalia's or other airlines' fly-drive schemes. No matter how you cross the Channel, it is a good two-day drive – about 1,600km from Calais to Rome.

Ferry information is available from any travel agent or direct from the ferry companies. You can cut many of the costly motorway tolls by going from Dover to Calais, travelling through France to Basle, Switzerland, and from there through the Gotthard Tunnel over the Alps. In the summer you can save the expensive tunnel tolls, and see some marvellous scenery, by taking one of the mountain passes instead.

Current motorway tunnel tolls are:

Fréjus Tunnel, *www.tunneldufrejus.com*, from Modane (France) to Bardonècchia. Prices from €25.60 one way.

Gran San Bernardo, *www.grandsaintbernard. ch*, from Bourg St Pierre (Switzerland) to Aosta. Prices from €25.60 one way.

You can avoid some of the driving by putting your car on the train (although again, balance the sizeable expense against the price of hiring a car for the period of your stay). There are **Motorail** links from Denderleeuw in Belgium to Bologna, Rimini, Rome and Venice (infrequently in winter: for further details contact **Rail Choice, t** (020) 8659 7300, *www.railchoice.co.uk*).

To bring a GB-registered car into Italy, you need a **vehicle registration document**, **full driving licence**, and **insurance papers** (these must be carried at all times when driving). If your driving licence is of the old-fashioned sort without a photograph you are also strongly recommended to apply for an international driving permit (available from the AA or RAC). Non-EU citizens should preferably have an international driving licence which has an Italian translation incorporated. Your vehicle should display a nationality plate indicating its country of registration. Before travelling, check everything is in perfect order. Minor infringements like worn tyres or burnt-out sidelights can cost you dearly in any country. Red triangular hazard signs and head-light converters are obligatory; also recommended are a spare set of bulbs, a first-aid kit and a fire extinguisher. Spare parts for non-Italian cars can be difficult to find, especially Japanese models. Before crossing the border, fill her up; *benzina* is very expensive in Italy.

Foreign-plated cars are no longer entitled to free breakdown service by the **Italian Auto Club** (ACI), but their prices are fair. Phone ACI on **t** (06) 44 77 to find out the current rates.

For more information on driving in Italy, contact the AA or RAC:

AA, t 0870 600 0371, *www.theaa.com*; breakdown cover **t** 0800 085 2840.

RAC, t 0800 092 2222, *www.rac.co.uk*; breakdown cover **t** 0800 828282 in the UK, **t** (407) 444 4000 in the USA.

AAA, (USA), **t** (212) 468 2600, **t** 800 AAA HELP *www.aaa.com*. The American Automobile Association.

Entry Formalities

Passports and Visas

To get into Italy you need a valid passport. EU nationals do not need a visa. US, Canadian and Australian nationals do not need a visa to enter Italy for stays of up to 90 days. If you mean to stay longer, you must get a *permesso di soggiorno*; you will need to state your reason for staying and be able to prove a source of income and medical insurance. According to Italian law, you must register with the police within eight days of your arrival. If you check into a hotel this is done automatically. Should you come to grief in the mesh of rules and forms, you can get someone to explain it to you in English by calling the Rome Police Office for visitors, **t** 06 4686, ext.2987.

Customs

Arrivals from non-EU countries have to pass through Italian Customs. For travellers entering the EU from outside, the duty-free limits are 1 litre of spirits or 2 litres of liquors (port, sherry or champagne), plus 2 litres of wine, 200 cigarettes and 50ml of perfume. Duty-free allowances have now been abolished within the EU, and much larger quantities – up to 10 litres of spirits, 90 litres of wine, 110 litres of beer and 800 cigarettes – bought locally and provided you are travelling between EU countries, can be taken through customs if you can prove they are for private consumption only and that taxes have been paid in the country of purchase. Under-17s are not allowed to bring tobacco or alcohol into the EU. **Pets** must be accompanied by a bilingual Certificate of Health from your local vet. You may not bring meat, vegetables or plants into the UK. Canadians can take home $300-worth of goods in a year, plus their tobacco and alcohol allowances.

Residents of the USA may each take home US$400-worth of foreign goods without attracting duty, including the tobacco and

Special-interest Holidays

A selection of specialist companies are listed below. Not all of them are necesssarily ABTA-bonded; check before booking.

In the UK

Abercrombie & Kent, Sloane Square House, Holbein Place, London SW1W 8NS, t 0845 0700 612, *www.abercrombiekent.co.uk*. City breaks in exotic mansions, restored palaces and family-run villas and *pensioni*.

Ace Study Tours, Babraham, Cambridge CB2 4AP, t (01223) 835 055, *www.study-tours.org*. Study courses led by art historians: includes accommodation and most meals.

Alternative Travel, 69–71 Banbury Road, Oxford OX2 6PE, t (01865) 315678, *www.atg-oxford.co.uk*. Walking and cycling tours.

Bellini Travel, 15 Savile Row, London W1X 1AE, t (020) 7437 8918, *www.bellinitravel.co.uk*. Superior, tailor-made tours in all three cities: can organize private visits to the Sistine Chapel, expert guides, visits to private collections, tours for children, etc.

British Airways Holidays, t 0870 442 3828, *www.batravelshops.com*. City breaks in 3–5- star hotels.

Brompton Travel, Brompton House, 64 Richmond Road, Surrey KT2 5EH, t (020) 8549 3334, *www.bromptontravel.co.uk*. Tailor-made and specialist opera tours in Venice and Florence.

Citalia, Marco Polo House, 3–5 Lansdowne Road, Croydon CR9 1LL, t (020) 8686 5533, *www.citalia.com*. Flexible city breaks, from hand-picked guest houses to 5 star hotels.

Cox & Kings, Gordon House, 10 Greencoat Place, London SW1P 1PH, t (020) 7873 5027, *www.coxandkings.co.uk*. Short breaks, music festivals, gourmet and escorted cultural tours with guest lecturers in assocation with NADFAS.

Inscape Fine Art Tours, Austins, High Street, Stonesfield, Witney, Oxfordshire OX29 8SU, t (01993) 891 726, *www.inscapetours.co.uk*. Escorted study tours discovering the 'inscape' of noted works of art and architecture: includes 'Baroque Rome' and 'Renaissance Rome and Florence'.

Italiatour, 9 Whyteleafe Business Village, Whyteleafe Hill, Whyteleafe, Surrey CR3 0AT, t (01883) 621 900, f (01883) 625 255, *www.italiatour.co.uk*. City breaks and *à la carte* holidays; tickets to opera, concerts, exhibitions, museums and football matches.

Italian Journeys, European Travel Centre, 216 Earl's Court Rd, London SW5 9QB, t (020) 7370 6002. Specialists in package and tailored holidays to Italy, staying in a range of upmarket hotels.

JMB, Rushwick, Worcester WR2 5SN, t (01905) 425 628, *www.jmb-travel.co.uk*. Opera and music festivals, staying in first-class *pensioni* and stylish hotels..

Kirker, 3 New Concordia Wharf, Mill Street, London SE1 2BB, t (020) 7231 3333, *www.kirkerholidays.com*. Exclusive tailor-made two- and three-centre breaks; can pre-book opera, museums, theatre and concerts.

alcohol allowance. For more information, US citizens can telephone the US Customs Service, t (202) 354 1000, or look at *www.customs.gov*.

strikes usually last only a day, just long enough to throw a spanner in the works if you have to catch a plane. Keep your ears open and watch for notices posted in the stations.

Getting Around

Italy has an excellent network of airports, railways, highways and byways and you'll find getting around fairly easy – until one union or another takes it into its head to go on strike (to be fair they rarely do it during the high holiday season, but learn to recognize the word in Italian: *sciopero* (SHO-per-o), and do as the Romans do – quiver with resignation). There's always a day or two's notice, and

By Air

Air traffic within Italy is intense, with up to ten flights a day on popular routes. Domestic flights are handled by Alitalia, ATI (its internal arm) or Avianova.

Air travel makes most sense when hopping between north and south. Shorter journeys are often just as quick (and much less expensive) by train or even bus if you include check-in and airport travelling times.

Magic of Italy, 227 Shepherds Bush Rd, London W6 7AS, t 0870 888 0228, *www.magictravel group.co.uk*. Flexible holidays and charters.

Martin Randall Travel, 10 Barley Mow Passage, Chiswick, London W4 4GF, t (020) 8742 3355, *www.martinrandall.com*. Cultural tours to inaccessible places: first-rate lecturers; small groups staying in 4-star hotels.

Page & Moy, 135–140 London Road, Leicester LE2 1EN, t 0870 010 6212, *www.page-moy.co.uk*. Escorted art, history, architectural and opera tours including 'Secret Venice'.

Prospect Music & Art, 36 Manchester Street, London W1U 7LH, t (020) 7486 5705, *www.prospecttours.com*. Fully guided art, architecture, music and archaeology tours; also exhibitions, festivals, etc.

Simply Tuscany & Umbria, Kings House, Wood Street, Kingston-upon-Thames, Surrey KT1 1UG, t (020) 8541 2206, *www.simply-travel.com*. Short breaks in Venice, Rome and Florence.

Special Tours, 2 Chester Row, London SW1W 9JH, t (020) 7730 2297, *www.specialtours. co.uk*. Tours include Classical and Early Christian Rome, and the Festa di Santa Maria della Salute in Venice: run by a small private travel company for National Art Collections Fund members.

Travelsphere, Compass House, Rockingham Road, Market Harborough, Leicestershire LE16 7QD, t (01858) 410 818, *www.travel sphere.co.uk*. 8–15-day escorted coach tours.

Voyages Jules Verne, 21 Dorset Square, London NW1 6QG, t (020) 7616 1000, *www.vjv.co.uk*.

Rome, Venice and Florence in a week, also Venice Lagoon cruises.

In the USA/Canada

Abercrombie & Kent, 1520 Kensington Rd, Oak Brook, IL 60523 2141, t 800 323 7308, *www.abercrombiekent.com*. City breaks in Rome, Florence and Venice.

American Express Travel Service, t 800 346 3607, *http://travel.americanexpress.com*. Pre-packaged and tailor-made tours.

CIT Tours, 15 West 44th St, New York, NY 10036, t 800 CIT-TOUR, *www.cit-tours.com*; in Canada, 80 Tiverton Ct, Suite 401, Markham, ON L3R OG4, t 800 387 0711. City breaks.

Esplanade Tours, 160 Commonwealth Ave, Boston, MA 02116, t (617) 266 7465, 800 426 5492, *www.esplanadetours.com*. Cultural tours, specialized tours, and FIT itineraries.

Europe Train Tours, 7578 N Broadway Suite 4, Red Hook, NY 12571, t (845) 758 1777 or t 800 551 2085, f (845) 758 1776, *www.etttours.com*. Take the Orient Express to Venice.

Italiatour, 666 5th Ave, New York, NY 10103, t 800 845 3365 (US) and 888 515 5245 (Canada), *www.italiatourusa.com*. Fly-drive holidays and city breaks by Alitalia.

Maupintour, 10650 W Charleston Blvd, Summerlin, NV 89135, t 800 255 4266, *www. maupintour.com*. Independdent city stays, includes sightseeing by car with driver.

Trafalgar Tours, 11 East 26th Street, New York, NY 10010, t (212) 689 8977, *www.trafalgar tours.com*. Rome, Venice and Florence in eight days.

Domestic flight costs are comparable to those in other European countries, and a complex system of discounts is available (some only at certain times of year). Each airport has a bus terminal in the city; ask about schedules as you purchase your ticket to avoid hefty taxi fares. Baggage allowances vary between airlines. Tickets can be bought at CIT offices and other large travel agencies.

By Rail

FS national train information: t 1478 88 088 (open 7am–9pm); www.fs-on-line.com.

Italy's national railway, the **FS** (Ferrovie dello Stato), is well run and often a pleasure to ride.

There are also several private rail lines that may not accept rail passes. Train **fares** have increased greatly over the last couple of years and only those without extra supplements can still be called cheap.

There is a strict hierarchy of **trains**. A *Regionale* travels short-ish distances, and tends to stop at all the stations. There are only a few *Espressi* trains left in service, but they are in poor condition, and mostly serve the long runs from the south of Italy. No supplement is required. *Intercity* trains link Italian cities, with minimum stops. Some carry an obligatory seat reservation requirement (free in this case), and all have a supplement. The true 'Kings of the Rails' are the super-swish and super-fast

(Florence–Rome in 1½ hours) *Eurostars*. These make very few stops, offer both first and second class carriages, and carry a supplement that includes an obligatory seat reservation. So, the faster the train, the more you pay. Make sure you check all fares at the time of booking.

The FS offers several **passes**. A flexible option is the **Flexi Card** (also available through CIT, Rail Choice or Rail Europe *see* p.78) which allows you unlimited travel either for four days within a month (€144), 8 days within a month (€150) or 12 days within a month (€259), plus supplements and seat reservations on Eurostars. Another ticket, the **Kilometrico**, gives you 3,000km of travel, made on a maximum of 20 journeys, and is valid for two months (2nd class €177, 1st class €181, plus supplements). One advantage is that it can be used by up to five people at the same time. However, supplements are payable on Intercity trains.

Other **discounts**, available only once you're in Italy, are 15% off same-day return tickets and three-day returns (depending on the distance involved), and discounts for families of at least four travelling together. Senior citizens (60 and over) can also get a *Carta d'Argento* ('silver card') for €25, entitling them to a 20% reduction in fares. A *Carta Verde* bestows a 20% discount on people under 26 and costs €25. The *Carto Amicotreno*, €50 for one year, gets you discounts from 10 to 50 %.

On Friday nights, weekends and in the summer, **reserve a seat** in advance (*fare una prenotazione*). The fee is small and can save you hours of standing.

Tickets may be purchased at the station or at many travel agents; it's wise to buy them in advance as queues may be long. Do check when you purchase your ticket in advance that the date is correct; tickets are only v alid the day they're purchased unless you specify otherwise.

Always remember to **stamp your ticket** (*convalidare*) in the not-very-obvious yellow machine at the head of the platform before boarding the train. Failure to do so will result in a fine. If you get on a train without a ticket you can buy one from the conductor, with an added 20 per cent penalty.

Refreshments on long-distance routes are provided by bar cars or trolleys. Station bars often have good take-away travellers' fare.

FS stations also have other services. Most offer a *depòsito*, where you can leave luggage for a small fee. Some even have an *albergo diurno* (with showers, shaving facilities, etc.), currency exchanges open at weekends (not the best rates), hotel-booking services, etc. You can also arrange to have a hire car awaiting you at your destination – Avis, Hertz and Maggiore provide this service (*see* opposite).

Details on tickets, discount passes and advance reservations are available at:

CIT (**UK**), Marco Polo House, 3–5 Lansdowne Rd, Croydon, Surrey, **t** (020) 8686 0677, *www.citalia.com*.

CIT (**USA**), 15 West 44th Street, 10th Floor, New York, NY 10036, **t** (212) 730 2121.

CIT (**Canada**), 80 Tiverton Court, Suite 401, Markham, Toronto L3R O94, **t** (905) 415 1060.

Beyond that, some words need to be said about riding the rails on the most serendipitous national line in Europe. The FS may have its strikes and delays, its petty crime and bureaucratic inconveniences, but when you catch it on its better side it will treat you to a dose of the real Italy before you even reach your destination. If there's a choice, try for one of the older cars, depressingly grey outside but fitted with comfortably upholstered seats, Art Deco lamps and old pictures of the towns and villages of the country. The washrooms are invariably clean and pleasant. Best of all, the FS is relatively reliable, and even if there has been some delay you'll have an amenable station full of clocks to wait in; some of the station bars have astonishingly good food, but at any of them you may accept a well-brewed cappuccino and look blasé until the train comes in. Try to avoid travel on Friday evenings, when the major lines out of the big cities are packed. The FS is a lottery; you may find a train uncomfortably full of Italians (in which case stand by the doors, or impose on the salesmen in first class, where the conductor will be happy to change your ticket). Now and then, you may just have a beautiful 1920s compartment all to yourself for the night – even better if you're travelling with your beloved – and be serenaded on the platform.

By Coach and Bus

Inter-city coach travel is sometimes quicker than train travel, but also a bit more expensive; you will find regular coach connections only where there is no train to offer competition. Coaches almost always depart from the vicinity of the train station, and tickets usually need to be purchased before you get on. If you can't get a ticket before the coach leaves, get on anyway and pretend you can't speak a word of Italian; the worst that can happen is that someone will make you pay for a ticket.

By Car

If you're planning a tour of the cities with few excursions into the countryside around, you'll be better off not driving at all. In town centres, **parking** is always a problem. Some areas are marked *zona disco blu* after the blue time discs, obtainable in many shops and fixed inside the windscreen, where you set the hour of your arrival and get an hour or two of free parking. Elsewhere an old gent with a book of receipts will shamble up to your car and hit you for a couple of euros or so, or there may be a parking ticket machine; blue stripes on the pavement instead of white always mean pay-parking.

Worse than parking, sometimes, can be simply driving. The Italian *centro storico* was just not made for cars. Often, sensibly, it is closed to them; the red circle sign at the entrance will have a notice underneath explaining hours and vehicles forbidden. You'll notice enforcement isn't very strict, and exceptions are usually made if you are loading or unloading at a hotel. Even when you can get into the centre, finding that the main street soon funnels into a 12ft passage full of pedestrians makes driving lose much of its charm. One false move, and you may be driving down a stairway, or through an alley where your car gets stuck between the walls. Give these fine old towns, and their residents, a break, and leave your beast in the parking areas signposted around the walls.

Third-party insurance is a minimum requirement in Italy (and you should be a lot more than minimally insured, as many of the locals have none whatever!). Obtain a Green Card

from your insurer, which gives automatic proof that you are fully covered. Also get hold of a **European Accident Statement** form, which may simplify things if you are unlucky enough to have an accident. Always insist on a full translation of any statement you are asked to sign. Breakdown assistance insurance is obviously a sensible investment.

Petrol (*benzina*; unleaded is *benzina senza piombo*, and diesel *gasolio*) is still very expensive in Italy (over €1.55 per litre). Many petrol stations close for lunch in the afternoon, and few stay open late at night, though you can usually always find a 'self-service' where you feed a machine nice smooth 5- or 20-euro notes. **Motorway** (*autostrada*) **tolls** are quite high (the journey from Milan to Rome on the A1 will cost you around €35 at the time of writing). Rest stops and petrol stations along the motorways stay open 24 hours.

Italians are famously anarchic behind a wheel. The only way to beat the locals is to join them by adopting an assertive and constantly alert driving style. Bear in mind the ancient maxim that he/she who hesitates is lost (especially at traffic lights, where the danger is less great of crashing into someone at the front than being rammed from behind). All drivers from boy racers to elderly nuns seem to tempt providence by overtaking at the most dangerous bends, and no matter how fast you are hammering along the *autostrada* (toll motorway), plenty will whizz past at apparently supersonic rates. North Americans used to leisurely speed limits and gentler road manners will find the Italian interpretation of the highway code especially stressful. **Speed limits** (generally ignored) are officially 130kph on motorways (110kph for cars under 1,100cc or motorcycles), 110kph on main highways, 90kph on secondary roads, and 50kph in built-up areas. For speeding, if you're especially unlucky you may be slapped with a *super multa*, or superfine, of €130–260 or more

If you are undeterred by these caveats, you may actually enjoy driving in Italy, at least away from the congested tourist centres. Signposting is generally good, and roads are usually excellently maintained. Some of the roads are feats of engineering that the Romans themselves would have admired –

Car Rental Agencies

UK

Auto Europe, t 0800 169 6414, *www.auto-europe.co.uk.*

Avis, t 0870 60 60 100, *www.avis.co.uk.*

Europcar, t 0870 607 5000 *www.europcar.com.*

Hertz, t 08705 99 66 99, *www.hertz.co.uk.*

National, t 0870 400 4502, *www.nationalcar.com.*

Netsmart, t 0870 758 9935, *www.car-hire. me.uk.*

Thrifty, t 01494 751600, *www.thrifty.co.uk.*

USA and Canada

Auto Europe, t 888 223 5555, *www.autoeurope. com.*

Avis, t 800 831 2847, *www.avis.com.*

Budget, t 800 527 0800, *www.drivebudget.com.*

Europcar, t 877 940 6900, *www.europcar.com.*

bravura projects suspended on cliffs, crossing valleys on vast stilts and winding up hairpins.

Buy a good road map (the Italian Touring Club series is excellent). The **Automobile Club of Italy** (ACI), **t** (06) 44 77, is a good friend to the foreign motorist.

Hiring a Car

Hiring a car is simple but not particularly cheap (around €50 a day for a smallish car, €300 for a week). Italian car rental firms are called *autonoleggi*. Remember to take into account that some hire companies require a deposit amounting to the estimated cost of the hire. The minimum age limit is usually 25 (sometimes 23) and the driver must have held their licence for over a year. Most major rental companies have offices in airports or main stations, though it may be worthwhile checking prices of local firms. If you need a car for longer than three weeks, leasing may be a more economic alternative. Non-residents are not allowed to buy cars in Italy.

It is probably easiest to arrange your car hire with a domestic firm before you depart and, in particular, to check-out fly-drive discounts.

Hitchhiking

It is illegal to hitch on the *autostrade*, though you may pick up a lift near one of the toll booths. Don't hitch from the city centres, head for suburban exit routes. For the best chances of getting a lift, travel light, look respectable and take your shades off. Hold a sign indicating your destination if you can. Risks for women are lower in northern Italy than in the more macho south, but it is not advisable to hitch alone.

By Moped

Mopeds, Vespas and scooters are the vehicles of choice for a great many Italians. You will see them everywhere. In the traffic-congested towns this is a ubiquity born of necessity; when driving space is limited, two wheels are always better than one. Despite the obvious dangers of this means of transport, there are clear benefits to moped-riding in Italy. For one thing it is cheaper than car hire and can prove an excellent way of covering a town's sites in a limited space of time. Furthermore, because Italy is such a scooter-friendly place, car drivers are more conditioned to their presence and so are less likely to hurtle into them when taking corners. Nonetheless, you should only consider hiring a moped if you have ridden one before (Italy's hills and alarming traffic are no place to learn) and, despite local examples, you should always wear a helmet. Also, be warned, some travel insurance policies exclude claims resulting from scooter or motorbike accidents.

Hire costs for a *motorino* (moped) range from about €26 per day; Vespas (scooters) are somewhat more (from about €35).

Practical A–Z

06

Children

Children are still the royalty of Italy, and are pampered, often obscenely spoiled, probably more fashionably dressed than you are, and never allowed to get dirty. Surprisingly, most of them somehow manage to be well-mannered little charmers. If you're bringing your own *bambini* to Italy, they'll receive a warm welcome everywhere. Many hotels offer advantageous rates for children and have play areas, and most of the larger cities have permanent **Luna Parks**, or funfairs. Rome's version in the EUR is huge and charmingly old-fashioned (a great trade-off for a day in the Vatican Museums). Italians don't like zoos and there are only a few small ones, but there's a small one in Rome's Villa Borghese which may amuse for a while. Apart from endless quantities of pizza, spaghetti and ice cream, **Venice** could have been specifically designed for kids, and there's always the **Carnival**. If your kids know some Italian, there is a **puppet theatre** in Rome, and if a **circus** visits town, you're in for a treat: it will either be a sparkling showcase of daredevil skill or a poignant, family-run, modern version of Fellini's *La Strada*. In **Florence**, museums such as the Archaeological Museum have a lot of gruesome mummies, and the Museo dei Ragazzi in Palazzo Vecchio organizes activities and special tours for children; there's also a wonderful old-fashioned merry-go-round in Piazza Strozzi.

Climate and When to Go

'*O Sole Mio*' notwithstanding, all of Italy isn't always sunny; it rains just as much in Rome every year as in London. **Summer** comes on dry and hot in the south and humid and hot in much of the northern lowlands and inland hills; and Venice tends to swelter. You can probably get by without an umbrella, but take a light jacket for cool evenings. For average touring, August is probably the worst month to stomp through Italy. Transport facilities are jammed to capacity, prices are at their highest, and the large cities are abandoned to hordes of tourists while the locals take to the beach.

Spring and **autumn** are perhaps the loveliest times to go; the weather is mild, places aren't crowded, and you won't need your umbrella much, at least until November. **Winter** is the best time to go if you want the museums to yourself. Beware though, it can rain and rain.

Crime

Police t 113.

There is a fair amount of petty crime in Italy – purse-snatchings, pickpocketing, minor thievery of the white-collar kind (always check your change) and car break-ins and theft – but violent crime is rare. Nearly all mishaps can be avoided with adequate precautions. Scooter-borne purse-snatchers can be foiled if you stay on the inside of the pavement and keep a firm hold on your property (sling your bag-strap across your body, not dangling from one shoulder); pickpockets strike in crowded buses or trams and gatherings; don't carry too much cash, and split it so you won't lose the lot at once. In cities and popular tourist sites, beware groups of scruffy-looking women or children with placards, apparently begging for

Average Temperatures in °C (°F)

	January	April	July	October
Rome	7.4 (44)	14.4 (58)	25.7 (79)	17.7 (63)
Venice	3.8 (38)	12.6 (54)	23.6 (74)	15.1 (59)
Florence	5.6 (42)	13.3 (55)	25.0 (77)	15.8 (60)

Average Monthly Rainfall in millimetres (inches)

	January	April	July	October
Rome	74 (3)	62 (3)	06 (3)	123 (5)
Venice	58 (2)	77 (3)	37 (1)	66 (3)
Florence	61 (3)	74 (3)	23 (1)	96 (4)

money. The smallest and most innocent-looking child is generally the most skilful pickpocket. If you are targeted, the best technique is to grab sharply hold of any vulnerable possessions or pockets and shout furiously. (Italian passers-by or plain-clothes police will often come to your assistance if they realize what is happening.) Be extra careful in train stations, don't leave valuables in hotel rooms, and always park your car in garages, guarded lots or on well-lit streets, with portable temptations well out of sight.

Political terrorism, once the scourge of Italy, has declined greatly in recent years, mainly thanks to special quasi-military squads of black-uniformed national police, the *Carabinieri*. Local matters are usually in the hands of the *Polizia Urbana*; the nattily dressed *Vigili Urbani* concern themselves with directing traffic and handing out parking fines.

Disabled Travellers

Recent access-for-all laws in Italy have improved the once dire situation: the number of ramps and stair lifts has increased probably a hundredfold in the past few years, and

Specialist Organizations for Disabled Travellers

In Italy
CO.IN (Consorzio Cooperative Integrate), Via Enrico Giglioli 54a, 00169 Rome, freephone **t** 06 800 437631, **t** 06 712 9011, **f** 06 2326 7505, *www.coinsociale.it/turismo*. Their tourist information centre (*open Mon–Fri 9–5*) offers advice and information on accessibility.

Centro Studi Consulenza Invalidi, Via Gozzadini 7, 20148 Milan. Publishes an annual guide,*Vacanze per Disabili*, with details of suitable accommodation in Italy.

In the UK and Ireland
RADAR (Royal Association for Disability & Rehabilitation), 12 City Forum, 250 City Road, London EC1V 8AF, **t** (020) 7250 3222, *www. radar.org.uk*. For information and books.

Holiday Care Service, Imperial Building, Victoria Rd, Horley, Surrey, RH6 7PZ, **t** (01293) 774535, *www.holidaycare.org.uk*. Information on accommodation, transportation, equipment hire, services, tour operators and contacts.

Royal National Institute for the Blind (RNIB), 105 Judd St, London WC1H 9NE, **t** 0845 766 9999, *www.rnib.org.uk*. Its mobility unit offers a advice for visually impaired people travelling by plane. Also advises on finding accommodation.

Tripscope, The Vassall Centre, Gill Avenue, Bristol BS16 2QQ, **t** 0845 758 5641, **f** (01179) 397736, *www.tripscope.co.uk*. Offers expert practical advice and information to people with impaired mobility on every aspect of travel and transport. Information can be provided by letter or tape.

Irish Wheelchair Association, Blackheath Drive, Clontarf, Dublin 3, **t** (01) 818 6400, **f** (01) 833 3873, *www.iwa.ie*. Publishes guides with advice for disabled holidaymakers.

In the USA and Canada
American Foundation for the Blind, 11 Penn Plaza, Suite 300, New York NY 10001, **t** (212) 502 7600, toll free **t** 800 AFB LINE, **f** (212) 502 7777, *www.afb.org*. The best source of information in the USA for visually impaired travellers.

Federation for the Handicapped, 211 West 14th Street, New York, NY 10011, **t** (212) 747 4262. Organizes summer tours for members; there is a nominal annual fee.

SATH (Society for Accessible Travel and Hospitality), 347 5th Avenue, Suite 610, New York NY 10016, **t** (212) 447 7284, **f** (212) 725 8253, *www.sath.org*. Travel and access information. Website has good links and a list of relevant on-line publications.

Internet Sites
Emerging Horizons, *www.emerginghorizons. com*. International on-line travel newsletter for people with disabilities.

Can Be Done, **t** (020) 8907 2400, **f** (020) 8909 1854, *www.canbedone.co.uk*. Tailor-made accessible tours: can book accommodation, flights or whole itinerary.

nearly every hotel has one or two rooms with facilities for the disabled – although the older ones may not have a lift, or not one large enough for a wheelchair. Although service stations on the *autostrade* have equipped restrooms, you could get very stuck in the middle of a city – **Florence**, visited by zillions of tourists is notoriously lacking in accessible toilets. Local tourist offices are helpful, and have been known to find someone to give you a hand on the spot.

Thanks to the efforts of **Venice**'s Institute for Architecture and its *Veneziapertutti* (Venice For All) campaign launched several years ago, the labyrinth opened up a little for visitors with disabilities or limited access. The city's 407 bridges still present the major obstacle in getting around, but by judicious use of the *vaporetti* a good proportion of the city becomes accessible. The tourist office's Venice–Lido map no.1 indicates the parts of the city easily accessible by wheelchair.

Italian churches are a problem in themselves. Long flights of steps in front were designed to impress on the would-be worshipper the feeling of going upwards to God – another raw deal for the disabled.

Eating Out

When you leave a restaurant you will be given a receipt (*scontrino* or *ricevuto fiscale*) which according to Italian law you must take with you out of the door and carry for at least 60 metres. If you aren't given one, it means the restaurant is probably fudging on its taxes and thus offering you lower prices. There is a slim chance the tax police (*Guardia di Fianza*) may have their eye on you and the restaurant, and if you don't have a receipt they could slap you with a heavy fine.

Price-ranges quoted for meals throughout this guide are for an average complete meal, Italian-style with wine, for one person. We have divided restaurants into price categories (*see* box, below).

Restaurant Price Categories
very expensive over €45
expensive €30–45
moderate €20–30
cheap below €20

When you eat out, mentally add to the bill (*conto*) the bread and cover charge (*pane e coperto*, between €1 and 3), and a 15% service charge. This is often included in the bill (*servizio compreso*); if not, it will say *servizio non compreso*, and you'll have to do your own arithmetic. Additional tipping is at your own discretion, but never do it in family-owned and -run places.

For further information about eating in Italy, including local specialities, wines and a menu decoder, *see* the **Food and Drink** chapter, pp.69–74.

Electricity

Your electric appliances will work if you adapt them to run on 220 AC with two round prongs on the plug. American appliances need transformers as well.

Embassies and Consulates

UK: Lungarno Corsini 2, **Florence**, t 055 284 133; Palazzo Querini, Accademia, Dorsoduro 1051, **Venice**, t 041 522 7207; Via XX Settembre 80/a, **Rome**, t 06 4220 0001, *www.britain.it*.

Ireland: 3 Piazza di Campitelli, **Rome**, t 06 697 9121.

USA: Lungarno A. Vespucci 38, **Florence**, t 055 239 8276; Via V. Veneto 119/a, **Rome**, t 06 46741, *www.usembassy.it*.

Canada: Via G.B. de Rossi 27, **Rome**, t 06 445 981, *www.canada.it*.

Australia: Via Alessandria 215, **Rome**, t 06 852 721, *www.australian-embassy.it*.

New Zealand: Via Zara 28, **Rome**, t 06 440 2928, *www.nzemb.org*.

Festivals

There are literally thousands of festivals answering to every description in Italy. Every *comune* has at least one or two honouring patron saints, at which the presiding Madonna is paraded through the streets decked in fairy lights and gaudy flowers. Shrovetide and Holy Week are great focuses of activity. *Carnival*, having been suppressed and ignored for decades, has been revived in many places, displaying the gorgeous music and

Calendar of Events

February Carnival, in all three cities.

March/April Holy Week and Easter, Procession of the Cross, **Rome**: *Scoppio del Carro* (Explosion of the Cart), **Florence**; Good Friday Procession led by the Pope, **Rome**.

May *Vogolonga*, **Venice** (the 'long row' from San Marco to Burano).

May/June *Maggio Musicale Fiorentino*, **Florence**.

June Historical Regatta of the Four Ancient Maritime Republics (boat race between the rival sea-towns of Pisa, **Venice**, Amalfi and Genoa – location alternates).

June 21 *Infiorata*, Genzano, **Rome**.

June 24 *Calcio Storico in Costume*, **Florence** (football in medieval costume); *Festa di San Giovanni*, Florence.

July Feast of the Redeemer, **Venice** (fireworks, gondola procession).

July and August Outdoor opera, Terme di Caracalla, **Rome**.

August International Film Festival, **Venice**.

September Historic Regatta, **Venice**; *Festa delle Rificolona*, 7 Sept, **Florence** – a children's festival.

November Festa della Salute, **Venice**.

December Opera and ballet at La Fenice (when it reopens) and Teatro Goldoni, **Venice**; Feast of St Lucy, **Venice** (torchlight procession and balloon launch); Advent and Christmas.

---

pageantry of the *Commedia dell'Arte* with Harlequin and his motley crew. In Venice the handmade carnival masks now constitute a new art form and make delightful, if expensive, souvenirs. In Rome the Supreme Pontiff himself officiates at the Easter ceremonies.

Other festivals are more earthily pagan, celebrating the land and the harvest in giant phallic towers. Some are secular affairs sponsored by political parties (especially the Communists and Socialists), where everyone goes to meet friends. There are great costume pageants dating back to the Middle Ages or Renaissance, an endless round of carnivals, music festivals, opera seasons and antique fairs.

Whatever the occasion, eating is a primary pastime at all Italian jamborees, and all kinds of regional specialities are prepared. Check at the local tourist office for precise dates, which alter from year to year and often slide into the nearest weekend.

Health and Emergencies

Fire t 115.
Ambulance t 113.

You can insure yourself for almost any possible mishap – cancelled flights, stolen or lost baggage and health. While national health coverage in the UK takes care of its citizens while travelling, in the USA it doesn't. Check any current policies you hold to see if they cover you while abroad, and in what circumstances, and judge whether you need a special **traveller's insurance policy**.

Citizens of EU countries are entitled to **reciprocal health care** in Italy's National Health Service and a 90 per cent discount on prescriptions (bring **Form E111** with you, available from post offices). The E111 does not cover all medical expenses (no repatriation costs, for example, and no private treatment), and it is advisable to take out separate travel insurance for full cover. Citizens of non-EU countries should check carefully that they have adequate insurance for any medical expenses, and the cost of returning home. Australia has a reciprocal health care scheme with Italy, but New Zealand, Canada and the USA do not. If you already have health insurance, a student card, or a credit card, you may be entitled to some medical cover abroad.

In an **emergency**, dial t 115 for fire and t 113 for an ambulance (*ambulanza*) or to find the nearest hospital (*ospedale*). Less serious problems can be treated at a *Pronto Soccorso* (casualty/first aid department) at any hospital clinic (*ambulatorio*), or at a local health unit (*Unita Sanitarial Locale – USL*). Airports and main railway stations also have **first-aid posts**. If you have to pay for any health treatment, make sure you get a receipt, so that you can make any claims for reimbursement later.

Dispensing **chemists** (*farmacia*) are generally open from 8.30am to 1pm and from 4 to 8pm. Pharmacists are trained to give advice for minor ills. Any large town will have a *farmacia* that stays open 24 hours; others take turns to stay open (the rota is posted in the window).

No specific **vaccinations** are required or advised for citizens of most countries before visiting Italy; the main health risks are the usual travellers' woes of upset stomachs or the effects of too much sun. Take a supply of **medicaments** with you (insect repellent, anti-diarrhœal medicine, sun lotion and antiseptic cream), and any drugs you need regularly.

Many Italian doctors speak at least rudimentary English, but if you can't find one, contact your embassy or consulate.

Maps and Publications

The maps in this guide are for orientation only and to explore in any detail it is worth investing in a good, up-to-date regional map before you arrive from any of the following:

Stanford's, 12–14 Long Acre, London WC2 9LP, **t** (020) 7836 1321.

The Travel Bookshop, 13 Blenheim Crescent, London W11 2EE, **t** (020) 7229 5260.

The Complete Traveller, 199 Madison Ave, New York, NY 10016, **t** (212) 685 9007.

Excellent maps are produced by **Touring Club Italiano**, **Michelin** and **Istituto Geografico de Agostini**. They are available at major bookshops in Italy or sometimes on news-stands. Italian tourist offices are helpful and can often supply good area maps and town plans.

Books are more expensive in Italy than in the UK, but some excellent shops stock English-language books. A few useful ones are listed below.

Anglo-American Book Co., Via della Vite 57, Rome.

Corner Bookshop, Via del Moro 48, Rome.

Economy Book Center, Via Torino 135a, Rome.

Lion Bookshop, Via dei Greci 36, Rome.

Open Door Bookshop, Via della Lungaretta 25, Rome.

Sangiorgio, San Marco 2087, Calle Larga XXII Marzo, Venice.

Feltrinelli, Via Cavour 12–20r, Florence.

The Paperback Exchange, Via Fiesolana 31r, Florence.

Money

The **euro** is the official currency in Italy (and 10 other nations of the European Union) and the official exchange rate was set at **1 euro = L1,936.27**. Since February 2002, the lira has no longer been legal tender. Euros come in denominations of €500, €200, €100, €50, €20, €10 and €5 (banknotes) and €2, €1, 50 cents, 20 cents, 10 cents, 5 cents, 2 cents and 1 cent (coins).

Remember that Italians indicate decimals with commas and thousands with full points.

It's a good idea to have a wad of euros to hand when you arrive in Italy. Take care how you carry it, however (don't keep it all in one place).

Most ATMs (Bancomats – automatic cash dispensers) will spout cash with your bank card and PIN number – for a significant commission – but check with your bank first. They also take Eurocheque cards and credit cards. Large hotels, resort area restaurants, shops and car-hire firms will accept plastic as well; smaller places may not. Visa, American Express and Diner's are more widely accepted than MasterCard (Access).

Obtaining money is often a frustrating task, involving much queueing and form-filling. The major banks and exchange bureaux licensed by the Bank of Italy give the best exchange rates for currency or traveller's cheques. Hotels, private exchanges in resorts and FS-run exchanges at train stations usually have less advantageous rates, but are open outside normal banking hours. In addition there are exchange offices at most airports.

Opening Hours

Although it varies from region to region, most of Italy closes down at 1pm until 3 or 4pm to eat and properly digest the main meal of the day. Afternoon hours are from 4 to 7, often from 5 to 8 in the hot summer months. Bars are often the only places open during the early afternoon. In any case, don't be surprised if you find anywhere in Italy unexpectedly closed, whatever its official stated hours.

Banks

Open Mon–Fri 8.30–1 and 3–4, closed weekends and on local and national holidays.

Shops

Open Mon–Sat 8–1 and 3.30–7.30. Some supermarkets and department stores stay open throughout the day.

Offices

Government-run dispensers of red tape (e.g. visa departments) often open for quite limited periods, usually during the mornings (*Mon–Fri*). It pays to get there as soon as they open (or before) to spare your nerves in an interminable queue. Anyway, take something to read, or write your memoirs.

Museums and Galleries

Many of Italy's museums are magnificent, many are run with shameful neglect, and many have been closed for years for 'restoration' with slim prospects of reopening in the foreseeable future. With two works of art per inhabitant, Italy has a hard time financing the preservation of its national heritage; it would be as well to enquire at the tourist office to find out exactly what is open and what is 'temporarily' closed before setting off.

Churches

Italy's churches have always been a prime target for art thieves and as a consequence

National Holidays

Most museums, as well as banks and shops, are closed on the following national holidays:

1 January (New Year's Day)
6 January (Epiphany)
Easter Monday
25 April (Liberation Day)
1 May (Labour Day)
15 August (Assumption, or *Ferragosto*, the climax of the Italian holiday season)
1 November (All Saints' Day)
8 December (Immaculate Conception)
25 December (Christmas Day)
26 December (*Santo Stefano*, St Stephen's Day)

are usually locked when there isn't a sacristan or caretaker to keep an eye on things. All churches, except for the really important cathedrals and basilicas, close in the afternoon at the same hours as the shops, and the little ones tend to stay closed. Always have a pocketful of coins for the light machines in churches, or whatever work of art you came to inspect will remain clouded in ecclesiastical gloom. Don't do your visiting during services, and don't come to see paintings and statues in churches the week preceding Easter – you will probably find them covered with mourning shrouds.

In general, Sunday afternoons and Mondays are dead periods for the sightseer – you may want to make them your travelling days. Places without specified opening hours can usually be visited on request – but it is best to go before 1pm. We have listed the hours of important sights and museums, and specified which ones charge admission. Entrance charges vary widely; major sights are fairly steep , but others may be completely free. EU citizens under 18 and over 65 get free admission to state museums, at least in theory.

Packing

You simply cannot overdress in Italy; whatever grand strides Italian designers have made on the international fashion merry-go-round, most of their clothes are purchased domestically, prices be damned. Whether or not you want to try to keep up with the natives is your own affair. It's not that the Italians are very formal; they simply like to dress up with a gorgeousness that adorns their cities just as much as those old Renaissance churches and palaces. The few places with dress codes are the major churches and basilicas (no shorts, sleeveless shirts or strappy sundresses – women should carry a scarf or wrap to throw over the shoulders), casinos and a few posh restaurants.

Photography

Film and developing are much more expensive than they are in either the UK or the USA, though there are plenty of outlets where you can obtain them. You are not allowed to take pictures in most museums and in some churches. Most cities now offer one-hour processing if you need your pics in a hurry.

Post Offices

In cities usually open Mon–Sat 8–6 or 7.

La posta italiana is one of the most expensive and slowest **postal services** in Europe. Note, however, that the Vatican City has a special speedy and efficient postal service (which requires special Vatican stamps), so if you're anwhere in Rome, make sure you post your cards from the Holy See.

Stamps (*francobolli*) are available in post offices or at tobacconists (*tabacchi*, identified by blue signs with a white T). Prices fluctuate.

Shopping

'Made in Italy' has become a byword for style and quality, especially in fashion and leather, but also in home design, ceramics, kitchenware, jewellery, lace and linens, glassware and crystal, chocolates, bells, Christmas decorations, hats, straw work, art books, engravings, handmade stationery, gold and silverware, bicycles, sports cars, woodworking, a hundred kinds of liqueurs, aperitifs, coffee machines, gastronomic specialities and antiques (both reproductions and the genuine article).

If you are looking for **antiques**, be sure to demand a **certificate of authenticity** – reproductions can be very, very good. To get your antique or modern art purchases home, you will have to apply to the Export Department of the Italian Ministry of Education – a possible hassle. You will have to pay an **export tax** as well; your seller should know the details. Be sure to save receipts for Customs on the way home.

Italians don't much like **department stores**, but there are a few chains – the classiest is the oldest, Rinascente, while COIN stores often have good buys in almost the latest fashions. Standa and UPIM are more like Woolworth's; they have good clothes selections, housewares, etc., and often contain basement supermarkets. The main attraction of Italian shopping, however, is to buy classy luxury items; for less expensive clothes and household items you can do better at home.

Telephones and Internet

Public telephones for international calls may be found in the offices of **Telecom Italia**, Italy's telephone company. They are the only places where you can make reverse-charge calls (*a erre*, collect calls) but be prepared for a wait, as all these calls go through the operator. Rates for long-distance calls are among the highest in Europe. Calls within Italy are cheapest after 10pm; international calls after 11pm.

Most **phone booths** now take either coins or phone cards; snap off the small perforated corner or they won't work. Coin phones accept €0.10, €0.20, €0.50 and €1 coins (€0.10 should be enough for a short, inter-city call). *Scheda Telefonica* are available from tobacconists for €2.58, €5.16 and €7.75.

Try to avoid telephoning from hotels; this used to be a major rip-off, but is less so today; small hotels will usually do it without a mark-up, but others might add 25% to the bill or lots more.

For **international calls** from Italy, dial 00, then dial the country code (UK 44; USA and Canada 1; Ireland 353, New Zealand 64), then the local code (minus the 0) and number. Calls within Italy are cheapest after 10pm, international calls after 11pm. If you're **calling Italy from abroad**, dial 39 and then the whole number, including the first zero.

Weights and Measures

1 kilogram (1,000g) – 2.2 lb	1 lb – 0.45 kg
1 etto (100g) – 0.25 lb (approx)	1 pint – 0.568 litres
1 litre – 1.76 pints	1 quart – 1.136 litres
1 metre – 39.37 inches	1 Imperial gallon – 4.546 litres
1 kilometre – 0.621 miles	1 US gallon – 3.785 litres
1 foot – 0.35 metres	1 mile – 1.16 kilometres

Clothing Sizes

Clothes sizes are tailored for slim Italian builds. Shoes, in particular, tend to be narrower than in most other Western countries.

Women's Shirts/Dresses

UK	10	12	14	16	18		
USA	8	10	12	14	16		
Italy	40	42	44	46	48		

Sweaters

UK	10	12	14	16			
USA	8	10	12	14			
Italy	46	48	50	52			

Women's Shoes

UK	3	4	5	6	7	8	
USA	4	5	6	7	8	9	
Italy	36	37	38	39	40	41	

Men's Shirts

UK/USA	14	14.5	15	15.5	16	16.5	17	17.5
Italy	36	37	38	39	40	41	42	43

Men's Suits

UK/USA	36	38	40	42	44	46	
Italy	46	48	50	52	54	56	

Men's Shoes

UK	5	6	7	8	9	10	11	12
USA	7.5	8	9	10	10.5	11	12	13
Italy	38	39	40	41	42	43	44	45

Many places have public **fax** machines, but the speed of transmission may make costs very high; a hotel-keeper might help.

Internet points have popped up at almost every street corner in Rome and Florence; rates charged will range from €2 to €3 per hour.

Time

Italy is on Central European Time, one hour ahead of Greenwich Mean Time and six hours ahead of Eastern Standard Time. From the last weekend of March to the end of September, Italian Summer Time is in effect.

Toilets

Frequent travellers have noted a steady improvement over the years in the cleanliness of Italy's public conveniences, although as ever you will only find them in places like train and bus stations and bars. Ask for the *bagno*, *toilette* or *gabinetto*; in stations and the smarter bars and cafés there are washroom attendants who expect a few cents. You'll probably have to ask them for paper (*carta*). Don't confuse the Italian plurals: *signori* (gents), *signore* (ladies).

Tourist Offices

Known under various initials as EPT, APT or AAST, Italian tourist offices usually stay open from 8am to 12.30 or 1pm, and from 3 to 7pm, possibly longer in summer. Few open on Saturday afternoons or Sundays. Information booths can also be found at major railway stations and can provide hotel lists, town plans and terse information on local sights and transport. Queues can be maddeningly long. If you're stuck, you may get more sense out of a friendly travel agency than an official tourist office.

The official state tourist website is *www.enit.it*. Nearly every city and province now has a web page, and you can often book your hotel direct through the Internet.

UK: 1 Princes Street, London W1R 8AY, **t** (020) 7408 1254, *italy@italiantouristboard.co.uk*.

USA: 630 Fifth Ave, Suite 1565, New York, NY 10111, **t** (212) 245 4822, *www.italiantourism. com*.

12400 Wilshire Blvd, Suite 550, Los Angeles, CA 90025, **t** (310) 820 1898.

500 N. Michigan Ave, Suite 1046, Chicago IL 60611, **t** (312) 644 1996.

Australia: Level 26, 44 Market St, NSW 2000, Sydney, **t** (02) 926 21666, *enitour@ihug. com.au*.

Canada: 175 Bloor St E, Suite 907, South Tower, M4W 3R8, **t** (416) 925 4882, *www.italian tourism.com*.

Tourist and travel information may also be available from **Alitalia** (Italy's national airline) or **CIT** (Italy's state-run travel agency) offices in some countries.

Where to Stay

All accommodation in Italy is classified by the Provincial Tourist Boards. Price control, however, has been deregulated since 1992. Hotels now set their own tariffs, which means that in some places prices have rocketed. After a period of rapid and erratic price fluctuation, tariffs are at last settling down again to more predictable levels under the influence of market forces. Good-value, interesting accommodation in cities can be very difficult to find.

The quality of furnishings and facilities has generally improved in all categories in recent years. Many hotels have installed smart bathrooms and electronic gadgetry. At the top end of the market, Italy has a number of exceptionally sybaritic hotels, furnished and decorated with real panache. But you can still find plenty of older-style hotels and *pensioni*, whose eccentricities of character and architecture (in some cases undeniably charming) may frequently be at odds with modern standards of comfort or even safety.

Hotels and Guesthouses

Italian *alberghi* come in all shapes and sizes. They are rated from one to five stars, depending what facilities they offer (not their character, style or charm). The star ratings are some indication of price levels, but for tax reasons not all hotels choose to advertise themselves at the rating to which they are entitled, so you may find a modestly rated hotel just as comfortable (or more so) than a higher-rated one. Conversely, you may find a hotel offers few stars in hopes of attracting budget-conscious travellers, but charges just as much as a higher-rated neighbour.

Pensioni are generally more modest establishments, though nowadays the distinction between these and ordinary hotels is becoming blurred. *Locande* are traditionally an even more basic form of hostelry, but these days the term may denote somewhere fairly chic. Other inexpensive accommodation is sometimes known as *alloggi* or *affittacamere*. There are usually plenty of cheap dives around railway stations; for somewhere more salubrious, head for the historic quarters. Whatever the shortcomings of the décor, furnishings and fittings, you can usually rely at least on having clean sheets.

Price lists, by law, must be posted on the door of every room, along with meal prices and any extra charges (such as air-conditioning, or even a shower in cheap places). Many hotels display two or three different rates, depending on the season. Low-season rates may be about a third lower than peak-season tariffs. During high season you should always book ahead to be sure of a room (a fax or email reservation may be less frustrating to organize than one by post). If you have paid a deposit, your booking is valid under Italian law, but don't expect it to be

Hotel Price Categories

For a double room with bath in high season.

luxury over €250
very expensive €180–250
expensive €130–180
moderate €75–130
inexpensive up to €75

refunded if you have to cancel. Tourist offices publish annual regional lists of hotels and *pensioni* with current rates, but do not generally make reservations for visitors. Major city business hotels may offer significant discounts at weekends.

Main railway stations generally have accommodation-booking desks; inevitably, a fee is charged. Chain hotels or motels are generally the easiest hotels to book, though not always the most interesting to stay in. Top of the list is CIGA (*Compagnia Grandi Alberghi*) with some of the most luxurious establishments in Italy, many of them grand, turn-of-the-century places that have been exquisitely restored. Venice's legendary Cipriani is one of its flagships. The French consortium *Relais et Châteaux* specializes in tastefully indulgent accommodation, often in historic buildings. At a more affordable level, one of the biggest chains in Italy is *Jolly Hotels*, always reliable if not all up to the same standard.

If you arrive without a reservation begin looking or phoning round for accommodation early in the day. If possible, inspect the room (and bathroom facilities) before you book, and check the tariff carefully. Italian hoteliers may legally alter their rates twice during the year, so printed tariffs or tourist board lists (and prices quoted in this book!) may be out of date. Hoteliers who wilfully overcharge should be reported to the local tourist office. You will be asked for your passport for registration.

Prices listed in this guide are for double rooms; you can expect to pay about two-thirds the rate for single occupancy, though in high season you may be charged the full double rate. Extra beds are usually charged at about a third more of the room rate. Rooms without private bathrooms generally charge 20–30% less, and most offer discounts for children sharing parents' rooms, or children's meals. A *camera singola* (single room) may be much more than half the price of a double.

If you want a double bed, specify a *camera matrimoniale*.

Breakfast is usually optional in hotels, though obligatory in *pensioni*. It is usually better value to eat breakfast in a bar or café if you have any choice. In high season you may be expected to take half-board if the hotel has a restaurant, and one-night stays may be refused.

Hostels and Budget Accommodation

There aren't many youth hostels (known as *alberghi* or *ostelli per la gioventù*), but they are generally pleasant and sometimes located in historic buildings.

The **Associazione Italiana Alberghi per la Gioventù** (Italian Youth Hostel Association, or AIG) is affiliated to the International Youth Hostel Federation (*www.iyhf.org*). For a full list of hostels, contact AIG at Via Cavour 44, 00184 Roma (**t** 06 487 1152; **f** 06 488 0492, *www.ostellionline.org*). An international membership card will enable you to stay in any of them. You can obtain these in advance from:

UK: International Youth Hostel Federation, 1st Floor, Fountain House, Parkway, Welwyn Garden City, Hertfordshire, AL8 6JH, **t** (01707) 324170, **f** (01707) 323980, *iyhf@iyhf.org*, *www.iyhf.org*

USA: American Youth Hostels Inc., 733 15th St NW, Suite 840, Washington DC 20005, **t** (202) 783 6161, *www.hiayh.org*.

Australia: Youth Hostels Association, 422 Kent St, Sydney, **t** (02) 926 11111, *www.yha.org.au*.

Canada: Youth Hostelling International, Room 400, 205 Catherine St, Ottowa, Ontario, K2P 1C3, **t** 800 663 57777, *www.hihostels.ca*.

Cards can usually be purchased on the spot in many hostels if you don't already have one. You can book youth hostel accommodation online at *www.hostellinginternational.com*.

Religious institutions also run hostels; some are single-sex, others will accept Catholics only. Discounts are available for senior citizens, and some family rooms are available. You generally have to check in after 5pm, and pay for your room before 9am.

Hostels usually close for most of the daytime, and many operate a curfew. During the spring, noisy school parties cram them for field trips. In the summer, it's advisable to book ahead.

Women Travellers

Italian men, with the heritage of Casanova, Don Giovanni and Rudolf Valentino as their birthright, are very confident in their role as Great Latin Lovers, but the old horror stories of gangs following the innocent tourist maiden and pinching her bottom are way behind the times. Italian men these days are often exquisitely polite and flirt on a much more sophisticated level, especially in the more 'Europeanized' north.

Still, women travelling alone may frequently receive hisses, wolf-whistles and unsolicited comments (complimentary or lewd, depending on your attitude) or 'assistance' from local swains – usually of the balding, middle-age-crisis variety. A confident, indifferent poise is usually the best policy. Failing that, a polite 'I am waiting for my *marito*' (avoiding damaged male egos which can turn nasty), followed by a firm '*No!*' or '*Vai via!*' (Scram!) will generally solve the problem. Flashers and wandering hands on crowded buses may be an unpleasant surprise, but rarely present a serious threat (unless they're after your purse).

Risks can be greatly reduced if you use common sense and avoid lonely streets or parks and train stations after dark. Choose hotels and restaurants within easy and safe walking distance of public transport. Travelling with a companion of either sex will buffer you considerably from such nuisances (a guardian male, of course, instantly converts you into an inviolable chattel in Italian eyes). Avoid hitchhiking alone in Italy.

Rome

07

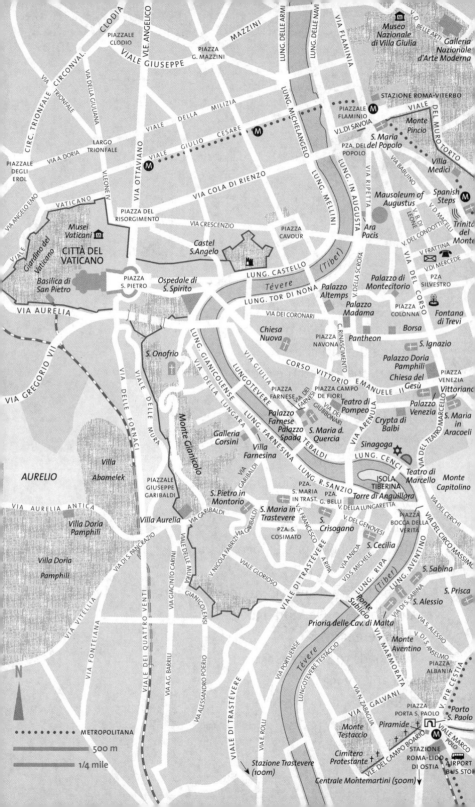

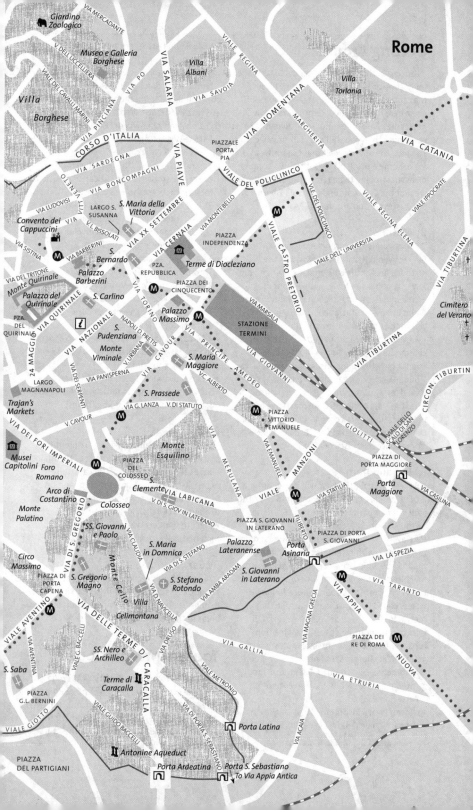

Rome

Giardino Zoologico

VIA MERCADANTE

Museo e Galleria Borghese

V. DELL'UCCELLIERA

VIALE DEI CAVALLI MARINI

Villa Borghese

VIA PO

VIA SALARIA

VIA SAVOIA

Villa Albani

VIA REGINA

VIA NOMENTANA

VIA CATANIA

Villa Torlonia

CORSO D'ITALIA

VIA SARDEGNA

VIA PIAVE

PIAZZALE PORTA PIA

VIALE DEL POLICLINICO

VIA PINCIANA

VIA V. VENETO

VIA LUDOVISI

VIA BONCOMPAGNI

VIALE DEL POLICLINICO

VLE DEL POLICLINICO

VIALE IPPOCRATE

VIA LATINA

LARGO S. SUSANNA

S. Maria della Vittoria

VIA MONTEBELLO

VIALE REGINA ELENA

VIALE DELLA UNIVERSITA

VIA TIBURTINA

Convento dei Cappuccini

V. L. BISSOLATI

VIA XX SETTEMBRE

VIA CERNAIA

PIAZZA INDEPENDENZA

VIALE CASTRO PRETORIO

Cimitero del Verano

VIA SISTINA

VIA BARBERINI

S. Bernardo

PZA. REPUBBLICA

Terme di Diocleziano

VIA MARSALA

Monte Quirinale

Palazzo Barberini

S. Carlino

PIAZZA DEI CINQUECENTO

STAZIONE TERMINI

VIA TIBURTINA

VIA DEL TRITONE

Palazzo del Quirinale

VIA QUIRINALE

VIA TORINO

Palazzo Massimo

VIA GIOVANNI

CIRCON. TIBURTIN

PZA. DEL QUIRINALE

24 MAGGIO

VIA NAZIONALE

NAPOLI DI PRETIS

S. Pudenziana

VIA CAVOUR

VIA PRINCIPE - AMEDEO

VIALE DELLO SCALO DI SAN LORENZO

Largo MAGNANAPOLI

VIA DEI SERPENTI

URBANA

Monte Viminale

VIA PANISPERNA

S. Maria Maggiore

V.C. ALBERTO

GIOLITTI

Trajan's Markets

V. CAVOUR

S. Prassede

VIA G. LANZA

V. DI STATUTO

VIA ALBERTO

PIAZZA VITTORIO EMANUELE

PIAZZA DI PORTA MAGGIORE

Musei Capitolini

VIA DEI FORI IMPERIALI

PIAZZA DEL COLOSSEO

Monte Esquilino

VIA MERULANA

VIA EMANUELE

VIALE MANZONI

Porta Maggiore

VIA CASILINA

Foro Romano

Arco di Costantino

Colosseo

S. Clemente

VIA LABICANA

V. DI S. GIOV IN LATERANO

VIA STATILIA

Porta Asinaria

Monte Palatino

VIA DI S. GREGORIO

SS. Giovanni e Paolo

VIA CLAUDIA

S. Maria in Domnica

VIA DI S. STEFANO

Palazzo Lateranense

PIAZZA S. GIOVANNI IN LATERANO

PIAZZA DI PORTA S. GIOVANNI

VIA LA SPEZIA

Circo Massimo

Monte Celio

S. Stefano Rotondo

VIA D. NAVICELLA

S. Giovanni in Laterano

VIA FILIBERTO

VIA TARANTO

VIALE AVENTINO

PIAZZA DI PORTA CAPENA

S. Gregorio Magno

Villa Celimontana

VIA DRUSO

VIA AMBA ARADAM

VIA MAGNA GRECIA

VIA APPIA

PIAZZA DEI RE DI ROMA

VIA AVENTINA

VIA G. BACCELLI

SS. Nero e Archilleo

VIA GALLIA

VIA ETRURIA

NUOVA

S. Saba

PIAZZA G.L. BERNINI

Terme di Caracalla

VIALE METRONIO

VIA ACAIA

VIALE GIOTTO

VIALE GUIDO BACCELLI

VIA DI PORTA S. SEBASTIANO

Porta Latina

PIAZZA DEL PARTIGIANI

Antonine Aqueduct

Porta Ardeatina

Porta S. Sebastiano

To Via Appia Antica

Getting Around

Looking at the map, Rome seems to be made for getting around on foot. This may be so in the *centro storico* around Piazza Navona, but elsewhere it's deceptive – city blocks in the newer areas are huge, and it will always take you longer than you think to walk anywhere. The hills, the outsize scale and the traffic also make Rome a tiring place, but there is some pleasant strolling to be had in the old districts west of the Corso, around the Isola Tiberina, in old Trastevere and around the Monte Celio.

By Metro

Rome's underground system is not particularly convenient as it seems to avoid the historic parts of the city; imagine trying to dig any sort of hole in Rome, with legions of archaeologists ready to pounce. The two lines, A and B, cross at Stazione Termini and will take you to the Colosseum, around the Monte Aventino, to Piazza di Spagna, San Giovanni in Laterano, San Paolo Fuori le Mura, Piazza del Popolo, or within eight blocks of St Peter's.

Single tickets (€0.77), also good for city buses – valid for 75mins from obliteration in the turnstile – are available from machines in metro stations, tobacconists, bars and kiosks. Daily and weekly tickets are also available from tobacconists (*see* below).

By Bus and Tram

Buses are by far the best way to get around. Pick up a map of the bus routes from the **ATAC** (city bus company) booth outside Stazione Termini. Bus tickets cost €0.77, and are good for travel on any ATAC city bus or tram and one metro ride – within 75mins of the first use of the ticket – which must be stamped in the machines in the back entrance of buses or trams. There are also special-price full-day tickets called BIG (which also include the metro) for €3, as well as weekly passes (CIS, €12.40) and monthly passes available from tobacconists. Some useful bus routes:

3 (tram) Villa Borghese–Viale Regina Margherita–San Lorenzo–S. Giovanni in Laterano–Colosseum–Viale Aventino–Porta San Paolo.
19 (tram) Piazza Risorgimento (near the Vatican)–Viale delle Milizie–Villa Borghese–Viale Regina Margherita–Porta Maggiore–San Lorenzo and Via Prenestina.
23 Musei Vaticani–Castel Sant'Angelo–Tiber banks–Porta San Paolo–S. Paolo.
36 Termini–Via Nomentana (Sant'Agnese).
46 Piazza Venezia–Corso V. Emanuele– Vatican.
63 Largo Argentina–Via del Corso–Via del Tritone–Via Vittorio Veneto.
64 Termini–Via Nazionale–Corso Vittorio Emanuele–Vatican (the main bus route from the *centro storico* to the Vatican and famous for its pickpockets so be extra careful).
116T Piazza della Repubblica–Via Nazionale– Via del Tritone–Via del Corso–Piazza Venezia–Largo Argentina–Mausoleo di Augusto (*8pm–1.30am*).
116 Via Veneto–Piazza Barberini–Via del Tritone–Piazza del Parlamento–Corso Rinascimento–Corso Vittorio Emanuele – Campo de' Fiori–Piazza Farnese–Via Giulia (a circular minibus, *weekdays 8am–9pm, Sat 8am–midnight*).
119 Piazza del Popolo–Via del Babuino–Piazza di Spagna–Piazza Barberini–Via Veneto– Porta Pinciano (and back).
218 San Giovanni in Laterano–Porta San Sebastiano–Via Appia Antica–Via Ardeatina (passing the catacombs and tombs).

By Taxi

Official taxis (painted white) are plentiful, and easier to get at a rank in one of the main piazzas than to flag down. They are quite expensive, with surcharges for luggage, on Sundays and after 10.30pm. Fares are clearly explained in English inside every taxi. Don't expect to find one when it's raining. To phone for a taxi, call **t** 06 3570, or **t** 06 4994.

By Car

Absolutely not recommended! Rome isn't as chaotic as Naples, but nearly so. Parking is expensive and difficult to find, and many areas in the centre are closed to traffic.

Tourist Information

Azienda di Promozione Turistica (APT), Via Parigi 11, 00185, **t** 06 488 991, **f** 06 4889 9238. *Open Mon–Fri 9.30–12.30*, Mon and Thurs also 2.30–4.30. The central office, near the Baths of Diocletian and Termini. The APT offices are the best source of information about what's on in Rome and its province.

APT (Fiumicino Airport), **t** 06 6595 6074. *Open Mon–Sat 8.15–7.* A useful branch office.

Comune di Roma Tourist Information Office, Termini Station. *Open daily 8–8.* Inside Rome's main train station. You'll find more information about the city here. Ask for free city maps and brochures in English. The free ATAC public transport map is very useful.

Comune di Roma helpline, **t** 06 3600 4399 (*select 2 for an English-speaking operator*). *Open daily 9–7.30.* Contact the efficient call centre or visit *www.romaturismo.com*.

In addition, there are tourist kiosks (*all open daily 9.30–7.30*) at Largo Goldoni, Piazza Pia, Piazza del Tempio della Pace, Piazza delle Cinque Lune, Via Marco Minghetti, Via Nazionale, Piazza Sonnino, Piazza San Giovanni in Laterano, Via dell'Olmata and Stazione Termini.

The Hotel Reservation Service, **t** 06 699 1000 (*open daily 8am– 10.45pm*) offers commission-free reservations.

Enjoy Rome, Via Varese 39, **t** 06 445 1843, also near Stazione Termini, is an English-speaking information service.

To make the most of the sights, you can buy a cumulative ticket called the **Roma Archeologia Card**, valid 7 days, which includes the Palatino, Colosseum, Crypta Balbi, Palazzo Massimo, Palazzo Altemps, Terme di Diocleziano, Baths of Caracalla, Tomb of Cecilia Metella and Villa dei Quintili; the ticket can be acquired at any of these sites and costs €20.

24-hour pharmacies: **Piram**, Via Nazionale 228, **t** 06 488 0754; **Arenula**, Via Arenula 73, **t** 06 6880 3278, near Largo Argentina. Outside banking hours money can be exchanged at **American Express**, Piazza di Spagna 38, **t** 06 67641 (*open Mon–Fri 9–5.30, Sat 9–12.30*); **Thomas Cook**, Via della Conciliazione 23, **t** 06 6830 0435 (*open Mon–Sat 8–6, Sun 8–5*). **Main post office**: Piazza San Silvestro 19, **t** 06 160, *www.poste.it*.

Shopping

Rome isn't as exciting for big-game shoppers as Milan, though when it comes to clothing you will find all the major designers and labels well represented. Serious shoppers

should check out the website *www.made-in-italy.com*. There is no shortage of shops selling **antiques**, a great number of them between the Tiber and Piazza Navona; look especially off Via Monserrato, Via dei Coronari and Via dell'Anima. For **old prints**, generally inexpensive, try Casali, Piazza Rotonda 81A; Alinari, Via Alibert 16/a is a good address for artistic **black and white pictures of old Rome**. L'Art Nouveau, Via dei Coronari 221, offers just what its name implies. **Antiques** also show up in the celebrated Sunday morning flea market at Porta Portese, as well as anything else you can imagine (*open dawn–1*).

The most **fashionable shopping** is on the streets between Piazza di Spagna and the Corso, with Via Condotti still the designer shopping street *par excellence*. Some special items: Massoni, Largo Goldoni 48, near Via Condotti, much frequented by film stars, sells some of Rome's finest **jewellery**; for **menswear**, Testa, Via Borgognona 13 and Via Frattina 42, or Valentino Uomo, Via Condotti 12, or for **custom tailoring**, Battistoni, Via Condotti 61/a. For **women's clothes** try the outlets of the big designers in the same area: Missoni, Via del Babuino 96, Giorgio Armani, Via Condotti 76–7 and Via del Babuino 140, Mila Schöen, Via Condotti 51, or the Rome-based Fendi, Via Borgognona 36/e. For **leather**, the Gucci outlet is at Via Condotti 8, and do not miss Fausto Santini, Via Frattina 120.

Discounted designer fashion may be had at Il Discount dell'Alta Moda, Via Gesù e Maria 16/a; for **high-fashion shoes**, try Barrilà, Via Condotti 29 and Via del Babuino 33; and for **Borsalino hats**, Troncarelli, Via della Cuccagna 15, near Piazza Navona.

For a special bottle of **wine**, try Enoteca Costantini, Piazza Cavour 16, for a wide selection. If you wish to stock up on Italian **coffee**, Tazza d'Oro, Via degli Orfani 84, has special bags of the city's best, the 'Aroma di Roma'.

If you need a good **book**, try the Anglo-American Book Co., Via della Vite 27, the Lion Bookshop, Via dei Greci 36, the Economy Book Center, Via Torino 135/a, near Via Nazionale, or Feltrinelli Internationalat Via Orlando 84–86 (this also stocks guides and maps).

For an amazing selection of **fancy kitchen gear**, there's C.U.C.I.N.A., Via Mario dei Fiori 65, while for serious, professional **pans, pots and** tools head to Zucchi, Via Sant'Antonio all'Esquilino 15, near Santa Maria Maggiore. Try Image, Via della Scrofa 67, for **posters, postcards and photographs**; and De Ritis, Via de' Cestari 1, for the latest **ecclesiastical fashions**, along with Madonnas and crucifixes.

Sports and Activities

Rome's main public **swimming pool** is the Piscina delle Rose, Viale America 20, in EUR, t 06 5425 2185 (Ⓜ EUR Fermi) (*open June–mid-Sept daily 9–7; adm €10.50*). There is also an attractive private pool at the Centro Sportivo Italiano, Lungotevere Flaminio 55, about a half-mile north of Piazza del Popolo, t 06 323 7333 (*open in summer*).

Rome's two first-division **football** clubs, AS Roma and Lazio, both play on Saturday or Sunday pm at the Stadio Olimpico, Viale dei Gladiatori 2 (Ⓜ Linea A to Ottaviano, then bus no.32) during the season (*Sept–May*). Tickets (€18–110) on sale 10–14 days ahead; contact Lazio Point, Via Farini 34, t 06 6482 6688; or *Orbis*, Piazza Esquilino 37, t 06 474 4776.

Where to Stay

Rome ✉ 00100

Prices are higher and service and quality lower than elsewhere in Italy, and places with a history, a view or quiet gardens are rare. That said, the city went into overdrive building, renovating and sprucing up its hotels for 2000. Much of the city's accommodation is around the Stazione Termini district, but it is overbuilt, dingy and down-at-heel, and inconvenient for most of the sights. At least it's close to the newly trendy San Lorenzo district.

Rooms can be difficult to find at short notice, but the free **Hotel Reservation Service**, t 06 699 1000, will do the looking for you. The private **Enjoy Rome** (*see* p.101) will also make commission-free hotel bookings.

Luxury
*****Art** by the Spanish Steps, Via Margutta 56, 00187, t 06 421 281, f 06 3600 3995, *www.hotelart.it*. Sleek boutique hotel decorated with a mixture of antiques and contemporary design, set in a former *palazetto* near the Spanish Steps. The extras include a Turkish bath, sauna and jacuzzi.
*****Excelsior**, Via Veneto 125, 00187, t 06 47081, f 06 482 6205, *www.westin.com/ excelsiorroma*. Also located in a choice area, though lacking the aura it had in the 1950s. The reception areas have thicker carpets, bigger chandeliers and more gilded plaster than anywhere in Italy, and most of the rooms are just as good – don't let them give you a modernized one. There are saunas, a famous bar, and a tiny cinema.
*****Hassler-Villa Medici**, Piazza Trinità dei Monti 6, 00187, t 06 699 340, f 06 678 9991, *www.hotelhasslerroma.com*, *hasslerroma@ mclink.it*. One of Rome's best hotels, with a fine location at the top of the Spanish Steps and wonderful views over the city. Beautiful courtyard, rooftop terrace, deferential service, and large wood-panelled rooms.
****D'Inghilterra**, Via Bocca di Leone 14, 00187, t 06 699 811, f 06 6992 2243, *www. hoteldinghilterraroma.it*. Another favourite near Piazza di Spagna. Parts of this building date from the 15th century, when it served as a prince's guest house; in its career as a hotel, since 1850, it has played host to most of Europe and America's literati and artists. Don't miss the beautiful roof garden.
****Columbus**, Via della Conciliazione 33, 00193, t 06 686 5435/ t 06 6819 9360, f 06 686 4874, *www.hotelcolumbus.net*. Staid but reliable, this is slightly geared towards business travellers; attractive, well-equipped rooms, some with views over St Peter's.
****Forum**, Via Tor de' Conti 25, 00184, t 06 679 2446, f 06 678 6479, *info@ hotelforum.com*, *www.hotelforum.com*. The only fancy establishment near the ancient Forum; it's somewhat worn, but has unbeatable views from the roof terrace.
****Raphael**, Largo di Febo 2, 00186, t 06 682 831, f 06 687 8993, *info@hotelraphael.com*, *www.raphaelhotel.com*. Very near Piazza Navona, a vine-covered old charmer, decorated with antiques. TV, bar, restaurant, air-conditioning and business facilities. Breakfast extra.

Very Expensive
****La Residenza**, Via Emilia 22, 00187, t 06 488 0789, f 06 485 721, *www.venere.it/roma/*

laresidenza. Near the Via Veneto; stands out as a very pleasant base, with beautifully appointed rooms in an old town house, and some luxuries more common to the most expensive hotels. Non-smoking.

★★★**Carriage**, Via delle Carrozze 36, 00187, **t** 06 699 0124, **f** 06 678 8279, *www.hotel carriage.net*. Almost at the foot of the Spanish Steps; a sleepy but charming spot with tastefully refurbished rooms and welcoming staff. Book well in advance.

★★★**Fontana**, Piazza di Trevi 96, 00187, **t** 06 678 6113, **f** 06 679 0024, *www.fontanahotel.com*. Would be a good hotel anywhere; it is also right across the street from the Trevi Fountain – something to look at out of your window that will guarantee nice dreams. Prices can reach luxury category.

★★★**Celio**, Via del Santio Quattro 35c, **t** 06 7049 5333, **f** 06 709 6377, *www.hotelcelio.com*. A welcoming, idiosyncratic hotel close to the Colosseum; each room bears the name of a famous opera singer and the bathrooms have mosaic-style floors. Prices range from luxury to expensive categories.

★★★**Due Torri**, Vicolo del Leonetto 23, 00186, **t** 06 687 6983, **f** 06 686 5442, *www. hotelduetorri.roma.it*. On a tiny, quiet street, this attractive little hotel was once the home of a famous prelate and offers comfortable, if slightly small, rooms (try to get one with rooftop views).

★★★**Fontanella Borghese**, Largo Fontanello Borghese 84, **t** 06 6880 9504, **f** 06 686 1295, *wwwfontanellaborghese.com*. Set in a 15th-century *palazzo*, this is a delightful and atmpospheric little hotel with tastefully decorated rooms and large bathrooms.

★★★**Locarno**, Via della Penna 22, **t** 06 361 0841, *www.hotellocarno.com*. Close to the Piazza del Popolo, this welcoming Art Nouveau-style hotel has plenty of charm. The elegant rooms are well-equipped – some have hi fi, video and and modem connections. There's also a lovely roof terrace. Book in advance.

★★★**Villa San Pio**, Via Santa Melania 19, 00153, **t** 06 574 8119, **f** 06 578 3604, *www.aventino hotels.com*. A glorious Aventine villa with a gorgeous, secluded statue-studded garden. The recently refurbished rooms are quietly elegant and some lead out onto the garden. Linked to Hotel Sant'Anselmo (*see* below).

Expensive

★★★**Hotel Sant'Anselmo**, Piazza Sant'Anselmo 2, 00153, **t** 06 574 8119, **f** 06 578 3604, *www. aventinohotels.com*. Up on the Monte Aventino, a peaceful hotel with a garden and comfortable, individually decorated rooms. Ask for one with views of the city.

★★★**Lancelot**, Via Capo d'Africa 47, **t** 06 7045 0615, **f** 06 7045 0616, *www.lancelothotel. com*. A charming, family-run hotel full of knick-knacks close to the Colosseum with recently refurbished rooms.

★★★**Portoghesi**, Via dei Portoghesi 1, 00186, **t** 06 686 4231, **f** 06 687 6976, *www. hotelportoghesi.roma.com*. A small, well-kept hotel in an former mansion on a quiet street north of Piazza Navona, with antique-filled rooms.

★★★**Teatro di Pompeo**, Largo del Pallaro 8, 00186, **t** 06 6830 0170, **f** 06 6880 5531, *hotel. teatrodipompeo@tiscalinet.it, web.tiscali.it/ hotel_teatrodipompeo*. A small, very welcoming hotel with plain rooms, which is built on the Teatro di Pompeo by Campo de' Fiori, perfect for peace and quiet.

★★★**Hotel Scalinata di Spagna**, Piazza Trinità dei Monti 17, **t** 06 679 3006, **f** 06 6994 0598. With a perfect location at the top of the Spanish Steps, this small hotel has just 15 rooms which book up quickly. The price is worth it for the views from the breakfast terrace alone. Prices soar to luxury price category in the high season.

Expensive–Moderate

★★**Campo de' Fiori**, Via del Biscione 6, 00186 **t** 06 6880 6865, **f** 06 687 6003, *www. campodefiori.com*. A revamped hotel covered in a sheet of ivy with hall-of-mirrors corridor, and theme-park bedrooms. Vertiginous views from the roof garden. Bar and air conditioning. Some cheaper rooms are available. Breakfast extra.

Moderate

★★**Sole**, Via del Biscione 76, 00186, **t** 06 687 9446, **f** 06 689 3787 *info@solealbiscione*. Near Campo de' Fiori, on the foundations of Pompey's Theatre, a family-run favourite of backpackers, grandparents and everyone else under the sun. Book in advance and request a room facing the pretty garden overlooked by a church. Cheaper rooms without bath available (*moderate*). No breakfast.

★★Nardizzi, Via Firenze 38, t 06 488 035, f 06 4880 0368, *www.hotelnadarzzi.it*. A very reasonably priced, simple option close to Termini. It doesn't ooze charm, but has friendly staff, clean, well-equipped rooms (with a/c), and a roof garden.

Moderate–Inexpensive

★★Abruzzi, Piazza della Rotonda 69, 00186, t 06 679 2021. Directly across the square from the Pantheon. A bit ragged, but amenable. Showers in the hall. TV, bar, air-conditioning.

★★Hotel Boccaccio, Via del Boccaccio 25, t/f 06 488 5962, *www.hotelboccaccio.it*. Delightful, simple little hotel (just eight rooms) not far from the Piazza di Spagna. The rooms are plain, but there's a pretty plant-filled courtyard and utterly charming staff.

Inexpensive

The area around **Stazione Termini** offers a wide choice of inexpensive hotels, ranging from plain, family-run establishments to bizarre dives with exposed plumbing.

Accommodation Planet 29, Via Gaeta 29, t 06 48 65 20, f 06 48 41 41, *cristina@mclink. it*, *www.mclink.it/com/travel*. A friendly place which has 15 simple rooms – some with kitchenette tucked away in a cupboard.

The City Guesthouse, Viale Opita Oppio 78, 00174, t 06 7698 3140, f 06 7696 7961, *www.cityguesthouse.com*. Out of the centre, but still only a 20min metro ride to Termini or the Spanish Steps. Rooms are individually decorated with trendy bold prints and slick, minimalist furniture. The staff couldn't be friendlier and there are plenty of great restaurants in the neighbourhood.

Colors Hotel and Hostel, Via Boezio 31, t 06 687 4030, *www.colorshotel.com*. One of the few budget places not in the Termini area. It's a popular, bright hotel and hostel close to the Vatican with dorm rooms (€19 per person), doubles (around €75), and self-catering. Kitchen, terrace, TV lounge and laundry.

Freedom Traveller, Via Gaeta 25, t 06 478 23 862, *info@freedom-traveller.it*, *www. freedom-traveller.it*. Big, brash backpacker hostel near Termini with an Internet café, kitchen facilities, common room, terrace and organized pub crawls. Dorm rooms from €18 per person; doubles from €50 per room. Breakfast is included.

★★Pensione Primavera, Piazza San Pantaleo 3, 00186, t 06 6880 3109, f 06 6880 3109. A little-known *pensione* with eight simple rooms, two minutes' walk from both Campo de' Fiori and Piazza Navona.

★Restivo, Via Palestro 55, t 06 446 2172, f 06 445 2629. Immaculate *pensione* run by a sweet Sicilian lady, whose hall is cluttered with gifts from affectionate visitors. If it's full, try the plain, but very cheap **Cervia** (t 06 491 057, f 06 491 056, *www.hotel cerviaroma.com*) in the same *palazzo*.

Bed and Breakfast

The APT tourist office publish a comprehensive list of bed and breakfast establishments. In addition, the Rome Chamber of Commerce provides a free booking service for establishments which have been given its quality award: t 06 679 5937, f 06 678 6521, *www.hotelreservation.it*.

Eating Out

Unlike many other Italians, the Romans aren't afraid to try something new. Chinese restaurants have appeared in droves, not to mention Arab, Korean and macrobiotic places. This should not be taken as a reflection on local cooking. Rome attracts talented chefs from all over Italy, giving a microcosm of Italian cuisine you'll find nowhere else.

The grand old tradition of Roman cooking has specialities such as *saltimbocca* (paper-thin slices of veal cooked with *prosciutto*), *stracciatella* (a soup with eggs, parmesan cheese and parsley), fried artichokes called *carciofi alla giudia* and veal *involtini*. In the less expensive places you are likely to encounter such favourites as *baccalà* (salt cod), *bucatini all'amatriciana* (in a tomato and bacon sauce) or *alla carbonara*, tripe and *gnocchi*. The wine will probably come from the Castelli Romani – light, fruity whites, of which the best come from Frascati and Velletri.

Though you can drop as much as €150 (without wine) if you follow the politicians and the TV crowd, prices somehow manage to keep close to the Italian average – Rome is much more reasonable than Milan. Watch out for tourist traps – places near a major sight with a 'tourist menu'. Hotel restaurants, those in the de luxe class, can often be quite good.

Very Expensive

La Pergola dell'Hotel Hilton, Via Cadlolo 101, **t** 06 3509 2152. Perched high above the city, this is one of the city's top restaurants for *alta cucina* served in elegant surroundings with all of Rome at your feet. Meals can be enjoyed on the roof terrace. Reserve well ahead. *Open Feb–Dec Tues–Sat 7.30–11.45pm*.

La Rosetta, Via della Rosetta 8, near the Pantheon, **t** 06 686 1002. Rome's best fish-only restaurant, with a Sicilian touch; even if you aren't dining, step in to admire the heap of shiny fish, oysters and sea-urchins arranged on the marble slab in the hall. Reserve well ahead. *Open Sept–July Mon–Sat 7.45–11.45pm and Thurs–Fri 1–3pm*.

Alberto Ciarla, Piazza San Cosimato 40, **t** 06 581 8668. Some way south of Santa Maria in Trastevere; the French-trained owner, proud enough to put his name on the sign, sees to it that everything is delicately and perfectly done, and graciously served: oysters, seafood ravioli and quite a few adventurous styles of *pesce crudo* (raw fish) are among the most asked for. *Open Mon–Sat 7.30–midnight, except 2 weeks in Jan and 1 week in Aug*.

Il Convivio, Vicolo dei Soldati 31, **t** 06 686 9432. Some of the most innovative cuisine in Rome – unbeatable chilled fruit soups, baked *zucchini* flowers and exquisite pastries. Reserve. *Open Tues–Sat 1–2.30 and 8–10.30, Mon 8–10.30 only, except 1 week in Aug*.

Checchino dal 1887, Via di Monte Testaccio 30, **t** 06 574 3816. The acknowledged temple of old Roman cooking, which has been owned by the same family for 107 years – the longest known in Rome. Both the fancy and humble sides of Roman food are well represented, with plenty of the powerful offal dishes that Romans have been eating since ancient times, and the setting is unique – on the edge of Monte Testaccio, with one of Rome's best cellars excavated under the hill. *Open Sept–July Tues–Sat 12–3 and 8–11.30. Closed Aug and over Christmas*.

Expensive

Il Toscano, Via Germanico 58, **t** 06 397 25717. Perhaps your best option in the tourist-trap Vatican area: family-run and very popular with Roman families, offering well-prepared Tuscan specialities like *pici* (rough, fresh spaghetti rolled by hand) in game sauce, and *fiorentina* steak – and home-made desserts. Reserve. *Open Sept–July Tues–Sat 12.30–3 and 8–11, except last week of Dec*.

Papà Giovanni, Via dei Sediari 4, **t** 06 686 5308. An intimate setting for some of the most heavenly food in Rome, based on availability in the market. This is your chance to dine like Caesar; the chef specializes in reviving old Roman recipes. *Open Mon–Sat 1–4 and 8–12, except first 2 weeks in Aug*.

Piperno, Via Monte de' Cenci 9, **t** 06 6880 6629. There is no better place to try *carciofi alla giudia* than right on the edge of the old ghetto at Rome's most famous purveyor of Roman-Jewish cooking – simple dishes on the whole, but prepared and served with refinement. *Open Sept–July Tues–Sat 12.45–2.30 and 8–10.30, Sun 12.30–3pm*.

Camponeschi, Piazza Farnese, **t** 06 687 4927. One of the top spots for star-spotting, this fine restaurant has views of the elegant Palazzo Farnese. Charming, knowledgeable service. *Closed 10–24 Aug*.

Vecchia Roma, Piazza di Campitelli 18, **t** 06 686 4604. Good food, an imaginative seasonal menu and fine wine list in a lovely quiet setting with tables outdoors; not far from Piazza Venezia. *Open Sept–July Thurs–Tues 1–3.30 and 8–11*.

Margutta Vegetariano, Via Margutta 119, **t** 06 3600 1805. One of Rome's few vegetarian restaurants. Rather chic and somewhat over-priced by international vegetarian standards, but it's got a lovely plant-filled terrace on a quiet square. *Open Mon–Sat 12.30–3 and 7.30–11.30*.

Dal Bolognese, Piazza del Popolo 1, **t** 06 361 1426. With tables outside on the grand piazza and a view of the Pincio, this is the place to go to sample Emilian specialities – don't miss the tortellini, and finish with *fruttini*, a selection of real fruit shells each filled with its own sorbet flavour. *Open Tues 8.15–11, Wed–Sun 12.45–3 and 8.15–11. Closed Aug and Christmas*.

Da Paris, Piazza San Calisto 7/a, **t** 06 581 5378. Just beyond Piazza Santa Maria in Trastevere; serves classic Roman-Jewish cuisine; come here for the *minestra di arzilla* (skate soup), *tagliolini con scampi e fiori di zucca* ('little cut' pasta with prawns and pumpkin flowers). *Open Sept–July Tues–Sat 12–3 and 8–11, Sun 12–3.*

The quarters just outside the Aurelian wall and north and east of the Villa Borghese are more good places to look for restaurants:

Al Ceppo, Via Panama 2, **t** 06 841 9696. In the heart of the Parioli neighbourhood, with an open grill and warm, comfortable, elegant décor reminiscent of a bourgeois drawing room. Traditional Italian cuisine with specialities from the Marches. Tables outside in summer. *Reserve for Sunday lunch. Open Tues–Sun 1–3 and 8–11, except 3 weeks in Aug.*

Moderate

Less expensive places are not hard to find in the *centro storico*, although chances to eat anything different from Roman cuisine are pretty low.

Albistrò, Via dei Banchi Vecchi 140, **t** 06 686 5274. Sample the lamb with honey sauce or the chicken with leeks in this family-run restaurant. Arrive early to secure a table in the inner courtyard. Tapas served on Mon, Thurs, Fri and Sat between 5.30 and 7.15. *Open late Aug–early July Thurs–Tues 7.30–11, Sun 12.30–3 and 7.30–11.*

Armando al Pantheon, Salita dei Crescenzi 31, **t** 06 6880 3034. An authentic Roman trattoria famous for *spaghetti cacio e pepe* (with pecorino cheese and black pepper) or *all' amatriciana*, *saltimbocca*, and a delicious ricotta tart. *Open Mon–Fri 12.30–3 and 7–11, Sat 12.30–3 only. Closed Aug.*

Checco er Carettiere, Via Benedetta 10, **t** 06 580 0985. One of Trastevere's oldest inns, with well-prepared versions of Roman specialities like *coda alla vaccinara* and seafood. Famous for making even tripe taste good. The fish is just right. *Open Mon–Sat 12–3 and 7–12, Sun 12–4.30. Closed May.*

La Cantina Tirolese, Via Vitelleschi 23, **t** 06 686 9994. A cheerful cellar in the Tyrolese style, with wooden benches, ironwork chandeliers and more than 30 Tyrolese fabric calendars on the walls. Hearty, delicious food from the Alpine region. *Open Mon 8–1, Tues–Sun 12–4 and 8–1, except 2 weeks in Aug.*

Ditirambo, Piazza della Cancelleria, **t** 06 687 1626. A favourite with young Romans; you'll have to take the noise along with the good food. A large selection of home-made pasta and vegetarian dishes. *Open Tues–Sun 1–3.30 and 8–11.30, Mon 8–11.30 only. Closed 3 weeks in Aug.*

L'Eau Vive, Via Monterone 85, **t** 06 6880 1095. An exception to the above: only in Rome would you find a good French restaurant run by a Catholic lay missionary society – *sole meunière* and onion soup in the well-scrubbed and righteous atmosphere not far from the Pantheon. A nourishing meal at a modest price, served with serenity, will have you joining in a prayer to the Virgin before dessert; the fixed lunch menu is a great bargain. *Open Sept–July Mon–Sat 12.30–3 and 7.30–10.30.*

Café Romana de l'Hotel d'Inghilterra, Via Bocca di Leone 14, **t** 06 699 81500. Another exception: an elegant retreat in the heart of the shopping district at the foot of the Spanish Steps; if you like their style you can return for a very expensive dinner.

Grappolo d'Oro, Piazza della Cancelleria 80, **t** 06 689 7080. Near Campo de' Fiori; offers good value traditional Roman cooking. One of the best places to sit outside at night. *Open Sept–July Mon–Sat 12–3 and 8–11.*

Cheap

Africa, Via Gaeta 26, **t** 06 494 1077. A great Ethiopian/Eritrean restaurant that offers spicy meals at very low prices. *Open for breakfast; closed Mon.*

Acchiappafantasmi, Via del Capillari 66, **t** 06 687 3462. Rustically decorated trattoria close to the Campo de' Fiori, where you'll find delicious home cooking at reasonable prices. *Closed Tues and 2 weeks in Aug.*

Enoteca Corsi, Via del Gesù 87, 06 679 0821. This buzzy, down-to-earth trattoria in the heart of the city is enormously popular thanks to the economical menu which is short but changes regularly. *Closed Aug.*

Tram Tram, Via dei Reti 44, **t** 06 490 416. Crowded and trendy restaurant in the arty San Lorenzo neighbourhood east of Termini. *Closed Mon.*

Pizzerias

Roman pizza is crisp and thin, although the softer, thicker Neapolitan-style pizza has recently won a fat slice of the market. Most pizzerias have tables outside and are open only for dinner, often until 2am.

Blu, Via de Sabelli 193, **t** 06 494 0863. Good pizza and pasta at this mellow, candle-lit bistro in San Lorenzo. *Open Mon 6.30–12, 12–3 and 6.30–12. Closed 2 weeks in Aug.*

Dar Poeta, Via del Bologna 46, **t** 06 588 0516. Enormously popular pizzeria in Trastevere, which also serves good *bruschette* and salads. Try the famous *calzone* with ricotta and nutella. *Open Mon, Wed–Sun 12.30–3 and 6.30–12.30, Tues 6.30–12.30. Closed Sept.*

La Montecarlo, Vicolo Savelli 12, **t** 06 686 1877. Sit elbow to elbow with your neighbours and duck as brilliant pizzas, chairs and tables are whipped over your head. *Open May–Oct daily 12–3 and 6.30–1, except 2 weeks in Aug; Nov–April Tues–Sun only.*

Pizzaré, Via di Rapetta 14, **t** 06 321 1468. A properly Neapolitan pizza – including a '*pizza sostanziosa*' with everything on it. *Open all year except 2 weeks in Aug, daily 12.45–3.30 and 7.30–12.30.* Another branch, **Pizzaré 2**, at Via Oslavia 39, Prati, to6 372 1173.

Frontoni, Viale Trastevere 52, **t** 06 3630 7865. Choose what to put in your pizza sandwich from a large selection of fillings. *Open Mon–Thurs 11am–1am, Fri and Sat 11am–2am.*

Supplì e Pizza al Taglio, Via San Francesco a Ripa, **t** 06 588 0516. Besides slices of pizza and roasted chicken, try the famous *supplì* – deep-fried rice balls with melted mozzarella in the middle. *Open noon–midnight.*

Wine Bars/*Enoteche*

Consider lunch in a wine bar, which will offer good selections of cured meat and cheese, soups, salads and occasional quiches and flans, and desserts (usually) made in-house. Choose from about 20 wines *in mescita* (by the glass) and hundreds by the bottle:

Semidivino, Via Alessandria 230, **t** 06 4425 0795. A classy and intimate wine bar run by an Iranian expatriate. Good for a first-rate meal based on excellent salads, interesting cheeses, pork-cured meat and comforting soups. *Open Sept–July Mon–Fri 12.30–2 and 7.30–11.30, Sat 7.30–11.30.*

Trimani, Via Cernaia 37/b, not far from Termini, **t** 06 446 9630. A haven of sanity where business types and intellectuals with demanding tastebuds flock at lunchtime. *Open Mon–Fri 12–12, Sat 8–12, except 2 weeks in Aug.*

Cul de Sac, Piazza Pasquino 73, **t** 06 6880 1094. A tiny – and always crammed – bottle-lined bar with a few tables outside which serves light meals to gastronomes (cured meats, cheeses, salads) as well as home cooked lasagne and other dishes. *Open daily 12–12.30, closed May.*

Cavour 313, Via Cavour 313, **t** 06 678 5496. A civilized wood-beamed bar which serves delicious, high-quality snacks and light meals, lunchtime and evenings, to accompany whichever of its 500 wines you care to drink. *Open Mon–Sat 12.30–2.30 and 7.30–12.30, Sun 7.30–12.30 only; closed all day Sun between June and Sept.*

Il Cantinere de Santa Dorotea, Via Santa Dorotea, **t** 06 581 9025. Tucked away in Trastevere, this warm and welcoming *enoteca* has delicious soups, pastas and cured meats to accompany its excellent selection of wines.

Entertainment and Nightlife

The best entertainment in Rome is often in the passing cosmopolitan spectacle of its streets; as nightlife goes, it can be a real snoozer compared with other European cities. If you're determined, the back streets around the Piazza Navona or Campo de' Fiori swarm with people in the evenings, and these are the places to come to plan your night ahead, as leaflets and free tickets are always being handed out. Often these are to new places that have opened. Another source is *Romac'e'* (€1 from news-stands, *www.romace.it*), with comprehensive listings and a small section in English, or the weekly *Time Out* with listings and articles (in Italian). The current hip neighbourhoods for going out are San Lorenzo, east of Termini station, and Testaccio.

Rome can be uncomfortably sticky in August, but there's plenty going on. The *Estate Romana* (Roman Summer, *www.estateromana.caltanet.it*, **t** 06 3600 4399) is a three-month-long festival of outdoor events, music, theatre and film (shown on outdoor screens around the city), and most museums run longer hours. A far older Roman party is the traditional **Festa de' Noantri** in Trastevere (16–31 July), where you may well find a gust of old Roman spontaneity along with music from all across the spectrum, acrobats, dancing and stall upon stall down Viale Trastevere.

Opera, Classical Music, Theatre, Film

Orbis, Piazza Esquilino 37, t 06 474 4776, *www.ticketone.it*, is a reliable agency for concert, opera and theatre tickets (*open Mon–Sat 9.30–1 and 4–7.30*).

From November until May you can take in a performance at the **Teatro dell'Opera di Roma**, Piazza B. Gigli, off Via del Viminale, t 800 016665, *www.opera.roma.it*. Other concerts are performed at and by the **Accademia Nazionale di Santa Cecilia**, in the auditorium on Via della Conciliazione 4, t 06 361 1044, and by the **Accademia Filarmonica Romana**, Via Flaminia 118, box office, t 06 6880 9222. Medieval, Baroque, chamber and choral music are performed at the **Oratorio del Gonfalone**, Via del Gonfalone 32/a, t 06 687 5952.

Traditionally during the summer there has been a range of special seasons. Evening concerts are held outside in the **Teatro di Marcello**, t 06 481 4800, or t 06 780 4314 (*mid-June–Sept*), and concerts are performed by the Accademia di Santa Cecilia and visiting international orchestras at **Villa Giulia** (*July*). The opera moves outside in the summer – to the **Villa Borghese** and the **soccer stadium**.

You can find films in *versione originale* at:
Alcazar, Via Cardinal Merry del Val 14, Trastevere, t 06 588 0099 (*Mon*).
Nuovo Sacher, Largo Ascianghi 1, Trastevere, t 06 5811 8116 (*Mon and Tues*). One of the best places to see new cinema in Rome.
Quirinetta, Via M. Minghetti 4, t 06 679 0012.
Pasquino, Piazza Sant'Egidio, near Santa Maria in Trastevere, t 06 580 3622 (*daily*).

Cafés and Bars

Caffè Greco, Via Condotti 86, t 06 679 1700. Rome's oldest café (1760), where Keats and Casanova sipped their java.
Rosati, Piazza del Popolo 4, t 06 322 5859. Another *grand café*: an elegant place

founded in 1922, and popular with Roman intelligentsia; extravagant ice-creams.
Babington's Tea Rooms, Piazza di Spagna 23. 150 years old; serves scones and tea or a full lunch in the proper Victorian atmosphere.
Sant'Eustachio, Piazza Sant'Eustachio 82, near Piazza Navona. Trendy home of Rome's most famous coffee; tell them to mind the sugar.
Bar della Pace, Via della Pace 5. Another kind of Roman bar is represented by this ultra-hip place frequented by celebrities.
Vineria Reggio, Campo de' Fiori 15. A more funky and friendly atmosphere can be found most evenings here at this relaxed traditional wine bar/shop with tables outside.
Il Gelato di San Crispino, Via della Panetteria 42, near the Trevi Fountain. It's not hard to find *gelato* on every corner in Rome, but hold out for the best the city has to offer.
Forno del Ghetto, Via del Portico d'Ottavia 2 (*closed Sat*). Sweets from the Jewish bakery.

Rock, Jazz and Clubs

Rome has a select band of clubs with music.
Il Locale, Vicolo del Fico 3, t 06 687 9075. Features hip and trendy Italian bands.
Big Mamma, Vicolo San Francesco a Ripa 18, in Trastevere, t 06 581 2451, *www.bigmamma.it*. Mainly rock venue.
Alpheus, Via del Commercio, 36, in Ostiense, t 06 574 7826. A blues club.
Caffè Latino, Via de Monte Testaccio 96, t 06 5728 8556. Dance club with live Latin music.

For *jazz* – which has a strong local following – try the following venues.
Alexanderplatz, Via Ostia 9, t 06 3972 2171.
Gregory's, Via Gregoriana 54, t 06 679 6386, *www.gregorysjazzclub.it*.

For serious **dancing** try the clubs below. All are what Italians call *di tendenza*, meaning they keep up with current UK and US trends. Most venues close down in late July and Aug.
Akab Cave, Via Monte Testaccio 69, t 06 578 2390. A hip favourite on two levels in Testaccio with live music and DJ sessions.
Alien, Via Velletri 13, near Piazza Fiume, t 06 841 2212.
Alpheus, Via del Commercio 36, off Via Ostiense, t 06 574 7826.
Gilda, Via Mario de' Fiori 97, close to the Spanish Steps, t 06 678 4838. Less juvenile (jacket required).

To know what Rome is, visit the little church of San Clemente, unobtrusively hidden away on the back streets behind the Colosseum. The Baroque façade conceals a 12th-century basilica with a beautiful marble choir screen 600 years older. In 1857 a cardinal from Boston discovered the original church of 313, one of the first great Christian basilicas, just underneath. And beneath *that* are two buildings and a Temple of Mithras from the time of Augustus; from it you can walk out into a Roman alley that looks exactly as it did 2,000 years ago, now some 28ft below ground level. There are commemorative plaques in San Clemente, placed there by a Medici duke, a bishop of New York, and the last chairman of the Bulgarian Communist Party.

You are not going to get to the bottom of this city, whether your stay is for three days or a month. With its legions of headless statues, acres of paintings, 913 churches and megatons of artistic sediment, this metropolis of aching feet will wear down even the most resolute of travellers (and travel writers). The name Rome passed out of the plane of reality into legend some 2,200 years ago, when princes as far away as China first began to hear of the faraway city and its invincible armies. At the same time the Romans were cooking up a personified goddess, the Divine Rome, and beginning the strange myth of their destiny to conquer and pacify the world, a myth that would still haunt Europe a thousand years later.

In our prosaic times, though, you may find it requires a considerable effort of the imagination to break through to the past Romes of the caesars and popes. They exist,

Lazio

On a Saturday night variety show, the television host discusses the founding of Rome with two comedians dressed up as Romulus and Remus; turning to Remus, the sillier-looking of the pair, he asks: 'What did you ever do?' Remus gets a big laugh by proudly claiming, 'Well, I founded Lazio.'

Despite being the location of the capital city, Lazio does not get much respect from the average Italian, who thinks of it as a sort of vacuum that needs to be crossed to get to Rome. Northerners often lump it in with Campania and Calabria as part of the backward south. To an extent it is, though great changes have come in the last 60 years with land reclamation and new industry. Lazio's problem is a simple one: Rome, that most parasitic of all cities. Before there was a Rome this was probably the wealthiest and most densely populated part of non-Greek Italy, the homeland of the Etruscans as well as the rapidly civilizing nations of Sabines, Aequi, Hernici, Volscii and the Latins themselves, from whom Lazio (*Latium*) takes its name.

After the Roman triumph the Etruscan and Italic cities shrivelled and died; those Romans who proved such good governors elsewhere caused utter ruin to their own backyard. A revival came in the Middle Ages when Rome was only one of a score of squabbling feudal towns, but once again, when the popes restored Rome, Lazio's fortunes declined. To finance their grandiose building projects, Renaissance popes literally taxed Lazio into extinction; whole villages and large stretches of countryside were abandoned, and land drained in medieval times reverted to malarial swamps. Modern Rome, at least since Mussolini's day, has begun to mend its ways; the government still considers Lazio a development area, and pumps a lot of money into it.

but first you will need to peel away the increasingly thick veneer of the 'Third Rome', the burgeoning, thoroughly up-to-date creation of post-Reunification Italy. Ancient Rome at the height of its glory had perhaps a million and a half people; today there are four million, and at any given time at least half of them will be pushing their way into the metro train while you are trying to get off. The popes, for all their centuries of experience in spectacle and ceremony, cannot often steal the show in this new Rome, and have to share the stage with a deplorable overabundance of preposterous politicians, with *Cinecittà* and the rest of the cultural apparatus of a great nation, and of course with the tourists, who sometimes put on the best show in town. The old guard Romani, now a minority in a city swollen with new arrivals, bewail the loss of Rome's slow and easy pace, its vintage brand of *dolce vita* that once impressed other Italians, let alone foreigners. Lots of money, lots of traffic and an endless caravan of tour buses have a way of compromising even the most beautiful of cities. Don't concern yourself; the present is only one snapshot from a 2,600-year history, and no one has ever left Rome disappointed.

History

The beginnings are obscure enough. Historians believe the settlement of the Tiber Valley began some time about 1000 BC, when an outbreak of volcanic eruptions in the Alban Hills to the south forced the Latin tribes down into the lowlands. Beyond that there are few clues for the archaeologists to follow. But remembering that every ancient legend conceals a kernel of truth – perhaps more poetic than scientific – it would be best to follow the accounts of Virgil, the poet of the Empire, and Livy, the great 1st-century chronicler and mythographer.

When Virgil wrote, in the reign of Augustus, Greek culture was an irresistible force in all the recently civilized lands of the Mediterranean. For Rome, Virgil concocted the story of Aeneas, fleeing from Troy after the Homeric sack and finding his way to *Latium*. Descent from the Trojans, however specious, connected Rome to the Greek world and made it seem less of an upstart. As Virgil tells it, Aeneas' son Ascanius founded Alba Longa, a city that by the 800s was leader of the Latin Confederation. Livy takes up the tale with Numitor, a descendant of Ascanius and rightful king of Alba Longa, tossed off the throne by his usurping brother Amulius. In order that Numitor should have no heirs, Amulius forced Numitor's daughter Rhea Silvia into service as a Vestal Virgin. Here Rome's destiny begins, with an appearance in the Vestals' chambers of the god Mars, staying just long enough to leave Rhea Silvia pregnant with the precocious twins **Romulus and Remus**.

When Amulius found out he of course packed them away in a little boat, which the gods directed up the Tiber to a spot near today's Piazza Bocca della Verità. The famous she-wolf looked after the babies, until they were found by a shepherd, who brought them up. When Mars revealed to the grown twins their origin, they returned to Alba Longa to sort out Amulius, and then returned (in 753 BC, traditionally) to found the city the gods had ordained. Romulus soon found himself constrained to kill Remus, who would not believe the auguries that declared his brother should be king, and thus set the pattern for the bloody millennium of Rome's history to come.

The legends portray early Rome as a glorified pirates' camp, and the historians are only too glad to agree. Finding themselves short of women, the Romans stole some from the Sabines. Not especially interested in farming or learning a trade, they adopted the hobby of subjugating their neighbours and soon polished it to an art.

Seven Kings of Rome

Romulus was the first, followed by Numa Pompilius, who laid down the forms for Rome's cults and priesthoods, its auguries and College of Vestals. Tullius Hostilius, the next, made Rome ruler of all *Latium*, and Ancus Martius founded the port of Ostia. The next king, **Tarquinius Priscus**, was an Etruscan, and probably gained his throne thanks to a conquest by one of the Etruscan city-states. Tarquin made a city of Rome, building the first real temples, the Cloaca Maxima or Great Drain, and the first Circus Maximus. His successor, **Servius Tullius**, restored Latin rule, inaugurated the division between patricians (the senatorial class) and plebeians, and built a great wall to keep the Etruscans out. It apparently did not work, for as next king we find the Etruscan **Tarquinius Superbus** (about 534 BC), another great builder. His misfortune was to have a hot-headed son like **Tarquinius Sextus**, who imposed himself on a noble and virtuous Roman maiden named Lucretia (cf. Shakespeare's *Rape of Lucrece*). She committed public suicide; the enraged Roman patricians, under the leadership of **Lucius Junius Brutus**, chased out proud Tarquin and the Etruscan dynasty forever. The republic was established before the day was out, with Brutus as first consul, or chief magistrate.

The Invincible Republic

Taking an oath never to allow another king in Rome, the patricians designed a novel form of government, a **republic** (*res publica* – public thing) governed by the two consuls elected by the Senate, the assembly of the patricians themselves; later innovations in the Roman constitution would include a tribune, an official with inviolable powers elected by the plebeians to protect their interests. The two classes fought like cats and dogs at home but combined with impressive resolve in their foreign wars. Etruscans, Aequi, Hernici, Volscii, Samnites and Sabines – all powerful nations – were defeated by Rome's citizen armies. Some of Livy's best stories come from this period, such as the taking of Rome by marauding Gauls in 390 BC, when the cackling of geese awakened the Romans and saved the citadel on the Capitoline Hill.

By 270 BC Rome had eliminated all its rivals to become master of Italy. It had taken about 200 years, and in the next 200 Roman rule would be established from Spain to Egypt. The first stage had proved more difficult. In Rome's final victory over the other Italians the city digested its rivals: whole cities and tribes simply disappeared, their peoples joining the mushrooming population of Rome. After 270 it was the same story, but on a wider scale. In the three **Punic Wars** against Carthage (264–146 BC) Rome gained almost the whole of the western Mediterranean; Greece, North Africa and Asia Minor were absorbed in small bites over the next 100 years. Rome's history was now the history of the Western world.

Imperial Rome

The old pirates' nest had never really changed its ways. Rome, like old Assyria, makes a fine example of that species of carnivore that can only live by continuous conquest. When the Romans took Greece they first met Culture, and it had the effect on them that puberty has on little boys. After some bizarre behaviour, evidenced in the continuous civil wars (**Sulla**, **Marius**, **Pompey**, **Julius Caesar**), the Romans began tarting up their city in the worst way, vacuuming all the gold, paintings, statues, cooks, poets and architects out of the civilized East. Beginning perhaps with Pompey, every contender for control of the now constitutionally deranged republic added some great work to the city centre: Pompey's theatre, the Julian Basilica, and something from almost every emperor up to Constantine. Julius Caesar and Augustus were perhaps Rome's greatest benefactors, initiating every sort of progressive legislation, turning dirt lanes into paved streets and erecting new forums, temples and the vast network of aqueducts. In their time Rome's population probably reached the million mark, surpassing Antioch and Alexandria as the largest city in the western world. It was **Augustus** who effectively ended the Republic in 27 BC, by establishing his personal rule and reducing the old constitution to formalities. During the imperial era that followed his reign, Rome's position as administrative and judicial centre of the empire kept it growing, drawing in a new cosmopolitan population of provincials from Britain to Mesopotamia. The city became the unquestioned capital of banking and finance – and religion; Rome's policy was always to induct everyone's local god as an honorary Roman, and every important cult image and relic was abducted to the Capitoline Temple. The emperor himself was *Pontifex Maximus*, head priest of Rome, whose title derives from the early Roman veneration of bridges (*pontifex* means keeper of bridges). **St Peter**, of course, arrived, and was duly martyred in AD 67. His successor, Linus, became the first **pope** – or *pontiff* – first in the long line of hierophants who would inherit Rome's long-standing religious tradition.

For all its glitter, Rome was still the complete predator, producing nothing and consuming everything. No one with any spare *denarii* would be foolish enough to go into business with them, when the only real money was to be made from government, speculation or real estate. At times almost half the population of Roman citizens (as opposed to slaves) was on the dole. Naturally, when things went sour they really went sour. Uncertain times made **Aurelian** give Rome a real defensive wall in AD 275. By AD 330 the necessity of staying near the armies at the front led the western emperors to spend most of their time at army headquarters in Milan. Rome became a bloated backwater, and after three sackings (Alaric the Goth in 410, Gaiseric the Vandal in 455 and Odoacer the Goth in 476), there was no reason to stay. The sources disagree: perhaps 100,000 inhabitants were left by the year 500, perhaps 10,000.

Rome in the Shadows

Contrary to what most people think, Rome did not ever quite go down the drain in the Dark Ages. Its lowest point in prestige undoubtedly came in the 14th century, when the popes were at Avignon. The number of important churches built in the Dark Ages (most, unfortunately, Baroqued later) and the mosaics that embellished them, equal in number if not in quality to those of Ravenna, testify to the city's importance. There was certainly enough to attract a few more sacks (Goths and Greeks in the 6th-century wars, Saracens from Africa in 746).

As in many other Western cities, but on a larger scale, the bishops of Rome – the popes – picked up some of the pieces when civil administration disintegrated and extended their power to temporal offices. Chroniclers report fights between them and the local barons, self-proclaimed heirs of the Roman Senate, as early as 741. It must have been a fascinating place, much too big for its population though still, thanks to the popes, thinking of itself as the centre of the Western world. The forum was abandoned, as were the gigantic baths, rendered useless as the aqueducts decayed. Almost all the temples and basilicas survived, converted to churches. **Hadrian**'s massive tomb on the banks of the Tiber was converted into a fortress, the Castel Sant'Angelo, an impregnable haven for the popes in troubled times.

The popes deserve credit for keeping Rome alive, but the tithe money trickling in from across Europe confirmed the city in its parasitical behaviour. With two outrageous forgeries, the 'Donation of Constantine' and the 'Donation of Pepin', the popes staked their claim to temporal power in Italy. **Charlemagne** visited the city after driving the Lombards out in 800; during a prayer vigil in St Peter's on Christmas Eve, Pope Leo III sneaked up behind the Frankish king and set an imperial crown on his head. The surprise coronation, which the outraged Charlemagne could not or would not undo, established the precedent of Holy Roman Emperors having to cross over the Alps to receive their crown from the pope.

Arnold of Brescia and Rienzo

Not that Rome ever spoke with one voice; over the next 500 years it was only the idea of Rome, as the spiritual centre of the universal Christian community, that kept the actual city of Rome from disappearing altogether. Down to some 20–30,000 people in this era, Rome evolved a sort of stable anarchy, in which the major contenders for power were the popes and noble families. First among the latter were the Orsini and the Colonna, racketeer clans who built fortresses for themselves among the ruins and fought like gangs in 1920s Chicago. Very often outsiders would get into the game. A remarkable woman of obscure birth named **Theodora** took the Castel Sant'Angelo in the 880s; with the title of Senatrix she and her daughter Marozia ruled Rome for decades. Various German emperors seized the city, but were never able to hold it. In the 10th century, things got even more complicated as the Roman people began to assert themselves. Caught between the people and the barons, nine of the 24 popes in that century managed to get themselves murdered. The 1140s was a characteristic period of this convoluted history. A Jewish family, the Pierleoni, held power, and a Jewish antipope sat enthroned in St Peter's. Mighty Rome occupied itself with a series of wars against its neighbouring village of Tivoli, and usually lost. A sincere monkish reformer appeared, the Christian and democrat **Arnold of Brescia**; he recreated the Senate and almost succeeded in establishing Rome as a free *comune*, but in 1155 he fell into the hands of the German emperor Frederick Barbarossa, who sold him to the English pope (Adrian IV) for hanging.

Too many centuries of this made Rome uncomfortable for the popes, who frequently removed themselves to Viterbo. The final indignity came when, under French pressure, the papacy decamped entirely to Avignon in 1309. Pulling strings from a distance, the popes only made life more complicated. Into the vacuum they created stepped one of the noblest Romans of them all, later to be the subject of Wagner's first opera. **Cola di Rienzo** was the son of an innkeeper, but he had a good enough education to read the Latin inscriptions that lay on ruins all around him, and Livy, Cicero and Tacitus wherever he could find them. Obsessed by the idea of re-establishing Roman glory, he talked at the bewildered inhabitants until they caught the fever too. With Rienzo as Tribune of the People, the Roman Republic was reborn in 1347. Power does corrupt, however, in Rome more than any spot on the globe, and an increasingly fat and ridiculous Rienzo was hustled out of Rome by the united nobles before the year was out. His return to power, in 1354, ended with his murder by a mob after only two months. Rome was now at its lowest ebb, with only some 15,000 people, and prosperity and influence were not to be completely restored until the reign of Pope Nicholas V after 1447.

The New Rome

The old papacy, before Avignon, had largely been a tool of the Roman nobles; periods when it was able to achieve real independence were the exception rather than the rule. In the more settled conditions of the 15th century, a new papacy emerged, richer and more sophisticated. Political power, as a guarantee of stability, was its goal, and a series of talented Renaissance popes saw their best hopes for achieving this by rebuilding Rome. By the 1500s this process was in full swing. Under **Julius II** (1503–13) the papal domains for the first time were run like a modern state; Julius also laid plans for the rebuilding of St Peter's, beginning the great building programme that transformed the city. New streets were laid out, especially Via Giulia and the grand avenues radiating from Piazza del Popolo; Julius' architect, Bramante, knocked down medieval Rome with such gay abandon that Raphael nicknamed him 'Ruinante'.

Over the next two centuries the work continued at a frenetic pace. Besides St Peter's, hundreds of churches were either built or rebuilt, and cardinals and noble families lined the streets with new palaces, imposing if not beautiful. A new departure in urban design was developed in the 1580s, under **Sixtus V**, recreating some of the monumentality of ancient Rome. Piazzas linked by a network of straight boulevards were cleared in front of the major religious sites, each with an Egyptian obelisk.

The New Rome, symbol of the Counter-Reformation and the majesty of the popes, was, however, bought at a terrible price. Besides the destruction of Bramante, buildings that had survived substantially intact for 1,500 years were cannibalized for their marble; the popes wantonly destroyed more of ancient Rome than Goths or Saracens had ever managed. To pay for their programme, they taxed the economy of the Papal States out of existence. Areas of Lazio turned into wastelands as exasperated farmers simply abandoned them; the other cities of Lazio and Umbria were set back centuries in their development. The New Rome was proving as voracious a predator as the old. Worst of all, the new papacy in the 16th century instituted terror as an instrument of public policy. In the course of the previous century the last vestiges of Roman liberty had been gradually extinguished. The popes tried to extend their power by playing a game of high-stakes diplomacy between Emperor Charles V of Spain and King Francis I of France, but reaped a bitter harvest in the 1527 Sack of Rome. An out-of-control imperial army occupied the city for almost a year, causing tremendous destruction, while the disastrous Pope Clement VII looked on helplessly from the Castel Sant'Angelo. Afterwards the popes were happy to become part of the Imperial-Spanish system. Political repression was fiercer than anywhere else in Italy; the **Inquisition** was refounded in 1542 by Paul III, and book burnings, torture of free-thinkers and executions became even more common than in Spain itself.

The End of Papal Rule

By about 1610 there was no Roman foolish enough to get burned at the stake; at the same time workmen were adding the last stones to the cupola of St Peter's. It was the end of an era, but the building continued. A thick accretion of Baroque collected, like coral, over Rome. Bernini did his Piazza Navona fountain in 1650, and the Colonnade for St Peter's 15 years later. The political importance of the popes, however, disappeared with surprising finality. As Joseph Stalin was later to note, the popes had plenty of Bulls but few army divisions, and they drifted into irrelevance in the power politics of modern Europe during the Thirty Years' War.

Rome was left to enjoy a decadent but pleasant twilight. A brief interruption came when revolutionaries in 1798 again proclaimed the Roman Republic, and a French army sent the pope packing. Rome later became part of **Napoleon**'s empire, but papal rule was restored in 1815. Another republic appeared in 1848, on the crest of that romantic year's revolutionary wave, but this time a French army besieged the city and had the pope propped back on his throne by July 1849. **Garibaldi**, the republic's military commander, barely escaped with his life.

For twenty years **Napoleon III** maintained a garrison in Rome to look after the pope, and consequently Rome became the last part of Italy to join the new Italian kingdom. After the French defeat in the war of 1870, Italian troops blew a hole in the old Aurelian wall near the Porta Pia and marched in. Pius IX, who ironically had decreed papal infallibility just the year before, locked himself in the Vatican and pouted; the popes were to be 'prisoners' until Mussolini's Concordat of 1929, by which they agreed to recognize the Italian state.

As capital of the new state, Rome underwent another building boom. New streets like Via Vittorio Veneto and Via Nazionale made circulation easier; villas and gardens disappeared under blocks of speculative building (everything around Stazione Termini, for example); long-needed projects like the Tiber embankments were built; and the new kingdom strove to impress the world with gigantic, absurd public buildings and monuments, such as the Altar of the Nation (Il Vittoriano) and the Finance Ministry on Via XX Settembre, as big as two Colosseums. Growth has been steady; from some 200,000 people in 1879, Rome has since increased twentyfold.

The Twentieth Century

In 1922 the city was the objective of **Mussolini**'s 'March on Rome', when the Fascist leader used his blackshirt squads to demand, and win, complete power in the Italian government, though he himself famously made the journey into town by train, and in his best suit. Mussolini was one more figure who wanted to create a 'New Roman Empire' for Italy. For twenty years Piazza Venezia was the chosen theatre for his oratorical performances. He also had big ideas for the city itself: it was under Fascism that many of the relics of ancient Rome were first opened up as public monuments in order to remind Italians of their heritage, and Via dei Fori Imperiali was driven past the Forum, destroying some of the archaeological sites in the process. His greatest legacy was the EUR suburb, the projected site of a world exhibition for 1942, and a showcase of his preferred Fascist-classical architecture. At the end of the war it was only half built, but the Italians, not wishing to waste anything, decided to finish the project, and it now houses a few of Rome's museums and sports venues.

Since the war Rome has continued to grow fat as the capital of the often ramshackle, notoriously corrupt political system thrown up by the Italian Republic, and the headquarters of the smug *classe politica* that ran it. Rome has been accused by Lombard regionalists of drawing off wealth from the productive areas of Italy in much the same way that it once demanded to be fed by the Empire; nevertheless, Romans have joined in Italy's 'Moral Revolution' of the last few years, abusing the old-style political bosses, despite the fact that a great many in this city of civil servants themselves benefited from the system.

Today's visitors to the city enjoy the benefits of substantial improvements made for the Holy Year 2000, including over 700 public works projects (restorations, refurbished museums, upgraded transportation and additional car parks). Among the highlights for those who have not been to Rome for a few years are the Domus Aurea, Musei Capitolini, the façade of Saint Peter's, the Vittoriano monument on Piazza Venezia, and Trajan's Markets.

Art and Architecture

The Etruscans

Although Rome stood on the fringes of the Etruscan world, the young city could hardly help being overwhelmed by the presence of a superior culture almost on its doorstep. Along with much of its religion, customs and its engineering talent, early Rome owed its first art to the enemies from the north. Thanks to the Villa Giulia Museum (*see* p.140), Rome can show you much of the best of Etruscan art. Enigmatic, often fantastical and always intensely vital, Etruria's artists stole from every Greek style and technique, and turned it into something uniquely their own.

The Romans Learn Building and Just Can't Stop

The Romans learned how to build roads and bridges from the Etruscans, perfected the art, and built works never dreamed of before. Speaking strictly of design, the outstanding fact of Roman building was its conservatism. Under the Republic, Rome

A Little Orientation

Two Walls

Of Rome's earliest wall, built by king Servius Tullius before the Republic, little remains; you can see one of the last surviving bits outside Stazione Termini. The second, built by Aurelian in AD 275, is one of the wonders of Rome, though taken for granted. With its 19km length and 383 towers, it is one of the largest ever built in Europe – and certainly the best-preserved of antiquity.

Three Romes

Historians and Romans often think of the city in this way. **Classical Rome** began on the Monte Palatino, and its business and administrative centre stayed nearby, in the original Forum and the great Imperial Fora built around it. Many of the busiest parts lay to the south, where now you see only green on the tourist office's map. After Rome's fall these areas were never really rebuilt, and even substantial ruins like Trajan's Baths remain unexcavated. The **Second Rome**, that of the popes, had its centre in the Campus Martius, the plain west and north of the Capitoline Hill, later expanding to include the 'Leonine City' around St Peter's, and the Baroque district around Piazza del Popolo and the Spanish Steps. The **Third Rome**, capital of United Italy, has expanded in all directions; the closest it has to a centre is Via del Corso.

Seven Hills

Originally they were much higher; centuries of building, rebuilding and river flooding have made the ground level in the valleys much higher, and emperors and popes shaved bits off their tops in building programmes. The **Monte Capitolino**, smallest but most important, now has Rome's City Hall, the Campidoglio, roughly on the site of ancient Rome's greatest temple, that of Jupiter Greatest and Best. The **Palatino**, adjacent to it, was originally the most fashionable district, and got entirely covered by the palaces of the emperors.

The plebeian **Aventino** lies to the south of it, across the Circus Maximus. Between the Colosseum and the Stazione Termini, the **Esquilino**, the **Viminale** and the **Quirinale** stand in a row. The Quirinale was long the residence of the popes, and later of the Italian kings. Finally, there is the **Monte Celio** south of the Colosseum, now an oasis of parkland and ancient churches.

Rome has other hills not included in the canonical seven: **Monte Vaticano**, from which the Vatican takes its name, **Monte Pincio**, including the Villa Borghese, and the **Gianicolo**, the long ridge above Trastevere the ancients called the Janiculum.

Fourteen Regions

Ancient Rome had neither street lights nor street signs; modern Rome has plenty of both. This being Rome, of course, the street signs are of marble. In the corner, you will notice a small number in Roman numerals; this refers to the *rione*, or ward. In the Middle Ages, there were 14 of these, descendants of the 14 *regii* of the ancient city; even after the fall of Rome they maintained their organization.

adopted Greek architecture, with a predilection for the more delicate Corinthian order. When the money started rolling in, the Romans began to build in marble. But for 400 years, until the height of Empire under Trajan and Hadrian, very little changed. As Rome became the capital of the Mediterranean, its rulers introduced new building types to embellish it: the series of **Imperial Fora**, variations on the **Greek agora**, the first of which was begun by Julius Caesar; **public baths**, a custom imported from Campania; **colonnaded streets**, as in Syria and Asia Minor; and **theatres**.

Concrete may not seem a very romantic subject, but in the hands of Imperial builders it changed both the theory and practice of architecture. Volcanic sand from the Bay of Naples, used with rubble as a filler, allowed the Romans to cover vast spaces cheaply. First in the palaces, and later in the Pantheon's giant concrete dome and in the huge public baths, an increasingly sophisticated use of arches and vaults was developed. Concrete seating made the Colosseum and the vast theatres possible, and allowed *insulae* – Roman apartment blocks – to climb six storeys and more. Near the Empire's end, the tendency towards gigantism becomes an enduring symptom of Roman decadence; the clumsy forms of late monsters like Diocletian's Baths and the Basilica of Maxentius show a technology far outstripping art.

Roman Sculpture, Painting and Mosaics

Even after the conquests of the 2nd century BC and the looting of the cultured East, it was a long time before Rome produced anything of its own. As in architecture, the other arts were dependent for centuries on the Greeks. Portrait sculpture, inherited from the Etruscans, is the notable exception, with a tradition of almost photographic busts and funeral reliefs. Sculpture, most of all, provides a vivid psychological record of Rome's history. In the 3rd century, as its confidence was undergoing its first crisis at the hands of German and Persian invaders, sculpture veers slowly towards the introverted and strange. Under the late Antonines the tendency is apparent, with grim, realistic battle scenes on Marcus Aurelius' column, and troubled portraits of the Emperor himself. Later portraits are even more unsettling, with rigid features and staring eyes, concerned more with psychological depth than outward appearances.

During the 3rd and 4th centuries there was little public art at all. There was a brief revival under Constantine, and no work better evokes the Rome of the psychotic, totalitarian late Empire than his weird, immense head in the Capitoline Museum. Gigantism survived the final disappearance of individuality and genuinely civic art, while the Imperial portraits freeze into eerie icons. Painting and mosaics were present from at least the 1st century BC, but Romans considered them little more than decoration, rarely entrusting to them any serious subjects.

Early Christian and Medieval Art

Almost from the beginning, Rome's Christians sought to express their faith in art. On dozens of finely carved sarcophagi and statues the figure of Christ is represented as the 'Good Shepherd', a beardless youth with a lamb slung over his shoulder. Occasionally he wears a Roman toga. Familiar New Testament scenes are common, along with figures of the early martyrs. The 4th-century building programme financed by Constantine filled Rome with imposing Christian basilicas, though little remains. Through the 5th and early 6th centuries, Christian art – now the only art permitted – changed little in style but broadened its subject matter, including scenes from the Old Testament and the Passion of Christ.

An impressive revival of Roman building came in the late 8th century, with peace, relative prosperity, and enlightened popes such as Hadrian, Leo III and Paschal I. New churches went up, decorated with mosaics by Greek artists. The return of hard times after the collapse of the Carolingian Empire put an end to this little Renaissance. When Rome began building again, it was largely with native artists, and stylistically there was almost a clean break with the past. The **Cosmati**, perhaps originally a single family, but eventually a name for a whole school, ground up fragments of coloured glass and precious stone and turned them into intricate pavements, altars, candlesticks and pulpits, geometrically patterned in styles derived from southern Italy, and ultimately from the Muslim world. Perhaps the greatest Roman artist of the Middle Ages was **Pietro Cavallini** (*c.* 1250–1330), whose freedom in composition and talent for expressive portraiture make him a genuine precursor of the Renaissance, equally at home in mosaics and fresco painting.

The Renaissance in Rome

Rome's High Renaissance begins with Julius II (1503–13). **Michelangelo Buonarroti** had already arrived, to amaze the world of art with his *Pietà* in St Peter's (1499), but the true inauguration of Rome's greatest artistic period was the arrival of **Donato Bramante**. This new marriage of the Renaissance and ancient Rome can best be seen at Bramante's Tempietto at San Pietro in Montorio (1503), or at his cloister for Santa Maria della Pace (1504).

For painting and sculpture, the High Renaissance meant a greater emphasis on emotion, dynamic movement and virtuosity. **Raphael**, following in Bramante's footsteps, arrived from Florence in 1508 and was the most influential painter of his time, with a virtuosity and sunny personality that patrons found irresistible. In the frescoes in the Vatican Stanze, he combined the grand manner from antique sculpture and the ancient approach to decoration from Nero's recently unearthed Golden House to create one of the definitive achievements of the age, and also excelled at portraiture, mythological frescoes, and even almost visionary religious work.

The Sack of Rome in 1527 rudely interrupted artistic endeavours, and many artists left Rome for ever. Among those who returned to Rome was, of course, Michelangelo, who in 1536 began the *Last Judgement* in the Sistine Chapel, whose sombre tones and subject matter illustrate more clearly than any other work the change in mood that had come over Roman art.

The Art of the Counter-Reformation

The Counter-Reformation and the Inquisition put a chill on the Italian imagination that would never really be dispelled. In 1563 the Council of Trent decreed the new order for art: conformist and naturalistic, propaganda entirely in the service of the totalitarian Church, with a touch of Spanish discipline and emotionalism. Rome was to become the symbol of the Church resurgent, the most modern and beautiful city in the world. Under Sixtus V, **Domenico Fontana** and other architects planned a scheme to unite the sprawling medieval city with a network of straight avenues sighted on obelisks in the major piazzas.

The Age of Baroque

During this period art was reduced to mere decoration, forbidden to entertain any thoughts that might be politically dangerous or subversive to Church dogma. But in this captive art there was still talent and will enough for new advances to be made, particularly in architecture. Plenty of churches, fountains and palaces were built, and . there was every opportunity for experimentation. In sculpture it meant a new emphasis on cascading drapery and exaggerated poses, typecasting emotion, saintliness or virtue in a way the Renaissance would have found slightly trashy. Here **Bernini** led the way, with such works as his early *David* in the Galleria Borghese (1623). Painting however was on a definite downward spiral, though one usually had to look up to see it. Decorative ceiling frescoes, such as those of **Pietro da Cortona**, were all the rage, though few artists could bring anything like Cortona's talent to the job.

The Last of Roman Art

From Rome, the art of the High Baroque reached out to all Europe – just as the last traces of inspiration were dying out in the city itself. After the death of Pope Alexander VII (1667) there was less money and less intelligent patronage, and by this time, a more introspective Rome was looking backwards. Meaningful sculpture and painting were gone for ever.

In the 19th century art in Rome continued to lose ground. After 1870 the fathers of the new Italy believed that liberation and Italian unity would unleash a wave of creativity, and they spent tremendous sums to help it along. They were mistaken. The sepulchral, artless monuments they imposed on Rome helped ruin the fabric of the city and provided an enduring reminder of the sterility of the Risorgimento and the subsequent corrupt regimes.

Mussolini too wanted his revolution to have its artistic expression. The sort of painting and sculpture his government preferred is best not examined too closely, but his architecture, mashing up Art Deco simplicity with historical pomposity, now and then reached beyond the level of the ridiculous. Rome today is moribund as an art centre, and even architecture has not recovered. There are no first-rate contemporary buildings. Not few – none. Efforts at planning the city's post-war growth resulted in confusion and concrete madness, and the hideous apartment and office blocks of the suburbs. Until recently it seemed impossible that Rome could ever again produce inspired architecture. However, Paolo Portoghesi's mosque, a playful postmodern extravaganza out near the Villa Ada, together with plans for a glass case by Richard Meier to go around the Ara Pacis in Rome, could be a sign that the tide is about to turn.

Around the City

Piazza Venezia and the Monte Capitolino

This traffic-crazed, thoroughly awful piazza may be a poor introduction to Rome, but it makes a good place to start, with the ruins of old Rome on one side and the boutiques and bureaucracies of the new city on the other. The piazza takes its name from the **Palazzo Venezia**, built for the Venetian Cardinal Pietro Barbo (afterwards Pope Paul II) in 1455, but long the Embassy of the Venetian Republic. Mussolini made it his residence, leaving a light on all night to make the Italians think he was working. His famous balcony, from which he would declaim to the 'oceanic' crowds in the square (renamed the Forum of the Fascist Empire in those days) still holds its prominent place, a bad memory for the Italians. Nowadays the *palazzo* holds a **museum of Renaissance and Baroque decorative arts** (*t 06 679 8865; open Tues–Sun 8.30–7.30; adm*), a frankly dull collection, which might be worth a glance for the palace's vast gloomy stone staircase and carved wooden ceilings. The palace complex was built around the ancient church of **San Marco** (*t 06 679 5305; open 9,30–1 and 4.30–6.45; no entrance during services*), with a 9th-century mosaic in the apse. Parts of the building are as old as AD 400, and the Renaissance façade is by Benedetto di Maiano.

Long ago the southern edge of this piazza had approaches up to the Monte Capitolino. The hill is still there, though it's now entirely blocked out by the **Altar of the Nation**, also known as **Il Vittoriano**, the 'Wedding Cake' or the 'Typewriter' (*t 06 699 1718; open Tues–Sun 10.30–6.30, last adm 5.30; adm free*), Risorgimento Italy's own self-inflicted satire and one of the world's apotheoses of kitsch. Its size and its solid marble walls are explained by the 1880s prime minister who commissioned it; he happened to have a marble quarry in his home district of Brescia. Recounting its sculptural allegories would take pages – but of the two big bronze imperial-style *quadrigae* on top, one represents Italian Liberty and the other Italian Unity. In the centre, the modest virtues of Vittorio Emanuele II have earned him a 38ft bronze equestrian statue, perhaps the world's largest. Beneath him, Italy's Unknown Soldier sleeps peacefully with a round-the-clock guard. It's worth the climb to the top terrace for staggering views across the city (without the blight of the Typewriter itself to spoil them). Il Vittoriano is home to a pair of **exhibition galleries** (*times depend on exhibition; adm*), another temporary exhibition space, and two military museums: the **Sacrario Militare della Bandiera** (a flag museum; *open Tues–Sun 9–1; free*) and the **Museo Centrale del Risorgimento** (*open Tues–Sun 10.30–6.30, last adm 5.30; free*). On the left-hand side of the monument you can see the remains of the republican Roman tomb of C. Publius Bibulus.

Behind the Vittoriano, two stairways lead to the top of the **Capitoline Hill**. This is a fateful spot; in 121 BC the great reformer Tiberius Gracchus was murdered here by what today would be called a 'right-wing death squad'. Almost a millennium and a half later Cola di Rienzo was trying to escape Rome in disguise when an enraged mob recognized him by the rings on his fingers and tore him to pieces. Rienzo built the

left-hand staircase, and was the first to climb it. It leads to **Santa Maria in Aracoeli** (*Scalinata d'Aracoeli*; **t** *06 679 8155; open 6.30–5.30*), begun in the 7th century over the temple of Juno Moneta – the ancient Roman Mint was adjacent to it. The Aracoeli, which in Rienzo's time served as a council hall for the Romans, is one of the most revered of churches; legend has it that one of the Sibyls of Tivoli prophesied the

Central Rome

Villa Medici

Spanish Steps

Trinità del Monte

V. D. DEL MACELLI

V. DEL CONDOTTI

V. FRATTINA

V. DELLA MERCEDE

PIAZZA SAN SILVESTRO

Fontana di Trevi

Pasta Museum

VIA LUDOVISI

VIA SISTINA

VIA DEL TRITONE

Monte Quirinale

Palazzo del Quirinale

VIA QUIRINALE

PZA. DEL QUIRINALE

24 MAGGIO

VIA VITT. VENETO

VIA BONCOMPAGNI

Convento dei Cappuccini

VIA BARBERINI

Palazzo Barberini

S. Maria della Vittoria

V. L. BISSOLATI

Largo S. Susanna

VIA XX SETTEMBRE

S. Bernardo

PZA. REPUBBLICA

V. TORINO

S. Carlino

VIA NAZIONALE

NAPOLI D.

Monte Viminale

V. URBANA

PRETIS

S. Pudenziana

VIA CERNAIA

Terme di Diocleziano

Palazzo Massimo

PIAZZA DEI CINQUECENTO

VIA PRINCIPE AMEDEO

PIAZZA INDEPENDENZA

VIA MONTEBELLO

VIA MARSALA

STAZIONE TERMINI

VIA GIOVANNI

S. Maria Maggiore

VIA CAVOUR

V.C. ALBERTO

Palazzo Doria Pamphili

Torre delle Milizie

Chiesa del Gesù

PIAZZA VENEZIA

Trajan's Markets

Foro Traiano

Vittoriano

Palazzo Venezia

S. Maria in Aracoeli

V. DEL TEATRO MARCELLO

PZA D. CAMPIDOGLIO

Musei Capitolini

Monte Capitolino

LARGO MAGNANAPOLI

VIA PANISPERNA

Foro di Augusto

V. CAVOUR

VIA DEI FORI IMPERIALI

Carcere Mamertino

Foro Romano

Basilica di Massenzio

S. Giorgio in Velabro

Tempio di Fortuna

V. DEL CERCHI

Tempio di Vesta

PIAZZA BOCCA DELLA VERITÀ

S. Maria in Cosmedin

LUNG. AVENTINO

VIA DEL CIRCO MASSIMO

Monte Palatino

Circo Massimo

VIA DEI SERPENTI

VIA G. LANZA

V. DI STATUTO

S. Prassede

S. Pietro in Vincoli

Monte Esquilino

Domus Aurea

PIAZZA DEL COLOSSEO

Arco di Tito

Colosseo

Arco di Costantino

VIA DI S. GREGORIO

SS. Giovanni e Paolo

S. Gregorio Magno

Monte Celio

Villa

PIAZZA DI PORTA CAPENA

V. CLAUDIA

VIA LABICANA

S. Clemente

V. DI S. GIOV IN LATERANO

VIA MERULANA

VIA DI S. STEFANO

VIA AMBA ARADAM

coming of Jesus and told Augustus to build a temple here to the 'first born of God'. Inside you can seek out frescoes by Pinturicchio (*San Bernardino of Siena*) and Gozzoli (*San Antonio of Padua*), and a tombstone by Donatello, near the entrance.

The second stairway takes you to the real heart of Rome, Michelangelo's **Piazza del Campidoglio**, passing a rather flattering statue of Rienzo set on a bronze pedestal.

Bordering the piazza, a formidable cast of statues includes the Dioscuri, who come from Pompey's Theatre, and Marforio (in the Musei Capitolini courtyard), a river god once employed as a 'talking statue', decorated with graffiti and placards commenting on current events. The great 2nd-century AD bronze equestrian statue of the benign and philosophical emperor **Marcus Aurelius**, that stood on the plinth in the middle of the piazza from the 16th century until 1981, has been fully restored and regilded and is now in the Musei Capitolini – fortunately enough, since it was an old Roman saying that the world would end when all the gold flaked off. The Christians of old only refrained from melting him down for cash because they believed he was not Marcus Aurelius, but Constantine. A faithful copy now stands in the piazza.

The Musei Capitolini

Michelangelo's original plans may have been adapted and tinkered with by later architects, but nevertheless his plan for the Campidoglio has come out as one of the triumphs of Renaissance design. The centrepiece, the **Palazzo Senatorio**, Rome's city hall, with its distinctive stairway and bell tower, is built over the ruins of the Roman *tabularium*, the state archive. At the base of the stair note the statue of Minerva, in her aspect as the allegorical goddess Roma.

Flanking it, Michelangelo redesigned the façade of the Palazzo dei Conservatori on the right, and projected the matching building across the square, the Palazzo Nuovo, built in the early 18th century. Together they make up the **Capitoline Museums**. Founded by Pope Clement XII in 1734, the oldest true museum in the world (*t 06 6710 2071, www.capitolium.org; open Tues–Sun 9–8, last adm 7pm, hols 9–1.45; adm, free last Sun of every month, audioguide €3.50*) reopened in 2000 after a massive restoration project which added an echoing subterranean corridor lined with sculpture, columns and sarcophagi, connecting the two palaces and giving access to the Tabularium, an arched gallery offering fantastic views of the Forum below. The Capitolini display both the heights and depths of ancient society and culture. For the heights there are the reliefs from the triumphal arch of Marcus Aurelius in the **Palazzo dei Conservatori** – first-class work in scenes of the emperor's clemency and piety, and his triumphal receptions in Rome. Marcus always looks a little worried in these, perhaps considering his good-for-nothing son Commodus, and the empire he would inherit, sinking into corruption and excess. What was to come is well illustrated by the degenerate art of the 4th century, like the colossal bronze head, hand and foot of Constantine, parts of a colossal statue in the Basilica of Maxentius, scattered around the courtyard or the immense frescoed halls of the 'Appartamento dei Conservatori' on the first floor. These halls also contain the the *Capitoline She-Wolf*, the very symbol of Rome (note that the suckling twins were added to the Etruscan bronze she-wolf in the Renaissance), and the gentle *Spinario*, a 1st-century BC bronze of a boy pulling out a thorn from his foot. On the second floor, there's a small **Pinacoteca**, with some digni-fied Velázquez gentlemen, looking scornfully at the other paintings, and two major works by Caravaggio, the *Fortune Teller* and *John the Baptist*. There are also some lovely 18th-century porcelains – orchestras of monkeys in powdered wigs, and such. As part of the millennial renovations, the Palazzo dei Conservatori was given new spaces for temporary exhibitions on the third floor, and there's an excellent café with a vast terrace and city views.

The **Palazzo Nuovo**, reached via the underground corridor, hasn't changed since the 18th century and holds statues of most of the emperors, busts of Homer, Sophocles and Pythagoras; the voluptuous *Capitoline Venus*; a big baby Hercules (who may have inspired Donatello's famous *Amor* in Florence); and the *Muse Polyhymnia*, one of the most delightful statues of antiquity. Later works include lots of papal paraphernalia, a statue of Charles of Anjou by Arnolfo di Cambio, and the regilded statue of Marcus Aurelius (just off the courtyard with its enormous Neptune fountain).

Carcere Mamertino

The best overview of the Roman Forum is to be had from behind Palazzo Senatorio. A stairway leads down from the left side to Via dei Fori Imperiali and the entrance to the Forum. On the way, beneath the church of San Giuseppe Falegnami, you can visit the **Carcere Mamertino** (*Via del Carcere Tulliano; open 9–12 and 2.30–5; donation requested*), the small calaboose used by the ancient Romans for their most important prisoners – the Catiline conspirators, Vercingetorix (the Gaulish chief captured by Caesar), and finally St Peter. The southern end of the Capitol, one of the quietest corners of Rome, was the site of the temple of Jupiter Optimus Maximus (Greatest and Best), built originally by the Etruscan kings. At the time it was the largest in Italy, testimony to Rome's importance as far back as 450 BC. Along the southern edge of the hill, the cliffs you see are the somewhat reduced remains of the **Tarpeian Rock**, from which traitors and other malefactors were thrown in Rome's early days.

Along the Tiber

The early emperors did their best to import classical Greek drama to Rome, and for a while, with the poets of the Latin New Comedy, it seemed the Romans would carry on the tradition. Great theatres were built like the **Teatro di Marcello** (*open by prior arrangement only, send a fax to f 06 689 2115*), begun by Caesar and completed by Augustus. By the second century AD, however, theatre had already begun to degenerate into music hall, lewd performances with naked actresses and grisly murders (condemned prisoners were sometimes butchered on stage), and shows by celebrity actors. Marcellus' theatre survived into the Middle Ages, when the Orsini family converted it into their palace-fortress, the strongest after the Castel Sant'Angelo. You can still see the tall arches of the circumference surmounted by the rough medieval walls, a dramatic backdrop for occasional concerts.

The streets to the west contain a mix of some of Rome's oldest houses with new buildings; the latter have replaced the old walled **ghetto**. There has been a sizeable Jewish community in Rome since the 2nd century BC; after conquering the Jews at the end of the 1st century AD, Pompey and Titus brought them to Rome as slaves. They helped finance the career of Julius Caesar, who would prove to be their greatest benefactor. For centuries they lived near this bend in the river and in Trastevere. Paul IV took time off from burning books and heretics to wall them into the tiny ghetto in

1555; at the same time he forced them to wear orange hats and to attend Mass on Sunday, and limited them to the rag and old iron trades. Tearing down the ghetto walls was one of the first acts of the Italian kingdom after the entry into Rome in 1870. The exotic, eclectic main **synagogue** was built in 1904; there are guided tours, and a small **Museum of the Jewish Community** (*Museo Ebraico, Lungotevere dei Cenci, t 06 6840 0661; open Mon–Thurs 9–7.30, last adm 7pm, Fri and Sun 9–1.30, closed Jewish hols; adm*), which includes a wrenching section on the Holocaust. Opposite the synagogue, the **Isola Tiberina** is joined to both sides of the river by surviving ancient bridges. In imperial times the island was sacred to Aesculapius, god of healing; a legend records how serpents brought from the god's shrine in Greece escaped and swam to the spot, choosing the site by divine guidance. Now, as in ancient times, most of the lovely island is taken up by a hospital, the Ospedale Fatebenefratelli; in place of the Temple of Aesculapius, there is also the church of **San Bartolomeo** (*t 06 687 7973; open 9–10.30 and 4–6.30*), most recently rebuilt in the 1690s.

The **Velabrum**, in the earliest days of Rome, was a cattle market (interestingly, in the Middle Ages, the Roman Forum itself was used for the same purpose). In this area, east of the Isola Tiberina, is **San Giorgio in Velabro** (*Via del Velabro 19; open 9–1 and 3–6.30*), in parts as old as the 7th century; there is a Cosmatesque altar, and early Christian fragments on the left wall. The lovely portico has been restored after a Mafia bombing in 1993. Of the two ancient arches outside, the **Arco degli Argentari** was erected by the moneychangers in honour of Septimius Severus. The larger, the unfinished, four-sided **Janus Quadrifons**, dates from the time of Constantine.

Piazza Bocca della Verità

Tourists almost always overlook this beautiful corner along the Tiber, but here you can see two well-preserved Roman temples. Both go under false names: the round **Temple of Vesta**, used as an Armenian church in the Middle Ages, and the **Temple of Fortuna Virilis** – it now seems almost certain that they were actually dedicated to Hercules Victor and Portunus (the god of harbours) respectively. Some bits of an exotic Roman cornice are built into the brick building opposite, part of the **House of the Crescenzi** (*Via Luigi Petroselli*), a powerful family in the 9th century, descended from Theodora Senatrix. Look over the side of the Tiber embankment here and you can see the outlet of the **Cloaca Maxima** (*Lungotevere Pierleoni*), the sewer begun by King Tarquin. Big enough to drive two carriages through, it is still in use today.

Just upstream, past the Ponte Palatino, a single arch decorated with dragons is all that remains of the Pons Aemilius. Originally built in the 2nd century BC, it collapsed twice and was last restored in 1575 by Gregory XIII, only to fall down again 20 years later. Now it is known as the 'broken bridge', or **Ponte Rotto**.

Across from the temples, the handsome medieval church with the lofty campanile is **Santa Maria in Cosmedin** (*t 06 678 1419; open summer 10–6.30, winter 10–5*), built over an altar of Hercules in the 6th century and given to Byzantine Greeks escaping from the Iconoclast emperors in the 8th. The name (like 'cosmetic') means 'decorated', but little of the original art has survived; most of what you see is from the 12th century, including some fine Cosmatesque work inside. In the portico, an ancient, ghostly image in stone built into the walls has come down in legend as the **Bocca della Verità** – the Mouth of Truth. Medieval Romans would swear oaths and close business deals here; if you tell a lie with your hand in the image's mouth he will most assuredly bite your fingers off. Try it.

The Heart of Ancient Rome

In the 1930s Mussolini built a grand boulevard between the Vittoriano and the Colosseum to ease traffic congestion and show off the ancient sites. He called it the Via del Impero, coinciding with his aspirations of returning Rome to greatness through a new empire in Africa. After Mussolini's demise the road was re-christened **Via dei Fori Imperiali**, after the Imperial Fora which it part covers.

The **Imperial Fora** of Augustus, Nerva and Trajan were built to relieve congestion in the original Roman Forum. **Trajan's Forum** (*Foro Traiano*), built with the spoils of his conquest of Dacia (modern Romania), was perhaps the grandest architectural and planning conception ever built in Rome, a broad square surrounded by colonnades, with a huge basilica flanked by two libraries and a covered market outside (the world's first shopping mall). A large part of **Trajan's Markets** (*Mercati di Traiano*) still stands and has recently been expensively converted into a massive and very striking exhibition space (*entrance on Via IV Novembre; t 06 679 0048; open Tues–Sun 9–5; adm*), and the network of surrounding paths and viewing points which pick over the ruins are due to be expanded. Behind it, you can see Rome's own leaning tower, the 12th-century **Torre delle Milizie**. All that remains of Trajan's great square is the paving and its centrepiece, **Trajan's Column** (*Colonna Traiana*). The spiralling bands of reliefs, illustrating the Dacian Wars, reach to the top, some 96ft high. They rank with the greatest works of Roman art. Behind the column, **Santa Maria di Loreto** (*Piazza Madonna di Loreto; open 7.30–12 and 4–6*) is a somewhat garish High Renaissance bauble, built by Bramante and Antonio da Sangallo the Younger. The Romans liked the church so much that in the 1730s they built another one just like it next door, the **Santissimo Nome di Maria**. Scanty remains of **Caesar's Forum** (*Foro di Cesare*) and **Augustus' Forum** (*Foro di Augusto*) can be seen along the boulevard to the south.

The Roman Forum

The entrances are on Via dei Fori Imperiali at Via Cavour, and at the end of the ramp that approaches the Forum from the Colosseum side; t 06 699 0110; open daily 9–1hr before sunset. There's a visitor centre for the Fori Imperiali on the Via dei Fori Imperiali with small exhibitions and an information desk.

For a place that was the centre of the Mediterranean world, there is surprisingly little to see; centuries of use as a quarry have seen to that. The word *forum* originally meant 'outside' (like the Italian *fuori*), a marketplace outside the original Rome that became the centre of both government and business as the city expanded.

The **Via Sacra**, ancient Rome's most important street, runs the length of the Forum. At the end of it beneath the Capitoline Hill you will be facing the **Arch of Septimius Severus** (AD 203), with reliefs of some rather trivial victories over the Arabs and Parthians; conservative Romans of the time must have strongly resented this upstart African emperor planting his monument in such an important spot. The arch also commemorated Septimius' two sons, Geta and Caracalla; when the nasty Caracalla did his brother in, he had his name effaced from it. In front of it, the **Lapis Niger**, a mysterious stone with an underground chamber beneath it, is the legendary tomb of Romulus (*closed to the public*). The inscription down below – a threat against the profaning of this sacred spot – is one of the oldest ever found in the Latin language. The famous Golden Milestone also stood here, the 'umbilicus' of Rome and the point from which all distances in the Empire were measured. To the right is the **Curia** (the Senate House), heavily restored after centuries' use as a church (the good Baroque church behind it is **SS. Luca e Martina** (*Clivo Argentario; closed for restoration*), built by Pietro da Cortona in the 1660s). To the left of the arch the remains of a raised stone area were the **Rostra**, the speakers' platform under the Republic, decorated with ships' prows (*rostra*) taken in a sea battle in about 320 BC. Of the great temples on the Capitol slope only a few columns remain: from left to right, the **Temple of Saturn**, which served as Rome's treasury, the **Temple of Vespasian** (three standing columns) and the **Temple of Concord**, built by Tiberius to honour the peace – so to speak – that the emperors had enforced between patricians and plebeians.

In front of the Rostra, in the open area once decorated with statues and monuments, the simple standing **column** was placed in honour of Nikephoros Phocas, Byzantine Emperor in 608 – the last monument ever erected in the Forum; the Romans had to steal the column from a ruined building. Just behind it a small pool once marked the spot of one of ancient Rome's favourite legends. In 362 BC, according to Livy, an abyss suddenly opened across the Forum, and the sibyls predicted that it would not close unless the 'things that Rome held most precious' were thrown in. A consul, Marcus Curtius, took this as meaning a Roman citizen and soldier. He leapt in fully armed, horse and all, and the crack closed over him.

This section of the Forum was bordered by two imposing buildings, the **Basilica Aemilia** to the north and the **Basilica Julia** to the south, the latter built by Caesar with the spoils of the Gallic Wars. The **Temple of Caesar** closes the east end, built by Augustus as a visual symbol of the new imperial mythology.

The adjacent **Temple of the Dioscuri** is a good example of how temples were used in ancient times. This one was a meeting hall for men of the equestrian class (the knights, though they were really more likely to be businessmen); they had safe-deposit boxes in the basement, where the standard weights and measures of the empire were kept. Between them, the round pedestal was the foundation of the small **Temple of Vesta**, where the sacred hearth-fire was kept burning by the Vestal Virgins; ruins of their extensive apartments can be seen next door.

Two more Christian churches stand in this part of the Forum. **SS. Cosma e Damiano** (*open daily 9–1 and 3–6.30*) was built on to the **Temple of Antoninus Pius and Faustina** in the 6th century; most of the columns survive, with a fine sculptural frieze of griffons. **Santa Francesca Romana** (*open daily 9.30–12 and 4–7*) is built over a corner of Rome's largest temple, that of **Venus and Rome**. Built by Hadrian, this was a curious, double-ended shrine to the state cult, one side devoted to the Goddess Roma and the other to Venus – in the imperial mythology she was the ancestress of the Caesars.

The church entrance is outside the Forum, but the adjoining convent, inside the monumental area, houses the **Antiquarium Forense**, a tired collection of Iron-Age burial urns and other paraphernalia from the Forum excavations. Between the two churches the mastodontic **Basilica of Maxentius**, finished by Constantine, remains the largest ruin of the Forum, its clumsy arches providing an illustration of the ungainly but technically sophisticated 4th century.

Near the exit, the **Arch of Titus** commemorates the victories of Titus and his father Vespasian over the rebellious Jews (AD 60–80), one of the fiercest struggles Rome ever had to fight. The reliefs show the booty being carted through Rome in the triumphal parade – including the famous seven-branched golden candlestick from the holy of holies in the Temple at Jerusalem.

South of the arch a path leads up to the **Monte Palatino** (*t 06 3996 7700; open daily 9–1hr before sunset; adm or Roma Archeologia Card, see p.101*). Here, overlooking the little corner of the world that gave our language words like *senate, committee, rostrum, republic, plebiscite* and *magistrate*, you can leave democracy behind and visit the etymological birthplace of *palace*. The ruins of the imperial *Palàtium* once covered the entire hill. As with the Forum, almost all the stone has been cannibalized, and there's little to see of what was once a complex half a mile long, to which a dozen of the emperors contributed.

There are good views across the Circus Maximus from just above what was once the portico from which the emperor could watch the races. Don't miss the chance to take a stroll through the gardens planted by the Farnese family (*currently closed for renovation*) over what were the imperial servants' quarters. The one modern building on the Palatino houses the **Museo Palatino** (*adm included in ticket for Palatine*), a good little collection of relics found within a stone's throw of the building, plus a history of the hill with models of the huts built by its first inhabitants.

The Colosseum

Piazza del Colosseo; open daily 9–1hr before sunset; adm; see Roma Archeologia Card p.101; audioguide in English €4. Daily guided tours in English at 3pm, plus 4.15 and 5.15 in summer, €3.50.

Its real name was the Flavian Amphitheatre, after the family of emperors who built it, beginning with Vespasian in AD 72; Colosseum refers to the *Colossus*, a huge gilded statue of Nero (erected by himself, of course) that stood in the square in front. There doesn't seem to be much evidence that Christians were literally thrown to lions here – there were other places for that – but what did go on was perhaps the grossest and best-organized perversity in all history. Gladiatorial contests began under the republic, designed to make Romans better soldiers by rendering them indifferent to the sight of death. Later emperors introduced new displays to relieve the monotony –

men versus animals, lions versus elephants, women versus dwarfs, sea-battles (the arena could be flooded at a moment's notice), public tortures of criminals, and even genuine athletics, a Greek import the Romans never much cared for. In the first hundred days of the Colosseum's opening, 5,000 animals were slaughtered. The native elephant and lion of North Africa and Arabia are extinct thanks to this.

However hideous its purpose, the Colosseum ranks with the greatest works of Roman architecture and engineering; all modern stadia have its basic plan. One surprising feature was a removable awning that covered the stands. Sailors from Cape Misenum were kept to operate it; they also manned the galleys in the mock sea-battles. Originally there were statues in every arch and a ring of bronze shields around the cornice. The concrete stands have eroded away, showing the brick structure underneath. Renaissance and Baroque popes hauled away half the travertine exterior – enough to build the Palazzo Venezia, the Palazzo Barberini, a few other palaces and bridges and part of St Peter's. Almost all of the construction work under Vespasian and Titus was performed by Jewish slaves after the suppression of their revolt.

Just outside the Colosseum, the **Arch of Constantine** marks the end of the ancient Triumphal Way (now Via di San Gregorio) where victorious emperors and their troops would parade their captives and booty. The arch, with a coy inscription mentioning Constantine's 'divine inspiration' (the Romans weren't sure whether it was yet respectable to mention Christianity), is covered with reliefs stolen from older arches and public buildings – a sad commentary on the state of art in Constantine's day.

Domus Aurea and the Monte Esquilino

When Nero decided he needed a new palace, money was no object. Taking advantage of the great fire of AD 64 (which he apparently did *not* start), he had a huge section of Rome (temporarily renamed Neropolis) cleared to make a rural estate in the middle of town. The **Golden House** (*Colle Oppio; t 06 3996 7700; open Wed–Mon 9–7.45; advance booking essential; adm; audioguide €2 recommended*) was probably the most sumptuous palace ever built in Rome, decorated in an age when Roman art was at its height, but Nero never lived to see it finished – he committed suicide during an army coup by Spanish legions. When the dust settled, the new emperor Vespasian realized that this flagrant symbol of imperial decadence had to go. He demolished it, and Titus and Trajan later erected great bath complexes on its foundations; Nero's gardens and his enormous lake became the site of the Colosseum. In the 1500s some beautifully decorated rooms of the Domus Aurea were discovered underground, saved for use as the basement of Titus' baths. Raphael and other artists studied them closely and incorporated some of the spirit of the fresco decoration into the grand manner of the High Renaissance (our word 'grotesque', originally referring to the leering faces and floral designs of this time, comes from the finds in this 'grotto').

The **Monte Esquilino** is better known today as the Colle Oppio. Much of it is covered with parks; besides the Domus Aurea there are very substantial ruins of the **Terme di Traiano**, still unexcavated. On the northern slope of the hill, **San Pietro in Vincoli** (*t 06 488 2865; open daily 7–12.30 and 3.30–6*) takes its name from relics supposed to be the chains Peter was locked in before Nero had him crucified. They are kept over the main altar, though the real attraction of this church for non-Catholics is the famous, ill-fated **tomb of Julius II** which tortured Michelangelo for many years. Of the original project, planned as a sort of tabernacle with 40 individual statues, the artist completed, as well as the statues of *Leah* and *Rachel*, the powerful figure of *Moses*, perhaps the closest anyone has ever come to capturing prophetic vision in stone. All the other statues on the tomb are the work of Michelangelo's students.

San Clemente

Via San Giovanni in Laterano; t 06 7045 1018; open weekdays 9–12.30 and 3–6, weekends and hols 10–12.30 and 3–6; adm to the excavations.

This church, a little way to the east of the Colosseum, is one of the more fascinating remnants of Rome's many-layered history. One of the first substantial building projects of the Christians in Rome, the original basilica of *c.* 375 burned along with the rest of the quarter during a sacking by the Normans in 1084. It was rebuilt soon afterwards with a new Cosmatesque pavement, and the 6th-century choir screen – a rare example of sculpture from that ungifted time – saved from the original church. The 12th-century mosaic in the apse represents the *Triumph of the Cross*, and the chapel at the entrance contains a beautiful series of quattrocento frescoes by Masolino. From a vestibule, nuns sell tickets to the **Lower Church**. This is the lower half of the original San Clemente, and there are remarkable, though deteriorated, frescoes from the 900s and the 12th century. The plaque from Bulgaria, mentioned on p.109, commemorates SS. Cyril and Methodius, who went from this church to spread the Gospel among the Slavs; they translated the Bible into Old Slavonic, and invented the first Slavic alphabet (Cyrillic) to do it.

From here, steps lead down to the lowest stratum, 1st and 2nd century AD buildings divided by an alley; this includes the **Mithraeum**, the best-preserved temple of its kind after the one in Capua. The larger, neighbouring building was filled with rubble to serve as a foundation for the basilica, and the apse was later added over the Mithraeum. Father Mulhooly of Boston started excavating in the 1860s, and later excavations have revealed a Mithraic antechamber with a fine stuccoed ceiling, a Mithraic school with an early fresco, and the temple proper, a small caven-like hall with benches for initiates to share a ritual supper.

Mithraism was a mystery religion, full of secrets closely held by the initiates (all male, and largely soldiers) and it is difficult to say what else went on down here. Two altars were found, each with the usual image of the Persian-import god Mithras despatching a white bull, including a snake, a scorpion and a crow, and astrological symbolism. Underneath all this, there is yet a fourth building level, some foundations from the republican era. At the end of the 1st-century building you can look down into an ancient sewer or underground stream, one of a thousand entrances to the surreal sub-Roma of endless subterranean caves, buildings, rivers and lakes, mostly unexplored and unexplorable. A century ago a schoolboy fell in the water here; they found him, barely alive, in open country several kilometres from the city.

Along Corso Vittorio Emanuele

This street, chopped through the medieval centre in the 1880s, still hasn't quite been assimilated into its surroundings; nevertheless, this ragged, smoky traffic tunnel will come in handy when you find yourself lost in the tortuous, meandering streets of Rome's oldest quarter. Starting west from Piazza Venezia, the church of **Il Gesù** (1568–84; *Piazza del Gesù*; *t 06 697 001*; *open 7–12 and 3–7.30*) was a landmark for a new era and the new aesthetic of cinquecento Rome. The transitional, pre-Baroque fashion was often referred to as the 'Jesuit style', and here in the Jesuits' head church architects Vignola and della Porta laid down Baroque's first law: an intimation of paradise through decorative excess. It hasn't aged well, though at the time it must have seemed to most Romans a perfect marriage of Renaissance art and a reformed, revitalized faith. St Ignatius is buried in the left transept right under the altar, Spanish-style; the globe in the sculpted Trinity is the biggest piece of lapis lazuli in the world.

Further west the street opens into a ghastly square called Largo Argentina. Remains of several republican-era temples, unearthed far below ground level, occupy the centre. The square teems with cats: tucked beneath the square at one end is the **Roman Cat Sanctuary** (**t** 06 687 2133, *www.romancats.com*). Take a short detour around the corner, halfway down Via delle Botteghe Oscure at No.31, to find the newest addition to the Museo Nazionale d'Arte Romana: the **Crypta Balbi** (*open Tues–Sun 9–7.45*; *adm, or part of Roma Archeologia Card or Museum Card, see pp.101 and 135*). This modern, glassy museum is built over the ruins of a theatre, which was almost as large as the huge theatres of Pompey and Marcellus. A medieval church grew up on the ruins, before becoming submerged by the modern street.

Back up on Via Corso Emanuele, just beyond the Largo Argentina, is another grand Baroque church, **Sant'Andrea della Valle** (**t** 06 686 1339; *open 8–12 and 4.30–7*), with the city's second-tallest dome. Maderno, one of the architects of St Peter's, did most of the work. The curving façade across the street belongs to **Palazzo Massimo alle Colonne** (*open 16 Mar only 7–1; adm*), the masterpiece of the Renaissance architect Baldassare Peruzzi; he transplanted something of the Florentine style of monumental palaces, adding some light-hearted proto-Baroque decoration. If you can, have a look at the adjacent church of **San Pantaleo de Parione** (*opposite Via dei Baullari; open, rarely, for Mass*), with its outlandish sculptural frieze of shields, trays and popes' hats piled like a rubbish heap. The sumptuous Palazzo Braschi next door houses the **Museo di Roma** (*Piazza San Pantaleo 10; t 06 8207 7384; open Tues–Sun 9–7, guided tours Sat and Sun, call for times; adm, audioguide €3.62*), which reopened in 2002 after a decade of restoration but has a disappointing collection of artefacts, virtually meaningless without the audioguide. The views over the Piazza Navona are good, though.

Right across the street is one of the earliest and best of the palaces on Corso Vittorio Emanuele, the delicate **Piccola Farnesina** by Antonio da Sangallo the Younger. It houses another little museum, a collection of sculpture called the **Museo Barracco** (*t 06 6880 6848; open Tues–Sun 9–7; adm*). Just around the corner from Sant'Andrea, the **Burcardo Library and Theatre Collection**, Via Sudario 44 (*open Sun–Fri 9–1.30, closed hols*) is a collection of fascinating relics from the Roman theatrical tradition.

The biggest palace on the street, attributed to Bramante, is **Palazzo della Cancelleria** (*t 06 6989 3405; open for visits by reservation at least one month in advance*), once the seat of the papal municipal government. St Philip Neri, the gifted, irascible holy man who is patron saint of Rome, built the **Chiesa Nuova** (*open 8–12 and 4.30–7*) near the eastern end of the Corso (1584). Philip was quite a character, with something of the Zen Buddhist in him. He forbade his followers any sort of philosophical speculation, but made them sing and recite poetry; two of his favourite pastimes were insulting popes and making initiates walk through Rome with a foxtail sewn to the back of their coat to learn humility. As was common in those times, sincere faith and humility were eventually translated into flagrant Baroque. The Chiesa Nuova is one of the larger and fancier of the species. Its altarpiece is a *Madonna with Angels* by Rubens. Even more flagrant, outside the church you can see the curved arch-Baroque façade of the **Oratorio dei Filippini** by Borromini. The form of music called the *oratorio* takes its name from this chapel, a tribute to St Philip's role in promoting sacred music.

Campo de' Fiori

Few cities can put on such a variety of faces; depending on where you spend your time in Rome, you may come away with the impression of a city that is one great Baroque stage set, a city of grimy early 1900s *palazzi* and bad traffic, or a city full of nothing but ruins and parks. Around Campo de' Fiori, one of the spots dearest to the hearts of Romans themselves, you may think yourself in the middle of some scruffy south Italian village. Rome's market square, disorderly, cramped and chaotic, is easily the liveliest corner of the city, full of market barrows, buskers, teenage bohemians and the folkloresque types who have lived here all their lives. The best time to see the square is during the morning market (*Mon–Sat dawn–1*) or at night along with the adjacent Piazza Fornese. During papal rule the old square was also used for executions – most notoriously the burning of Giordano Bruno in 1600. This well-travelled philosopher was the first to take Copernican astronomy to its logical extremes – an infinite universe with no centre, no room for Heaven, and nothing eternal but change. The Church had few enemies more dangerous. Italy never forgot him; the statue of Bruno in Campo de' Fiori went up only a few years after the end of papal rule.

Just east of the square, the heap of buildings around Piazzetta di Grottapinta is built over the cavea of **Teatro di Pompeo**, ancient Rome's biggest. This complex included a curia, the place where Julius Caesar was assassinated in 44 BC. Walk south from Campo de' Fiori and you will be thrown from cosy medievalism into the heart of the High Renaissance with the **Palazzo Farnese** (*open for group visits by arrangement with the cultural section of the French Embassy*), one of the definitive works of that Olympian style. The younger Sangallo began it in 1514, and Michelangelo contributed to the façades and interiors. The building is now the French Embassy, and the square it overlooks is one of the most romantic in the city.

Most of the palaces that fill up this neighbourhood have one thing in common – they were made possible by someone's accession to the papacy, the biggest jackpot available to any aspiring Italian family. Built on the pennies of the faithful, they provide the most outrageous illustration of Church corruption at the dawn of the

Reformation. Alessandro Farnese, who as Pope Paul III was a clever and effective pope – though perhaps the greatest nepotist – managed to build this palace 20 years before his election, with the income from his 16 absentee bishoprics.

Palazzo Spada, just to the east on Via Capo di Ferro 13, was the home of a mere cardinal, but its florid stucco façade (1540) almost upstages the Farnese. Inside, the **Galleria Spada** (*t 06 6880 9814; open Tues–Sat 9–7.30, Sun 9–6.30; adm*) is one of Rome's great collections of 16th- and 17th-century painting. Guido Reni, Guercino and the other favourites of the age are well represented. Don't miss the courtyard, which has decoration similar to the façade, and a glass window with a view through the library to one of Rome's little Baroque treasures: the recently restored *trompe l'œil* corridor, designed by Borromini to appear four times its actual length (the statue at the end of the path is actually less than a yard in height). To the south, close to the Tiber, **Via Giulia** was laid out by Pope Julius II: a pretty thoroughfare lined with churches and *palazzi*. Many artists (successful ones) have lived here, including Raphael.

Piazza Navona

In 1477 the area now covered by one of Rome's most beautiful piazzas was a field full of huts and vineyards, tucked inside the imposing ruins of the Stadium of Domitian. A redevelopment of the area covered the long grandstands with new houses, but the decoration had to wait for the Age of Baroque. In 1644, the Pamphili family won the papal sweepstakes with the election of Innocent X. Innocent, a great grafter and such a villainous pope that when he died no one – not even his newly wealthy relatives – would pay for a proper burial, built the ornate **Palazzo Pamphili** (now the Brazilian Embassy) and hired Borromini to complete the gaudy church of **Sant'Agnese in Agone** (*open Tues–Sun 10–7 and for Mass*), begun by Carlo and Girolamo Rainaldi.

Borromini's arch-rival, Bernini, got the commission for the piazza's famous fountains; the Romans still tell stories of how the two artists carried on. Borromini started a rumour that the tall obelisk atop the central **Fontana dei Fiumi** was about to topple; when the alarmed papal commissioners arrived to confront Bernini with the news, he tied a piece of twine around it, secured the other end to a lamppost, and laughed all the way home. The fountain is Bernini's masterpiece, Baroque at its flashiest and most lovable. Among the travertine grottoes and fantastical flora and fauna under the obelisk, the four colossal figures represent the Ganges, Danube, Rio de la Plata and Nile (with the veiled head because its source was unknown). Bernini also designed the smaller **Fontana del Moro**, at the southern end. The third fountain, that of *Neptune*, was an empty basin until the nineteenth century, when the statues by Giacomo della Porta were added to make the square seem more symmetrical. Off the southern end of the piazza, at the back of Palazzo Braschi, **Pasquino** is the original Roman 'talking statue', embellished with placards and graffiti ('*pasquinades*') since the 1500s – one of his favourite subjects in those days was the insatiable pigginess of families like the Farnese; serious religious issues were usually too hot to touch.

Piazza Navona seems mildly schizoid these days, unable to become entirely part of high-fashion, tourist-itinerary Rome, yet no longer as comfortable and unpretentious as the rest of the neighbourhood. One symptom will be readily apparent should you step into any of the old cosy-looking cafés and restaurants around the piazza: they're as expensive as in any part of Rome. The best time to come to Piazza Navona is at night when the fountain is illuminated – or, if you can, for the noisy, traditional toy fair of the **Befana**, set up between just before Christmas and Epiphany. **Palazzo Altemps**, on Piazza Sant'Apollinare, now contains part of the excellent **Museo Nazionale Romano** (*t 06 683 3759; open Tues–Fri 9–7.45, Sun 9am–11pm; adm; admission included with the Roma Archeologia Card, see p.101, or with the Museum Card, which is valid 7 days, costs €9 and covers the four sites run by the Museo Nazionale Romano: the Palazzo Altemps, the Palazzo Massima, Baths of Diocletian and the Crypta Balbi*). The beautiful palace makes a stunning setting for the busts and statues: the *piano nobile* still contains fragments of 16th-century frescoes and there's a glorious painted loggia lined with busts of the Caesars, as well as a tiny, forlorn gilded theatre in the basement. Some of the churches in the area are worth a look, such as **Santa Maria della Pace** (*Vicolo del Arco della Pace 5; t 06 686 1156; open Tues–Sat 10–12 and 4–6, Sun 9–11*), with Raphael's series of *Sibyls and Prophets* on the vaulting and a cloister by Bramante. **San Luigi dei Francesi** (*t 06 688 271; open Mon–Wed and Fri–Sun 8.30–12.30 and 3.30–7; Thurs 8.30–12.30 only*), the French church in Rome, contains the great *Life of St Matthew* by Caravaggio in a chapel on the left aisle. Towards the Pantheon, **Sant'Ivo alla Sapienza** (*Corso del Rinascimento 40, t 06 686 4987; open Sun am for Mass*) once served the English community in Rome. Borromini built them one of his most singular buildings (1660), with its dome and spiralling cupola.

The Pantheon

Piazza della Rotonda, t 06 6830 0230; open Mon–Sat 8.30–7.30, Sun 9–6.

When we consider the fate of so many other great buildings of ancient Rome we begin to understand what a slim chance it was that allowed this one to come down to us. The first Pantheon was built in 27 BC by Agrippa, Emperor Augustus' son-in-law and right-hand man, but was destroyed by fire and replaced by the present temple in AD 119–128 by the Emperor Hadrian, though curiously retaining Agrippa's original inscription on the pediment. Its history has been precarious ever since. In 609 the empty Pantheon was consecrated to Christianity as 'St Mary of the Martyrs'.

Becoming a church is probably what saved it, though the Byzantines hauled away the gilded bronze roof tiles soon after, and for a while in the Middle Ages the portico saw use as a fish market. The Pantheon's greatest enemy, however, was Gian Lorenzo Bernini. He not only 'improved' it with a pair of Baroque belfries over the porch (demolished in 1887), but he had Pope Urban VIII take down the bronze covering on the inside of the dome to melt down for his *baldacchino* over the altar at St Peter's. Supposedly there was enough left over to make the pope 60 cannons.

You may notice that the building seems perilously unsound. There is no way a simple vertical wall can support such a heavy, shallow dome (steep domes push downwards, shallow ones outwards). Obviously the walls will tumble at any moment. That is a little joke the Roman architects are playing, for here they are showing off as shamelessly as in the Colosseum, or the aqueduct with four storeys of arches that used to run *up* to the Monte Palatino. The wall that looks so fragile is really 23ft thick and the dome on top isn't a dome at all; the real hemispherical dome lies underneath, resting easily on the walls inside. The ridges you see on the upper dome are courses of cantilevered bricks, effectively almost weightless. The real surprise, however, lies behind the enormous original bronze doors: an interior of precious marbles and finely sculpted details, the grandest and best-preserved building to have survived from the ancient world. The movie directors who made all those Roman epics in the 1950s and '60s certainly took many of their settings from this High Imperial creation, just as architects from the early Middle Ages onwards have tried to equal it.

Brunelleschi learned enough from it to build his dome in Florence, and a visit here will show you at a glance what Michelangelo and his contemporaries were trying so hard to outdo. The coffered dome, the biggest cast concrete construction ever made before the 20th century, is the crowning audacity. At 141ft in diameter it is probably the largest in the world (a little-known fact – but St Peter's dome is 6ft less, though much taller). Standing in the centre and looking at the clouds through the 28ft *oculus*, the hole at the top, is an odd sensation you can experience nowhere else.

Inside, the niches around the perimeter held statues of the Pantheon's 12 gods, plus those of Augustus and Hadrian; in the centre, illuminated by a direct sunbeam at midsummer noon, stood Jove. All these are gone, of course, and the interior decoration is limited to an *Annunciation*, attributed to Melozzo da Forlì, and the tombs of eminent Italians such as Raphael and kings Vittorio Emanuele II and Umberto I. The Pantheon simply stands open, with no admission charges, probably fulfilling the same purpose as in Hadrian's day – no purpose at all, save that of an unequalled monument to art and the builder's skill.

Just behind the Pantheon, the big church of **Santa Maria sopra Minerva** (*t 06 679 1217; church open daily 7–7.30, cloister open Mon–Sat 8–1 and 4–7*) is interesting for being one of the few medieval churches of Rome (*c.* 1280) to escape the Baroque treatment; its Gothic was preserved in restoration work in the 1840s. Two Medici popes, Leo X and Clement VII, are buried here, as is Fra Angelico. Santa Maria's Florentine connection began with the Dominican monks who designed it; they also did Florence's Santa Maria Novella. A work of Michelangelo, *Christ with the Cross*, can be seen near the high altar; the Carafa Chapel off the right aisle, where you can pay your respects to Pope Paul IV, has a series of frescoes (1489) on the *Life of St Thomas* by Filippino Lippi, his best work outside Florence.

Via del Corso

The Campus Martius, the open plain between Rome's hills and the Tiber, was the training ground for soldiers in the early days of the Republic. Eventually the city swallowed it up and the old path towards the Via Flaminia became an important thoroughfare, *Via Lata* (Broad Street). Not entirely by coincidence, the popes of the 14th and 15th centuries laid out a new boulevard almost in the same place. **Via del Corso**, or simply the Corso, has been the main axis of Roman society ever since. Goethe left a fascinating account of the Carnival festivities of Rome's benignly decadent 18th century, climaxing in the horse-races that gave the street its name. Much of its length is taken up by the overdone palaces of the age, such as the Palazzo Doria (1780), where the **Galleria Doria Pamphili** (*Piazza del Collegio Romano 2, t 06 679 7323, www.doriapamphili.it; open Fri–Wed 10–5; adm, includes audioguide in English*), still owned by the Pamphili, has a fine painting collection – with Velazquez' *Portrait of Innocent X*, Caravaggio's *Flight into Egypt*, and works by Rubens, Titian, Brueghel and more. Guided tours of the apartments (in English by request) give an idea of the lifestyle a family expected when one of its members hit the papal jackpot.

Continuing northwards, the palaces have come down in the world somewhat, tired-looking blocks that now house banks and offices. Look on the side-streets for some hidden attractions: **Sant'Ignazio** (*Piazza di Sant'Ignazio; open 7.30–12.30 and 4–7.15*) is another Jesuit church with spectacular *trompe l'œil* frescoes on the ceiling; a block north on Piazza di Pietra, columns of the ancient **Temple of Hadrian** are incorporated into the north side of the city's tiny Stock Exchange. **Piazza Colonna** takes its name from the column of Marcus Aurelius, whose military victories are remembered in a column (just like those of Trajan); atop stands a statue of St Paul. The obelisk in adjacent Piazza di Montecitorio once marked the hours on a gigantic sundial in Emperor Augustus' garden; **Palazzo di Montecitorio**, begun by Bernini, now houses the Italian Chamber of Deputies.

A little way east of Piazza Colonna is the **Fontana di Trevi**, into which you can throw your coins to guarantee your return trip to Rome. The fountain, completed in 1762, was originally planned to commemorate the restoration of Agrippa's aqueduct by Nicholas V in 1453. The source was called the 'Virgin Water' after Virgo, a young girl who had shown thirsty Roman soldiers the hidden spring. It makes a grand sight – enough to make you want to come back; not many fountains have an entire palace for a stage backdrop. The big fellow in the centre is Oceanus, drawn by horses and tritons through cascades of travertine and blue water. Across from the fountain, little **SS. Vincenzo and Anastasio** (*t 06 678 3098; open 7–9am*) has the distinction of caring for the pickled hearts and entrails of dozens of popes, kept down in the crypt.

Just a short walk from the Trevi Fountain is the **Museo delle Paste Alimentari**, on Piazza Scanderbeg 117 (*t 06 699 1119; open daily 9.30–5.30; adm*), where a small, modern display traces the history of Italy's most famous food.

Further north, the Corso reaches close to the Tiber and the dilapidated and overgrown **Mausoleo di Augusto** (*closed to the public*), a cylinder of shabby brick once covered in marble and golden statues. All the Julian emperors except Nero were interred here, in the middle of what were Augustus' enormous gardens. After the centuries had despoiled the tomb of its riches the Colonna family turned the hulk into a fortress. Further indignities were in store. Until 1823, when the pope forbade them, bullfights were popular in Rome, and a Spanish entrepreneur found the circular enclosure perfect for the *toreros*. After that the tomb was used as a circus, before Mussolini, wishing to afford the founders of Imperial Rome due respect (and perhaps intending to be buried there himself), declared it a national monument and had trees planted around it. Even so, no one quite seems to know what to do with it; it sits locked and empty.

Across the street, Augustus' **Ara Pacis**, Altar of Peace (*Via di Ripetta, t 06 6710 3819; closed for restoration*), has had a better fate. Bits and pieces of the beautiful sculpted reliefs, dug up in 1937, were joined with casts of others from museums around Europe to recreate the small building almost in its entirety, one of antiquity's noblest (and least pretentious) conceptions. Among the mythological reliefs, note the side facing the river, with the emperor and his family dedicating a sacrifice. At the time of writing it's shrouded in scaffolding while Richard Meier's glassy new visitor centre takes shape around it.

Piazza di Spagna

The shuffling crowds of tourists who congregate here at all hours of the day are not a recent phenomenon; this supremely sophisticated piazza has been a favourite with foreigners ever since it was laid out in the early 16th century. The Spaniards came first, as their embassy to the popes was established here in 1646, giving the square and the steps their name. Later, the English Romantic poets made it their headquarters in Italy; typical mementoes – locks of hair, fond remembrances, death masks – are awaiting your inspired contemplation at the **Keats-Shelley Memorial House** at No.26 (*t 06 678 4235; open Mon–Fri 9–1 and 3–6; Sat 11–2, and 3–6; adm*). Almost every artist, writer or musician of the last century spent some time here, but today the piazza often finds itself bursting at the seams with refreshingly Philistine gawkers and wayward youth from all over the world, caught between the charms of McDonald's (the first one built in Rome) and the fancy shops around nearby Via Condotti.

All these visitors need somewhere to sit, and the popes obliged them in 1725 with the construction of the **Spanish Steps** (*Scalinata di Trinità dei Monti*), an exceptionally beautiful and exceptionally Baroque ornament. The youth who loll about here are taking the place of the hopeful artists' models of the more picturesque centuries who once crowded the steps, striking poses of antique heroes and Madonnas, waiting for some easy money. At the top of the stairs the simple but equally effective church of **Trinità dei Monti** (*t 06 679 4179; open 9–8*) by Carlo Maderno (early 16th century) was paid for by the king of France. At the southern end of Piazza di Spagna, a Borromini palace housed the papal office called the *Propaganda Fide*, whose job was just what the name implies. The column in front (1857) celebrates the proclamation of the Dogma of the Immaculate Conception. Via del Babuino, a street named after a siren on a fountain so ugly that Romans called her the 'baboon', connects Piazza di Spagna with Piazza del Popolo. Besides its very impressive antique shops, the street carries on the English connection, with All Saints' Church, a sleepy neo-pub and an English bookshop just off it.

Piazza del Popolo

If you have a choice of how you enter Rome, this is the way to do it, through the gate in the old Aurelian wall and into one of the most successful of all Roman piazzas, copied on a smaller scale all over Italy. No city has a better introduction, and the three diverging boulevards direct you with thoughtful efficiency towards your destination. Valadier, the pope's architect after the Napoleonic occupation, gave the piazza the form it has today, but the big obelisk of Pharaoh Ramses II, punctuating the view down the boulevards, arrived in the 1580s. It is 3,200 years old but, like all obelisks, it looks mysteriously brand-new. Augustus brought it to Rome from Heliopolis and planted it in the Circus Maximus; it was transferred here by Pope Sixtus V. The two domed churches designed by Rainaldi, set like bookends at the entrance to the three boulevards, are from the 1670s, part of the original plan for the piazza to which Bernini and Fontana may have contributed. Nero's ashes were interred in a mausoleum here, at the foot of the Monte Pincio. The site was planted with walnut trees and soon everyone in Rome knew that Nero's ghost haunted the grove, sending out demons in the form of flocks of ravens to perform deeds of evil. In about 1100 Pope Paschal II destroyed the grove and scattered the ashes; to complete the exorcism he built a church on the site, **Santa Maria del Popolo** (*t 06 361 0636; open Mon–Fri 6–1 and 5–7.30, Sat–Sun 8–1 and 5–7.30*). Rebuilt in the 1470s, it contains some of the best painting in Rome: Caravaggio's stunning *Crucifixion of St Peter* and *Conversion of St Paul* (in the left transept), and frescoes by Pinturicchio near the altar. Raphael designed the Chigi Chapel, off the left aisle, including its mosaics.

Villa Borghese

From Piazza del Popolo a winding ramp leads up to Rome's great complex of parks. Just by coincidence this was mostly parkland in ancient times. The **Monte Pincio** once formed part of Augustus' imperial gardens, and the adjacent **Villa Medici** (*Viale della Trinità dei Monti 1, t 06 676 1305, www.villamedici.it; open for guided tours of the gardens 1 Mar–31 May and 6–25 Oct, Sun every half-hour 10–12.30*) occupies the site of the Villa of Lucullus, the 2nd-century BC philosopher and general who conquered northern Anatolia and first brought cherries to Europe. Now the home of the French Academy, the Villa Medici was a posh jail of sorts for Galileo during his Inquisitorial trials. The Pincio, redesigned by Valadier as a lovely formal garden, offers rare views over Rome. It is separated from the **Villa Borghese** (*open dawn–sunset*) proper by the Aurelian wall and the modern sunken roadway that borders it; its name, Viale del Muro Torto (crooked wall), refers to a section that collapsed in the 6th century and was left as it was because it was believed to be protected by St Peter.

Exploring the vast spaces of Villa Borghese, you will come across charming vales, woods and a pond (rowing boats for hire), an imitation Roman temple or two, rococo avenues where the bewigged dandies and powdered tarts of the 1700s came to promenade, bits of ancient aqueduct and a **zoo** (*Piazzale del Giardino Zoologico, t 06 360 8211, www.bioparco.it; open daily Mar–Oct 9.30–6, Oct–Mar 9.30–5; adm*), which is finally becoming more eco-friendly and has rechristened itself the Bioparco. On the northern edge of the park is a ponderous boulevard called **Viale delle Belle Arti**, where academies have been set up by foreign governments to stimulate cultural exchange. The **Galleria Nazionale d'Arte Moderna** (*t 06 322 981; open Tues–Sun 8.30–7.30; adm; guided tours in English by reservation, Sun 11am, €4 extra*) makes its home here in one of Rome's most inexcusable buildings (1913), but the collection includes some great works of Modigliani and the Futurists, as well as a fair sampling of 19th- and 20th-century artists from the rest of Europe.

From there, gingerly skirting the Romanian Academy, you come to the **Museo Etrusco Nazionale di Villa Giulia** (*t 06 321 7224; open Tues–Sun 8.30–7.30; adm, entrance on Piazzale di Villa Giulia*). If you cannot make it to Tarquinia, this is the place to get to know the Etruscans. Some of their best art has been collected here, as well as laboriously reconstructed terracotta façades to give you some idea of how an Etruscan temple looked. As usual, the compelling attraction is the Etruscans' effortless, endearing talent for portraiture: expressive faces that bridge the gap between the centuries can be seen in terracotta ex-votos (some of children), sarcophagi and even architectural decoration. Serious art is often more stylized; fine examples are the charming couple on the *Sarcophago dei Sposi* from Cerveteri, and the roof statues from the Temple of Portonaccio at Veii – these by Vulca, the only Etruscan artist whose name has survived along with his work. The museum building and its courts and gardens are attractions in themselves; Julius III had Vignola and Ammannati build this quirky Mannerist villa in 1553, and Vasari and Michelangelo may also have helped.

The fantastic trove of ancient relics and late-Renaissance and Baroque painting and sculpture – including masterpieces by Bernini and Caravaggio – at the **Museo e Galleria Borghese** (*t 06 32810; open Tues–Sun 9–7; adm, advance booking (€1 fee) recommended and essential in summer; guided visits of museum at 9.10 and 11.10, €5; guided tours of the Villa's Secret Gardens Sat at 10.30, free, call to reserve, t 06 8107 7304*) is testimony to the legendary greed and avarice of Cardinal Scipione Borghese, nephew of Pope Paul IV. He amassed, by any means available, one of the great private collections of the 17th century and built a magnificently decorated palace on the family's property to hold it. The display today is all the more impressive because a descendant of the Cardinal 'sold' many pieces to his brother-in-law, Napoleon Bonaparte, who put them in the Louvre. The Museo Borghese (ground floor) offers an intriguing mix of great art and Roman preciosity. Often the two go hand-in-hand, as with the sensuously charged showpieces of Bernini: *Apollo and Daphne*, *The Rape of Proserpina* and especially his *David*, which the artist modestly chiselled in his own image. Canova, the hot item among sculptors in Napoleon's day, contributes a titillatingly languorous statue of Pauline Borghese (Napoleon's sister) as the *Conquering Venus*. Even the ancient world joins in the fun, with such works as the famous Hellenistic *Sleeping Hermaphrodite*. Also downstairs are several Caravaggios, including the *Madonna of the Palafrenieri*, *David with the Head of Goliath* and *St Jerome*. No less impressive are the paintings in the gallery upstairs (entrance through the basement café), representing many of the finest 16th- and 17th-century painters: Titian, Bernini, Raphael, Correggio and Rubens.

Via Veneto and the Quirinale

This chain of gardens was once much bigger, but at the end of the last century many of the old villas were lost to the inevitable expansion of the city. Perhaps the greatest loss was the Villa Ludovisi, praised by many as the most beautiful of all Rome's parks. Now the choice 'Ludovisi' quarter, it has given the city one of its most famous streets, Via Veneto, the long winding boulevard of grand hotels, cafés and boutiques that stretches down from Villa Borghese to Piazza Barberini. A promenade for the smart set in the 1950s, it wears something of the forlorn air of a jilted beau.

Pull yourself away from the passing show on the boulevard to take in the unique spectacle provided by the **Convento dei Cappuccini** at the southern end of the street, just up from Piazza Barberini (*entrance halfway up the stairs of Santa Maria della Concezione; open daily 9–12 and 3–6; adm*). Unique, that is, outside Palermo, for, much like the Capuchin convent there, the Roman brethren have created a loving tribute to our friend Death. In the cellars 4,000 dead monks team up for an unforgettable *Danse Macabre* of bones and grinning skulls, carefully arranged by serious-minded Capuchins long ago to remind us of something we know only too well.

On the other side of Piazza Barberini, up a gloomy Baroque avenue called Via delle Quattro Fontane, you'll find the Palazzo Barberini, one of the showier places in Rome, decorated everywhere with the bees from the family arms. Maderno, Borromini and Bernini all worked on it, with financing made possible by the election of a Barberini as Pope Urban VIII in 1623. Currently it houses the **Galleria Nazionale d'Arte Antica** (*t 06 481 4591; open Tues–Sun 8.30–7.30; adm*) – a misleading title, since this is a gallery devoted to Italian works of the 12th–18th centuries. Often the original decoration steals the show from the pictures: Bernini's Great Hall, for example, with a ceiling fresco by Pietro da Cortona, the *Triumph of Divine Providence*, or the ceiling in Room 7, with a fresco by Andrea Sacchi where the enthroned Virgin looking down on the round earth seems like a Baroque attempt to create a new Catholic astronomy. Works present include a Bernini self-portrait, Raphael's famous portrait of his beloved mistress *La Fornarina*, the 'baker's girl', more portraits by the Genoese artist Baciccio, lots of Caravaggios, Lippi's *Madonna* and two rather sedate pictures by El Greco.

San Carlino (*t 06 488 3261; open Mon–Fri 9–1 and 3–4, Sat 9–12.30, Sun 10.30–1*), on the corner of Via delle Quattro Fontane and Via Quirinale, is one of Borromini's best works – and his first one (1638), a purposely eccentric little flight of fancy built exactly the size of one of the four massive pillars that hold up the dome in St Peter's. Just down the street, his rival Bernini counters with **Sant'Andrea al Quirinale** (1658–70), a small, richly decorated elliptical church that is one of the great architectural *tours de force* of the Baroque. Continue down **Via Quirinale** and you'll reach the summit of that hill, covered with villas and gardens in ancient times, and abandoned in the Middle Ages. During the reign of Sixtus V they were excavated to reveal monumental Roman statues of the **Dioscuri** (Castor and Pollux), probably copied from Phidias or Praxiteles. Together with a huge basin found in the Forum, they make a centrepiece for Piazza del Quirinale. Behind it, stretching for a dreary half-kilometre along the street is the **Palazzo del Quirinale** (*t 06 46991; open late Sept–early July Sun 8.30–12.30; adm*), built in 1574 to symbolize the political domination of the popes, later occupied by the kings of Italy, and now the residence of the country's president.

Around Stazione Termini

Rome's great big station takes its name from the nearby **Terme di Diocleziano** (*open Tues–Sun 9–7; adm; adm included with Roma Archeologia Card, see p.101, and Museum Card, see p.135, t 06 3996 7700*), just on the other side of Piazza dei Cinquecento,

which is part of the **Museo Nazionale Romano**, the greatest Italian collection of antiquities after the museum in Naples. Until the popes dismantled the baths for building
stone this was by far Rome's biggest ruin; its outer wall followed the present-day lines
of Via XX Settembre, Via Volturno and Piazza dei Cinquecento, and the big semicircular **Piazza della Repubblica**, with its mouldering, grandiose 1890s *palazzi* and
huge fountain, occupies the site of the baths' exercise ground, or *palaestra*. All
together the complex covered some 11 hectares. Michelangelo, not on one of his
better days, converted a section of the lofty, vaulted central bathhouse into the
church of **Santa Maria degli Angeli**, conserving some of the building's original form
and adding a broad new cloister. The cloister and the adjoining building now house
part of the Museo Nazionale Romano's enormous collection.

Across the street, you can see more of the Museo Nazionale's holdings at the
unmissable **Palazzo Massimo alle Terme** (*t 06 3996 7700; open Tues–Sun 9–7; adm;
adm included with Roma Archeologia Card, see p.101, and Museum Card, see p.135*). The
basement, courtyard and first floor contain coins, jewellery, busts and statuary, but it's
the delicate frescoes and mosaics from the Villa di Livia, the Villa della Farnesina and
other aristocratic homes which really stand out (*visits by guided tour only because of
the fragility of the collection; the time will be marked on your admission ticket*). There's
a shimmering sea-green forest of fruit trees and exotic birds which once covered the
dining room of the Villa di Livia, and a lively fresco from the old fish market.

A block north of the baths, Piazza San Bernardo has two interesting churches: **San
Bernardo**, built out of a circular library that once occupied a corner of the baths' walls,
and **Santa Maria della Vittoria** (*t 06 482 6190; open 7–12 and 4.30–7*), home to one of
the essential works of Baroque sculpture, the disconcertingly erotic *St Teresa in Ecstasy*
by Bernini (in a chapel off the left aisle).

Two Patriarchal Basilicas

Besides St Peter's there are three Patriarchal Basilicas, ancient and revered churches
under the care of the pope that have always been a part of the Roman Pilgrimage.
Santa Maria Maggiore, San Paolo Fuori le Mura (*see p.150*) and San Giovanni in
Laterano are all on the edges of the city, away from the political and commercial
centre; by the Middle Ages they stood in open countryside, and only recently has the
city grown outwards to swallow them once more.

Santa Maria Maggiore

Santa Maria Maggiore, on Monte Esquilino, was probably begun about 352, when a
rich Christian saw a vision of the Virgin directing him to build a church; Pope Liberius
had received the same vision at the same time, and the two supposedly found the
site marked out for them by a miraculous August snowfall. The church (*t 06 483 195;
open 7–7; call for info on guided visits to the Loggia delle Benedizioni, which has 13th-
century mosaics depicting the legend of the church's foundation*) took its current
form in the 1740s, with a perfectly elegant façade by Fernando Fuga and an equally

impressive rear elevation by other architects; the obelisk behind it came from the Mausoleum of Augustus. Above everything rises the tallest and fairest **campanile** in Rome, an incongruous survival from the 1380s. Inside, the most conspicuous feature is the coffered ceiling by Giuliano da Sangallo, gilded with the first gold brought back from the New World by Columbus, a gift from Ferdinand and Isabella of Spain. In the apse there are splendid but faded mosaics from 1295 of the *Coronation of the Virgin*; others, from the 5th century, decorate the nave and the 'triumphal arch' in front of the apse. Santa Maria Maggiore has a prize relic – nothing less than the genuine manger from Bethlehem, preserved in a sunken shrine in front of the altar; in front, kneeling in prayer, is a colossal, rather grotesque statue of Pope Pius IV added in the 1880s.

In 822, two decades after Charlemagne visited Rome, Pope Paschal I found the money and the talent to build works he hoped would be compared to the magnificent ruins that lay on every side. The churches he had rebuilt near Santa Maria

Santa Maria Maggiore

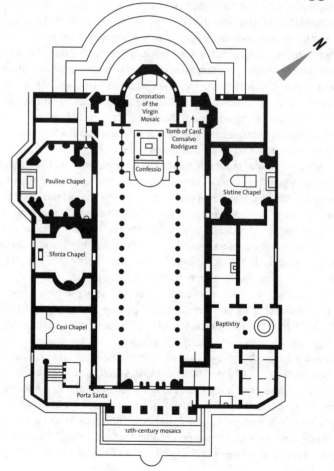

Maggiore commemorating two sisters, early Christian martyrs of the 1st century, were not large, but they were a start, and to embellish them he imported Byzantine artists who originated a rebirth of mosaic work and painting in Rome. **Santa Pudenziana** (*Via Urbana 160; t 06 481 4622; open 7–7*) conserves a mosaic of *Christ and the Apostles* from the 4th century, a thoroughly classical work from the very beginnings of Christian art. At **Santa Prassede** the mosaics reveal a different world: the shadowy Rome of the not-entirely Dark Ages. The jewel of Santa Prassede (*Via Santa Prassede 9/a, t 06 488 2456; open 7–12 and 4–6.30*) is the small San Zeno Chapel, which Paschal intended as a mausoleum for his mother. The square vaulted chamber is entirely covered with gold-ground mosaics of Christ Pantocrator, saints and some very dignified, classical angels who look as if they never heard anything about the fall of Rome. The 9th-century mosaics around the altar are even better, if less golden.

San Giovanni in Laterano (St John Lateran)

Where is Rome's cathedral? It isn't St Peter's, and never has been. The true seat of the Bishop of Rome, and the end of a Roman Pilgrimage, is here in the shadow of the Aurelian wall, a church established by Constantine himself (*t 06 6988 6433; open daily 7–6.45, Museo Sacro and cloister open 9–6*). The family of Plautius Lateranus, according to ancient records, had their property here confiscated after a failed coup against Nero in AD 66. It eventually became part of the imperial real estate and Constantine and his wife Fausta (whom he later executed) once kept house in the Lateran Palace. Later he donated it to Pope Miltiades as a cult centre for the Christians of Rome. Almost nothing remains of the original basilica; the sacks of the Vandals and Normans, two earthquakes and several fires have resulted in a building made up of bits and pieces from each of the last 16 centuries.

Like Santa Maria Maggiore, this church has an 18th-century exterior that is almost miraculously good considering other Italian buildings from that age, with a west front by Alessandro Galilei (1736) that confidently and competently re-uses the High Renaissance architectural vernacular. The equally fine north façade is older, done by Domenico Fontana in 1586, and incorporates the twin medieval bell towers. Entering at the west front you pass an ancient statue of Constantine, found at the baths he built on the Quirinale; the bronze doors in the central portal once graced the Senate House in the Forum. Inside, the nave is dominated by giant statues of the Apostles (*c.* 1720), glaring down like Roman emperors of old. There is some carefree Baroque work in the side chapels – also remains of a fresco by Giotto, behind the first column on the right. Near the apse, decorated with 13th-century mosaics (of a reindeer worshipping the cross, an odd conceit probably adapted from older mosaics in Ravenna), the Papal Altar supposedly contains the heads of Peter and Paul. Below floor level is the tomb of Pope Martin V; pilgrims drop flowers and coins for luck.

Rome in the later Middle Ages had evolved an architectural style entirely its own, uninterested in Gothic or reviving classicism, or, for that matter, in anything else that was going on in the rest of Italy. Sadly, almost all of it disappeared in the Renaissance and Baroque rebuildings. The towers of Santa Maria in Cosmedin and Santa Maria Maggiore are good examples of it, as well as the expressive mosaics of Pietro Cavallini and his school and the intricate, geometrical Cosmatesque pavements in this church and so many others. Perhaps the most striking survival of this lost chapter in art is the Lateran **cloister** (*open daily 9–6, until 5 in winter; adm*), with its pairs of spiral columns and 13th-century Cosmatesque mosaics; it completely upstages everything else in the church. All around the cloister walls, fragments from the earlier incarnations of the basilica have been assembled, a hoard of broken pretty things that includes a tomb of a 13th-century bishop, perhaps the work of Arnolfo di Cambio.

The Lateran's **baptistry** (*open daily 8–12.30 and 3.30–7*) is no ordinary baptistry – nothing less than the first one in Christendom, converted from an older temple by Constantine; its octagonal form has been copied in other baptistries all over Italy. Inside there are unusual pairs of bronze doors on either side: one from 1196 with scenes of how the Lateran basilica appeared at that time, and the other from the Baths of Caracalla, 'singing' doors that make a low, harmonic sound when you open them slowly. Built around the baptistry are three venerable chapels with more mosaics from the early Middle Ages. The entrance to the baptistry is in Piazza San Giovanni in Laterano, behind the **Lateran Palace** (*t 06 6988 6452; open Mon–Sat 8–1; adm*) rebuilt in 1588 over the original building that had served as home for the popes from the 4th to the 14th centuries.

Across the piazza you will see the **Scala Santa** (*t 06 6988 6392; open daily 6.15–12 and 3.30–6.45, in winter 3–6*), supposedly the stairs of Pilate's palace in Jerusalem, ascended by Christ on his way to Judgement and brought to Rome by Constantine's mother, St Helena. Serious pilgrims ascend them on their knees. The Chapel of San Lorenzo at the top, a part of the medieval Papal Palace, contains two miraculous portraits of Jesus, painted by angels. While you're here, you have a good opportunity to explore the Aurelian Wall. The stretch of it behind the Lateran Palace probably looks much as it did originally, and the nearby **Porta Asinara** (next to Porta San Giovanni) is one of the best-preserved monumental ancient gateways.

Monte Celio

South of the Colosseum you can see nothing but trees, but, on every inch of this vast tract of parkland, ancient neighbourhoods wait just a few feet beneath the surface. Modern Rome never expanded in this direction, and almost the whole of it has been preserved as open space. It's a fascinating place to walk around, if you can avoid the traffic thundering down the big boulevards towards the southern suburbs. The Monte Celio is only a small part of it, but it is one of the least known and most delightful corners of Rome. Have a picnic in the **Villa Celimontana** (*behind Piazza della Navicella; open daily 7am–sunset*) and you may have only squirrels for company.

Some of Rome's most ancient churches repose in quiet settings here, all worth a look inside if they are open. **Santo Stefano Rotondo** (*Piazza della Navicella, at Via de Santo Stefano Rotondo, t 06 7049 3717; open Tues–Sat 9–1 and 3.30–6, Mon 3.30–6 only*), the oldest circular church in Italy, was built around 470 over the ruins of a marketplace of Nero's time. Across the street more mosaics from the age of Paschal I

(c. 820) can be seen in **Santa Maria in Domnica** (t 06 700 1519; open 9–12 and 3.30–7, in winter until 6) standing in **Piazza della Navicella**, with a fountain made in the form of an ancient Roman ship. Take the narrow road (just downhill from the church) that cuts down into the hill to **SS. Giovanni e Paolo** (open 8.30–12 and 3–6.30), built in the 4th century in the top floor of three Roman houses, which have just emerged from restoration and can be visited (adm). Down the western slope you reach **San Gregorio Magno** (t 06 5526 1617; open 8–12.30 and 4–6.30), begun by Pope Gregory the Great in 590. St Augustine lived here before being sent by Gregory to convert the Angles and Saxons of Britain. Adjacent to the church are several chapels with frescoes.

Circus Maximus and Terme di Caracalla (Caracalla's Baths)

Piazza Porta Capena, at the foot of the Monte Celio, has an odd decoration, an obelisk erected by Mussolini to commemorate his conquest of Ethiopia – he stole it from the Ethiopian city of Axum, although at long last it is scheduled to be returned. The piazza itself is a vortex of Mussolinian pretensions; the dictator built himself a new Triumphal Way (now Via San Gregorio) along the route of the original one, to celebrate his piddling triumphs in Roman imperial style. An enormous building that was to house the Ministry of Africa to administer Mussolini's colonies found a more agreeable use after the war – as home of the UN Food and Agricultural Organization (FAO). To the west, a broad green lawn is all that's left of the **Circus Maximus**. Archaeologists have estimated that as many as 300,000 Romans could squeeze in here and place their bets on the chariot races. Founded by King Tarquin and completed by Trajan, the stadium proved simply too convenient a quarry; the banked, horseshoe-shaped depression, however, still follows the line of the grandstands.

The **Terme di Caracalla** (AD 206–220), in a large park south of Porta Capena, rank with those of Diocletian as the largest and most lavish (t 06 975 8626; open Tues–Sun 9–1hr before sunset, Mon 9–2; adm, or with Roma Archeologia Card, p.101; guided tours Sat and Sun 10.30, audioguide €4). Roughly 1,000ft square, with libraries and exercise courts, the baths probably boasted more gold, marble and art than any building complex in Rome; here the Farnese family dug up such masterpieces as the Hercules and the Farnese Bull, now in the Naples Museum. In the 1700s these baths were one of the obligatory sights of the Grand Tour; their lofty, broken arches and vaults appealed to the Romantic love of ruins like no other. Much of the central building survives, with its mosaic-decorated hot and cold rooms, great hall and swimming pool. A large tunnel connects the baths with the area around Palazzo Venezia, a mile away; its purpose was to transport the vast amounts of wood needed to keep the baths hot. Mussolini initiated the custom (now provisionally discontinued owing to the frailty of the ruins) of holding summer operas here; he liked to drive his roadster through the tunnel and pop out dramatically on stage at the start of the festivities.

Behind the baths a stretch of the **Antonine Aqueduct** that supplied it can still be seen. On the other side, facing Via Terme di Caracalla, **SS. Nereo e Achilleo** (open daily 10–12 and 4–6; ring for custodian) has more mosaics from the time of Leo III (c. 800), a Cosmatesque floor and choir and some gruesome 16th-century frescoes of the martydoms of the saints.

The Via Appia: Rome's Catacombs

The hop-on, hop-off 'Archeobus' minibus departs from the Piazza Venezia and heads down the Via Appia to the Villa dei Quintili. There are hourly departures, and tickets (available on the bus) are valid all day, priced €7.75.

Rome's 'Queen of Roads', the path of trade and conquest to Campania, Brindisi and the East, was begun in 312 BC by Consul Appius Claudius. Like most of the consular roads outside Rome, over the centuries it became lined with cemeteries and the elaborate mausolea of the wealthy, since ancient Roman practice, inherited from the Etruscans, prohibited any burials within the *pomerium*, the sacred ground of the city itself. Later the early Christians built extensive catacombs here – the word itself comes from the location, *ad catacumbas*, referring to the dip in the Via Appia near the suburban Circus of Maxentius. The Via Appia Antica (as distinguished from the modern Via Appia Nuova) makes a pleasant excursion outside the city, especially on Sundays when the road is closed to traffic all the way back to Piazza Venezia.

The road passes under the Aurelian wall at **Porta San Sebastiano**, one of the best-preserved of the old gates. It houses the **Museo delle Mura** (*t 06 7047 5284; open Tues–Sun 9–7, in winter until 5.30; adm*), admission to which also gives you access to a well-preserved section of the 4th-century wall alongside it. Continuing along the road, after about ½km, with some ruins of tombs along the way, there is the famous church of **Domine Quo Vadis?** (*t 06 512 0441; open 7.30–6.45*), on the spot where Peter, fleeing from the dangers of Rome, met Christ coming the other way. 'Where goest thou, Lord?' Peter asked. 'I am going to be crucified once more,' was the reply. As the vision departed the shamed Apostle turned back, to face his own crucifixion in Rome.

Another kilometre or so takes you to the **Catacombe di San Callisto**, off on a side road to the right (*open for guided tours only, summer Thurs–Tues 8.30–12 and 2.30–5, winter 8.30–12 and 2.30–5, closed Feb; adm*). Here the biggest attraction is the 'Crypt of the Popes', burial places of 3rd- and 4th-century pontiffs with some well-executed frescoes and inscriptions. A word about catacombs: popular romance and modern cinema notwithstanding, these were never places of refuge from persecution, but simply burial grounds. The word 'catacombs' was only used after the 5th century; before that the Christians simply called them 'cemeteries'. The burrowing instinct is harder to explain. Few other places have ancient catacombs (Naples, Syracuse, Malta and the Greek island of Milos are among them). One of the requirements seems to be tufa, or some other stone that can be easily excavated. Even so, the work involved was tremendous, and not explainable by any reasons of necessity. Christians were still digging them after they had become a power in Rome, in Constantine's time. No one knows for certain what sort of funeral rites were celebrated in them, just as no one knows much about any of the prayers or rituals of the early Christians; we can only suspect that a Christian of the 4th century and one of the 16th would have had considerable difficulty recognizing each other as brothers in the faith.

Most catacombs began small, as private family cemeteries; over generations some grew into enormous termitaries extending for miles. Inside, most of the tombs you see will be simple *loculi*, walled-up niches with only a symbol or short inscription.

Others, especially the tombs of popes or the wealthy, may have paintings of scriptural scenes, usually very poor work that reflects more on the dire state of the late Roman imagination than on the Christians.

You can detour from here another ½km west to the **Catacombe di Santa Domitilla** (*Via delle Sette Chiese 283, t 06 511 0342; open Feb–Dec for guided tours only, Wed–Mon 8.30–12 and 2.30–5.30; adm*). She was a member of a senatorial family and, interestingly, the catacombs seem to incorporate parts of earlier pagan hypogea, including a cemetery of the Imperial Flavian family; the paintings include an unusual *Last Supper* scene, portraying a young and beardless Jesus and Apostles in Roman dress. There is an adjacent basilica, built about the tombs of SS. Nereus and Achilleus, on Via delle Sette Chiese. Not far away on Via Ardeatina 174 is a monument to martyrs of a very different sort, the **Mausoleum of the Fosse Ardeatine** (*t 06 513 6742; open Mon–Fri 8.15–6.45, weekends 8.15–3.30*), dedicated to the 335 Romans massacred by the Nazis on this spot in 1944 in retaliation for a partisan attack. Back on the Via Appia Antica, there are several catacombs near the corner of Via Appia Pignatelli, including a Jewish one (*closed*); the largest are the **Catacombe di San Sebastiano** (*t 06 788 735; open for guided tours only Fri–Wed 8.30–12 and 2.30–5.30, closed Nov; adm*). This complex, too, began as a pagan cemetery and has intriguing paintings and incised symbols throughout. The place had some special significance for the early Christians, and it has been conjectured that Peter and Paul were originally buried here, before their removal to the basilicas in Constantine's time.

Further south, by now in fairly open country, there are the ruins of the **Circus of Maxentius** (*t 06 780 1324; open April–Sept, Tues–Sat, 9–7 and Sun 9–1; Oct–Mar Tues–Sat 9–5, Sun 9–1; adm*), built in the early 4th century, and then the imposing cylindrical **tomb of Cecilia Metella** (*t 06 780 2465; open Tues–Sun 9–7; adm, or with Roma Archeologia Card, see p.101*), from the time of Augustus. In the Middle Ages the Caetani family turned the tomb into a family fortress, guarding the road to the south; at other times, before and since, it was a famous rendezvous for *banditti*. The road continues, flanked by tombs and stately pines, with stretches of the original paving, for 16km beyond the walls of Rome. Further out still are the extensive, marble-strewn remains of the **Villa dei Quintili** (*open 9am–one hour before sunset; adm, or with Roma Archeologia Card, see p.101*), built in the 2nd century AD by the Quintilius brothers and once the largest villa outside the city walls.

Monte Aventino

Every now and then, when left-wing parties walk out of negotiations, Italian newspapers may call it an 'Aventine Secession', a reference to events in Rome 2,500 years ago. Under the Republic, the Monte Aventino was the most solidly plebeian quarter of the city. On several occasions, when legislation proposed by the senate and consuls seriously threatened the rights or interests of the people, they retired *en masse* to the Aventino and stayed there until the plan was dropped. Rome's unionists are probably unaware that their ancestors had the honour of inventing the general strike.

The Aventino had another distinction in those times. In its uninhabited regions – the steep, cave-ridden slopes towards the south – Greek immigrants and returning soldiers introduced the midnight rituals of Dionysus/Bacchus. Though secret, such goings-on soon came to the attention of the senate, which rightly saw the orgies as a danger to the state and banned them in 146 BC. They must not have died out completely, however, as in the Middle Ages the Aventino had a reputation as a haunt of witches. The early Christian community also prospered here, and their churches are the oldest relics on the Aventino today.

Coming up from the Circus Maximus along Via Santa Sabina, **Santa Sabina** (*Piazza Pietro d'Illiria; open daily 6.30–12 and 3.30–7*) is a simple, rare example of a 5th-century basilica, with an atrium at its entrance like a Roman secular basilica, and an original door of cypress carved with scriptural scenes. This has been the head church of the Dominicans ever since a 13th-century pope gave it to St Dominic. Both Santa Sabina and the church of **Sant'Alessio** (*open daily 8.30–8*) down the street have good Cosmatesque cloisters. At the end of this street, one of the oddities only Rome can offer stands on its quiet square, oblivious of the centuries: the **Priorato dei Cavalieri di Malta** (*open for guided tours by prior arrangement; call t 06 577 9193*), a fancy rococo complex designed by Giambattista Piranesi. The Knights of Malta – or more properly, the Knights Hospitallers of St John – no longer wait for the popes to unleash them against Saracen and Turk. Mostly this social club for nobles bestirs itself to assist hospitals, its original job during the Crusades. The Order's ambassadors to Italy and the Vatican still live here. You can't go inside, but you can look through the keyhole.

Elsewhere on the Aventino, **Santa Prisca** (*t 06 3996 7700; open by appointment only*) has beginnings typical of an early Roman church; its crypt, the original church, was allegedly converted from the house of the martyr Prisca, host to St Peter; the Apostle must have often presided over Mass here. **San Saba** (*Via San Saba; open 7–12 and 4–7*) was founded in the 7th century by monks fleeing the Arabs in Jordan and Syria, with a 1205 rebuilding, including some Cosmatesque details, a superb mosaic floor and a crypt with 7th–11th-century frescoes.

Rome's Pyramid and Monte Testaccio

Porta San Paolo stands in one of the best-preserved sections of the Aurelian wall. The gate itself looks just as it did 1,700 years ago, when it was the *Porta Ostiense*; its change of name came about because Paul passed through it on the way to his execution. Near the gate is something unique: the 92ft **Pyramid of Caius Cestius** (AD 12) may seem a strange self-tribute for a Roman, but at least Cestius, who had served in Egypt, paid for the tomb himself.

Behind it, inside the walls, the lovely **Cimitero Protestante** (*Via Caio Cestio 6, t 06 574 1900; open Tues–Sun 9–5.30, in winter until 4.30; ring the bell at the gate; donation expected*) is a popular point of Romantic pilgrimage. The graves of Shelley and Keats are there, recently joined by 400 British soldiers who died during the march on Rome in 1944. Just to the west is the youngest of Rome's hills, **Monte Testaccio**, made up almost entirely of pot-shards. In ancient times, wine, oil, olives and nearly everything else were shipped in big *amphorae*; here, in what was Rome's port warehouse district, all the broken, discarded ones accumulated in one place. The vast cellars the Romans left beneath it are now used as workshops, wine cellars and nightclubs that make Testaccio a swinging area after dark.

San Paolo Fuori le Mura (Outside the Walls)

t 06 541 0341; basilica open 7–6.30, cloister 9–1 and 3–6.

Paul was beheaded near the Ostia road; according to an old legend, the head bounced three times, and at each place where it hit a fountain sprung up. The Abbazia delle Tre Fontane, near EUR, occupies the site today. Later, Constantine built a basilica alongside the road as a fitting resting place for the saint. Of the five patriarchal basilicas this one has had the worst luck. Today it sits in the middle of factories, gasworks and concrete flats. Once St Paul's was the grandest of them all; 9th-century chroniclers speak of the separate walled city of 'Giovannipolis' that had grown up around it, connected to the Aurelian wall by a 1½km-long colonnade built by Pope John VIII in the 870s. The Norman sack of 1084, a few good earthquakes, and finally a catastrophic fire in 1823 wiped Giovannipolis off the map, and left us with a St Paul's that for the most part is barely more than a century old. Still, the façade of golden mosaics and sturdy Corinthian columns is pleasant to look at, and some features survive – the 11th-century door made in Constantinople, a Gothic *baldacchino* over Paul's tomb by Arnolfo di Cambio, a 13th-century Cosmatesque cloister, and 5th-century mosaics over the 'Triumphal Arch' in front of the apse, the restored remains of the original mosaics from the façade, contributed by Empress Galla Placidia. Art Deco is not what you would expect from those times, but Americans at least will have a hard time believing these mosaics were not done by President Roosevelt's WPA. The apse itself has some more conventional mosaics from the 13th-century Roman school, and the nave is lined with the portraits of all 263 popes. According to one Roman legend, when the remaining eight spaces are filled, the world will end.

On the same road as San Paolo (Via Ostiense), is the **Centrale Montemartini** (*open Tues–Sun 9.30–7; adm, combined ticket available with Musei Capitolini (see p.124); metro to Garbatella and cross the flyover towards the Via Ostiense, or take a bus to the Via Ostiense*). The Capitoline Museums have found an unusual home for the overflow of their great hoard of ancient art; this converted power station makes a dramatic setting for busts, mosaics and statuary which are arranged around two enormous power generators. There's a peaceful café on the top floor.

Trastevere

So often just being on the wrong side of the river encourages a city district to cultivate its differences and its eccentricities. Trastevere isn't really a Left Bank – more of a pocket-sized Brooklyn, and as in Brooklyn those differences and eccentricities often turn out to be the old habits of the whole city, preserved in an out-of-the-way corner. The people of Trastevere are more Roman than the Romans. Indeed, they claim to be the real descendants of the Romans of old; one story traces their ancestry back to the sailors who worked the great awning at the Colosseum. Such places have a hard time surviving these days, especially when they are as trendy as Trastevere is right now. But even though such things as Trastevere's famous school of dialect poets may be mostly a memory, the quarter remains the liveliest in Rome.

Just over Ponte Garibaldi is Piazza Sonnino, with the **Torre degli Anguillara**, an uncommon survival of the defence towers that once loomed over medieval Rome, and the 12th-century church of **San Crisogono** (*t 06 581 8225; open Mon–Sat 7am–7.30pm, Sun 8–1 and 4.15–7.30*), with mosaics by Pietro Cavallini, built over the remains of an earlier church. Near the bridge, the statue in the top hat is Giuseppe Gioacchino Belli, one of Trastevere's 19th-century dialect poets. Turn left on to one of the narrow streets off Viale di Trastevere and make your way to the church of **Santa Cecilia in Trastevere** (*t 06 589 9289; open daily 9.30–1 and 4–7.15*), founded over the house of the 2nd-century martyr whom centuries of hagiography have turned into one of the most agreeable of saints, the inventor of the organ and patroness of music. Cecilia was disinterred in 1599, and her body was found entirely uncorrupted. Clement VIII commissioned Maderno to sculpt an exact copy from sketches made before her body dissolved into thin air; this charming work can be seen near the altar.

Nearby there is a *Tabernacle* by Arnolfo di Cambio similar to the one in St Paul's, and 9th-century mosaics in the apse. The church has other treasures: Renaissance tombs, including one of a 14th-century cardinal from Hertford; frescoes by the school of Pinturicchio in a chapel on the right; and a crypt built in the underlying Roman constructions, thought to be Cecilia's home (*adm*). Up in the singing gallery (*visits to Cavallini's frescoes Sun 11.15–12, Tues and Thurs 10–12; adm*) are the remains of the original church wall decoration – a wonderful fresco of the *Last Judgement* by Cavallini.

Across Viale di Trastevere – an intrusive modern boulevard that slices the district in two – lies the heart of old Trastevere, around **Piazza Santa Maria in Trastevere** and its church. Most of this building dates from the 1140s, though the original church, begun perhaps in 222, may be the first anywhere dedicated to the Virgin Mary. The medieval building is a treasure-house of Roman mosaics. The piazza, and the streets around it, has been for decades one of the most popular spots in Rome for restaurants; tables are spread out wherever there's room, and there is always a crowd in the evening.

Two Roads to St Peter's

One is broad and straight, the route of the many; the other is tortuous and narrow, and after it but few enquire. **Via della Lungara**, the route of the slothful from Trastevere, takes you past **Villa Farnesina** (*open Mon–Sat 9–1; adm*), an early 1500s palace built for the Chigi family. Inside are some of the best frescoes in Rome: the *Galatea* by Raphael and the *Cupid and Psyche Gallery*, designed by Raphael, a prospect of the constellations and a room of false perspectives by Baldassare Peruzzi, who also designed the building; and works of Sodoma. Across the street, the **Palazzo Corsini** (*t 06 6880 2323; open Tues–Sat 8.30–6.30, Sun 9–1; adm*) contains an exceptional collection of 16th- and 17th-century art, including works by Caravaggio, Van Dyck, Guido Reni, Salvatore Rosa and many others – it's out of the way, but this may be the best of all Rome's many small state picture galleries.

The other road may be more difficult to find, but repays the effort with lovely gardens and views over Rome from the Gianicolo, the ancient *Janiculum*. First find Via Garibaldi, in the back streets behind Ponte Sisto, and continue up to the Renaissance church of **San Pietro in Montorio** (*t 06 581 3940; open 9–12 and 4–6; if closed, ring bell at door to right of church*), once erroneously believed to be the spot of St Peter's upside-down crucifixion. A popular church for weddings, it has several fine paintings in the shallow chapels, including a marvellous *Flagellation* by Sebastiano del Piombo – but the real draw here is Bramante's famed **Tempietto** in the adjacent courtyard. In so many Renaissance paintings – Perugino's *Donation of the Keys* in the Sistine Chapel or Raphael's *Betrothal of the Virgin* in Milan – the characters in the foreground take second place in interest to an ethereal, round temple centred at the perspectival vanishing point. These constructions, seemingly built not of vulgar stone but of pure intelligence and light, could stand as a symbol for the aspirations of the Renaissance. Bramante was the first actually to try to build one; his perfect little Tempietto (1502), the first building to re-use the ancient Doric order in all of its proportions, probably inspired Raphael's painting two years later.

Via Garibaldi continues up the *Janiculum* to the gushing **Acqua Paola Fountain**, where you should turn right along the Passeggiata del Gianicolo. The **Garibaldi Monument** stands at the summit, overlooking the Botanical Gardens and the rest of Rome. At the other end of the hill, going towards the Vatican, the road curves downwards, passing the Renaissance church of **Sant'Onofrio** (*open daily 9–1*), with frescoes by Peruzzi in the apse. After descending the Passeggiata del Gianicolo, cross the modern Piazza della Rovere into the Borgo district. On your right is the hospital of Santo Spirito and the church of **Santo Spirito in Sassia** (*open daily 7.30–12 and 3–7.30*). This name may ring a bell for antiquarians. 'Sassia' refers to the Saxons of England, who upon their conversion became among the most devoted servants of the Church. English princes founded this hospital in the 8th century. The Angles and Saxons who settled in Rome made up almost a small village unto themselves at this bend of the Tiber, and their 'burgh' gave its name to the neighbourhood called the Borgo today.

Castel Sant'Angelo

Lungotevere Castello 50, t 06 3996 7600; open Tues–Sun 9–8; adm; English audioguide €4. Guided visits, by reservation (extra charge), of the castle in English Tues–Fri 10.30am, Sat–Sun 10.30, 12.15 and 4.30; and of the prisons in English Sun 2.30pm. Times of guided tours change, so call in advance.

Though intended as a resting place for a most serene emperor, this building has seen more blood, treachery and turmoil than any in Rome. Hadrian designed his own mausoleum three years before his death in 138, on an eccentric plan consisting of a huge marble cylinder surmounted by a conical hill planted with cypresses. The marble, obelisks and gold and bronze decorations did not survive the 5th-century sacks, but in *c.* 590, during a plague, Pope Gregory the Great saw a vision of St Michael over the mausoleum, ostensibly announcing the end of the plague, but perhaps also mentioning discreetly that here, if anyone cared to use it, was the most valuable fortress in Europe.

There would be no papacy, perhaps, without this castle – at least not in its present form. Hadrian's cylinder is high, steep and almost solid – impregnable even after the invention of artillery. With rebellions of some sort occurring on average every two years before 1400 the popes often had recourse to this place of safety. It last saw action in the sack of 1527, when the miserable Clement VII withstood a siege of several months while his city went up in flames. The popes also used Castel Sant'Angelo as a prison; famous inmates included Giordano Bruno, Benvenuto Cellini and Beatrice Cenci. Tosca tosses herself off the top at the end of Puccini's opera.

Inside, the recently restored spiral ramp leads up to the **Papal Apartments**, decorated as lavishly by 16th-century artists as anything in the Vatican. The **Sala Paolina** has frescoes by Perin del Vaga of events in the history of Rome, and the **Sala di Apollo** is frescoed with grotesques attempting to reproduce the wall decorations of Nero's Golden House. A mighty statue of Michael commemorates Gregory's vision. Castel Sant'Angelo makes a great place to rest after the Vatican. The views from the roof are some of the best in Rome, and there's a café on the 4th floor. The three central arches of the **Ponte Sant'Angelo** were built by Hadrian, although the statues of angels added in 1688 steal the show; at once dubbed Bernini's Breezy Maniacs, they battle a never-ending Baroque hurricane to display the symbols of Christ's Passion.

Vatican City

The world's smallest country contains the world's largest museum, piazza, and church. It is next to impossible to see the Vatican Museums, St Peter's and Castel Sant'Angelo all in one day, let alone the **Vatican Gardens**, easily Rome's most beautiful park, with a remarkable Renaissance jewel of a villa inside: the Casino of Pius IV (1558–62) by Pietro Ligorio and Peruzzi (*morning tours May–Sept, Mon–Tues and Thurs–Sat; Oct–April on Sat; €9 per person; reserve a few days in advance with the Vatican information office*). Nor will you fit in the afternoon tour of the ancient **necropolis** under St Peter's – underneath the crypt, archaeologists in the 1940s discovered a street of Roman tombs, perfectly preserved with many beautiful paintings (*open by reservation only for 1½-hour guided visits (in English); adm €8. Call the Ufficio degli Scavi, just to the left of St Peter's, t 06 6988 5318, for information; then fax them, f 06 6988 5518, with your name, nationality, the language you want a tour in, the dates you are in Rome, an email address and a contact number in Rome – they will then confirm a date and time*).

Michelangelo also designed the **wall** that since 1929 has marked the Vatican boundaries. Behind it are things most of us will never see: several small old churches, a printing press, the headquarters of L'Osservatore Romano and Vatican Radio (run, of course, by the Jesuits), a motor garage, a 'Palazzo di Giustizia' and even a big shop –

Vatican Practicalities

The **museums** are *open Mar–Oct Mon–Fri 8.45–2.20, Sat 8.45–12.20, Nov–Feb Mon–Sat 8.45–12.20; adm; also open (and free) the last Sun of each month 8.45–12.20.* Times are subject to change so confirm in advance. The entrance is on Viale Vaticano, to the north of Piazza San Pietro.

St Peter's is *open daily Nov–March 7–6, April–Oct 8–7;* the basilica is closed when there are official ceremonies in the piazza, although visitors are allowed during Mass. The **dome** is *open summer 8.30–5.45, winter 8.30–4.45* and the **Treasury,** *9–6.15.* The dress code – no shorts, short skirts or sleeveless dresses – is strictly controlled by the papal gendarmes. Free guided visits to St Peter's in English on Sun at 2.30, Mon, Wed–Sun at 3pm.

The **Vatican Information Office, t** *o6 6988 1662,* in Piazza San Pietro *(open daily 8.30–7)* is very helpful, and there are Vatican post offices on the opposite side of the square and inside the Vatican Museums for distinctive postcards home. The information office arranges 2hr-long morning tours of the **Vatican Gardens,** The rest of the Vatican is strictly off limits, patrolled by Swiss Guards (still recruited from the three Catholic Swiss cantons).

For tickets to the Wednesday morning **papal audience,** usually held at 10.30am in the piazza *(May–Sept)* or in the Nervi Auditorium *(Oct–April),* apply in advance at the Papal Prefecture – through the bronze door in the right-hand colonnade of Piazza San Pietro *(open Mon–Sat 9–1.30, t o6 6988 3114, f o6 6988 5863; collect tickets Mon–Sat 3–8 at the Portone del Bronzo on Piazza San Pietro).*

everything the world's smallest nation could ever need. Modern popes, in contrast to their predecessors, do not take up much space. The current Papal Apartments are in a corner of the Vatican Palace overlooking Piazza San Pietro; John Paul II usually appears to say a few electrically amplified words from his window at noon on Sundays.

St Peter's

Along Borgo Sant'Angelo, leading towards the Vatican, you can see the famous **covered passageway,** used by the popes since 1277 to escape to the castle when things became dangerous. The customary route, however, leads up **Via della Conciliazione**, a broad boulevard drilled by Mussolini through the tangled web of medieval streets. Critics have said it spoils the surprise, but no arrangement of streets and buildings could really prepare you for Bernini's Brobdingnagian **Piazza San Pietro**. Someone has calculated there is room for about 300,000 people in the piazza, with no crowding. Few have ever noticed Bernini's little joke on antiquity; the open space almost exactly meets the size and dimensions of the Colosseum. Bernini's **Colonnade** (1656), with 284 massive columns and statues of 140 saints, stretches around it like 'the arms of the Church embracing the world' – perhaps the biggest cliché in Christendom by now, but exactly what Bernini had in mind. Stand on either of the two dark stones at the foci of the elliptical piazza and you will see Bernini's forest of columns resolve into neat rows, a subtly impressive optical effect like the hole in the top of the Pantheon. Flanked by two lovely fountains, the work of Maderno and Fontana, the Vatican **obelisk** seems nothing special as obelisks go, but is actually one of the most fantastical relics in all Rome. This obelisk comes from Heliopolis, founded as a capital and cult centre by Akhnaton, the half-legendary Pharaoh who, according to Sigmund Freud and others, founded the first monotheistic religion, influencing Moses and all that came after. Caligula brought it over to Rome in AD 37 to decorate the now-disappeared Circus Vaticanus (later referred to as the Circus of Nero) where it

St Peter's

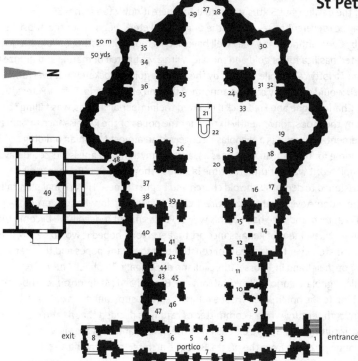

50 m
50 yds

N

exit

entrance

portico

1   Statue of Constantine/ Scala Regia
2   Holy Door
3   Crocetti Door
4   Filarete Door
5   Manzù Door
6   Minguzzi Door
7   Giotto's Navicella
8   Statue of Charlemagne
9   Michelangelo's *Pietà*
10   Queen Christina Monument
11   Cappella di San Sebastino
12   Countess Matilda Monument
13   Innocent XII Monument
14   Cappella del Santissimo Sacramento
15   Gregory XIII Monument
16   Cappella Gregoriana
17   Madonna del Soccorso
18   Lift up to Dome
19   Altar of St Wenceslas
20   Statue of St Peter
21   High Altar/Bernini's Baldacchino
22   Confessio
23   St Longinus / entrance to Grottoes
24   St Helen
25   St Veronica
26   St Andrew
27   Tribune / Cathedra of St Peter
28   Urban VIII Monument
29   Paul III Monument
30   Guercino's St Petronilla
31   Altar of the Navicella
32   Clement XIII Monument
33   St Bruno
34   Cappella della Colonna
35   Leo the Great Tomb
36   Alexander VII Monument
37   Cappella Clementina
38   Pius VII Monument
39   Leo XI Monument
40   Cappella del Coro
41   Innocent VIII Monument
42   Pius X Monument
43   Cappella della Presentazione
44   John XXIII Monument
45   Clementina Sobieska Monument/stairs and
     down lift from Dome
46   Monument to the last Stuarts
47   Baptistry
48   Pius VIII Monument / entrance to St Peter's
     Treasury
49   Sacristy

would have overlooked Peter's martyrdom. In the Middle Ages it was placed to the side of the basilica, but Sixtus V moved it to where it now stands in 1586.

It may be irreverent to say so, but the original St Peter's, begun over the Apostle's tomb by Constantine in 324, may well have been a more interesting building: a richly decorated basilica full of gold and mosaics with a vast porch of marble and bronze in front and a lofty campanile, topped by the famous golden cockerel that everyone believed would some day crow to announce the end of the world. This St Peter's, where Charlemagne and Frederick II received their imperial crowns, was falling to pieces by the 1400s, conveniently in time for the popes of the Renaissance to plan a replacement. In about 1450 Nicholas V conceived an almost Neronian building programme for the Vatican, ten times as large as anything his ancestors could have contemplated. It was not until the time of Julius II, however, that Bramante was commissioned to demolish the old church and begin the new. His original plan called for a great dome over a centralized Greek cross. Michelangelo, who took over in 1546, basically agreed, and if he had had his way St Peter's might indeed have become the crowning achievement of Renaissance art that everyone hoped it would be.

Unfortunately over the 120 years of construction too many popes and too many artists got their hand in – Rossellino, Giuliano da Sangallo, Raphael, Antonio da Sangallo, Vignola, Ligorio, della Porta, Fontana, Bernini and Maderno all contributed something to the hotchpotch we see today. The most substantial tinkering came in the early 17th century, when a committee of cardinals decided that a Latin cross was desired, resulting in the huge extension of the nave that blocks the view of Michelangelo's dome from the piazza. Baroque architects, mistaking size and virtu-osity for art, found perfect patrons in the Baroque popes, interested in the power and majesty of the papacy. Passing through Maderno's gigantic façade seems like entering a Grand Central Station full of stone saints and angels, keeping an eye on the clocks overhead as they wait for trains to Paradise. All along the nave, markers showing the length of other proud cathedrals prove how each fails to measure up to the Biggest Church in the World. This being Rome, not even the markers are honest – Milan's cathedral is actually 63ft longer.

The best is on the right: Michelangelo's *Pietà*, now restored and kept behind glass to protect it from future madmen. Sculpted when he was only 25, it helped make Michelangelo's reputation. Its smooth and elegant figures, with the realities of death and grief sublimated on to some ethereal plane known only to saints and artists, were a turning point in religious art. From here the beautiful, unreal art of the reli-gious Baroque was the logical next step. Michelangelo carved his name in small letters on the band around the Virgin's garment after overhearing a group of tourists from Milan who thought the *Pietà* the work of a fellow Milanese. Not much else in St Peter's really stands out. In its vast spaces scores of popes and saints are remem-bered in assembly-line Baroque; the paintings over most of the altars have been replaced by mosaic copies. The famous bronze statute of St Peter, its foot worn away by the touch of millions of pilgrims, is by the right front pier. Stealing the show, as he knew it would, is Bernini's great, garish **baldacchino** over the high altar, cast out of bronze looted from the Pantheon roof.

Many visitors head straight for Michelangelo's **dome** (*open summer 8.30–5.45, winter 8.30–4.45; adm €5 with lift, €4 without. There are still 320 steps AFTER the lift to get right up to the cupola viewing terrace*). To be in the middle of such a spectacular construction is worth the climb itself. You can walk out on to the roof for a view over Rome, but even more startling is the chance to look down from the interior balcony over the vast church 250ft below. In the **treasury** (*open 9–6.15; adm*), built in the 18th century, there are a number of treasures – those the Saracens, the imperial soldiers of 1527, and Napoleon couldn't steal. Do not pass up a descent to the **Sacred Grottoes** (*same hours as basilica*), the foundation of the earlier St Peter's converted into a crypt. Dozens of popes are buried here, along with distinguished friends of the Church like Queen Christina of Sweden and James III, the Stuart pretender. Perhaps the greatest work of art here is the bronze tomb of Sixtus IV, a definitive Renaissance confection by Pollaiuolo, though the most visited is undoubtedly the monument to John XXIII.

The Musei Vaticani (Vatican Museums)

The admission (*currently €10, audioguides €5*) may be the most expensive in Italy, but for that you get 10 museums in one, with the Sistine Chapel and the Raphael rooms thrown in free. Altogether almost 7km of exhibits fill the halls of the Vatican Palace, and unfortunately for you there isn't much dull museum clutter that can be passed over lightly. Seeing this infinite, exasperating hoard properly would be the work of a lifetime. On the bright side, the pope sees to it that his museum is managed more intelligently and thoughtfully than anything run by the Italian state. A choice of two colour-coded itineraries, which you may follow according to the amount of time you have to spend, will get you through the labyrinth in two or four hours.

Near the entrance, the first big challenge is the large **Museo Egizio** – one of Europe's best Egyptian collections – and then some rooms of antiquities from the Holy Land and Syria, before the **Museo Chiaramonti**, full of Roman statuary (including famous busts of Caesar, Mark Antony and Augustus) and inscriptions. The **Museo Pio Clementino** contains some of the best-known statues of antiquity: the dramatic *Laocoön*, dug up in Nero's Golden House, and the *Apollo Belvedere*. No other ancient works recovered during the Renaissance had a greater influence on sculptors than these two. A 'room of animals' captures the more fanciful side of antiquity, and the 2nd-century 'Baroque' tendency in Roman art comes out clearly in a group called 'The Nile', complete with sphinxes and crocodiles – it comes from a Roman temple of Isis. The bronze papal fig-leaves that protect the modesty of hundreds of nude statues are a good joke at first – it was the same spirit that put breeches on the saints in Michelangelo's *Last Judgement*, ordered by Pius IV once Michelangelo was safely dead.

The best things in the **Museo Etrusco** are Greek, a truly excellent collection of vases imported by discriminating Etruscan nobles that includes the famous *Oedipus and the Sphinx*. Beyond that, there is a hall hung with beautiful high-medieval tapestries from Tournai (15th century), and the long, long **Galleria delle Carte Geografiche**, lined with carefully painted town views and maps of every corner of Italy; note the long scene of the 1566 Great Siege of Malta at the entrance. Anywhere else, with no Michelangelos to offer competition, Raphael's celebrated frescoes in the **Stanza della**

The Vatican Museums

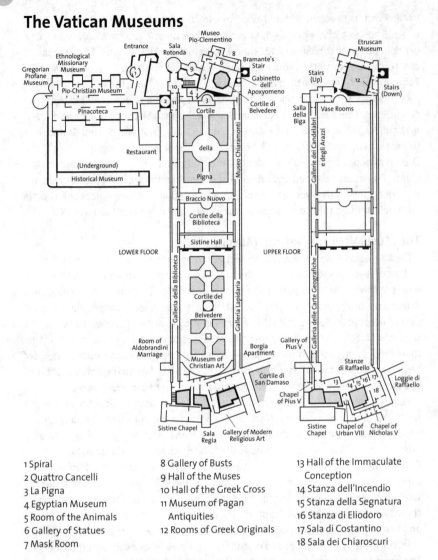

1 Spiral
2 Quattro Cancelli
3 La Pigna
4 Egyptian Museum
5 Room of the Animals
6 Gallery of Statues
7 Mask Room

8 Gallery of Busts
9 Hall of the Muses
10 Hall of the Greek Cross
11 Museum of Pagan Antiquities
12 Rooms of Greek Originals

13 Hall of the Immaculate Conception
14 Stanza dell'Incendio
15 Stanza della Segnatura
16 Stanza di Eliodoro
17 Sala di Costantino
18 Sala dei Chiaroscuri

Segnatura would have been the prime destination on anyone's itinerary. The *School of Athens* is too well known to require an introduction, but here is a guide to some of the figures: on Aristotle's side, Archimedes and Euclid surrounded by their disciples (Euclid, drawing plane figures on a slate, is a portrait of Bramante); off to the right, Ptolemy and Zoroaster hold the terrestrial and celestial globes. Raphael includes himself among the Aristotelians, between Zoroaster and the painter Sodoma. Behind Plato stand Socrates and Alcibiades, and to the left, Zeno and Epicurus. In the foreground, Pythagoras writes while Empedocles and the Arab Averroes look on. Diogenes sprawls philosophically on the steps, while isolated near the front is Heraclitus –

really Michelangelo; Raphael put him in at the last minute after seeing the work in progress in the Sistine Chapel.

Across from this apotheosis of philosophy, Raphael painted a Triumph of Theology to keep the clerics happy, the *Dispute of the Holy Sacrament*. The other frescoes include the *Parnassus*, a vision of the ancient Greek and Latin poets, the *Miracle of Bolsena*, the *Expulsion of Heliodorus*, an allegory of the triumphs of the Counter-Reformation papacy, the *Meeting of Leo I and Attila* and, best of all, the solemn, spectacularly lit *Liberation of St Peter*. Nearby, there is the **Loggia** of Bramante, also with decoration designed by Raphael, though executed by other artists (*only visitable with written permission*), and the chapel of **Nicholas V**, with frescoes by Fra Angelico. The **Appartamento Borgia**, a luxurious suite built for Pope Alexander VI, has walls decorated by Pinturicchio. These run into the **Opere d'Arte Religiosa Moderna**, a game attempt by the Vatican to prove that such a thing really exists.

The Sistine Chapel (*Cappella Sistina*)

To the sophisticated Sixtus IV, building this ungainly barn of a chapel may have seemed a mistake in the first place. When the pushy, despotic Julius II sent Michelangelo up, against his will, to paint the vast ceiling, it might have turned out to be a project as hopeless as the tomb Julius had already commissioned. Michelangelo spent four years of his life (1508–12) on the Sistine Ceiling. No one can say what drove him to turn his surly patron's whim into a masterpiece: the fear of wasting those years, the challenge of an impossible task, or maybe just to spite Julius – he exasperated the pope by making him wait, and refused all demands to hire assistants.

Everywhere on the Sistine Ceiling you will note the austere blankness of the backgrounds. Michelangelo always eschewed stage props; one of the tenets of his art was that complex ideas could be expressed in the portrayal of the human body alone. With sculpture, that takes time. Perhaps the inspiration that kept Michelangelo on the ceiling so long was the chance of distilling out of the Book of Genesis and his own genius an entirely new vocabulary of images, Christian and intellectual. Like most Renaissance patrons, Julius had asked for nothing more than virtuoso interior decoration. What he got was the way the Old Testament looks in the deepest recesses of the imagination. The fascination of the Sistine Ceiling, and the equally compelling *Last Judgement* on the rear wall, done much later (1534–41), is that while we may recognize the individual figures we still have not captured their secret meanings. Hordes of tourists stare up at the heroic Adam, the mysterious *ignudi* in the corners, the Russian masseuse sibyls with their longshoremen's arms, the six-toed prophets, the strange vision of Noah's deluge. They wonder what they're looking at, a question that would take years of inspired wondering to answer. Mostly they direct their attention to the all-too-famous scene of the Creation, with perhaps the only representation of God the Father ever painted that escapes being merely ridiculous. One might suspect that the figure is really some ageing Florentine artist, and that Michelangelo only forgot to paint the brush in his hand.

The restoration of the ceiling and *Last Judgement*, paid for by a Japanese television network, have accurately revealed Michelangelo's true colours – jarring, surprise colours that no interior decorator would ever choose, plenty of sea-green, with splashes of yellow and purple and dramatic shadows. No new paint was applied, only solvents to clear off the grime. Most visitors overlook the earlier frescoes on the lower walls, great works of art that would have made the Sistine Chapel famous by themselves: scenes from the *Exodus* by Botticelli, Perugino's *Donation of the Keys*, and Signorelli's Moses *Consigning his Staff to Joshua*.

More Miles in the Big Museum

There's still the **Vatican Library** to go, with its seemingly endless halls and precious manuscripts tucked neatly away in cabinets. The brightly painted rooms contain thousands of reliquaries and monstrances, medieval ivories, gold-glass medallions from the catacombs, and every sort of globe, orrery and astronomical instrument. If you survive this, the next hurdle is the new **Museo Gregoriano**, with a hoard of classical statuary, mosaics and inscriptions collected by Pope Gregory XVI. Then comes a museum of **carriages** (*closed for restoration*), the **Museo Pio-Cristiano** of early-Christian art and, finally, one of the most interesting of all, the museum of **ethnology**, with wonderful art from every continent, brought home to Italy by missionaries.

By itself the Vatican **Pinacoteca** would be by far the finest picture gallery in Rome, a representative sampling of Renaissance art from its beginnings, with some fine works of Giotto (*Il Redentore* and the *Martyrdoms of Peter and Paul*) and contemporary Sienese painters, as well as Gentile da Fabriano, Sano di Pietro and Filippo Lippi. Don't overlook the tiny but electrically surreal masterpiece of Fra Angelico, the *Story of St Nicolas at Bari*, or the *Angelic Musicians* of Melozzo da Forlì, set next to Melozzo's famous painting of Platina being nominated by Sixtus IV to head the Vatican Library – a rare snapshot of Renaissance humanism. Venetian artists are not well represented, but there is a *Pietà* by Bellini and a *Madonna* by the fastidious Carlo Crivelli. Perhaps the best-known paintings are the *Transfiguration of Christ*, Raphael's last work, and the *St Jerome* of Da Vinci.

EUR

By the late 1930s Mussolini was proud enough of his accomplishments to plan a world fair. A vast area south of Rome was cleared and transformed into a grid of wide boulevards and huge pavilions. War intervening, the Esposizione Universale di Roma never came off. After 1945 the Italians tried to make the best of it, turning EUR into a model satellite city and trade centre, on the lines of La Défense in Paris: a chilly nightmare of modernism. Some of the older corners reveal giant Fascist mosaics, and at the end of the Boulevard of Civilization and Labour you can have a look at the modest masterpiece of Mussolini architecture – a small, elegantly proportioned **Palazzo della Civiltà del Lavoro**, nicknamed the Square Colosseum. EUR is also home to a few good museums: the **Museo della Civiltà Romana**, Piazza G. Agnelli 10 (*open Tues–Sat 9–6.45, Sun 9–1.30; adm*), with exhibits including a huge scale-model of ancient Rome; a **museum of prehistory and ethnography**, Piazza Marconi 14 (*open Tues–Sun 9–8; adm*), and a **museum of the early Middle Ages**, Viale Lincoln 3 (*open Tues–Sat 9–8; adm*).

Venice

Venice

PONTE DELLA LIBERTA

Rio della Madonna dell'Orto

Madonna
dell'Orto

Rio della sensa

Palazzo
Mastelli

PONTE DEI
TRE ARCHI

Canale di Cannaregio

VECCHIO CAMPO
DEL
GHETTO

FONDAMENTA DELLA MISERICORDIA

GHETTO

CANNAREGIO

RIO TERÀ DI S. LEONARDO

Palazzo Correr
Contarini

Palazzo
Vendramin
Calergi

Scalzi

LISTA DI
SPAGNA

Casino

SS. Apostoli

Canal Grande

RIO DI S. FELICE

STRADA NUOVA

PONTE DEGLI
SCALZI

RIVA DI BIASIO

Fondaco
dei Turchi

Ca d'Oro

Stazione
S.Lucia

Canal Grande

FOND. S. SIMEON

S. Simeone
Piccolo

CAMPO
S. GIACOMO
DELL'ORIO

SANTA CROCE

CAMPO S.
BARTOLOMEO

Giardini
Papadopoli

CAMPO
S. STIN

RUGA VECCHIA

PONTE DI
RIALTO

Stazione
Marittima

PIAZZALE
ROMA

S. Rocco

Frari

CAMPO
S. POLO

RIO DI S. POLO

RIVA DEL VIN

Canale della Scomenzera

FOND. DEI TRE PONTI

FOND MINOTTO

SAN POLO

Casa del
Goldoni

Pal. Corner
Spinelli

Pal.
Corner

RIVA DEL CARBON

CALLE DEI FABBRI

Pal.
Bembo

Rio Nuovo

SALIZZADA S.
PANTALON

Pal. Pisani

Pal.
Fortuny

C. DELLA
MANDOLA

Teatro
Goldoni

FOND.
ROSSA

Rio delle Procuratie

Rio di S. Margherita

CAMPO S.
MARGHERITA

RIO. Ca' Foscari

Palazzo
Balbi

Palazzo
Mocenigo

CAMPO
S. ANGELO

CALLE VALLARESSO

Ca' Foscari

Palazzo
Grassi

SAN MARCO

Ca'
Rezzonico

S. Stefano

La Fenice

S. Moisè

San
Sebastiano

Rio di S. Barnaba

CAMPO
S. STEFANO

Ca'
Corner

Stazione
Marittima

CALLE LUNGA S. BARNABA

DORSODURO

Ca'
Giustinian

CAMPO S.
BASILIO

Rio Ognissanti

RIO S. TROVASO

PONTE
DELL'ACCADEMIA

Grande

Pal.
Pisani

Accademia

RIO TERRA A. FOSC.

Gesuati

FOND BRAGADIN

Peggy
Guggenheim
Collection

S. Maria
della Salute

Dogana
di Mare

ZATT. AI GESUATI

ZATT. AL SP SANTO

ZATT. AL SALONI

Canale della Giudecca

Palazzo
Vendramin

GIUDECCA

Redentore

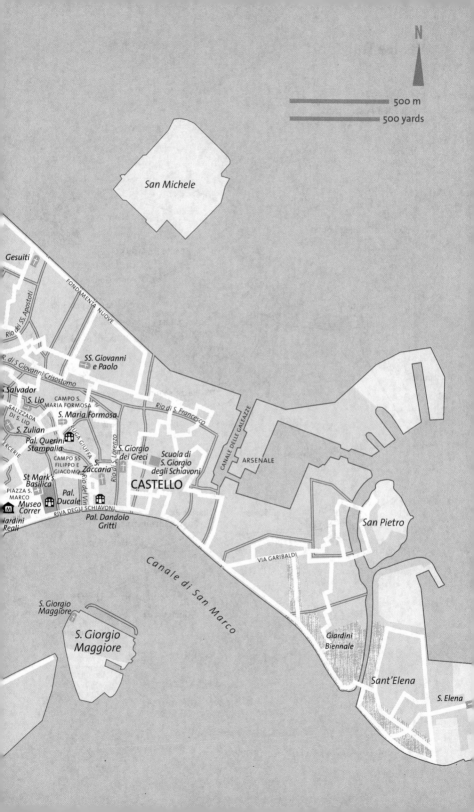

N

500 m
500 yards

San Michele

Gesuiti

FONDAMENTA NUOVE

Rio dei SS. Apostoli

R. di S Giovanni Crisostomo

SS. Giovanni e Paolo

S.Salvador

S. Lio

CAMPO S. MARIA FORMOSA

SALIZZADA DI S. LIO

S. Maria Formosa

Rio di S. Francesco

S. Zulian

MERCERIE

Pal. Querini Stampalia

RUGA GIUFFA

Rio di S. Lorenzo

S. Giorgio dei Greci

Scuola di S. Giorgio degli Schiavoni

CANALE DELLE GALEAZZE

ARSENALE

CAMPO SS FILIPPO E GIACOMO

St Mark's Basilica

S. Zaccaria

Rio del Vin

CASTELLO

PIAZZA S. MARCO

Pal. Ducale

Museo Correr

Giardini Reali

RIVA DEGLI SCHIAVONI

Pal. Dandolo Gritti

San Pietro

VIA GARIBALDI

Canale di San Marco

S. Giorgio Maggiore

S. Giorgio Maggiore

Giardini Biennale

Sant'Elena

S. Elena

Venice Transport

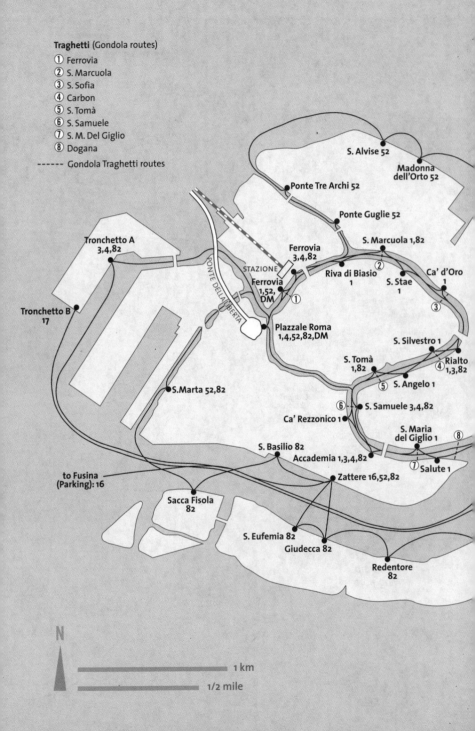

Traghetti (Gondola routes)
1. Ferrovia
2. S. Marcuola
3. S. Sofia
4. Carbon
5. S. Tomà
6. S. Samuele
7. S. M. Del Giglio
8. Dogana
------ Gondola Traghetti routes

S. Alvise 52

Madonna
dell'Orto 52

Ponte Tre Archi 52

Ponte Guglie 52

S. Marcuola 1,82

Tronchetto A
3,4,82

Ferrovia
3,4,82

STAZIONE

Ferrovia
1,52,
DM

Riva di Biasio
1

S. Stae
1

Ca' d'Oro
1

PONTE DELLA LIBERTÀ

Tronchetto B
17

Plazzale Roma
1,4,52,82,DM

S. Silvestro 1

S. Tomà
1,82

Rialto
1,3,82

S. Angelo 1

S.Marta 52,82

S. Samuele 3,4,82

Ca' Rezzonico 1

S. Maria
del Giglio 1

S. Basilio 82

Accademia 1,3,4,82

Salute 1

to Fusina
(Parking): 16

Zattere 16,52,82

Sacca Fisola
82

S. Eufemia 82

Giudecca 82

Redentore
82

N

1 km

1/2 mile

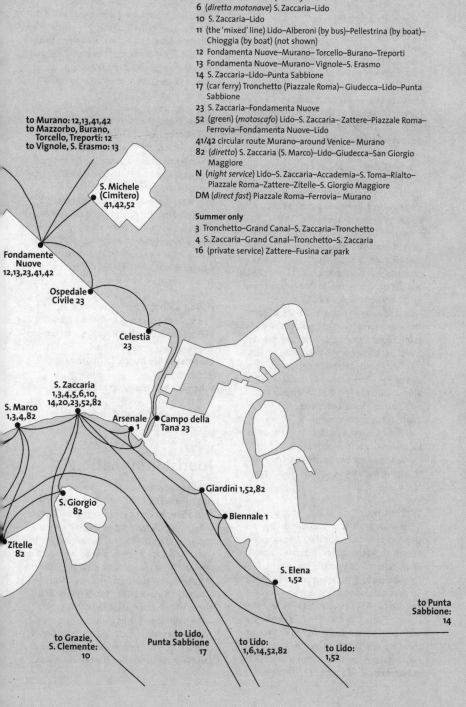

Regular Lines

1 (*accelerato*) Piazzale Roma–Ferrovia–Grand Canal–
San Marco–Lido: stops everywhere
6 (*diretto motonave*) S. Zaccaria–Lido
10 S. Zaccaria–Lido
11 (the 'mixed' line) Lido–Alberoni (by bus)–Pellestrina (by boat)–
Chioggia (by boat) (not shown)
12 Fondamenta Nuove–Murano–Torcello–Burano–Treporti
13 Fondamenta Nuove–Murano–Vignole–S. Erasmo
14 S. Zaccaria–Lido–Punta Sabbione
17 (car ferry) Tronchetto (Piazzale Roma)–Giudecca–Lido–Punta
Sabbione
23 S. Zaccaria–Fondamenta Nuove
52 (green) (*motoscafo*) Lido–S. Zaccaria–Zattere–Piazzale Roma–
Ferrovia–Fondamenta Nuove–Lido
41/42 circular route Murano–around Venice–Murano
82 (*diretto*) S. Zaccaria (S. Marco)–Lido–Giudecca–San Giorgio
Maggiore
N (*night service*) Lido–S. Zaccaria–Accademia–S. Toma–Rialto–
Piazzale Roma–Zattere–Zitelle–S. Giorgio Maggiore
DM (*direct fast*) Piazzale Roma–Ferrovia–Murano

Summer only

3 Tronchetto–Grand Canal–S. Zaccaria–Tronchetto
4 S. Zaccaria–Grand Canal–Tronchetto–S. Zaccaria
16 (private service) Zattere–Fusina car park

to Murano: 12,13,41,42
to Mazzorbo, Burano,
Torcello, Treporti: 12
to Vignole, S. Erasmo: 13

S. Michele
(Cimitero)
41,42,52

Fondamente
Nuove
12,13,23,41,42

Ospedale
Civile 23

Celestia
23

S. Zaccaria
1,3,4,5,6,10,
14,20,23,52,82

S. Marco
1,3,4,82

Arsenale
1

Campo della
Tana 23

Giardini 1,52,82

S. Giorgio
82

Biennale 1

Zitelle
82

S. Elena
1,52

to Punta
Sabbione:
14

to Grazie,
S. Clemente:
10

to Lido,
Punta Sabbione
17

to Lido:
1,6,14,52,82

to Lido:
1,52

Getting Around

Vaporetti and *Motoscafi*

Public transport in Venice means by water, on the grunting, canal-cutting *vaporetti* (the all-purpose water-buses), or the sleeker, faster *motoscafi*, run by the ACTV (t 041 528 7886). The only canals served by public transport are the Grand Canal, the Rio Nuovo, the Canale di Cannaregio and Rio dell'Arsenale; between them, you'll have to rely on your feet, which is not as gruelling as it sounds, as Venice is so small you can walk across it in an hour.

Single **tickets** (a flat rate of €3.10) should be purchased and validated in the machines at the landing-stages (random inspections aren't very frequent, but if you get caught you'll have to pay a €23 fine on the spot).

As some landing stages don't sell tickets, it's best to stock up (most *tabacchi* sell them in blocks of ten). You can also buy a single ticket on board, but tell the attendant immediately you get on. There are also family tickets and group tickets which are a bit cheaper.

Or, if you intend being on a boat at least three times in a given day, purchase a **24-hour tourist pass**, for €9.30, valid for unlimited travel on all lines, or the **3-day pass**, for €18.80.

Lines of most interest to visitors are listed on pp.164–5; most run until midnight. There is also an all-night line. Precise schedules are listed in the tourist office's free fortnightly guide, *Un Ospite di Venezia*.

At San Marco you can also find a number of **excursion boats** to various points in the Lagoon; they are more expensive than public transport, but may be useful if you're pressed for time.

Water-taxis

These are really tourist excursion boats – they work like taxis, but their fares are de luxe. Stands are at the station, Piazzale Roma, Rialto, San Marco, Lido and the airport. They can hold up to 15 passengers, and fares are set for destinations beyond the historic centre, or you can pay €73 per hour. Within the centre the minimum fare for up to four people is €73; additional passengers are up to €4 each, and there are surcharges for baggage, holiday or nocturnal service (after 10pm), and for using a radio taxi (t 041 522 2303 or t 041 723 112).

Gondolas

Gondolas, first mentioned in the city's annals in 1094, have a stately mystique that commands all other boats to give way. Shelley and many others have compared them to a funeral barque or the soul ferry to Hades, and not a few gondoliers share the infernal Charon's expectation of a solid gold tip for their services.

Once used by all and sundry, gondolas now operate frankly for tourists (and weddings). Official prices are €62 for a 50-minute ride (€77.50 after 8pm). Be sure to agree with the gondolier on where you want to go and how long you expect it to take before setting out.

In addition, gondolas retired from the tourist trade are used for **gondola *traghetti*** services across the Grand Canal at various points between its three bridges – your only chance to enjoy an economical, if brief, gondola ride for €0.40. *Traghetto* crossings are signposted in the streets nearby. For appearance's sake you'll have to stand up.

Hiring a Boat

Perhaps the best way to spend a day in Venice is by bringing or hiring your own motor boat, to drive, or chauffeured.
Cooperativa San Marco, San Marco 4267,
t 041 523 5775.
Veneziana Motoscafi, San Marco 4179,
t 041 716 000.
Serenissima Motoscafi, Castello 4545,
t 041 522 4281.

Tourist Information

The main information office is in the **Palazzina dei Santi**, in the Giardini Reali, by Piazza San Marco, t 041 522 5150. Branch offices at Palazzetto Selva, right by the San Marco *vaporetto* stop, the railway station and the bus station in Piazzale Roma offer accommodation services. There are also offices on the Rotonda Marghera, at Marco Polo Airport, and on the Lido at Gran Viale 6. The official tourist board website is *www.turismovenezia.it*.

The main source in English on any current events is the fortnightly magazine *Un Ospite di Venezia*, distributed free at tourist offices and in hotels. Otherwise, the two local daily papers *Il Gazzetino* and *Nuova Venezia* both have listings of films, concerts and so on in Venice and the *terra firma*.

For €12.91, people between the ages of 14 and 29 can buy a *Rolling Venice* card, which gives discounts on the city's attractions, from films at the Film Festival to museums, hostels, shops and restaurants (and access to the university canteen in Palazzo Badoer, Calle del Magazen 2840). It also allows you to buy a special reduced-price ticket for travelling on the *vaporetti*. Apply at one of the following (take a photo and your passport):

Agenzia Arte e Storia, Santa Croce 659, Corte Canal, **t** 041 524 0232 (*Mon–Fri 9–1 and 3–6*).

Assessorato alla Gioventù, San Marco 1553, Corte Contarina, **t** 041 274 7653 (*Mon–Fri 9.30–1, Tues and Thurs also 3–5*).

.**Associazone Italiana Alberghi per la Gioventù**, San Polo 3101, Calle del Castelforte, **t** 041 520 4414 (*Mon–Sat 8–1.30*).

Many churches now belong to an association called **Chorus** (**t** 041 275 0462, *www.chorus-ve.org*), and a collective ticket for all these churches costs €8. All Chorus churches have the same opening times (*Mon–Sat 10–5 and Sun 1–5*). Tickets are available from the churches, from VELA ticket offices, and from the Venice Pavilion tourist office.

VELA, *www.velaspa.com*, the commercial branch of the ACTV transport company, acts as a ticket office not only for bus and boat tickets but also for some concerts, operas, dance events and the Biennale. All are available from main *vaporetto* stops (Accademia, Ferrovia, Rialto, Tronchetto, Vallaresso, San Zaccaria, Lido) and VELA agencies (Calle dei Fuseri, **t** 041 241 8029, *open 7.30–7*, and Piazzale Roma, **t** 041 272 2249; *open 8.30–6.30*).

For the usual **internet** services:

The Netgate, Dorsoduro 3812/A, Crosera, **t** 041 244 0213.

Venetian Navigator, San Marco 676, Spadaria, **t** 041 241 1293;

Net House, San Marco, Campo Santo Stefano, **t** 041 277 1190 (*open 24 hours*).

If you lose something in the city, try the Comune, **t** 041 274 8225; or if you lost it on a train, **t** 041 785 238; or on a *vaporetto*, **t** 041 272 2179.

If you have an accident or become seriously ill, go to the *Pronto Soccorso* department of the **city hospital** in Castello, Campo Santi Giovanni e Paolo, or the **Ospedale del Mare**, Lido, 1 Lungomare d'Annunzio (**t** 041 529 4111); if you need a doctor at night or on holidays ring the *Guardia Medica*, **t** 041 529 4060.

Ambulance, t 041 523 0000.

Several *farmacie* are open all night on a rotating basis: the addresses are in the window of each, or ring **t** 041 531 1592 for a list; *Un Ospite di Venezia* has a list at the back.

Places that exchange money outside normal banking hours include:

American Express: San Moisè 1471, **t** 041 520 0844 (*open summer Mon–Sat 8–8; winter Mon–Sat 9–5*).

Thomas Cook, San Marco 5126, Riva del Ferro, **t** 041 528 7358, near the Rialto (*open Mon–Sat 9–6, Sun 9.30–5*).

The **main post office** is in the Fóndaco dei Tedeschi, near the Ponte Rialto (*open Mon–Sat 8.15–7.25*). There are smaller offices at the foot of Piazza San Marco (Calle dell'Ascensione) and at the western end of the Zattere. You can buy stamps at any tobacco shop.

Festivals

The Venice **Biennale** (*odd-numbered years; June–Sept*) is the most famous contemporary art show in the world (since 1895). The main exhibits of the forty or so countries officially represented are set up in the permanent pavilions in the Giardini Pubblici.

The city's other great cultural junket is the **Venice Film Festival** (*late August/early Sept*), in the Palazzo del Cinema and the Astra Cinema on the Lido. As well as spotting the stars, you can sometimes get in to see films if you arrive at the cinemas really early.

Venice's renowned **Carnival** (*10 days before Shrove Tues*), first held in 1094, was revived in 1979 after several decades of dormancy. It attracts huge crowds, but faces an uphill battle against the inveterate Italian love of *bella figura* – getting dressed up in elaborate costumes, wandering down to San Marco and taking each other's picture is as much as most of the revellers get up to. Concerts and shows are put on all over Venice, with city and corporate sponsorship, but there's very little spontaneity or serious carousing, and certainly no trace of what Byron called the 'revel of the earth'.

In 1988 Venice revived another crowd-pleaser, **La Sensa** (*first Sun after Ascension Day*), in which the Doge married the sea. Now the mayor plays the groom, in a replica of the state barge or *Bucintoro*. It's as corny and pretentious as it sounds, but on the same day you can watch the gondoliers race in the **Vogalonga**, or long row, from San Marco to Burano and back again.

Venice's most spectacular festival is **Il Redentore** (*third Sun in July*), with its bridge of boats (*see* p.211). The greatest excitement happens the Saturday night before, when Venetians row out for an evening picnic on the water, manoeuvring for the best view of the fabulous fireworks display over the Lagoon. For the thousands of landlubbers the prime viewing and picnicking spots are towards the eastern ends of either the Giudecca or the Zattere.

More perspiration is expended in the **Regata Storica** (*first Sun in Sept*), a splendid pageant of historic vessels and crews in Renaissance costumes and hotly contested races by gondoliers and a variety of other rowers down the Grand Canal.

Another bridge of boats is built on 21 November, this time across the Grand Canal to the Salute, for the feast of **Santa Maria della Salute**, which also commemorates the ending of another plague, in 1631. This event provides the only opportunity to see Longhena's unique basilica as it would have been when it was built, with its doors thrown open on to the Grand Canal.

Shopping

Since the Middle Ages, Venice has been one of Italy's top cities for shopping, whether you're looking for tacky bric-a-brac (just walk down the Lista di Spagna, the Riva degli Schiavoni or through the Rialto) or the latest in hand-crafted Venetian design.

Many Venetian shops neither have nor display a name, and some of those listed below will be mere addresses.

Shops are generally open Mon–Sat 8–1 or 9–1 and 4–7.30, although many tourist shops have longer hours. Many shops are closed Monday am (except grocers). Markets and grocers tend to close Wednesday pm.

Art and Antiques

Madera, Dorsoduro 2762, Campo San Barnaba, **t** 041 522 4181, *www.maderavenezia.it*. The contemporary *objets* in this small design shop are all hand-made using traditional methods, mostly by young Italian artisans. Jewellery made of Venetian glass beads, beautifully turned wooden bowls and utensils and some Japanese-inspired ceramics.

Sabbie e Nebbie, San Polo 2768A, Calle dei Nomboli, **t** 041 719 073. An interesting little shop with a carefully chosen mix of Japanese ceramics, ethnic papers and ceramics by Italian designers.

Antichità, Dorsoduro 1195, Calle Toletta, **t** 041 522 3159. A squeeze of a shop packed with beautiful antique glass beads, jewellery, lace, children's clothes, and bits and pieces.

Bastianello Arte, San Marco 5042, Campo San Bartolomeo. Western and oriental antiques, as well as Art Nouveau and jewellery.

Pietro Scarpa, San Marco 1464, Campo San Moisè; and San Marco 2089, Calle Larga XXII Marzo. The shops resemble museums; the second one sells old drawings.

Unnamed Shop, Dorsoduro 2609, Fondamenta del Soccorso. A real 'Old Curiosity Shop': from Baroque clocks to bills printed by the 1848 revolutionary government.

Books

Filippi, Castello 5763, Calle del Paradiso, **t** 041 523 6919. The city's best selection of Italian books about Venice, including facsimiles of antique books from the days when Venice was one of Europe's chief printing centres.

Libreria Cassini, San Marco 2424, Calle Larga XXII Marzo. Old prints and rare editions.

Libreria Goldoni, San Marco 4742, Calle dei Fabbri. Venice's largest general bookstore. Good for holiday reading.

The Museum Shop, Dorsoduro 710, Fondamenta Venier dei Leoni, **t** 041 240 5410. Next to the Guggenheim. A fine selection of art and photography books, children's books in English, gifts and postcards. Profits go to the museum. *Closed Tues.*

Punto Libri, Santa Croce, Salizzada di San Pantalon. Art and architecture books.

Sangiorgio, San Marco 2087, Calle Larga XXII Marzo. Books in English, especially about Venice, and some hefty art tomes.

Sansovino, San Marco 84, Bacino Orseolo (just outside the Procuratie Vecchie). Art and coffee-table books, and lots of postcards.

Clothes, Accessories and Shoes

Most of the big-name designer boutiques (Gucci, Prada, Versace, Louis Vuitton, Armani) are clustered around the outskirts of Piazza San Marco, along streets such as Mercerie, Frezzeria, Calle dei Fabbri, Calle Larga XXII Marzo and Salizzada San Moisè. Venetians buy their clothes at the COIN department store, while most tourists buy their 'Vuitton' and 'Prada' bags from the street-sellers paving the way to Piazza San Marco along Calle Larga XXII Marzo. Their first offer will be about three times what you should end up paying.

COIN, Cannaregio 5787, Fontego Salizzada San Giovanni Grisostomo, **t** 041 520 3581. Good department store. *Open daily.*

Emilio Ceccato, San Polo, Sottoportico di Rialto. Gondoliers' shirts, jackets and tight trousers.

Hibiscus, San Polo 1060, Ruga Rialto, **t** 041 520 8989. Beautiful, colourful silk garments and accessories, and original jewellery.

Kalimala, Castello 5387, Salizzada San Lio, **t** 041 528 3596. Beautiful and practical handmade leather goods: chunky bags, luggage, belts.

Risuola Tutto di Giovanni Dittura, Dorsoduro 871, Calle Nuova Sant'Agnese, **t** 041 523 1163. The best selection of colourful velvet slippers with cord and rubber soles. Cheaper than markets. Also shoe repairs. *Open daily.*

Rolando Segalin, San Marco 4365, Calle dei Fuseri, **t** 041 522 2115. 'Il Calzolaio di Venezia' stocks fabulous handmade shoes: from the sublimely elegant to the extraordinarily eccentric. *Open Mon–Fri and Sat am.*

Trois, San Marco 2666, Campo San Maurizio, **t** 041 522 2905. A Venetian institution, with Fortuny fabrics made to traditional specifications on the Giudecca.

Venetia Studium, San Marco 2403, Calle Larga XXII Marzo 2403; San Marco 723, Mercerie San Zulian, **t** 041 522 9281. Pleated silk Fortuny scarves, Fortuny lamps, pochettes, cushions, waistcoats and drawstring bags.

Vogini, San Marco 1257a, Calle Larga XXII Marzo 1300, **t** 041 522 2573. The greatest name in Venetian leather, with articles by Venetian designer Roberta di Camerino.

La Fenice, San Marco 2255, Calle Larga XXII Marzo, **t** 041 523 1273. Posh shoes by French and Italian designers.

No Name Cobbler, Castello 5268, Calle delle Bande. Old-fashioned shoe repair shop.

Food and Drink

Caffè Costarica, Cannaregio 1337, Rio Terrà San Leonardo. Gift packs for Java junkies. *Open Mon–Sat 9.30–1 and 4–7.*

Cantinone già Schiavi, Dorsoduro 992, Fondamenta Priuli. A fine old wine shop.

Panificio Volpe, Cannaregio 1143, Calle Ghetto Vecchio, **t** 041 715 178. Traditional Jewish pastries.

Pantagruelica, Dorsoduro 2844, Campo San Barnabà, **t** 041 523 6766; Giudecca 461, Fondamenta Sant' Eufemia, **t** 041 523 1809. Cheeses, hams and salamis, pastas, rice, preserves, wines, bread, oils and vinegars, all carefully sourced and much of it organic.

Il Pastaio, San Polo 219, Calle del Varoteri, Rialto markets. Pasta in a score of colours and shapes, including tagliatelle made with cuttlefish ink or curry.

Pastificio Artigiano, Cannaregio 4292, Strada Nuova. Venice's tastiest and most exotic pastas: *al cacao* (chocolate pasta), *al limone* (lemon), or beetroot, garlic, mushroom...

Rizzo Pane, San Marco, Calle delle Botteghe, (just off Campo F. Morosini). Everything you could ever need for a picnic.

Sacchi, Cannaregio 1815, Rio Terrà San Leonardo. Possibly the best fruit and veg shop in Venice, with a spectacular and mouthwatering display.

Supermercato Punto, Dorsoduro 3114, Rio Terrà Canal. One of the few supermarkets in the *centro storico.*

Unnamed Boat, Dorsoduro, Ponte dei Pugni. Near Campo San Barnabà, this boat houses the last floating greengrocer's in Venice. *Open Mon–Sat am.*

Glass and Ceramics

Arca, Santa Croce 1811, Calle Tintor. Intensely coloured, modern ceramic tiles, vases, plates.

CAM, Murano, Piazzale Colonna 1/b. One of the largest selections of glassware on Murano. Exceptionally friendly and unpushy.

Carlo Moretti, Murano, Fondamenta Manin 3, t 041 739 217. Contemporary glassware.

Domus Vetri d'Arte, Murano, Fondamenta Vetrai 82. A small glass shop with a tasteful selection by some top Italian designers.

Pauly, San Marco 4391, Calle Larga San Marco, t 041 709 899. Classic blown glassware.

San Vio, Dorsoduro 669, Campo San Vio 669. Striking modern designs.

Unnamed Shop, San Marco 1470, Salizzada San Moisè. Murano's most ambitious creations, at astronomical prices.

Jewellery

Jewellers are concentrated in Piazza San Marco and on the Ponte Rialto.

Codognato, San Marco 1295, Calle dell' Ascensione, t 041 522 5042. One of the oldest jewellers in Venice, with rare pieces by Tiffany and Cartier, and Art Deco baubles.

Missiaglia, San Marco 125, Piazza San Marco, near Quadri. Some of the most elegant work by Venetian gold and silversmiths, as well as necklaces, etc.

Nardi, San Marco 69/71, Piazza San Marco 69–71, next to Florian. One of Venice's luxury establishment jewellers, celebrated for its series of 'Othellos', elaborate jewelled pieces of carved ebony, each unique. Past customers include Grace Kelly and Liz Taylor.

Perle e Dintorni, San Marco 3740, Calle della Mandola, t 041 520 5068; San Marco 5468, Calle della Bissa, t 041 522 5624; Cannaregio 5622, Campo Santi Apostoli, t 041 520 6969. Glass beads to buy or have made into necklaces and bracelets in a couple of hours,

Lace

This is fiendishly hard to avoid on Burano, though the bargains you find are probably neither handmade nor Buranese.

Annelie, Dorsoduro 2748, Calle Lunga San Barnabà, t 041 520 3277. Exquisitely worked items, new and antique. *Closed Sat pm*.

La Fenice Atelier, San Marco 3537, Campo Sant' Angelo, t 041 523 9578. Exquisite bed linens, towels and nightwear in superb silks, satins and cotton lawn, decorated with lace and embroidery. Made-to-measure service.

Jesurum, San Marco 60/61, Piazza San Marco, t 041 522 9864. A vast quantity of lace (tablecloths, lingerie, etc.) on display in a former

12th-century church, plus an array of swimming costumes and summery togs.

Markets

Campo San Maurizio. A flea market appears periodically in this square, in the heart of the principal antiques area. *A week before Easter and Christmas, and third week of Sept.*

Rialto Markets. Venice's major markets, selling everything under the sun on the bridge and in all the streets to the north. There is a fish market, and fruit and veg, in the Peschiera, Fabbriche Vecchie and Fabbriche Nuove. *Open Mon–Sat 7–1 (fruit and veg), Tues–Sat 7–1 (fish, on Ruga degli Specializi)*.

Rio Terrà San Leonardo. Clothes, fish and food. *Open daily*.

Masks and Costumes

Giorgio Clanetti, Castello 6657, Barbaria delle Tolè, t 041 522 3110. Fine, traditionally crafted masks. *Rarely open, so call ahead*.

Mondonovo, Dorsoduro 3063, Rio Terrà Canal. Some of the best masks in town: camels, sphinxes, moonfaces and everything else.

Papier-mâché, Castello 5175; Calle Lunga Santa Maria Formosa. Exquisite paintwork and masks decorated in the style of Kandinsky.

Tragicomica, San Polo 2800, Calle dei Nomboli. Extraordinary variety of wonderfully shaped masks and costumes.

Paper and Stationery

Alberto Valese-Ebrû, San Marco 3471, Campo Santo Stefano. Persian/Italian styles in paper-making; also silk ties and masks.

Carta da Casetti, Dorsoduro 364, t 041 523 2804, *www.cartadacassetti.yahoo.it*. Tucked away in a tiny piazzetta between the Salute and the Guggenheim. Original designs: sheets of paper or original gifts.

Legatoria Piazzesi, San Marco 2511, Campiello Feltrina, t 041 522 1202. 'The Oldest Paper Shop in Italy': all sorts of gifts and papers.

Paolo Olbi, San Marco 3652, Calle della Mandola (near Campo San Angelo). Exquisite handmade paper, blank books and photo albums. Also leather-bound.

Il Pavone, Dorsoduro 721, Fondamenta Venier dei Leoni, t 041 523 4517. Paper products covered in unusual designs made on the premises. Bound books and other gifts.

Wood

Franco Furlanetto, San Polo 2768, Calle dei Nomboli. A workshop for *'remi e forcole'*, where you can buy gondola oars and oar-locks (more beautiful than practical).

Livio de Marchi, San Marco 3157, Salizzada San Samuele. Internationally renowned for everyday objects sculpted in natural wood – clothes hanging on pegs, benches in the form of giant paintbrushes, desks made from piles of oversized wooden books.

La Scialuppa, San Polo 2695, Calle Seconda dei Saoneri. Beautiful *forcole* (walnut gondola oar-locks), and make-your-own gondola kits.

Sports and Activities

Aero Club G. Ancillotto, Lido, **t** 041 526 0808, *aeroclub venezia.com*. A flying school that also offers excursion flights over Venice.

Alberoni Golf Course, Lido, Via del Forte Alberoni, **t** 041 731 333. This course on the southern tip of the Lido is among the best in Italy. Non-m embers are permitted, but need proof of membership of another club. *Open Oct–March Tues–Sat 8.30–6; April–Sept Tues–Fri 8.30–6, Sat and Sun 8.30–8.*

Giorgio Barbieri, Lido, Via Zara 5, **t** 041 526 1490. Rent a bike, or a touristy tricycle with a canopy, to explore the length of the Lido.

Where to Stay

Whatever class of hotel you stay in, expect it to cost around a third more than it would on the mainland, even without the often out-rageous charge for breakfast. Reservations are near-essential from about April to October and for Carnival; many hotels close in the winter, although many that do stay open offer substantial discounts. Single rooms are always very hard to find. If you arrive at any time without reservations, tourist offices at the station and Piazzale Roma have a free room-finding service. The tourist office in Piazza San Marco has a list of agencies that rent self-catering flats.

Luxury

★★★★★Cipriani, Giudecca 10, Fondamenta San Giovanni, **t** 041 520 7744, **f** 041 520 3930, *info@hotelcipriani.it*, *www.orientexpress hotels.com*. Since 1963 this has been one of Italy's most luxurious hotels, a villa isolated in a lush garden at one end of the Giudecca that's so quiet and comfortable you could forget Venice exists, even though it's only a few minutes away by the hotel's 24-hour private launch service. An Olympic-size pool, sauna, jacuzzis in each room, tennis courts and a superb restaurant are just some of its facilities. Nowhere could pamper you more.

★★★★★Danieli, Castello 4196, Riva degli Schiavoni, **t** 041 522 6480, **f** 041 520 0208, *www.luxurycollection.com*. The largest and most famous hotel in Venice, in what must be the most glorious location, overlooking the Lagoon and rubbing shoulders with the Palazzo Ducale. Formerly the Gothic palazzo of the Dandolo family, it has been an hotel since 1822; Dickens, Proust, George Sand and Wagner stayed here. Nearly every room has a story to tell, in a beautiful setting of silken walls, Gothic staircases, gilt mirrors and oriental rugs. The new wing is comfortable, but lacks the charm and the stories.

★★★★★Gritti Palace, San Marco 2467, Campo Santa Maria del Giglio, **t** 041 794 611, **f** 041 520 0942, *www.starwood.com/grittipalace*. The 15th-century Grand Canal palace that once belonged to the dashing glutton and womanizer Doge Andrea Gritti has been preserved as a true Venetian fantasy and elegant retreat. All the rooms are furnished with Venetian antiques, but for a real splurge do as Somerset Maugham did and stay in the Ducal Suite. Another of its delights is the restaurant, the **Club del Doge**, on a terrace overlooking the canal.

★★★★Londra Palace, Castello 4171, Riva degli Schiavoni, **t** 041 520 0533, **f** 041 522 5032, *www.hotelondra.it*. Tchaikovsky wrote his *Fourth Symphony* in room 108, and it was also a favourite of Stravinsky. The hotel was created by linking two palaces together, and it has an elegant interior, over half the rooms with a stunning canal view, and exceptionally good service. There is also an excellent restaurant, **Les Deux Lions**.

★★★★Des Bains, Lido, Lungomare Marconi 17, **t** 041 526 5921, **f** 041 526 0113, *www. sheraton.com*. A grand old luxury hotel in a large park designed for dalliance. Thomas

Mann stayed here on several occasions, and had Aschenbach sigh his life away on the private beach. It has a saltwater swimming pool, two tennis courts, a private pier and a motorboat service into Venice. There are 190 large rooms, a Liberty-style salon and a breeze-filled veranda dining room. Service is faultless. *Closed Dec–mid-Mar.*

★★★★**Kette**, San Marco 2053, Piscina San Moisè, **t** 041 520 7766, **f** 041 522 8964, *info@hotelkette.com, www.hotelkette.com.* 63 elegant rooms with pale striped walls, *mezzacorona* beds and smart bathrooms; colour schemes are dusty pink and green. Public rooms on the ground floor have been expanded and there are now conference facilities. Air-conditioning in all rooms.

★★★**San Moisè**, San Marco 2058, Piscina San Moisè, **t** 041 520 3755, **f** 041 521 0670, *info@sanmoise.it, www.sanmoise.it.* A major overhaul of this quiet hotel has swept aside the rather cloying Venetian style in favour of a cleaner look. Most bathrooms have a tub. Book early for a room overlooking the canal; there is a little terrace outside on the *calle.*

Very Expensive

★★★**Accademia**, Dorsoduro 1058, Fondamenta Bollani, **t** 041 521 0188, **f** 041 523 9152, *pensioneaccademia@flashnet.it.* A generous dollop of slightly faded charm in a 17th-century villa with a garden, just off the Grand Canal. Its 26 rooms are furnished with antiques, some of which look as if they were left behind by the villa's previous occupant – the Russian Embassy. Book well in advance.

★★★**American**, Dorsoduro 628, Fondamenta Bragadin, **t** 041 520 4733, **f** 041 520 4048, *www. hotel american.com.* An elegant, traditional hotel that has undergone extensive renovation, this overlooks the lovely San Vio canal (the best rooms, with windows on two sides, are 201 and 202). There's a pretty first-floor breakfast terrace and an internet point for guests' use. Staff are very friendly.

★★★**Locanda Cipriani**, Torcello, Piazza Santa Fosca, **t** 041 730 150, **f** 041 735 433, *www. locandacipriani.com.* There are only six rooms in this famous yellow-painted, green-shuttered country house hotel, in the most rural and tranquil spot in Venice. Some have views over the garden; you can sleep where

Hemingway wrote his Venice novel, *Across the River and Into the Trees.* All the rooms are spacious and fresh. The restaurant is excellent *(see* p.174). *Closed Jan.*

★★★**Locanda del Ghetto**, Cannaregio 2892, Campo del Ghetto Nuovo, **t** 041 275 9292, **f** 041 275 7987, *ghetto@veneziahotels.com, www.veneziahotels.com.* A delightful new hotel with a pretty canal-side breakfast room. Right by the synagogue (one room has a beamed ceiling that was part of the 16th-century version), it has nine stylish bedrooms with parquet floors, pale gold fabrics and smart furniture. Two have terraces overlooking the *campo.*

★★★**Pausania**, Dorsoduro 2824, San Barnaba, **t** 041 522 2083, **f** 041 522 2989. This traditional hotel is in an old *palazzo* in a quiet corner of Dorsoduro. The courtyard has an old well and a stone staircase leading to some of the rooms, and there is a garden.

Expensive

★★★**Do Pozzi**,San Marco 2373, Via XXII Marzo, **t** 041 520 7855, **f** 041 522 9413, *www. hoteldopozzi.it.* With 29 rooms on a charming little square where tables are set out for breakfast or a drink. Rooms on two of the floors have been renovated, and there are some in a nearby annexe.

★★**San Fantin**, San Marco 1930A, Campiello Fenice, **t/f** 041 523 1 401. Just around the corner from La Fenice in a quiet little *campo,* this simple hotel is out of a time-warp, with a reception area a bit like your granny's parlour, dated in a rather refreshing way. The 14 rooms (two without a bath) are pleasant, and the place is spotless.

★**Antica Locanda Montin**, Dorsoduro 1147, Fondamenta di Borgo, **t** 041 522 7151, **f** 041 520 0255, *locandamontin@libero.it.* An old-fashioned Venetian hostelry, with ten character-filled rooms, a bohemian atmosphere and an infamous arty restaurant.

Ca' del Dose, Castello 3801, Calle del Dose, **t/f** 041 520 9887, *www.cadeldose.com.* One of the new generation of good-value *affitta camere* or small B&Bs in Venice. Just off the Campo Bandiera e Moro, it has six comfortable rooms furnished stylishly with dark parquet floors and elegant fabrics. One large room at the top of the house has a terrace.

Moderate

Hotel Iris, San Polo 2910A, Calle del Cristo, **t 041 522 2882, *Htliris@tin.it*. The clean, pleasant rooms in this hotel have been recently redecorated; one has a pretty ceiling fresco and is really quite elegant. All rooms have phone and TV. *Closed Jan.*

*Silva, Castello 4423, Fondamenta del Remedio, **t** 041 522 7643, **f** 041 528 6817, *albergosilva@libero.it*. A bit hard to find – on one of the most photographed little canals in Venice, between the San Zaccaria *vaporetto* stop and Santa Maria Formosa. Fairly basic, but quiet; the staff are friendly.

Inexpensive

*Casa Boccassini, Cannaregio 5295, Calle del Fumo, **t** 041 522 9892, **f** 041 523 6877. In a quiet neighbourhood well away from the crowds, this is something of a find. The basic but clean-as-a-whistle rooms have the odd antique piece to add character, and there is a pleasant breakfast room and sitting area, though it's the delightful garden that is the real attraction. All rooms have a phone; three don't have a bath.

*Doni, Castello 4656, Calle del Vin, **t/f** 041 522 4267, *Albergodoni@libero.it*. A basic but clean little family-run hotel on a pretty canal; the best rooms (larger with creaky old wooden floors and overlooking the water) are the three without a bath.

Hostels and Campsites

The tourist office has a list of all inexpensive hostel accommodation in Venice; as sleeping in the streets is now discouraged, schools are often pressed into use to take in the summer overflow, charging minimal rates to spread out a sleeping bag.

Assocamping, t 041 968 071, **f** 041 537 1106, *assocamping@cavallino.net*, *www.cavallino.net*. Supply a list of campsites.

Fusina, Via Moranzini 79, **t 041 547 0055, **f** 041 547 0050, *info@camping-fusina.com*, *www.camping-fusina.com*. At least 1,000 places. Venice is 20mins away by boat; *vaporetto* 16 from San Zaccaria runs every hour (until 11pm in the summer). It has a restaurant, pizzeria, bar, breakfast bar, public Internet and email terminals, and a marina with slip access so you can yacht off to

Greece, leaving your car at Fusina. Tents are €4, plus €6pp; campers/cars plus a tent are €13 per night, then €6pp. There are also small self-catering bungalows for rent. *Open all year.*

Serenissima, Via Padana 334, Oriago, Mira, **t 041 920 286, **f** 041 920 286, *camping serenissima@shineline.it*, *www.camping serenissima. com*. 300 camping places and 60 bungalows just off the Brenta Canal; bus 53 connects with Venice every half-hour. *Open April–Oct.*

Ostello di Venezia, Giudecca 86, Fondamenta delle Zitelle, **t** 041 523 8211, **f** 041 523 5689. One of the most strikingly located youth hostels in Italy, right on the Giudecca Canal, with views of San Marco. No phone reservations; to be assured of a place in July or August, write well in advance. At other times, you can chance it and book in person any day after 6pm (doors open for queueing at midday). It's members only, but cards are sold at the door. Doors are open 7–9.30am and 1.30–11pm (curfew is 11.30pm). Rates are €16 a head, including breakfast.

Foresteria Valdese, Castello 5170, Calle della Madonetta, **t/f** 041 528 6797, *venezia foresteria@chiesavaldese.org*, *www.chiesa valdese.org/venezia*. An old *palazzo* converted into a dormitory/*pensione* by the Waldensians. Check-in 9–1 and 6–8. Doubles cost €54, beds in dorms with bath €22; breakfast included.

Istituto Canossiano, Giudecca 428, Fondamenta del Ponte Piccolo, **t/f** 041 522 2157. Women-only hostel run by nuns. Simple and clean, with 10.30pm curfew. Beds €13.

Eating Out

The Venetians are traditionally the worst cooks in Italy, and their beautiful city bears the ignominy of having a highest percentage of dud restaurants per capita. Not only is cooking in general well below the norm in Italy, but prices tend to be about 15% higher, and even the moderate ones can give you a nasty surprise at *conto* time with excessive service and cover charges. The cheap ones, serving up 500 tourist menus a day, are mere providers of calories to keep you on your feet; pizza is a good standby if you're on a budget.

Very Expensive

Antico Martini, San Marco 1983, Campo San Fantin, t 041 522 4121, *www.anticomartini. com*. A Venetian classic, all Romance and elegance. A Turkish coffeehouse in the early 18th century, but nowadays better known for seafood, a superb wine list and the best *pennette al pomodoro* in Venice. The intimate piano bar-restaurant stays open until 2am. Its romantic flavour is temporarily swallowed up by La Fenice's rebuilding works outside. *Closed Tues, and Wed midday.*

Danieli Terrace, Danieli Hotel, Castello 4196, Riva degli Schiavoni, t 041 522 6480, *www.starwoodhotels.com/danieli*. The Danieli's rooftop restaurant is renowned for classic cuisine (try the *spaghetti alla Danieli*, prepared at your table) and perfect service in an incomparable setting overlooking Bacino San Marco.

Da Fiore, San Polo 2202A, Calle del Scaleter, t 041 721 308. People 'in the know' believe this to be the best restaurant in Venice. Food is taken seriously here; the atmosphere is sober without any of the pretentious frills of many other Venetian eateries. Start with a plate of *misto crudo* or marinated raw fish or scallops *gratinati* in the oven with thyme before moving on to the classic *bigoli in salsa* (handmade spaghetti in a sauce of mashed anchovies and onions), penne with scallops and broccoli, or a wonderful, silky black squid ink risotto. Main courses include *involtini* of sole wrapped round radicchio, and a meaty tuna steak flavoured with rosemary. *Closed Sun and Mon, early Jan and Aug.*

Harry's Bar, San Marco 1323, Calle Vallaresso, t 041 528 5777, *www.cipriani.com*. In a class by itself, a favourite of Hemingway and assorted other luminaries, this is as much a Venetian institution as the Doge's Palace, though food has become secondary to its celebrity atmosphere. Best to avoid the restaurant upstairs and just flit in for a quick hobnob while sampling a sandwich or the justly famous cocktails (a Bellini, Tiziano or Tiepolo – delectable fruit juices mixed with Prosecco), at a table downstairs near the bar.

Hostaria da Franz, Castello 754, Fondamenta San Giuseppe, t 041 522 0861, *www.hostaria dafranz.com*. Booking advised. A fine restaurant well worth the fairly hefty outlay. Eat in the intimate, elegant dining room or outside on the enchanting canal-side terrace. The traditional fish dishes (with creative twists) contain only the freshest ingredients: giant prawns marinated in citrus fruits, ravioli stuffed with fish, and sea bass with fresh herbs. Eels are a speciality; Franz prepares them to a secret recipe. The wine list is excellent. *Closed Jan.*

Harry's Dolci, Giudecca 773, Fondamenta San Biagio, t 041 522 4844. Decked out like a trattoria, with tiled walls and wooden tables. Similar food to Harry's Bar, but considerably cheaper. Stunning views across the canal. *Closed Mon, Tues and Nov–Mar.*

Il Sole Sulla Vecia Cavana, Cannaregio 4624, Rio Terrà SS Apostoli, t 041 528 7106, *www.ilsolevenezia.it*. Traditional and more creative dishes are served at this elegant restaurant, all beautifully presented. The seafood salad with 'pearls' of melon and cucumber makes for an unusual antipasto; follow this with '*margherite*' (a kind of ravioli) stuffed with sea bass, and wonderful Sicilian-style tuna steaks seared on the grill and served with capers, tomato and oregano. Also some meat dishes. *Closed Mon, and 2 weeks Aug, 2 weeks Jan.*

Cipriani, Giudecca 10, t 041 240 8507, *www.orient-expresshotels.com*. Booking advised. A meal here may not be the ultimate gastronomic experience, but it certainly holds its own with romance and atmosphere, especially in summer when tables are laid on a magical terrace and a piano tinkles in the background. The wide variety of dishes, both local and otherwise, are well prepared and exquisitely presented: an interesting array of antipasti to start, fillet of John Dory in a potato crust and served with asparagus, and duck breast with polenta soufflé. No children under eight at dinner. For a less wallet-busting (and far less romantic) experience, come for lunch at the Cip's club. *Closed Nov–Mar.*

Locanda Cipriani, Torcello, Piazza Santa Fosca 29, t 041 730 150, *www.locandacipriani.com*. In spite of the high prices and merely average food, this is an idyllic place to eat, as Hemingway and Chaplin discovered in their time. Situated off sleepy Torcello's main square, it is rustic and cosy, with a lovely vine-covered terrace. There are six elegant bedrooms above the restaurant (*see* p.171). *Closed Tues.*

La Corte Sconta, Castello 3886, Calle del Pestrin, **t** 041 522 7024. It may be off the beaten track, but the reputation of this trattoria rests solidly on its exquisite molluscs and crustaceans, served in a setting that's a breath of fresh air. Locals claim it's even better in the off-season; be sure to order the house wine. Booking essential. *Closed Sun and Mon, and mid-July–mid-Aug.*

Da Ignazio, San Polo 2749, Calle dei Saoneri, **t** 041 523 4852. Booking advised. Cosy, traditional trattoria serving classic Venetian fish dishes for more than 50 years. Also such oddities as *moeche* (small, soft-shelled crabs eaten whole), *castraure* (spring artichokes) and *sparesee* (wild asparagus). Or delicious spaghetti with *vongole veraci* (giant clams). There is a pretty courtyard. *Closed Sat and 3 weeks July–Aug.*

Da Remigio, Castello 3416, Ponte dei Greci, **t** 041 523 0089. A neighbourhood favourite, with the freshest of fish dishes. Very popular with the locals. *Closed Mon eve and Tues.*

Expensive

Osteria San Marco, San Marco 1610, Frezzeria, **t** 041 528 5242. Plain white walls, exposed brickwork and wooden tables in this stylish new *osteria/enoteca*. The food is interesting too: gnocchi with crab and rosemary, ravioli stuffed with ricotta and mint and served with a lamb sauce, scallop salad with artichoke hearts, guinea fowl with balsamic vinegar, and fillet steak cooked with coffee (an ancient recipe). Open all day for a snack and a glass of wine. *Closed Sun and Jan.*

Alla Nuova Speranza, Castello 145, Campo Ruga, **t** 041 528 5225. Booking required for dinner (or the cook will go home early). No cards. Simple, friendly trattoria with a TV at one end of the wood-panelled room and football coupons on sale from a little booth at the other. Packed with local workmen at lunchtime. Fill up on great-value seafood: fat *capparossoli* (clams) sautéed in garlic and wine or tossed into spaghetti or monkfish. The tourist menu is good value at €15.

Vecio Fritolin, Santa Croce 2262, Calle della Regina, **t** 041 522 2881, *www.veciofritolin.com*.

A calm, civilized restaurant with a delightful owner, Irina. The day's catch is cooked without fuss and beautifully presented: baby shrimp on a bed of sautéed artichoke hearts; green tagliolini with nettles; courgette flowers and shrimp; steamed fillet of turbot with asparagus in a buttery vinaigrette. *Closed Sun eve and Mon.*

Le Bistrot de Venise, San Marco 4685, Calle dei Fabbri, **t** 041 523 6651, *www.bistrotdevenise. com*. This cosy restaurant presents poetry readings, live music and other cultural events as well as specializing in historical Venetian dishes full of unusual herbs and spices: pumpkin and cheese gnocchi flavoured with cinnamon, spicy pheasant soup, *baccalà* in a sweet and sour sauce, sturgeon cooked with prunes, grapes and balsamic vinegar and Turkish spiced rice pudding. *Open until 12.30am.*

Vini da Gigio, Cannaregio 3628A, Fondamenta San Felice, **t** 041 528 5140. Booking essential. Small restaurant with views over the canal, always crowded with local foodies. Still has the feel of an old *bacaro*, with low, beamed ceilings and rustic tiled floors. Traditional food: fish, game and meat, various kinds of raw, marinated fish, fish soup, *baccalà mantecato* (creamed stockfish), sautéed scallops, duck from the lagoon ('*masorini*') – and the superb wine list features some 600 labels from both Italy and beyond. *Closed Mon, 3 weeks Jan/Feb and 3 weeks July/Aug.*

Ribò, Santa Croce 158, Fondamenta Minotto, **t** 041 524 2486. The new young owners of this small restaurant have favoured an elegant, modern look, and food to match: carpaccio of octopus with shallot vinegar, risotto with scampi and asparagus, tuna steak with fresh herbs, tempura of scallops. There's a delightful garden. *Closed Mon.*

Al Mascaron, Castello 5225, Calle Lunga Santa Maria Formosa, **t** 041 522 5995. A favourite Venetian *osteria*, now somewhat spoilt by too many tourists, but nonetheless full of atmosphere and serving good food. Wine is served out of huge containers in the front and the atmosphere is noisy and unpretentious. Traditional Venetian specialities – both fish and meat – are served at marble-topped tables. Liver and sardines are served *in saor*, that is with pine nuts, raisins and marinated onions. *Closed Sun and Jan.*

L'Incontro, Dorsoduro 3062, Rio Terrà Canal, t 041 522 2404. If you can't stand the sight of another fish, head for this reasonably priced Sardinian restaurant where the menu is entirely meat- and vegetable-based: *gnocchi* with tomato and *pecorino*, ravioli flavoured with saffron, steaks (beef or horse) and roast suckling pig. *Closed Mon and Tues midday.*

Al'Aciugheta, Castello 4357, Campo SS. Filippo e Giacomo, t 041 522 4292, *www.aciugheta-hotelrio.it.* One of the best cheap restaurants and bars near the Piazza San Marco, with a good atmosphere. It's a touristy pizzeria at the front, but go early to the back room with a local for great *cicheti* and excellent wines.

Moderate

Osteria ai Assassini, San Marco 3695, Rio Terrà dei Assassini, t 041 528 7986. Popular *osteria* on a quiet street north of La Fenice. Fish features on Thursdays and Fridays, the rest of the week is for carnivores. The ambience is rustic (low ceilings, wood panelling and brickwork) and lively, and the place is full of Italians. Snack on *cicheti* if you're not up for a whole meal. *Closed Sat midday and Sun.*

Bancogiro: Osteria da Andrea, San Polo 122, Campo Giacometto, t 041 523 2061. Booking essential. This modern *osteria* enjoys a fabulous position overlooking the Grand Canal. In the street-level bar, excellent wines and snacks are served; above, those who have booked can choose creative dishes such as fish salad with apple and mandarin, roast fresh tuna with pine nuts and gratin of steamed vegetables flavoured with coriander. *Closed Sun eve and Mon.*

Anice Stellato, Cannaregio 3272, Fondamenta della Sensa, t 041 720 744. Booking advised. New-generation, family-run *bacaro/trattoria* near the remote church of Sant'Alvise. Traditional dishes are enlivened by the odd creative twist – spaghetti with *caparossoli* (local clams) or with sardines and balsamic vinegar, tagliatelle with scampi and cour-gette flowers, *dorade* flavoured with curry. *Closed Mon and 3 weeks Aug/Sept.*

Gam-Gam, Cannaregio 1122, Sottoportico di Ghetto Vecchio, t 041 715 284, *www.jewish venice.org.* No cards. A modern kosher bar

and restaurant by the entrance to the ghetto with tables on the canal. Excellent choice of antipasti (hummous, baba ganoush, tasty salads, etc.), fish, meat and vegetable couscous, shwarma and latkes. The odd Italian dish is thrown in too, and there are vegetarian options. *Closed Sat.*

Alla Vedova, Cannaregio 3912, Ramo Ca d'Oro, t 041 528 5324. Booking essential. One of the oldest and best-known *bacari* in Venice, where locals crowd round the bar to eat a selection of excellent *cicheti* (including wonderful spicy *polpette* or meatballs) while hungrier punters join a relaxed crowd of tourists at wooden tables in the adjoining room for tagliatelle with duck, *fritto misto* and *fegato alla veneziana* (and vegetarian options). The same family has run the place for some 130 years, and the décor and atmosphere have been carefully preserved. *Closed Sun midday, Thurs, Fri and Aug.*

Mistra, Giudecca 212A, t 041 522 0743. Booking advised. First-floor trattoria with watery views among boatyards on the south side of Giudecca. Specialities are fish and dishes from Liguria (so expect lots of pesto). *Closed Mon eve, Tues and Jan.*

Ai 4 Feri, Dorsoduro 2754, Calle Lunga San Barnabà, t 041 520 6978. No cards. A new *osteria* run along traditional lines, with excellent *cicheti* and full meals at honest prices: pumpkin soup, spaghetti with artichokes and shrimps, simple grilled fish, *seppie* with polenta or fresh tuna '*in saor*', a speciality of the house. *Closed Sun.*

Al Pantalon, Dorsoduro 3958, Calle del Scalater, t 041 710 849, *www.osteriaalpantalon.it.* Venetians and tourists alike pile into this popular rustic *osteria* near the Frari. Run by the same team as Alla Patatina (*see* p.177), it has *cicheti* at a front counter and tables in an adjoining room. *Closed Sun.*

Cheap

Rosticceria San Bartolomeo, San Marco 5424, Calle della Bissa, t 041 522 3569. No-frills trattoria with an even cheaper snack bar downstairs. Eat in or take away.

Vino Vino, San Marco 2007A, Calle del Caffettier, t 041 523 7027, *www.vinovino.co.it.* A pleasant little wine bar near La Fenice, offering some 350 wines from all over Italy and further afield. Choose from snacks at the bar or reasonably priced meals in the adjoining room.

Da Toni, Dorsoduro 1642, Fondamenta San Basegio, **t** 041 528 6899. No cards. Simple local trattoria harks back to pre-commercial days: scallops with parsley, garlicky sea snails, and excellent grilled monkfish. *Closed Mon and 3 weeks Aug.*

Il Réfolo, Santa Croce 1459, Campo San Giacomo dell'Orio, **t** 041 524 0016, *www. dafiore.com.* Excellent new pizzeria run by the same team behind the legendary Da Fiore (*see* p.173). *Closed Tues and Dec and Jan.*

Cafés and Bars

Between 5pm and dinner is the time to indulge in a beer and *tramezzini*, finger sandwiches that come in a hundred varieties.

Caffè Costarica, Cannaregio 1337, Rio Terrà San Leonardo. Brews Venice's most powerful *espresso* and great iced coffee (*frappé*). Also sells ground coffees and beans. *Closed Sun.*

Caffè Florian, San Marco 56/59, Piazza San Marco, **t** 041 520 5641, www.caffeflorian.com. Florian's has a charming and cosy 18th-century décor of mirrors and frescoes, and every Venetian learns to have coffee here rather than at Quadri (*see* below). The thimblefuls of espresso are good, if outrageously costly, and be warned that sitting on the outside terrace when there is live music carries an extra charge of €4.50 per head.

Gran Caffè Lavena, San Marco 133, Piazza San Marco, **t** 041 522 4070, *www.venetia.it/ lavena.* Excellent coffee in a beautiful old setting (1750), with fewer tourists and less stinging prices. *Open until midnight.*

Gran Caffè Quadri, San Marco 120, Piazza San Marco. **t** 041 522 2105, *www.quadrivenice. com.* Another of Venice's historic coffee-houses, Quadri fell from grace during the Second World War. It's an elaborate confection of stucco and mirrors. The food in the gorgeous restaurant upstairs is good. There's a charge for music on the terrace. *Open until midnight.*

Marchini, San Marco 676, Calle Spadaria, **t** 041 522 9109, *www.golosessi.com.* The smell of chocolate as you enter is almost overwhelming; it has a mouth-watering range of chocolates, cakes and pastries, all of them beautifully presented, including the prize-winning *Torta del Doge. Closed Sun.*

Rosa Salva, Castello 6779, Campo SS Giovanni e Paolo, **t** 041 522 7949 (also San Marco 4589, Campo San Luca, **t** 041 522 5385). Have breakfast in one of Venice's best cake shops with tables on the square.

Paolin, San Marco 2962, Campo Santo Stefano, **t** 041 522 5576. Known as the best *gelateria* in the city, above all for its divine pistachio.

Il Doge, Dorsoduro 3058, Campo Santa Margherita, **t** 041 523 4607. No cards. Lively gelateria. *Open until midnight.*

Gelateria Causin, Dorsoduro 2996, Campo Santa Margherita. Reassuringly old-fashioned *caffè/gelateria. Closed Sun.*

Nico, Dorsoduro 922, Fondamenta Zattere ai Gesuati, **t** 041 522 5293. Also a must on anyone's ice cream tour, if the late-night queues are anything to go by.

Il Caffè, Dorsoduro 2963, Campo Santa Margherita, **t** 041 528 7998. Known as Caffè Rosso, 'The Red Bar'. A lively local hang-out. Cocktails, coffee, pastries and snacks. *Open until 2am. Closed Sun.*

Alla Mascareta, Castello 55183, Calle Lunga Santa Maria Formosa, **t** 041 523 0744. *Enoteca* with an exceptional wine list and a wonderful choice of cheeses, hams and salamis. *Open 6pm–1am. Closed Sun.*

Rizzardini, San Polo 1415, Campiello dei Meloni, **t** 041 522 3835. No cards. An invitingly old-fashioned pastry shop and *caffè* (since 1742) with traditional Venetian cakes and biscuits, including marzipan cake and a mean-looking strudel. *Closed Tues and Aug.*

Dal Mas, Cannaregio 150A, Lista di Spagna, **t** 041 715 101. The home-made cakes and pastries at this *pasticceria* are probably the nearest decent sugar fix to the station. *Closed Tues and July.*

Bacari

The *bacaro* is Venice's answer to a tapas bar, although many of them also serve complete meals, often at long tables in a back room. Originally drinking places, they come in all shapes and sizes, from gloomy holes in the wall with standing room only to slick, new establishments with trendy décor. They all offer a choice of wines by the glass (*un ombra*), and an array of *cicheti* or tasty little snacks which are usually arranged on the counter: anything from fishy tit-bits to grilled vegetables, artichoke hearts, deep-fried courgette flowers, chunks of salami, ham or cheese, or squares of fried polenta. They are often speared with a toothpick off the main serving dish, or you can ask for a selection to be put on a plate, pointing at what takes your fancy even if you have no idea what it is. Prices are not usually displayed on each item so the bill can quickly mount up.

Venice is full of *bacari*, usually hidden away down narrow alleyways. Most are open all day (some have a couple of hours' siesta in mid-afternoon) but close at around 8pm; some of the newer ones stay open late. They rarely accept credit cards.

Al Bacareto, San Marco 3447, Calle della Botteghe, **t** 041 528 9336. Booking advised. A popular, traditional *bacaro* with a huge variety of excellent *cicheti*, plus some more substantial dishes for hungrier clientele. There's a small terrace too. *Closed Sat eve and Sun, and Aug.*

Al Volto, San Marco 4081, Calle Cavalli, **t** 041 522 8945. A cosy little *bacaro* near Campo San Luca. Choose a snack and a drink, or one of the handful of daily dishes such as *bigoli in salsa* or *calimari in umido. Closed Sun.*

Ai Do Mori, San Polo 429, Calle dei Do Mori, **t** 041 522 5401. This historic '*locale*' occupies a long, rather gloomy, wood-panelled room. There's nowhere to sit, so punters (a mix of locals and clued-up foreigners) prop up the bar. Good wine list, plus *cicheti. Closed Sun and 3 weeks Aug.*

Algiubagiò, Cannaregio 5039, Fondamenta Nuove, **t** 041 523 6084, *www.algiubagio.com*. Right by the *vaporetto* stop for the islands, with a large terrace and friendly staff. Good for a drink, snack or light meal. *Closed Jan.*

Da Codroma, Dorsoduro 2540, Fondamenta Briati, **t** 041 524 6789. At lunchtime the long communal tables are packed with students. In the evening the atmosphere is smoky and laid-back. *Closed Sun and 3 weeks Aug.*

Vino Vino (*see* restaurant section, p.176).

Al Bottegon, Dorsoduro 992, Fondamenta Nani, **t** 041 523 0034. An old-fashioned wine shop near the Zattere with an 18th-century

atmosphere and wine by the glass served with snacks. *Closed Sun afternoon.*

Alla Patatina, San Polo 2741A, Ponte San Polo, **t** 041 523 7238. A lively place famous for its home-made potato chips. *Closed Sat eve, Sun and 2 weeks Aug.*

Enoteca Due Colonne, Cannaregio 1814C, Rio Terrà del Cristo, **t** 041 524 0453. A fun, noisy bar full of Venetians, serving *cicheti*, panini and a wide variety of drinks. Closed Sat.

Entertainment and Nightlife

Sadly, in a city that's clearly made-to-order for revelry and romance, life after dark is notoriously moribund. The locals take an evening stroll to their local *campo* for a chat and an *aperitivo*, before heading home – the hot-blooded may go on to bars and discos in Mestre, Marghera or the Lido. Even so, there are places to go among all this peace and quiet, and there's always Venice's packed calendar of special events. For an up-to-date calendar of current events, exhibitions, shows, films and concerts in the city, consult *Un Ospite di Venezia*, free from tourist offices.

Visitors are left to become even poorer at the **Casinò di Venezia**, Cannaregio 2040, Ca'Vendramin-Calergi, **t** 041 529 7111, *www.casinovenezia.it (daily 3pm–2.30am; dress smartly)*. You might prefer a comparative bargain – a moonlit gondola ride – or you can do as most people do: wander about. Venice is a different city at night.

Opera, Classical Music and Theatre

La Fenice, **t** 041 786 511, *fenice@interbusiness.it*, *www.teatrolafenice.it*. **PalaFenice**, Tronchetto island. **Teatro Malibran**, Cannaregio 5850, Campo del Milion, **t** 041 786 601. Until restoration work at La Fenice is completed (*see* p.201), the orchestra and chorus perform at the PalaFenice, a vast tent on Tronchetto, and the restored Teatro Malibran.

I Frari, San Polo, Campo dei Frari, **t** 041 522 2637. Regular concerts in this huge church, *see* pp.204–5 (*May–July and Sept–Oct Fri 9pm*).

Palazzo delle Prigioni, Riva degli Schiavoni, **t** 041 984 252, *www.concertinvenice.com*. Venetian Baroque and classical concerts in the ex-prison next to the Palazzo Ducale (*Jan–May and summer*).

La Pietà, Castello, Riva degli Schiavoni, **t** 041 523 1096. Concerts in Vivaldi's lovely rococo church (*see* p.206). Prices are usually high, but the acoustics are well-nigh perfect.

Teatro Goldoni, San Marco 4650B, Calle del Teatro, **t** 041 240 2011, *www.teatro stabileveneto.it*. Italian classics (Goldoni, Pirandello and so on) in a beautiful state-run theatre. Big-name directors and actors appear regularly. Some concerts too.

Jazz, Clubs and Nightspots

Venice's few late-night bars and music venues can be fun, or just posey and dull, and what you find is pretty much pot luck.

Bacaro Jazz, San Marco 5546, Salizzada del Fóndaco dei Tedeschi, **t** 041 528 5249. A lively bar where you can eat and drink until late. Jazz and blues sounds, and the occasional live act. *Open Thurs–Tues 11am–2am.*

Caffè Blu, Dorsoduro 3778, Salizzada San Pantalon, **t** 041 710 227. A crowded, smoky bar with live music (blues, Latin, jazz) on Fri evenings (*Oct–April*). *Open Mon–Fri 8.30am–2am, Sat 5pm–2am.*

Il Caffè, Dorsoduro 2963, Campo Santa Margherita, **t** 041 528 7998. Café-by-day (*see* p.176), open-air nightspot after dark. *Open Mon–Sat 7am–1.20am.*

Casanova Disco, Cannaregio 158A, Lista di Spagna, **t** 041 275 0199. Large classic 'disco' with pop, rock and chart music and some house nights. *Open daily 9pm–4am.*

Da Codroma, Dorsoduro 2540, Fondamenta Briati, **t** 041 524 6789. This popular student eaterie and drinkerie (*see* p.177) turns into a crowded nightspot with live music (jazz and blues) on Tues. *Open Sun–Fri 8am–midnight.*

Al Delfino, Lido, Lungomare Marconi 96, **t** 041 526 8309. An 'American bar' with music, snacks and billiards. *Open until 2am.*

The Fiddler's Elbow, Cannaregio 3847, Campiello Testori, **t** 041 523 9930. An Irish pub behind Palazzo Fontana. *Open daily 5pm–1am.*

Iguana, Cannaregio 2515, Fondamenta della Misericordia, **t** 041 713 561. Latin club with great cocktails (*happy hour 7–9*), spicy food and dancing to Latin sounds. Live music Tues. *Open Tues–Sat 6pm–2am.*

Margaret Duchamp, Dorsoduro 3019, Campo Santa Margherita, **t** 041 528 6255. A designer 'disco bar' (as it calls itself); one of the few in Venice and frequented by a trendy mix of black-clad Venetians and foreigners. *Open daily 9am–2am (winter closed Tues).*

L'Olandese Volante, Castello 5658, Campo San Lio, **t** 041 528 9349. 'The Flying Dutchman' is a current favourite for young trendies and one of Venice's answers to a pub, open late with snacks. *Open Mon–Sat 10am–midnight.*

Paradiso Perduto, Cannaregio 2540, Fondamenta della Misericordia, **t** 041 720 581. The city's best-known and most popular late-night bar/restaurant, with inexpensive though variable food and a relaxed, bohemian atmosphere; live concerts (jazz and roots music), parties, exhibitions. *Open Thurs–Tues 7pm–2am; closed 2 weeks Aug.*

Piccolo Mondo, Dorsoduro 1056, Calle Contarini-Corfù, **t** 041 520 0371. Tiny and rather sleazy, but one of the few real clubs in Venice. *Open Tues–Sun 10pm–4am.*

Sound Code, Mestre, Via delle Industrie 32, **t** 041 531 3890. The best disco in the area. *Open Fri and Sat until 4am.*

Teranga, Mestre, Via della Crusca 34, **t** 041 531 7787. A popular and lively club playing mainly African sounds, and with regular live music. Membership required (about €10). *Open Fri and Sat 9.30pm–4am.*

Vitae, San Marco 4118, Calle Sant'Antonio, **t** 041 520 5205. Small, smoky and crowded, with designer décor and loud, laid-back music. Popular for cocktails. Summer nights see the hip crowd spill on to the street outside. *Open Mon–Fri 9am–1am, Sat 3pm–1am.*

Cipriani Hotel, Giudecca 10, Fondamenta San Giovanni, **t** 041 520 774. The Cipriani has two piano bars: the San Giorgio (*7pm–10pm*); and Bar Gabbiano (*10pm–2am*), where the pianist also sings, and you can dance.

T.A.G. Club, Mestre, Via Giustizia 19, **t** 041 921 970, *www.v4u.it/tag*. An excellent little club with live blues, jazz and rock. *Open Wed–Sat 10pm–5am.*

Al Vapore, Marghera, Via Fratelli Bandiera 8, **t** 041 930 796. Small venue near Mestre station very popular for excellent live jazz and blues concerts featuring both known and lesser-known names. *Open Tues–Sun noon–3pm and 6pm–2am.*

Venice seduces, Venice irritates, but Venice rarely disappoints. She is a golden fairy-tale city floating on the sea, a lovely mermaid with agate eyes and the gift of eternal youth. On the surface she is little changed from the days when Goethe called her the 'market-place of the Morning and the Evening lands', when her amphibious citizens dazzled the world with their wealth and pageantry, their magnificent fleet, their half-Oriental doges, their crafty merchant princes, their splendidly luminous art, their silken debauchery and their decline and fall into a seemingly endless carnival. One can easily imagine Julius Caesar bewildered by today's Rome, or Romeo and Juliet missing their rendezvous in the traffic of modern Verona, but Marco Polo, were he to return from Cathay today, could take a familiar gondola up the familiar Grand Canal to his house in the Rialto, astonished more by the motor-boats than anything else. Credit for this unique preservation goes to the Lagoon, the amniotic fluid of Venice's birth, her impenetrable 'walls' and the formaldehyde that has pickled her more thoroughly than many far more venerable cities on the mainland.

When to Go

Venice (Venezia) is as much a character as a setting, and the same may be said of its weather. In no other city will you be so aware of the light; on a clear, fine day no place could be more limpid and clear, no water as crystal-bright as the Lagoon. The rosy dawn igniting the domes of St Mark's, the splash of an oar fading in the cool mist of a canal, the pearly twilit union of water and sky are among the city's oldest clichés.

If you seek solitude and romance with a capital R, go in January. Pack a warm coat, water-resistant shoes and an umbrella, and expect frequent fogs and mists. It may even snow – in 1987 you could even ski-jump down the Rialto bridge. But there are also plenty of radiant diamond days, brilliant, sunny and chill; any time after October you take your chances.

As spring approaches there is Carnival, a game and beautiful but rather bland attempt to revive a piece of old Venice; Lent is fairly quiet, though in the undercurrent the Venetians are building up for their first major invasion of sightseers at Easter. By April the tourism industry is cranked up to full operational capacity; the gondolas are un-mothballed and the café tables have blossomed in the Piazza. In June even the Italians are considering a trip to the beach.

In July and August elbow-room is at a premium. Peripheral camping grounds are packed, queues at the tourist office's room-finding service stretch longer and longer, and the police are kept busy reminding the hordes that there's no picnicking in St Mark's Square. The heat can be sweltering, the ancient city gasping under a flood of cameras, shorts, sunglasses and rucksacks. Scores head off to the Lido for relief; a sudden thunderstorm over the Lagoon livens things up, as do the many festivals, especially the Redentore and its fireworks in July. In the autumn the city and the Venetians begin to unwind, the rains begin to fall, and you can watch them pack up the parasols and cabanas on the Lido with a wistful sigh.

As far as hotels are concerned, high season is from Carnival to mid-November, with prices coming down a bit in midsummer.

Venetia

Venetia, sometimes known as the Three Venetias, is one of Italy's ripest showpieces and most chic holiday playgrounds, bursting at the seams with brilliant art, palaces, villas and beautiful cities. To these add some of Europe's most ravishing mountains, alpine lakes and sophisticated winter sports facilities; add too a few of Italy's most famous wines, delicious seafood and a very noticeable cultural diversity and richness.

Venetia encompasses roughly the region controlled by Venice from the 14th and 15th centuries until the conquest of Napoleon. It includes three modern Italian regions – the Veneto itself, and the autonomous regions of Trentino-Alto Adige (Trento and Bolzano provinces) and Friuli-Venezia Giulia (Trieste, Udine, Pordenone and Gorizia) – stretching from the Po to the Dolomites, from Lake Garda to the border of Slovenia.

For 1,000 years Venice called herself the Most Serene Republic (La Serenissima), and at one point she ruled 'a quarter and a half' of the Roman Empire. The descent to an Italian provincial capital was steep and bittersweet; and sensitive souls find gallons of melancholy, or, like Thomas Mann, even death, brewed into the city's canals that have nothing to do with the more flagrant microbes. In the winter, when the streets are silent, Venice can be so evocative that you have to kick the ghosts out of the way to pass down the narrower alleys. But most people (some million or so a year) show up in the summer and, like their ancestors, have a jolly good time. For Venice is a most experienced old siren in her boudoir of watery mirrors. International organizations pump in the funds to keep her petticoats out of the water and smooth her wrinkles. Notices posted throughout the city acknowledge that she 'belongs to everybody', while with a wink she slides a knowing hand deep into your pocket. Venice has always lived for gold, and you can bet she wants yours – and you might just as well give it to her, in return for the most enchanting, dream-like favours any city can grant.

History

Venice has always been so different, so improbable, that one can easily believe the legend that the original inhabitants sprang up from the dew and mists on the mud banks of the Lagoon. Historians who don't believe in fairies say that Venice was born of adversity: the islands and treacherous shallows of the Lagoon provided the citizens of the Veneto with a refuge from **Attila the Hun** and the Arian heresies sweeping the mainland. According to Venetians' own legends, the city was founded at exactly noon, 25 March 413, when the refugees laid the first stone on the Rialto. Twelve Lagoon townships grew up between modern Chioggia and Grado; when Theodoric the Great's secretary Cassiadorus visited them in 523 he wrote that they were 'scattered like sea-birds' nests over the face of the waters'.

In 697 the 12 townships united to elect their first duke, or Doge. Fishing, trading – in slaves, among other things – and their unique knowledge of the Lagoon brought the Venetians their first prosperity, but their key position in between the Byzantine empire and the 'barbarian' kings on the mainland also made them a bone of contention. In 810 the Franks, who had defeated the Lombards in the name of the Pope and claimed dominion over the whole of northern Italy, turned their attention to the last hold-out, Venice: Doge Obelario de'Antenori, engaged in a bitter internal feud with other Venetian factions, even invited Charlemagne's son Pepin to send his army into the city.

The quarrelling Venetians, until then undecided whether to support Rome or Constantinople, united at the approach of Pepin's fleet, deposed the Doge, declared for Byzantium, and entrenched themselves on the Rialto. The shallows and queer humours of the Lagoon confounded Pepin, and after a gruelling six-month siege he threw in the towel. A subsequent treaty between the Franks and the Eastern Emperor Nicephorus (814) recognized Venice as a subject of **Byzantium**, with important trading concessions. As Byzantine authority over the city was never more than words, it in effect marked the birth of an independent republic.

The Venetians lacked only a dynamic spiritual protector; their frumpy St Theodore with his crocodile was simply too low in the celestial hierarchy to fulfil the destiny they had in mind. In 829 Venetian merchants, supposedly on secret orders from the Doge, carried off one of the Republic's greatest coups when they purloined the body of St Mark from Alexandria, smuggling him past Egyptian customs by claiming that the saint was pickled pork. To acquire an Evangelist for themselves was, in itself, a demonstration of the Venetians' new ambition.

Marriage to the Sea

As the East–West trade expanded, the Venetians designed their domestic and external policies to accommodate it. At home they required peace and stability, and by the beginning of the 11th century had squelched all notions of an hereditary doge-ship by exiling the most hyper-active families; Venice would never have the despotic *signori* who plagued the rest of Italy. Raids by Dalmatian pirates spurred the Venetians to fight and win their first major war in 997, under **Doge Pietro Orseolo**, who captured the pirates' coastal strongholds. The Venetians were so pleased with themselves that they celebrated the event with a splendidly arrogant ritual every Ascension Day, the Sensa or 'Marriage of the Sea', in which the Doge would sail out to the Lido in his sumptuous barge, the *Bucintoro*, and cast a diamond ring into the sea, proclaiming 'We wed thee, O sea, in sign of our true and perpetual dominion'.

Venice, because of her location and fleet, supplied a great deal of the transport for the first three Crusades, and in return received her first important trading concessions in the Middle East. Arch-rival Genoa became increasingly envious, and in 1171 convinced the Byzantine Emperor to all but wipe out the Venetian merchants in Constantinople. Rashly, the Doge Vitale Michiel II set off in person to launch a revenge attack upon the Empire, and failed utterly, and on his return he was killed by an angry mob. The Venetians learned from their mistakes: the Great Council, the *Maggior Consiglio*, was created to check the power of the Doge and avert future calamities.

Vengeance stayed on the back-burner until the next Doge, the spry and crafty Enrico Dandolo, was contracted to provide transport for the Fourth Crusade. When the

Crusaders turned up without their fare, Dandolo offered to forgo it in return for certain services: first, to reduce Venice's rebellious satellites in Dalmatia, and then, in 1204, to sail to Constantinople instead of Egypt. Aged 90 and almost blind, Dandolo personally led the attack; Christendom was scandalized, but Venice had gained, not only a glittering hoard of loot, but three-eighths of Constantinople and 'a quarter and a half' of the Roman Empire – enough islands and ports to control the trade routes in the Adriatic, Aegean, Asia Minor and the Black Sea.

To ensure their dominance at home, in 1297 the merchant élite limited membership in the *Maggior Consiglio* to themselves and their heirs (an event known in Venetian history as the **Serrata**, or Lock-out), their names inscribed in the famous **Golden Book**. The Doges were reduced to honorary chairmen of the board, bound up by an increasingly complex web of laws and customs to curb any possible ambitions; for the patricians, fear of revolution from above was as powerful as fear of revolt from below.

A Rocky 14th Century

First the people (1300) and then the snubbed patricians (the 1310 **Tiepolo Conspiracy**) rose up against their disenfranchisement under the *Serrata*. Both were unsuccessful, but the latter threat was serious enough that a committee of public safety was formed to hunt down the conspirators, and in 1335 this committee became a permanent institution, the infamous **Council of Ten**. Because of its secrecy and speedy decisions, the Council of Ten (in later years it was streamlined into a Council of Three) was more truly executive than the figurehead Doge: it guarded Venice's internal security, looked after foreign policy and, with its sumptuary laws, kept tabs on the Venetians' moral conduct as well.

Away from home the 14th century was marked by a fight to the death with Genoa over eastern trade routes. Each republic annihilated the other's fleet on more than one occasion before things came to a head in 1379, when the Genoese, fresh from a victory over the Venetian commander Vittor Pisani, captured Chioggia and waited for Venice to starve, boasting that they had come to 'bridle the horses of St Mark'. As was their custom, the Council of Ten had imprisoned Pisani for his defeat, but Venice was now in such a jam, with half of its fleet far away, that the people demanded his release to lead what remained of their navy. A brilliant commander, Pisani exploited his familiarity with the Lagoon and in turn blockaded the Genoese in Chioggia. When the other half of Venice's fleet came dramatically racing home, the Genoese surrendered (June 1380) and never recovered in the East.

Fresh Prey on the Mainland

Venice was determined never to feel hungry again, and set her sights on the mainland – not only for the sake of farmland, but to control her trade routes into the west that were being increasingly harried and taxed by the *signori* of the Veneto. Treviso came first, then opportunity knocked in 1402 with the sudden death of the Milanese duke Gian Galeazzo Visconti, whose conquests became the subject of a great land grab. Venice picked up Padua, Bassano, Verona and Belluno, and in 1454 added Ravenna, southern Trentino, Friuli, Crema and Bergamo. In 1489 the Republic's overseas empire reached its greatest extent when it was presented with Cyprus, a somewhat reluctant 'gift' from the king's widow, a Venetian noblewoman named Caterina Cornaro who received the hill town of Àsolo as compensation.

But just as Venice expanded, Fortune's wheel gave a creak and conspired to squeeze her back into her Lagoon. The Ottoman Turks captured Constantinople in 1453 and, although the Venetians tried to negotiate trading terms with the sultans (as they had previously done with the infidel Saracens, to the opprobrium of the West), they would be spending the next three centuries fighting a losing battle for their eastern territories. The discovery of the New World was another blow, but gravest to the merchants of Venice was Vasco da Gama's voyage around the Cape of Good Hope to India in 1497, blazing a cheaper and easier route to Venice's prime markets that broke her monopoly of oriental luxuries; Western European merchants no longer had to pay Venice for safe passage to the East. In just 44 years nearly everything that Venice had worked for over 500 years was undermined.

On the mainland, Venice's rapid expansion had excited the fear and envy of Pope Julius, who rallied Italy's potentates and their foreign allies to form the League of Cambrai to humble the proud Republic. They snatched her *terra firma* possessions after her defeat at Agnadello in 1509, but quarrelled amongst themselves afterwards, and before long all the territories they conquered voluntarily returned to Venice. Venice, however, never really recovered from this wound inflicted by the very people who should have rallied to her defence, and although her Arsenal produced a warship a day, and her captains helped to win a glorious victory over the Turks at Lepanto (1571), she was increasingly forced to retreat.

A Most Leisurely Collapse

The odds were stacked against her, but in her heyday Venice had accumulated enough wealth and verve to cushion her fall. Her noble families consoled themselves in the classical calm of Palladio's villas, while the city found solace in masterpieces of Venice's golden age of art. Carnival, ever longer, ever more licentious, was sanctioned by the state to bring in moneyed visitors, like Lord Byron, who dubbed it 'the revel of the earth, the masque of Italy'. In the 1600s the city had 20,000 courtesans, many of them dressed as men to whet the Venetians' passion. It didn't suit everyone: 'Venice is a stink pot, charged with every virus of hell,' fumed one Dr Warner, in the 18th century.

In 1797 **Napoleon**, declaring he would be 'an Attila for the Venetian state', took it with scarcely a whimper, ending the story of the world's longest-enduring republic, in the reign of its 120th doge. Napoleon took the horses of St Mark to Paris as his trophy, and replaced the old *Pax tibi, Marce, Evangelista Meus* inscribed in the book the lion holds up on Venice's coat-of-arms with 'The Rights of Men and Citizens'. Reading it, a gondolier made the famous remark, 'At last he's turned the page'. Yet while many patricians danced merrily around his Liberty trees, freed at last from responsiblity, the people wept. Napoleon gave Venice to Austria, whose rule was confirmed by the Congress of Vienna after the Emperor's defeat in 1815. The Austrians' main contribution was the railway causeway linking Venice irrevocably to the mainland (1846). Two years later, Venice gave its last gasp of independence, when a patriotic revolt led by

Daniele Manin seized the city and re-established the Republic, only to fall to the Austrian army once again after a heroic one-year siege.

Modern Venice

The former Republic did, however, finally join the new kingdom of Italy in 1866, after Prussia had conveniently defeated the Austrians. Already better known as a magnet to visitors than for any activity of its own, Venice played a quiet role in the new state. Things changed under Mussolini, the industrial zones of Mestre and Marghera were begun on the mainland, and a road was added to the railway causeway. The city escaped damage in the two World Wars, despite heavy fighting in the environs; according to legend, when the Allies finally occupied Venice in 1945 they arrived in a fleet of gondolas.

But Venice was soon to engage in its own private battle with the sea. From the beginning the city had manipulated nature's waterways for her own survival, diverting a major outlet of the Po, the Brenta, the Piave, the Adige, and the Sile rivers to keep her Lagoon from silting up. In 1782 Venice completed the famous *murazzi*, the 2½-mile-long, 20ft-high sea walls to protect the Lagoon. But on 4 November 1966 a deadly combination of wind, torrential storms, high tides and giant waves breached the *murazzi*, wrecked the Lido and left Venice under record *acque alte* (high waters) for 20 hours, with disastrous results to the city's architecture and art. The catastrophe galvanized the international community's efforts to save Venice. Even the Italian state, notorious for its indifference to Venice (historical grudges die slowly in Italy) passed a law in 1973 to preserve the city, and contributed to the construction of a new flood barricade similar to the one on the Thames.

This giant sea gate, known as 'Moses', has now been completed, but arguments continue over whether it will ever be effective if needed, and what its ecological consequences might be. Venice today is perennially in crisis, permanently under restoration, and seemingly threatened by a myriad potential disasters – the growth of algae in the Lagoon, the effects of the outpourings of Mestre on its foundations, the ageing of its native population, or perhaps most of all the sheer number of its tourists. Proposals have been made to charge admissions at the causeway and limit the number who come in daily. Fears of an environmental catastrophe have, though, receded of late; somehow, the city contrives to survive, as unique as ever, and recent proposals to give it more of a function in the modern world, as, for example, a base for international organizations, may serve to give it new life as well.

Architecture

At once isolated but linked to the traditions of East and West, Venice developed her own charmingly bastard architecture, especially in a style called Venetian Gothic, adopting only the most delightfully visual elements from each tradition. Ruskin's *The Stones of Venice* is the classic work on the city's buildings, which harsher critics – and Ruskin was one – disparage for being all artifice and show. The Venetians inherited the Byzantines' love of colour, mosaics, rare marbles and exotic effects, epitomized in the magnificently gaudy **St Mark's**. Venetian Gothic is only slightly less elaborate, and achieved its best products in the great palaces, most notably the **Palazzo Ducale** and the **Ca' d'Oro**, with their ogival windows and finely wrought façades.

The Renaissance arrived in Venice relatively late, and its early phase is called Lombardesque, after the **Lombardo** family (Pietro and sons Tullio and Antonio) who designed the best of it, including **Santa Maria dei Miracoli** and the rich **Scuola di San Marco**. Later Renaissance architects brought Venice into the mainstream of the classical revival, and graced Venice with the arcaded **Piazza San Marco**, the **Libreria** of Sansovino, the **San Michele** of Mauro Codussi (or Coducci), and two of **Palladio**'s finest churches. Venice's best Baroque works are by **Longhena**, the spiritual heir of Palladio.

To support all this on the soft mud banks, the Venetians drove piles of Istrian pine 16½ft into the solid clay – over a million posts hold up the church of Santa Maria della Salute alone. If Venice tends to lean and sink, it's due to erosion of these piles by the salty Adriatic, pollution, and the currents and wash caused by the deep channels dredged into the Lagoon for the large tankers sailing to Marghera. Or, as the Venetians explain, the city is a giant sponge.

The Face of Venice

Venice stands on 117 islets, divided by over 100 canals that are spanned by some 400 bridges. The longest bridges are the 4.2km rail and road causeways that link Venice to the mainland. The open sea is half that distance across the Lagoon, beyond the protective reefs or *lidi* formed by centuries of river silt and the Adriatic current. The Grand Canal, Venice's incomparable main street, was originally the bed of a river that fed the Lagoon; the other canals, its tributaries (called *rio*, singular, or *rii*, plural), were shallow channels meandering through the mud banks, and are nowhere as grand – some are merely glorified sewers.

A warren of 2,300 alleys, or *calli*, handle Venice's pedestrian-only traffic, and they come with a colourful bouquet of names – a *rio terrà* is a filled-in canal; a *piscina* a filled-in pool; a *fondamenta* or *riva* a quay; a *salizzada* is a street that was paved in the 17th century; a *ruga* is one lined with shops; a *sottoportico* passes under a building. A Venetian square is a *campo*, recalling the days when they were open fields; the only square dignified with the title of '*piazza*' is that of St Mark's, though the two smaller squares flanking the basilica are called *piazzette*, and there's one fume-filled *piazzale* (Piazzale Roma), the dead end for buses and cars.

All the *rii* and *calli* have been divided into six quarters, or *sestieri*, since Venice's earliest days: San Marco (by the *piazza*), Castello (by the Arsenal) and Cannaregio (by the Ghetto), all on the northeast bank of the Grand Canal; and San Polo (by the church), Santa Croce (near the Piazzale Roma), and Dorsoduro, the 'hard-back' by the Accademia, all on the southwest bank. Besides these, the modern *comune* of Venice includes the towns on the Lagoon islands, the Lido, and the mainland *comuni* of Mestre and Marghera, Italy's version of the New Jersey Flats, where most Venetians live today. There is some concern that historic Venice (population around 60,000 and falling , down from 170,000 in 1946) may soon become a city of second homes belonging to wealthy northern Italians and foreigners.

Most Venetian houses are four to six storeys high. On the tops of some you can see the wooden rooftop loggias, or *altane*, where the Renaissance ladies of Venice were wont to idle, bleaching their hair in the sun; they wore broad-brimmed hats to protect their complexions, and spread their tresses through a hole cut in the crown.

Venetian Art

Venice may have been a Renaissance Johnny-come-lately, but the city and its hinterland are rivalled only by Tuscany when it comes to top-notch painting. Before the 14th century the Venetians excelled primarily in mosaic, an art they learned from the Byzantines, shown at their very best in St Mark's and Torcello. In 1306 **Giotto** painted his masterpiece in Padua's Cappella Scrovegni and gave local painters a revolutionary eyeful. His naturalism influenced a school of artists in Padua and **Paolo Veneziano**, the first great Venetian painter of note, although many artists would continue painting decorative Gothic pieces for a long time to come, notably **Jacobello del Fiore**, **Michele Giambono** and the **Vivarini** family.

Things began to change in the mid 15th century, with the advent of two great masters. **Andrea Mantegna** (1431–1506), trained in Padua, influenced generations with his strong interests in antiquity, perspective and powerful sculptured figures. His more lyrical and humane brother-in-law, **Giovanni Bellini** (1440?–1516) founded the Venetian school. Bellini learned the technique of oil painting from **Antonello da Messina** during his visit in 1475, and he never looked back: his use of luminous natural light and colour to create atmosphere ('tonalism') and sensuous beauty are characteristics all of his followers adopted, if few ever equalled. Meanwhile Giovanni's brother, **Gentile Bellini**, and **Vittore Carpaccio** (1470–1523) avoided tonalism altogether in their charming and precise narrative works.

The Cinquecento–Settecento

For the heavy hitters of Venice's 16th-century Golden Age, however, tonalism was a religion: while other Italians followed the Romans in learning drawing and anatomy, the Venetians went their own way, obsessed by the dramatic qualities of atmosphere. The tragically short-lived **Giorgione di Castelfranco** (1475–1510) was the seminal figure in the new manner: his *Tempest* in the Accademia is a remarkable study in brooding tension. Giorgione also invented 'easel painting' – i.e. art that served neither Church nor State nor the vanity of the patron, but stood on its own for the pleasure of the viewer.

Giorgione's colleague, Tiziano Vecellio, or **Titian** (1485/90–1576), was the greatest master of the Venetian school. Known for his bold, spiralling compositions, his rich colours and his luscious mythologies, he was a revolutionary in his old age, using increasingly free brushstrokes and even applying paint with his fingers. **Tintoretto** (1518–94), of the famously quick brushstrokes, took his Mannerist compositions to unforgettable extremes, while his contemporary, **Paolo Veronese** (1528–88), painted lavish *trompe l'œil* canvases and frescoes that are the culmination of Venice at her most decorative. This was also the period of **Palma Vecchio**, the sensuous painter of

Signs and Directions

The Venetian language, Venetic or Venet, is still commonly heard – to the uninitiated it sounds like an Italian trying to speak Spanish with a numb mouth – and it turns up on the city's street signs. Your map may read 'San Giovanni e Paolo' but you should inquire for 'San Zanipolo'; 'San Giovanni Decollato' (decapitated John) is better known as 'San Zan Degola'. Still, despite the impossibility of giving comprehensible directions through the tangle of alleys (Venetians will invariably point you in the right direction, however, with a blithe *sempre diritto!* – straight ahead!), it's hard to get hopelessly lost in Venice. It only measures about 1.5 by 3 kilometres, and there are helpful yellow signs at major crossings, pointing the way to San Marco, Rialto and the Accademia, or the Piazzale Roma and the Ferrovia if you despair and want to go home. When hunting for an address in Venice, make sure you're in the correct *sestiere*, as quite a few *calli* share names. Also, beware that houses in each *sestiere* are numbered consecutively in a system logical only to a postman from Mars; numbers up to 5,000 are not unusual.

Venetian blonde goddesses, **Cima da Conegliano**, author of some of the loveliest landscapes, and **Lorenzo Lotto**, of the famous psychologically penetrating portraits, who was run out of Venice by Titian and his buddies.

Venetia enjoyed an artistic revival in the twilight years of the 18th century, when its art was in great demand at home and abroad. Much of the thanks goes to **Giambattista Tiepolo** (1697–1770), the first to cast aside Baroque gloominess to create an effervescent, light-filled, brilliantly coloured style; he was also the last great fresco-painter in Italy. His chief follower was his son Giandomenico, although his influence can also be seen in the luminous palettes of **Antonio Canaletto** (1697–1768) and **Francesco Guardi** (1712–93), who produced the countless views of Venice that were the rage among travellers on the Grand Tour; even now most of their works are in Britain and France. **Pietro Longhi**, their contemporary, devoted himself to genre scenes that offer a delightful insight into the Venice of 200 years ago.

Around the City

The Grand Canal

A ride down Venice's bustling and splendid main artery is most visitors' introduction to the city, and there's no finer one. The Grand Canal has always been Venice's status address, and along its looping banks the patricians of the Golden Book, or *Nobili Homini*, built a hundred marble palaces with their front doors giving onto the water, framed by peppermint-stick posts where they moored their watery carriages.

The highlights, from Piazzale Roma to Piazza San Marco, include: the 12th-century **Fóndaco dei Turchi** (with rounded arches, on the right after the Station Bridge), the Ottoman merchants' headquarters until 1838, and now the Natural History

Museum. Nearly opposite, Mauro Codussi's Renaissance **Palazzo Vendramin-Calergi**, where Richard Wagner died in 1883, is now the casino. Back on the right bank, just after the San Stae landing, the Baroque **Palazzo Pésaro** is adorned with masks by Longhena. And then comes the loveliest palace of all, the **Ca' d'Oro**, with an florid Venetian Gothic façade, formerly etched in gold, now housing the Galleria Franchetti (*see* p.209).

After the Ca' d'Oro Europe's most famous bridge, the **Ponte di Rialto**, swings into view. 'Rialto' recalls the days when the canal was the Rio Alto; originally it was spanned here by a bridge of boats, then by a 13th-century wooden bridge. When that was on the verge of collapse, the Republic held a competition for the design of a new stone structure. The winner, Antonio da Ponte, was the most audacious, proposing a single arch spanning 157ft; built in 1592, it has defied all the dire predictions of the day and still stands, even taking the additional weight of two rows of shops. The reliefs over the arch are of St Mark and St Theodore.

Byron Goes Swimming

Byron arrived in Venice in 1816, his heart full of romance as he rented a villa on the Brenta to compose the last canto of his *Childe Harold's Pilgrimage*. The city's canals at least afforded him the personal advantage of being able to swim anywhere (his club foot made him shy of walking); on one occasion he swam a race from the Lido to the Rialto bridge and was the only man to finish.

It wasn't long before the emotional polish of *Childe Harold* began to crack. To Byron's surprise, Venice didn't perfect his romantic temper, but cured him of it. He went to live in the Palazzo Mocenigo on the Grand Canal, in the company of 14 servants, a dog, a wolf, a fox, monkeys and a garlicky baker's wife, *La Fornarina*, who stabbed him in the hand with a fork – which so angered Byron that he ordered her out, whereupon she threw herself into the Grand Canal. Under such circumstances, all that had been breathless passion reeked of the ridiculous, as he himself admitted:

And the sad truth which hovers o'er my desk
Turns what was once romantic to burlesque

Venice, its women, its own ironic detachment and its love of liberty set Byron's mind free to write *Beppo: A Venetian Story*, spoofing Venice's *cavalieri serventi* (escort-lovers – even nuns had them) while celebrating the freedom of its people. He followed this with two bookish plays on Venetian themes, *Marino Faliero* and *The Two Foscari*, and most importantly began his satirical masterpiece, *Don Juan*.

Meanwhile debauchery was taking its toll: an English acquaintance wrote in 1818 that 'His face had become pale, bloated and sallow, and the knuckles on his hands were lost in fat'. Byron became infatuated with a young countess, Teresa Guiccioli, and left Venice to move in with her and her elderly husband in Ravenna. But, having tasted every freedom in Venice, Byron once more began to chafe; the *contessa* was 'taming' him. He bundled up the manuscript of *Don Juan* and left, only to die of fever at the age of 36 in the Greek War of Independence.

To the right stretch the extensive **Rialto Markets**, and on the left the **Fóndaco dei Tedeschi** (German Warehouse), once the busiest trading centre in Venice, where merchants from all over the north lived and traded. The building (now the post office) was remodelled in 1505 and adorned with exterior frescoes by Giorgione and Titian, of which only fragments survive (now in the Ca' d'Oro).

Beyond the Ponte di Rialto are two Renaissance masterpieces: across from the San Silvestro landing, Sanmicheli's 1556 **Palazzo Grimani**, now the Appeals Court, and Mauro Codussi's **Palazzo Corner-Spinelli** (1510), just before Sant'Angelo landing stage. A short distance further along the left bank are the **Palazzi Mocenigo**, actually three palaces in one, where Byron lived for two years (*see* p.189). A little way further on the same side, the wall of buildings gives way for the Campo San Samuele, dominated by the **Palazzo Grassi,** an 18th-century neoclassical residence, renovated by Fiat as a modern exhibition and cultural centre.

On the right bank, just after the bend in the canal, the lovely Gothic **Ca' Foscari** was built in 1437 for Doge Francesco Foscari; two doors down, by its own landing-stage, is Longhena's 1667 **Ca' Rezzonico**, where Browning died. Further on the canal is spanned by the wooden **Ponte dell'Accademia**, built in 1932 to replace the ungainly iron 'English bridge'. On the left bank, before Santa Maria del Giglio landing, the majestic Renaissance **Palazzo Corner** (Ca' Grande) was built by Sansovino in 1550. On the right bank, Longhena's Baroque masterpiece **Santa Maria della Salute** is followed by the Customs House, or **Dogana di Mare**, crowned by a golden globe and weathervane of Fortune, guarding the entrance to the Grand Canal. The next stop is San Marco.

Piazza San Marco

Venice's self-proclaimed Attila, Napoleon himself, described this asymmetrical showpiece as 'Europe's finest drawing-room', and, no matter how often you've seen it in pictures or in the flesh, its charm never fades. There are Venetians (and not all of them purveyors of souvenirs) who prefer it in the height of summer at its liveliest, when Babylonians from the four corners of the earth outnumber even the pigeons, who swoop back and forth at eye level, while the rival café bands provide a Fellini-esque accompaniment. Others prefer it in the misty moonlight, when the familiar seems unreal under hazy, rosy streetlamps.

The piazza and its two flanking *piazzette* have looked essentially the same since 1810, when the 'Ala Napoleonica' was added to the west end, to close in Mauro Codussi's long, arcaded **Procuratie Vecchie** (1499) on the north side and Sansovino's **Procuratie Nuove** (1540) on the south. Both, originally used as the offices of the 'procurators' or caretakers of St Mark's, are now filled with jewellery, embroidery and lace shops. Two centuries ago they contained an equal number of coffee-houses, the centres of the 18th-century promenade. Only two survive – the **Caffè Quadri** in the Procuratie Vecchie, the old favourite of the Austrians, and **Florian's**, in the Procuratie Nuove, its décor unchanged since it opened its doors in 1720, although with espressos at more than €3 a head the proprietors could easily afford to remodel it in solid gold.

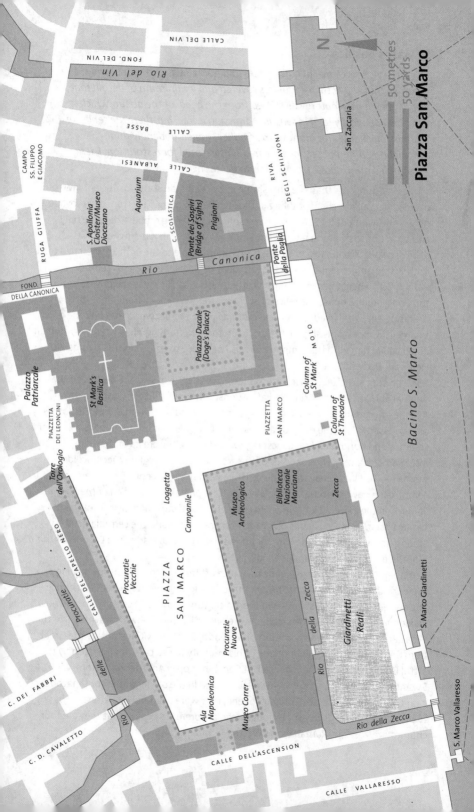

Piazza San Marco

N

50 metres
50 yards

CALLE DEL VIN
FOND. DEL VIN
Rio del Vin

CAMPO
SS. FILIPPO
E GIACOMO

CALLE BASSE

CALLE ALBANESI

San Zaccaria

RUGA GIUFFA

S. Apollonia
Cloister/Museo
Diocesano

Aquarium

C. SCOLASTICA

Ponte dei Sospiri
(Bridge of Sighs)

Prigioni

RIVA DEGLI SCHIAVONI

FOND.
DELLA CANONICA

Rio Canonica

Ponte
della Paglia

Palazzo
Patriarcale

PIAZZETTA
DEI LEONCINI

St Mark's
Basilica

Palazzo Ducale
(Doge's Palace)

MOLO

Column of
St Mark

Column of
St Theodore

PIAZZETTA
SAN MARCO

Bacino S. Marco

Torre
dell'Orologio

CALLE DEL CAPELLO NERO

Procuratie
Vecchie

Loggetta

Campanile

PIAZZA
SAN MARCO

Museo
Archeologico

Biblioteca
Nazionale
Marciana

Zecca

C. DEI FABBRI

Procuratie
delle

Rio

Procuratie
Nuove

Zecca

della

Zecca

Giardinetti
Reali

S. Marco Giardinetti

C. D. CAVALETTO

Rio

delle

Ala
Napoleonica

Museo Correr

Rio della Zecca

S. Marco Vallaresso

CALLE DELL'ASCENSION

CALLE VALLARESSO

St Mark's Basilica

Open to visitors Mon–Sat 9.30–5, Sun and hols 2–4.30. No shorts, and women must have their shoulders covered and a minimum of décolletage, or risk being peremptorily dismissed from the head of the queue, which can be diabolically long in season. Admission is free, but there are separate admission charges for many of the smaller chapels and individual attractions; different sections are frequently closed for restoration. There is disabled ramp access from Piazzetta dei Leoncini.

This is nothing less than the holy shrine of the Venetian state. An ancient law decreed that all merchants trading in the East had to bring back from each voyage a new embellishment for St Mark's. The result is a glittering robbers' den, the only church in Christendom that would not look out of place in Xanadu. Yet it was dismissed out of hand for centuries. 'Low, impenetrable to the light, in wretched taste both within and without,' wrote the Président de Brosses in the 18th century.

Until 1807, when it became Venice's cathedral, the basilica was the private chapel of the Doge, built to house the relics of St Mark after their 'pious theft' of his body from Alexandria in 828, a deed sanctioned by a tidy piece of apocrypha that had the good Evangelist mooring his ship on the Rialto on the way from Aquileia to Rome, when an angel hailed him with the famous '*Pax tibi*...' or 'Peace to you, Mark, my Evangelist. Here your body shall lie.'

The present structure, consecrated in 1094, was begun after a fire destroyed the original St Mark's in 976. Modelled after Constantinople's former Church of the Apostles, five rounded doorways, five upper arches and five round Byzantine domes are the essentials of the exterior, all frosted with a sheen of coloured marbles, ancient columns and sculpture ('As if in ecstasy,' wrote Ruskin, 'the crests of the arches break into marbly foam...'). The spandrils of the arches glitter with gaudy, Technicolor mosaics – the High Renaissance, dissatisfied with the 13th-century originals, saw fit to commission new painterly scenes, leaving intact only the *Translation of the Body of St Mark* on the extreme left, which includes the first historical depiction of the basilica itself. The three bands of 13th-century **reliefs** around the central portal, among Italy's finest Romanesque carvings, show Venetian trades, the Labours of the Months, and Chaos in the inner band.

Front and centre, seemingly ready to prance off the façade, the controversial 1979 copies of the bronze **horses of St Mark** masquerade well enough – from a distance. The ancient originals (cast between the 3rd century BC and 2nd century AD, and now inside the basilica's Museo Marciano) were one of the most powerful symbols of the Venetian Republic. Originally a 'triumphal quadriga' taken by Constantine the Great from Chios to grace the Hippodrome of his new city, it was carried off in turn by the artful Doge Dandolo in the 1204 Sack of Constantinople. Another prize from Byzantium are the four porphyry 'Moors' huddled in the corner of the south façade near the Doge's Palace; according to legend, they were changed into stone for daring to break into St Mark's treasury, though scholars prefer to believe that they are four chummy 3rd-century Roman emperors, the Tetrarchs.

The Interior

The best mosaics, most of them from the 13th century, cover the six domes of the **atrium**, or narthex, their old gold glimmering in the permanent twilight. The oldest mosaic in St Mark's is that of the *Madonna and Saints* above the central door, a survivor of the original 11th-century decoration of the basilica. A slab of red marble in the pavement marks the spot where the Emperor Barbarossa knelt and apologized to 'St Peter and his Pope' – Alexander III, in 1177. This, a favourite subject of Venetian state art, is one of the few gold stars the Republic ever earned with the papacy; mistrust and acrimony were far more common.

The interior, in the form of a Greek cross, dazzles the eye with the intricate splendour of a thousand details. The domes and upper vaults are adorned with golden mosaics on New Testament subjects, the oldest dating back to the 1090s, though there have been several restorations since. Ancient columns of rare marbles, alabaster, porphyry and verdantique, sawn into slices of rich colour, line the lower walls; the 12th-century pavement is a magnificent geometric mosaic of marble, glass and porphyry. Like a mosque, the nave is partially covered with carpets.

The first door on the right leads to the 14th-century **baptistry** (*currently closed; with any luck it may have reopened by the time you get there*), much beloved by John Ruskin and famous for its mosaics on the life of John the Baptist, with a lovely Salome in red who could probably have had just as many heads as she pleased. Attached to the baptistry, the **Cappella Zen** (*also currently closed*) was designed by Tullio Lombardo in 1504 to house the tomb of one Cardinal Zen, who had left a fortune to the Republic on condition he be buried in St Mark's. Further along the right transept you can visit the **treasury** (*open Mon–Sat 9.30–5, Sun 1.30–5; adm*), containing the loot from Constantinople that Napoleon overlooked – golden bowls and crystal goblets studded with huge coloured gems, straight from the cavern of Ali Baba. Near the Altar of the Sacrament, at the end of the right transept, a lamp burns 'eternally' next to one pillar: after the 976 fire, the body of St Mark was lost, but in 1094 (after Bari had beaten Venice to the relics of St Nicolaus) the good Evangelist staged a miraculous reappearance, popping his hand out of the pillar during Mass. St Mark is now safely in place in a crypt under the high altar, in the **sanctuary** (*open Mon–Sat 9–5, Sun 2–4; adm*). You can't visit his relics, but you can see the altar's retable, the fabulous, glowing **Pala d'Oro**, a masterpiece of medieval gold and jewel work. The upper section may originally have been in the Church of the Pantocrator in Constantinople, and the lower section was commissioned in that same city by Doge Pietro Orseolo I in 976. Over the years the Venetians added their own scenes, and the Pala took its present form in 1345.

In the left transept, the **Chapel of the Madonna of Nicopeia** shelters a 10th-century icon hijacked from Constantinople, the *Protectress of Venice*, formerly carried into battle by the Byzantine Emperors. More fine mosaics are further to the left in the Chapel of St Isidore (Venetian bodysnatchers kidnapped his relics from Chios – and in the mosaic he seems happy to go). In the **Chapel of the Madonna dei Máscoli**, the mosaics on the *Life of the Virgin* by Tuscan Andrea Castagno and Michele Giambono (1453) were among the first harbingers of the Renaissance in Venice.

1 *Translation of the Body of St Mark* (1270)

2 *Venice Venerating the Relics of St Mark* (1718)

3 Central door, with magnificent 13th-century carvings in arches

4 *Venice Welcoming the Relics of St Mark* (1700s)

5 *Removal of St Mark's Relics from Alexandria* (1700s)

6 Pietra del Bando, stone from which the Signoria's decrees were read

7 *Scenes from the Book of Genesis* (1200) and 6th-century Byzantine door of San Clemente

8 *Noah and the Flood* (1200s), tomb of Doge Vitale Falier (d. 1096)

9 *Madonna and Saints* (1060s); red marble slab where Emperor Barbarossa submitted to Pope Alexander III (1177); stair up to the Loggia and Museo Marciano

10 *Death of Noah and the Tower of Babel* (1200s)

11 *Story of Abraham* (1230s)

12 *Story of SS. Alipius and Simon, and Justice* (1200s)

14 Tomb of Doge Bartolomeo Gradenigo (d. 1342)

15 *Story of Joseph*, remade in 19th century

16 Porta dei Fiori (1200s); Manzù's bust of Pope John XXIII

17 *Christ with the Virgin and St Mark* (13th century, over the door)

18 Pentecost Dome (the earliest, 12th century)

19 On the wall: *Agony in the Garden* and *Madonna and Prophets* (13th century)

20 Baptistry, *Life of St John the Baptist* (14th century) and tomb of Doge Andrea Dandolo

21 Cappella Zen, by Tullio and Antonio Lombardo (1504–22)

22 On the wall: *Christ and Prophets* (13th century)

23 In arch: *Scenes of the Passion* (12th century)

24 Central Dome, the *Ascension* (12th century)

25 Tabernacle of the Madonna of the Kiss (12th century)

26 On wall: *Rediscovery of the Body of St Mark* (13th century)

27 Treasury

28 Dome of San Leonardo; Gothic rose window (15th century)

29 In arch, *Scenes from the Life of Christ* (12th century)

30 Altar of the Sacrament; pilaster where St Mark's body was rediscovered, marked by marbles

31 Altar of St James (1462)

32 Pulpit where newly elected doge was shown to the people; entrance to the sanctuary

33 Rood screen (1394) by Jacopo di Marco Benato and Jacobello and Pier Paolo Dalle Masegne

34 Singing Gallery and Cappella di San Lorenzo, sculptures by the Dalle Masegnes (14th century)

35 Dome, *Prophets Foretell the Religion of Christ* (12th century); Baldacchino, with Eastern alabaster columns (6th century?)

36 Pala d'Oro (10th–14th century)

37 Sacristy door, with reliefs by Sansovino (16th century)

38 Sacristy, with mosaics by Titian and Padovanino (16th century) and Church of St Theodore (15th century), once seat of the Inquisition, and now part of the sacristy: both are rarely open

39 Singing Gallery and Cappella di San Pietro (14th century): note the Byzantine capitals

40 Two medieval pulpits stacked together

41 *Miracles of Christ* (16th century)

42 Dome, with *Life of St John the Evangelist* (12th century)

43 Cappella della Madonna di Nicopeia (miraculous 12th-century icon)

44 Cappella di Sant'Isidoro (14th-century mosaics and tomb of the Saint)

45 Cappella della Madonna dei Máscoli: *Life of the Virgin* by Andrea del Castagno, Michele Giambono, Jacopo Bellini

46 On wall: *Life of the Virgin* (13th century)

47 Finely carved Greek marble stoup (12th century)

48 *Virgin of the Gun* (13th century – rifle ex-voto from 1850s)

49 Il Capitello, altar topped with rare marble ciborium, with miraculous Byzantine Crucifixion panel

St Mark's Basilica

Note how crooked it is!
In the Middle Ages symmetry
was synonymous with death.

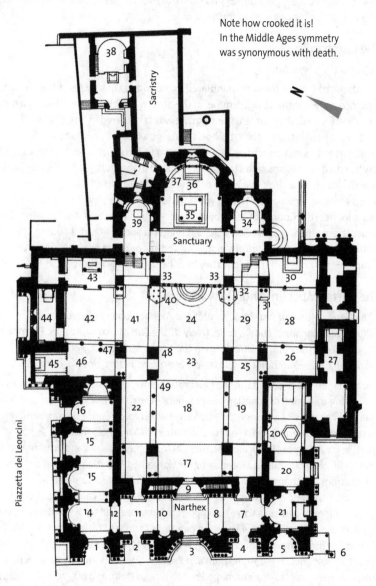

N

Piazza San Marco

Before leaving, climb the steep stone stair near the west door of the narthex, to the **Museo Marciano**, **Galleria** and **Loggia dei Cavalli** (*open daily 9.30–5; adm*) for a closer look at the dome mosaics from the women's gallery and a visit to the loggia, where you can inspect the replica horses and compare them with the excellently restored, gilded, almost alive originals in the museum.

The Campanile

Open daily 9–7; adm.

St Mark's bell tower, to those uninitiated in the cult of Venice, seems like an alien presence, a Presbyterian brick sentinel in the otherwise delicately wrought piazza. But it has always been there, at least since 912; it was last altered in 1515, and when it gently collapsed into a pile of rubble on 14 July 1902 (the only casualty a cat) the Venetians felt its lack so acutely that they began to construct an exact replica, only a few hundred tons lighter and stronger, completed in 1912. It is 332ft tall, and you can take the lift up for a bird's-eye vision of Venice and its Lagoon; from up here the city seems amazingly compact. Though you have to pay for the view, misbehaving priests had it for free; the Council of Ten would suspend them in cages from the windows. Under the campanile, Sansovino's elegant **loggetta** adds a graceful note to the brick belfry. Its marbles and sculptures glorifying Venice took it on the nose when the campanile fell on top of them, but they have been carefully restored.

The Correr Museum and Clock Tower

The Correr Museum also incorporates the Archaeological Museum and Biblioteca Marciana, known collectively as the San Marco museums. Entrance to all except the Palazzo Ducale is via the Correr Museum. Open April–Oct daily 9–7; Nov–Mar daily 9–5; last tickets 90mins before closing; adm.

At the far end of the piazza, in the Procuratie Nuove, the **Museo Correr** contains an interesting collection of Venetian memorabilia – the robes, ducal bonnets and old-maidish nightcaps of the doges, the 20-inch-heeled *zoccoli*, once the rage among Venetian noblewomen, and a copy of the statue of Marco Polo from the Temple of 500 Genies in Canton. There are also musical instruments, arms and armour, some wonderful old globes and an interesting section called 'Venetian Civilization' with objects from Venetian domestic life: pots and pans, and other domestic artefacts. There are also some antique games – roulette wheel, playing cards, draughts set, jigsaw, children's games (a yo-yo), a bingo set, dominoes – all from the 18th century. Upstairs, the fine collection of Venetian paintings includes two great works by Carpaccio, *The Courtesans* (or Ladies – in Venice it was hard to tell) and *A Visitation*; Ferrarese/Bolognese's the *Young Man in a Red Beret*, with his archetypal Venetian face; Antonello da Messina's damaged but luminous *Pietà*, and others by Cosme Turà and a young Giovanni Bellini; a lively early sculpture by Canova, *Daedalus and Icarus* (1779); and the Bosch-esque *Temptation of St Anthony* by Il Civetta (the little owl).

At the head of the Procuratie Vecchie two bronze wild men, called the 'Moors', sound the hours atop the clock tower, the **Torre dell'Orologio** (*currently being restored, with* *a view to reopening in 2004, but the innards of the clock itself are on display in the Ducal Palace*), built to a design by Mauro Codussi in 1499 above the entrance to Venice's main shopping street, the Mercerie. The old Italians were fond of elaborate astronomical clocks, but none is as beautiful as this, with its coloured enamel and gilt face, its Madonna and obligatory lion. The Council of Ten (which actually encouraged fearsome false rumours about itself, to make its job easier) allegedly blinded the builders to prevent them creating such a marvel for any other city. Below, flanking the basilica's north façade, a fountain and two porphyry lions stand in **Piazzetta Giovanni XXIII**, named after the Venetian patriarch who became pope in 1959.

Piazzetta San Marco

To the south of the basilica, the Piazzetta San Marco was the Republic's foyer, where ships would dock under the watchful eye of the Doge. The view towards the Lagoon is framed by two tall Egyptian granite **columns**, trophies brought to Venice in the 1170s. The Venetians had a knack for converting their booty into self-serving symbols: atop one of the columns several Roman statues were pieced together to form their first patron saint, St Theodore with his crocodile (or dragon, or fish), while on the other stands an ancient Assyrian or Persian winged lion, under whose paw the Venetians slid a book, creating their symbol of St Mark.

Opposite the Doge's Palace stands the **Biblioteca** (*entry via Correr Museum*), built in 1536 by Sansovino and considered by Palladio to be the most beautiful building since antiquity, especially notable for the play of light and shadow in its sculpted arcades. Sansovino, trained as a sculptor, was notorious for paying scant attention to architectural details, and the library was scarcely completed when its ceiling collapsed. The goof-up cost him a trip to the Council of Ten's slammer, and he was only released on the pleading of Titian. Scholars with permission from the director can examine such treasures as the 1501 Grimani breviary, a masterwork of Flemish illuminators; Homeric *codices*, the 1459 world map of Fra Mauro, and Marco Polo's will. But not the famous library Petrarch willed to the Republic – the Venetians misplaced it.

Next to the library, at No.17, Venice's **Archaeological Museum** (*entry via Correr Museum*) is one of the few museums in the city heated in the winter. It has an excellent collection of Greek sculpture, including a violent *Leda and the Swan* and ancient copies of the famous *Gallic Warriors of Pergamon*, all given to the city by collector Cardinal Grimani in 1523. On the other side of the Libreria, by the waterfront, is another fine building by Sansovino, the 1547 **Zecca**, or Old Mint, which once stamped out thousands of gold *zecchini*, and gave English a new word: 'sequin'.

The Doge's Palace (Palazzo Ducale)

Open April–Oct daily 9–7; Nov–Mar daily 9–5; adm exp – includes entry to the Museo Correr. Entrance and tickets on Riva degli Schiavoni.

What St Mark's is to sacred architecture, the **Doge's Palace** is to the secular – unique and audacious, dreamlike in a half-light, an illuminated storybook of Venetian history and legend. Like the basilica, it was founded shortly after the city's consolidation on the Rialto, though it didn't begin to take its present form until 1309 – with its delicate lower colonnade, its loggia of lacy Gothic tracery, and the massive top-heavy upper floor, like a cake held up by its own icing. Its weight is partly relieved by the diamond pattern of white Istrian stone and red Verona marble on the façade, which from a distance gives the palace its wholesome peaches-and-cream complexion. Less benign are the two reddish pillars in the loggia (on the Piazzetta façade) said to have been dyed by the blood of Venice's enemies, whose tortured corpses were strung out between them.

Some of Italy's finest medieval sculpture crowns the 36 columns of the lower colonnade, depicting a few sacred and many profane subjects – animals, guildsmen, Turks, and Venetians. Beautiful sculptural groups adorn the corners, most notably the 13th-century *Judgement of Solomon*, near the grand entrance, the 1443 **Porta della Carta** (Paper Door), a Gothic symphony in stone by Giovanni and Bartolomeo Bon.

Fires in 1574 and 1577 destroyed much of the palace, and at the time there were serious plans afoot to knock it down and let Palladio start again *à la* Renaissance. Fortunately, however, you can't teach an old doge new tricks, and the palace was rebuilt as it was, with Renaissance touches in the interior. Just within the Porta della Carta, don't miss Antonio Rizzo's delightful arcaded courtyard and his finely sculpted grand stairway, the **Scala dei Giganti**, named for its two Gargantuan statues of *Neptune* and *Mars* by Sansovino.

The new ticket office leads you straight into the big courtyard, designed by Antonio Rizzo and containing two of Venice's finest well-heads. First on the tour is the **Museo dell'Opera**, with its rooms full of vast bits of stone capitals, columns, chunks of stonework from the upper loggia, and models of the palace. Then you go back into the courtyard and begin the tour proper by ascending the **Scala dei Censori** to the first floor, or *primo piano nobile*, once the private apartments of the Doge, although its stripped-down unfurnished state offers few clues as to how the Doge lived in this gilded cage of pomp and ritual, leading public and private councils and rites as grand as the 'Marriage to the Sea'. Turn right, and Sansovino's **Scala d'Oro** continues up to the *secondo piano nobile*, from where the Venetian state was governed. After the fire that destroyed its great 15th-century frescoes, Veronese and Tintoretto were employed to paint the newly remodelled chambers with mythological themes and scores of allegories and apotheoses of Venice – a smug, fleshy blonde in the eyes of these two. These paintings are the palace's chief glory, and signboards in each room identify them. Visiting ambassadors and other foreign official guests would be required to wait in the first room, the **Anticollegio**, so the frescoes (Tintoretto's *Bacchus and Ariadne* and Veronese's *Rape of Europa*) had to be especially impressive; in the next room, the **Sala del Collegio**, with several masterpieces by both artists, they would be presented to the hierarchy of the Venetian state.

Tintoretto's brush dominates in the **Sala del Senato** – less lavish, since only Venetians were admitted here – while the main work in the **Sala del Consiglio dei Dieci** is Veronese's ceiling, *Old Man in Eastern Costume with a Young Woman*. Under this the Council of Ten deliberated and pored over the accusations deposited in the *Bocche dei Leoni* – the lions' mouths spread over the Republic. To be considered, an accusation had to be signed and supported by two witnesses, and anyone found making a false accusation would suffer the punishment that would have been meted out to the accused had it been true. Next to the Ten's chamber, the old **Armoury** (Sala d'Armi) houses a fine collection of medieval and Renaissance arms and armour.

From here the visit continues downstairs, to the vast and magnificent **Sala del Maggior Consiglio**, built in 1340 and capable of holding the 2,500 patricians of the Great Council. At the entrance hangs Tintoretto's crowded, and recently restored, *Paradiso* – the biggest oil painting in the world (23 by 72ft), all the Blessed looking up at Veronese's magnificent *Apotheosis of Venice* on the ceiling. The frieze along the upper wall portrays the first 76 doges, except for the space that would have held the portrait of Marin Falier (1355) had he not led a conspiracy to take sole power; instead, a black veil bears a dry note that he was decapitated for treason. The portraits of the last 44 doges, each painted by a contemporary painter, continue around the **Sala dello Scrutinio**, where the votes for office were counted. Elections for Doge were Byzantine and elaborate – and frequent; the Maggior Consiglio preferred to choose doges who were old, and wouldn't last long enough to gain a following.

At the end of the tour the **Bridge of Sighs** (*Ponte dei Sospiri*) takes you to the 17th-century **Palazzo delle Prigioni**, mostly used for petty offenders. Those to whom the Republic took real exception were dumped into uncomfortable *pozzi*, or 'wells' in the lower part of the Palazzo Ducale, while celebrities like Casanova got to stay up in the *piombi* or 'leads' just under the roof (*see* below).

The Secret Itinerary

In 1984 the section of the palace where the real nitty-gritty business of state took place, a maze of narrow corridors and tiny rooms, was restored and opened to the public. Because the rooms are so small the 1½-hour guided tour, the Itinerari Segreti ('Secret Itinerary') is limited to 20 people, and the reason why it's not better known is that it has previously only been available in Italian, but it is now available in French and English too (*tours 10am and 12 noon; adm includes visiting the state rooms; book at least a day in advance at the director's office on the first floor, or ring* **t** *041 522 4951*).

The tour begins at the top of the Scala d'Oro, with the snug wood-panelled offices of the **Chancellery** and the 18th-century **Hall of the Chancellors**, lined with cupboards for holding treaties, each bearing the arms of a Chancellor. In the justice department is the **Torture Chamber**, where the three Signori della Notte dei Criminali (judges of the night criminals) would 'put to the question' anyone suspected of treason, hanging them by the wrists on a rope that is still in place. This ended in the early 1700s, when Venice, along with Tuscany, became one of the first states in Europe to abolish torture.

Next is the ornate **Sala dei Tre Capi**, the chamber of the three magistrates of the Council of Ten, who had to be present at all state meetings. As this chamber might be visited by foreign dignitaries, it was lavishly decorated with works by Veronese, Antonello da Messina and Hieronymus Bosch. From here it's up to the notorious **Piombi**, which despite their evil reputation appear downright cosy, as prisons go. Casanova's cell is pointed out, and there's an elaborate explanation of his famous

A Doge's Life: Gormenghast with Canals

Senator in Senate, Citizen in City were his titles, as well as Prince of Clothes, with a wardrobe of gold and silver damask robes, and scarlet silks. Once the Doge was dressed, the rest of his procession would fall in line, including all the paraphernalia of Byzantine royalty: a naked sword, six silver trumpets, a damask parasol, a chair, cushion, candle and eight standards bearing the Lion of St Mark in four colours symbolizing peace, war, truth and loyalty. Yet for all the pomp this was the only man in Venice not permitted to send a private note to his wife, or receive one from her, or from anyone else; nor could he accept any gift beyond flowers or rose-water, or go to a café or theatre, or engage in any money-making activity, while nevertheless having to meet the expenses of his office out of his own pocket. Nor could he abdicate, unless requested to do so.

The office was respected, but often not the man. When a Doge died he was privately buried in his family tomb before the state funeral – which used a dummy corpse with a wax mask. First, an 'Inquisition of the Defunct Doge' was held over the dummy, to discover if the Doge had kept to his *Promissione* (his oath of coronation), if his family owed the state any money, and if it were necessary to amend the *Promissione* to limit the powers of his successor still further. Then the dead Doge's dummy was taken to St Mark's to be hoisted in the air nine times by sailors, to the cry of '*Misericordia!*' (Mercy), and then given a funeral service at the church of Santi Giovanni e Paolo.

escape through a hole in the roof. Near the end of the tour comes one of Venice's marvels: the **attic of the Sala del Maggior Consiglio**, where you can see how the Arsenale's shipwrights made a vast ceiling float unsupported over the room below; built in 1577, it has yet to need any repairs.

San Marco to Rialto

The streets between the piazza and the market district of the Rialto are the busiest in Venice, especially the **Mercerie**, which begin under the clock tower and are lined with some of the city's smartest shops. It was down the Mercerie that Baiamonte Tiepolo, miffed at being excluded from the Golden Book, led his rebel aristocrats in 1310, when an old lady cried 'Death to tyrants!' from her window and hurled a brick at his standard-bearer, killing him on the spot, and causing such disarray that Tiepolo was forced to give up his attempted coup. It was a close call that the Republic chose never to forget: the site, above the Sottoportego del Capello Nero, is marked by a stone relief of the heroine with her brick.

The Mercerie continue to the church of **San Zulian**, redesigned in 1553 by Sansovino, with a façade most notable for Sansovino's statue of its pompous and scholarly bene-factor, Tommaso Rangone. Sansovino also had a hand in **San Salvatore** in the next *campo*, adding the finishing touches to its noble Renaissance interior and designing the monument to Doge Francesco Venier. An 89-year-old Titian painted one of his more unusual works for this church, the *Annunciation*, which he signed with double emphasis *Titianus Fecit* – '*Fecit*' because his patrons refused to believe that he had painted it. In a chapel north of the altar is the *Supper at the House of Emmaus*, by the school of Giovanni Bellini.

Humming, bustling **Campo San Bartolomeo**, next on the Mercerie, has for centuries been one of the social hubs of Venice, and still gets packed with after-work crowds every evening. Its centre is graced by the **statue of Goldoni**, whose comedies in Venetian dialect still make the Venetians laugh; and by the look on his jolly face he still finds their antics amusing. Follow the crowds up to the **Ponte di Rialto** (*see* 'The Grand Canal', p.189), the geographical heart of Venice, and the principal node of its pedestrian and water traffic.

The city's central markets have been just across the bridge for a millennium, divided into sections for vegetables and for fish. Near the former you may pay your respects to Venice's oldest church, little **San Giacomo di Rialto**, founded perhaps as long ago as the 5th century and substantially reworked in 1071 and 1601. In the same *campo* stands a famous Venetian character, the 16th-century granite hunchback, **Gobbo di Rialto**, who supports a little stairway and marble podium from which the decrees of the Republic were proclaimed.

San Marco to the Accademia

Following the yellow signs 'To the Accademia' from the Piazza San Marco (starting by the tourist office), the first *campo* belongs to Baroque **San Moisè** (1668), Italy's most grotesque church, with a grimy opera-buffa façade, rockpile and altarpiece. For more opera and less buffa, take a detour up Calle Veste (the second right after Campo San Moisè) to monumental Campo San Fantin and **La Fenice** (1792), the Republic's last hurrah and one of Italy's most renowned opera houses, which saw the premieres of Verdi's *Rigoletto* and *La Traviata*. A fire set by a contractor during renovations ripped it apart in 1996, so expect to see a lot of scaffolding. Work on La Fenice is due to finish in 2004. It has been held up by endless bureaucratic and political wranglings, not to mention lack of money. Venice has a venerable musical tradition, albeit one that had become more tradition than music by the time of the era of grand opera – although Mozart's great librettist, Lorenzo da Ponte, was a Venetian.

Back en route to the Accademia, in the next *campo* stands **Santa Maria Zobenigo** (or del Giglio), on which the Barbaro family stuck a fancy Baroque façade in 1680, not for God but for the glory of the Barbari; the façade is famous for its total lack of religious significance. The signs lead next to the Campo Francesco Morosini, named after the Doge who recaptured the Morea from the Turks, but is remembered everywhere else as the man who blew the top off the Parthenon. Better known as **Campo Santo Stefano**, it's one of the most elegant squares in Venice, a pleasant place to sit outside at a café table – particularly at **Paolin**, Venice's best *gelateria*. At one end, built directly over a canal, the Gothic church of **Santo Stefano** has the most gravity-defying campanile of all the leaning towers in Venice (most alarmingly viewed from the adjacent Campo Sant'Angelo). The interior is worth a look for its striking wood ceiling, soaring like a ship's keel, as well as its wooden choir stalls (1488).

Dorsoduro

The Accademia

Open Mon 9–2, Tues–Fri 9–9, Sat 9am–11pm, Sun 9am–8pm; adm exp.
It's a good idea to get there early since only 300 visitors are allowed at a time, or pre-book a date and time, t 041 520 0345 (small booking fee).

Just over the bridge and Grand Canal from Campo Santo Stefano stands the Galleria dell'Accademia, the grand cathedral of Venetian art, ablaze with light and colour. The collection is arranged chronologically, beginning in the former refectory of the Scuola (**Room I**): among them, 14th-century altarpieces by Paolo and Lorenzo Veneziano, whose half-Byzantine Madonnas look like fashion models for Venetian silks. Later altarpieces fill **Room II**, most importantly Giovanni Bellini's *Pala di San Giobbe*, one of the key works of the quattrocento: the architecture repeats its original setting in the church of San Giobbe; on the left St Francis invites the viewer into a scene made timeless by the music of the angels at the Madonna's feet. Other beautiful altarpieces in the room are by Carpaccio, Basaiti and Cima da Conegliano (the subtle *Madonna of the Orange Tree*).

The next rooms are small but, like gifts, contain the best things: Mantegna's confidently aloof *St George*, the little allegories and a trio of Madonnas by Giovanni Bellini (including the lovely, softly coloured *Madonna of the Little Trees*) and Piero della Francesca's *St Jerome and Devotee*, a youthful study in perspective. In **Room V** you will find Giorgione's *La Vecchia*, with the warning '*Col Tempo*' ('With Time') in her hand, and the mysterious *The Tempest*, two of the few paintings scholars accept as being indisputably by Big George, but how strange they are! It is said Giorgione invented easel painting for the pleasure of bored, purposeless courtiers in Caterina Cornaro's Àsolo, but the paintings seem to reflect rather than lighten their ennui and discontent.

Highlights of the next few rooms include Lorenzo Lotto's *Gentleman in his Study*, which catches its sitter off-guard before he could clear the nervously scattered scraps of paper from his table, and Paris Bordenone's masterpiece, *Fisherman Presenting St Mark's Ring to the Doge* (1554), celebrating a miracle of St Mark.

The climax of the Venetian High Renaissance comes in **Room X**, with Veronese's *Christ in the House of Levi* (1573), set in a Palladian loggia with a ghostly white imaginary background, in violent contrast to the rollicking feast of Turks, hounds, midgets, Germans and the artist himself (in the front, next to the pillar on the left). The painting was originally titled *The Last Supper*, and fell foul of the Inquisition, which took umbrage (especially at the Germans). Veronese was cross-examined, and ordered to make pious changes at his own expense; the artist saved himself both the trouble and the money by simply giving it the title by which it has been known ever since.

Room X also contains Veronese's fine *Annunciation*, and some early masterworks by Tintoretto – *Translation of the Body of St Mark*, and *St Mark Freeing a Slave*, in which the Evangelist, in true Tintoretto-esque fashion, nosedives from the top of the canvas. The last great painting in the room was also the last ever by Titian, the sombre *La Pietà*, which he was working on when he died in 1576, aged about 90, from the plague; he intended it for his tomb, and smeared the paint on with his fingers.

Alongside several more Tintorettos, the following few rooms mainly contain work from the 17th and 18th centuries (Tiepolo, Sebastiano and Marco Ricci, Piazzetta, Longhi, Rosalba Carriera). Canaletto and Guardi, whose scenes of 18th-century Venice were the picture postcards of the British aristocracy on their Grand Tour, are represented in **Room XVII**.

The final rooms of the Accademia were formerly part of the elegantly Gothic church of Santa Maria della Carità, and house more luminous 15th-century paintings by Alvise Vivarini, Giovanni and Gentile Bellini, Marco Basaiti and Crivelli. **Room XX** has a fascinating series depicting the *Miracles of the True Cross* with Venetian backgrounds, painted by Gentile Bellini, Carpaccio and others. **Room XXI** contains the dreamily compelling and utterly charming *Cycle of St Ursula* by Carpaccio, from the former Scuola di Sant'Orsola. Finally, the last room, **Room XXIV**, the former *albergo* of the church, contains two fine paintings that were originally made for it: Titian's striking *Presentation of the Virgin* (1538) and a triptych by Antonio Vivarini and Giovanni d'Alemagna (1446).

Around Dorsoduro

The *sestiere* of Dorsoduro can also boast the second-most-visited art gallery in Venice, the **Peggy Guggenheim Collection** (*open Wed–Mon 10–6; 1 April–2 Nov also Sat 10–10; adm exp*), just down the Grand Canal from the Accademia in her 18th-century Venetian Palazzo Venier dei Leoni. In her 30 years as a collector, until her death in 1979, Ms Guggenheim amassed an impressive quantity of brand-name 20th-century art – Bacon, Brancusi, Braque, Calder, Chagall, Dali, De Chirico, Dubuffet, Duchamp, Max Ernst (her second husband), Giacometti, Gris, Kandinsky, Klee, Magritte, Miró, Mondrian, Moore, Picasso, Pollock, Rothko and Smith. Administered by the Solomon R. Guggenheim Foundation in New York, the collection can come as a breath of fresh air after so much high Italian art, and also sponsors temporary exhibitions, even in winter; look out for posters.

From here it's a five-minute stroll down to the serene, octagonal basilica of **Santa Maria della Salute** 'of Health' (1631–81, *open daily 9–12 and 3–5.30*), on the tip of Dorsoduro. One of five votive churches built after the passing of plagues (Venice, a busy international port, was particularly susceptible), La Salute is the masterpiece of Baldassare Longhena, its snow-white dome and marble jelly rolls dramatically set at the entrance of the Grand Canal. The interior is a relatively restrained white and grey Baroque, and the **sacristy** (*adm*) contains the *Marriage at Cana* by Tintoretto and several works by Titian, including his *St Mark Enthroned Between Saints*. Almost next to the basilica, on the point, stands the distinctive profile of the **Dogana di Mare**, the Customs House (*see* 'The Grand Canal', p.190).

The **Fondamenta delle Zattere**, facing away from the city towards the freighter-filled canal and the island of Giudecca, leads around to the **Gesuati**, the only church in Venice decorated by Umbrian artists. For a more elaborate feast, take the long stroll along the Fondamenta (or take *vaporetto* Line 5 to San Basegio) to Veronese's parish church of **San Sebastiano** on Rio di San Basilio (*open Mon–Sat 10–5; under restoration; adm*). Veronese, it is said, murdered a man in Verona and took refuge in this neighbourhood, and over the next 10 years he and his brother Benedetto Caliari embellished San Sebastiano – beginning in 1555 with the ceiling frescoes of the sacristy and ending with the magnificent ceiling, *The Story of Esther*, and illusionistic paintings in the choir (*the lights are always lit*).

From San Sebastiano you can head back towards the Grand Canal (Calle Avogaria and Calle Lunga San Barnaba); turn left up Calle Pazienza to visit the 14th-century church of the **Carmini** with a landmark red campanile and lovely altars by Cima da Conegliano and Lorenzo Lotto. The **Scuola Grande dei Carmini** (*open Mon–Sat 9–6 (winter 9–4), Sun 9–1; adm; sometimes also open for concerts*), next door, was designed by Longhena in the 1660s, and contains one of Tiepolo's best and brightest ceilings, *The Virgin in Glory*.

The Carmini is on the corner of the delightful **Campo Santa Margherita**. Traditionally the main marketplace of Dorsoduro, it's a good spot to find relatively inexpensive pizzerias, restaurants and cafés that are not aimed primarily at tourists. It is also close to **Ca' Rezzonico** (Rio Terrà Canal down to the Fondamenta Rezzonico), home to the **Museo dei Settecento** (*open Wed–Mon 10–5; adm*), Venice's attic of 18th-century art, with bittersweet paintings by Giandomenico Tiepolo, some wild rococo furniture by Andrea Brustolon, a pharmacy, genre scenes by Longhi (*The Lady and Hairdresser*), and a breathtaking view of the Grand Canal. The house was owned in the last century by Robert Browning's son, Pen, and the poet died there in 1889. One of the palaces you see opposite belonged to Doge Cristoforo Moro, whom the Venetians claim Shakespeare used as his model for Othello, confusing the Doge's name with his race.

San Polo and Santa Croce

From the Ponte di Rialto, follow the yellow signs to Piazzale Roma, passing the pretty **Campo San Polo** and church of **San Polo** (*open Mon–Sat 10–5, Sun 1–5; adm*), with Giandomenico Tiepolo's dramatic *Stations of the Cross* in the Oratory of the Crucifix. The signs next take you before a venerable Venetian institution: the huge brick Gothic church of the **Frari** (*open Mon–Sat 9–6, Sun 1–6; adm*), one of the most severe medieval buildings in the city, built between 1330 and 1469. Monteverdi, one of the founding fathers of opera and choir director at St Mark's, is buried here, as is Titian, whose tomb follows the Italian rule – the greater the artist, the worse the tomb (*see* Michelangelo's in Florence). The strange pyramid with a half-open door was intended by Antonio Canova to be Titian's tomb, but it eventually became the sculptor's own last resting place. The Frari is celebrated for its great art, and especially for the most over-rated painting in Italy, Titian's *Assumption of the Virgin* (1516–18), in the centre of the Monk's Choir. Marvel at the art, at Titian's revolutionary Mannerist use of space and movement, but its big-eyed, heaven-gazing Virgin has as much artistic vision as a Sunday school holy card.

That, however, is not true of Giovanni Bellini's *Triptych of Madonna with Child and Saints* in the sacristy, or Donatello's rustic statue of *St John the Baptist* in the choir chapel. In the north aisle Titian's less theatrical *Madonna di Ca' Pésaro* was modelled on his wife Celia; the painting had a greater influence on Venetian composition than the *Assumption*. Also note the beautiful Renaissance Tomb of Doge Nicolò Tron by Antonio Rizzo in the sanctuary, from 1476.

The Scuola di San Rocco

Next to the Frari, the **Scuola Grande di San Rocco** (*open daily 9–5.30; adm*) was one of Venice's most important *scuole*. San Rocco, renowned for his juju against the Black Death, was so popular among the Venetians that they stole his body from Montpellier and canonized him before the Pope did, and his confraternity was one of the city's wealthiest. The *scuola* has a beautiful, lively façade by Scarpagnino, and inside it contains one of the wonders of Venice – or rather, 54 wonders – all painted by Tintoretto, who worked on the project from 1562 to 1585 without any assistance.

Tintoretto always managed to look at conventional subjects from a fresh point of view; while other artists of the High Renaissance composed their subjects with the epic vision of a Cecil B. de Mille, Tintoretto had the eye of a 16th-century Orson Welles, creating audacious, dynamic 'sets', often working out his compositions in his little box-stages, with wax figures and unusual lighting effects. In the *scuola*, especially in the upper floor, he was at the peak of his career, and painted what is considered by some to be the finest painting cycle in existence, culminating in the *Crucifixion*, where the event is the central drama of a busy human world. Vertigo is not an uncommon response – for an antidote, look at the funny carvings along the walls by Francesco Pianta. In the same room there are also several paintings on easels by Titian, and a *Christ* that some attribute to Titian, some to Giorgione.

Just north, beyond Campo San Stin, the **Scuola Grande di San Giovanni Evangelista** (*open on request, call t 041 718 234, or try ringing the bell*) deserves a look for its beautiful Renaissance courtyard and double-ramp stairway (1498), Mauro Codussi's masterpiece, noted for the rhythms of its domes and barrel vaults.

From Campo San Stin, if you start along Calle Donà and keep as straight as possible, you should end up at **Ca' Pésaro** on the Grand Canal, a huge 17th-century pile by Longhena that is occupied by the **Galleria d'Arte Moderna** (*open Tues–Sun 10–5; adm*), with a collection principally of works exhibited in the Biennale exhibitions. Italian contemporary art, much of it unfamiliar to a foreign audience, is the mainstay, but some international figures are also represented, such as Gustav Klimt. Ca' Pésaro also houses a **Museum of Oriental Art** (*open Tues–Sun 9.15–2; adm*), with a higgledy-piggledy collection of Asian artefacts collected in the 19th century. If you really want to escape the crowds, however, head further up the canal to the stuffed Lagoon fowl in the **Natural History Museum** (*closed for major restoration; due to re-open in 2004; call t 041 275 0206 to check*) in the Venetian-Byzantine **Fóndaco dei Turchi**.

San Marco to Castello

From Piazzetta San Marco, the gracefully curving, ever-thronging **Riva degli Schiavoni** took its name from the Slavs of Dalmatia; in 1782 Venice was doing so much business here that the quay had to be widened. A few steps beyond the Palazzo Ducale, one of the city's finest Gothic *palazzi* was converted in 1822 to the famous **Hotel Danieli**, its name a corruption of the 'Dandolo' family who built it. The quay also has a robust **Memorial to Vittorio Emanuele II** (1887), where two of Venice's over 10,000 lions shelter – as often as not with members of Venice's equally numerous if smaller feline population between their paws.

From Riva degli Schiavoni, the Sottoportico San Zaccaria leads back to the lovely Gothic-Renaissance **San Zaccaria** (*open Mon–Sat 10–12 and 4–6, Sun 4–6*), begun by Antonio Gambello in 1444 and completed by Mauro Codussi in 1515. Inside, look for Bellini's recently restored and extraordinary *Madonna and Saints* in the second chapel to the right, and the refined Florentine frescoes by Andrea del Castagno in the chapel of San Tarasio. Another church, back on the Riva itself, **La Pietà** (*open only for concerts, see p.xxx*), served the girls' orphanage which the red-headed priest Vivaldi made famous during his years as its concert master and composer (1704–38). The church was rebuilt shortly afterwards by Giorgio Massari with a remarkable oval interior, in luscious cream and gold with G. B. Tiepolo's extravagant *Triumph of Faith* on top. It has particularly fine acoustics – Vivaldi helped design it.

Due north of La Pietà stands the city's Greek Orthodox church, the 16th-century **San Giorgio dei Greci**, with its tilting tower and *scuola*, next to the **Museo di Icone** (*open Mon–Sat 9–12.30 and 2–4.30, Sun 10–5; adm*), run by the Hellenic Centre for Byzantine and Post-Byzantine Studies. Many of its icons were painted in the 16th and 17th centuries by artists who fled the Turkish occupation. In Venice the Greeks came into contact with the Renaissance; the resulting Venetian-Cretan school nourished, most famously, El Greco.

Close by, another ethnic minority, the Dalmatians – present in Venice almost throughout the history of the Republic – began their tiny **Scuola di San Giorgio degli Schiavoni** in 1451 (*open Tues–Sat 9.30–12.30 and 3.30–6.30, Sun 9.30–12.30; adm*). Its minute interior is decorated with the most beloved art in all Venice: Vittore Carpaccio's frescoes on the lives of the Dalmatian patron saints – Augustine writing, watched by his patient little white dog; Jerome bringing his lion into the monastery; George charging a petticoat-munching dragon in a landscape strewn with maidenly leftovers from lunch; and more. Some of the greatest paintings by Carpaccio's more serious contemporaries, the Vivarini and Cima da Conegliano, hold pride of place in **San Giovanni in Brágora** (between San Giorgio degli Schiavoni and the Riva); the best work, Cima's *Baptism of Christ*, is in the sanctuary.

The Arsenale and Naval History Museum

From the Riva degli Schiavoni, the Fondamenta dell'Arsenale leads to the twin towers guarding the **Arsenale**. Founded in 1104, this first of all arsenals derived its name from the Venetian pronunciation of the Arabic *darsina'a*, or workshop, and up until the 17th century these were the greatest dockyards in the world, the very foundation of the Republic's wealth and power. In its heyday the Arsenale had a payroll of 16,000, and produced a ship a day to fight the Turks. Dante visited this great industrial complex twice, and, as Blake would later do with his Dark Satanic Mills, found its imagery perfect for the *Inferno*. The Biennale has now taken over a vast section of its empty shipyards as a year-round space for exhibitions, arts events, music and the like.

Look at the **Great Gateway** next to the towers. It was built in 1460 – almost entirely from marble trophies nicked from Greece. Among the chorus line of lions is an ancient beast that Doge Francesco Morosini found in Piraeus, with 11th-century runes carved in its back in the name of Harold Hardrada, the member of the Byzantine Emperor's Varangian Guard who was later crowned king of Norway. Other very innocent-looking lions, eroded into lambs, were taken from the island of Delos in 1718 when the Turks weren't looking.

Venice's glorious maritime history is the subject of the fascinating artefacts and models in the **Museo Storico Navale** (*open Mon–Fri 8.45–1.30, Sat 8.45–1; adm*) – most dazzling of all is the model of the Doge's barge, the *Bucintoro*. The museum is just past the gateway to the Arsenale, near the beginning of Via Garibaldi; in a neighbouring house lived two seafarers, originally from Genoa, who contributed more to the history of Britain than that of Venice, Giovanni and Sebastiano Caboto.

Via Garibaldi and Fondamenta Sant'Anna continue to the Isola di San Pietro, site of the unmemorable **San Pietro di Castello** (*open Mon–Sat 10–5, Sun 1–5; adm*), until 1807 Venice's cathedral, its lonely, distant site a comment on the Republic's attitude towards the papacy. The attractive, detached campanile is by Codussi, and, inside, there is a marble throne incorporating a Muslim tombstone with verses from the Koran, which for centuries was said to have been the Throne of St Peter in Antioch. To the south are the refreshing pines and planes of the **Public Gardens**, where the International Exhibition of Modern Art, or Biennale, takes place in even-numbered years in the artsy pavilions. This, and the **Parco delle Rimembranze** further on, were a gift to this sometimes claustrophobic city of stone and water by Napoleon, who knocked down four extraneous churches to plant the trees. From here you can take Line 1 or 2 back to San Marco, or to the Lido.

San Marco to Santi Giovanni e Paolo

The *calli* that lead from the Piazzetta dei Leoncini around the back of San Marco and over the Rio di Palazzo will take you to the Romanesque cloister of Sant'Apollonia and one of Venice's newest museums, the **Museo Diocesano** (*open Mon–Sat 10.30–12.30*), containing an exceptional collection of trappings and art salvaged from the city's churches. Through a web of alleys to the north there's more art in the 16th-century Palazzo Querini-Stampalia, home of the **Fondazione Querini-Stampalia** (*open Tues–Thurs and Sun 10–6, Fri and Sat 10–10; adm exp*), which has an endearing assortment of genre paintings – scenes of 18th-century Venetian convents, dinner parties, music lessons, etc. by Pietro Longhi and Gabriel Bella, as well as works by Bellini,

Palma il Vecchio, Vincenzo Catena (a 16th-century merchant and the first known amateur to dabble in painting) and G. B. Tiepolo – all in a suitably furnished 18th-century patrician's palazzo.

Santa Maria Formosa (*open Mon–Sat 10–5, Sun 1–5; adm*), in its charming *campo* just to the north, was rebuilt in 1492 by Codussi, who made creative use of its original Greek-cross plan. The head near the bottom of its campanile is notorious as being the most hideous thing in Venice, while, inside, Palma il Vecchio's *Santa Barbara* is famed as the loveliest of all Venetian blondes, modelled on the artist's own daughter. Another celebrated work, Bartolomeo Vivarini's *Madonna della Misericordia* (1473), is in the first chapel on the right; the parishioners shown under the protection of the Virgin's mantle earned their exalted position by paying for the painting.

The next *campo* to the north is dominated by **Santi Giovanni e Paolo** (or *San Zanipolo*), after St Mark's the most important church on the right bank (*open Mon–Sat 8–12.30 and 3–6, Sun 3–5.30*), a vast Gothic brick barn begun by the Dominicans in 1246, then almost entirely rebuilt after 1333, and finally completed in 1430, no one could accuse it of being beautiful, despite its fine front doorway. San Zanipolo was the pantheon of the doges; all their funerals were held here after the 1300s, and some 25 of them went no further, but lie in splendid Gothic and Renaissance tombs. Scattered among them are monuments to other honoured servants of the Venetian state, such as Marcantonio Bragadin, the commander who in 1571 was flayed alive by the Turks after he had surrendered Famagusta, in Cyprus, after a long siege; his bust sits on an urn holding his neatly folded skin. The adjacent chapel contains Giovanni Bellini's polyptych of *St Vincent Ferrer*, a fire-eating subject portrayed by the gentlest of painters; nearby there's a buoyant Baroque ceiling by Piazzetta in St Dominic's chapel, and a small shrine containing the foot of St Catherine of Siena. The right transept has paintings by Alvise Vivarini, Cima da Conegliano and Lorenzo Lotto; the finest tomb is in the chancel, that of Doge Andrea Vendramin, by Tullio and Antonio Lombardo (1478), while **Chapel of the Rosary** in the north transept, which was severely damaged by fire in the 19th century, has a ceiling by Veronese from the church of the Umiltà, long demolished.

Adjacent to San Zanipolo, the **Scuola Grande di San Marco** has one of the loveliest Renaissance façades in Italy, the fascinating *trompe-l'œil* lower half by Pietro and Tullio Lombardo, the upper floor by Mauro Codussi, and finished in 1495. The *scuola* is now used as Venice's municipal hospital, but it is possible to enter to see the lavish coffered ceiling in the library with the permission of the Direttore di Sanità.

Opposite stands the superbly dynamic **Equestrian Statue of Bartolomeo Colleoni**, the *condottiere* from Bergamo (1400–76) who had served the Republic so well on the mainland. In his lifetime proud of his emblem of *coglioni* (testicles – a play on his name), Colleoni envied Donatello's statue of his predecessor Gattamelata erected by the Venetians in Padua, and in his will he left the Republic 100,000 ducats if it would erect a similar statue of him in front of St Mark's. Greedy for the money but unable to countenance a monument to an individual in their sacred Piazza, the wily Venetians put the statue up before the *scuola* of St Mark. Verrocchio, the master of Leonardo and

Botticelli, had only finished the plaster moulds when he died in 1488, leaving Alessandro Leopardi to do the casting. Verrocchio never saw a portrait of his subject, and all resemblances to Klaus Kinski are purely accidental.

Santa Maria dei Miracoli and the Ca' d'Oro

From Campo San Zanipolo, Largo G. Gallina leads to the perfect little Renaissance church of **Santa Maria dei Miracoli** (*open Mon–Sat 10–5, Sun 1–5; adm*), built by Pietro Lombardo in the 1480s and often compared to an exquisite jewel box, elegant, graceful, and glowing with a soft marble sheen, inside and out. Just to the south are two enclosed courtyards, known as the **Corte Prima del Milion** and the **Corte Seconda del Milion**, where Marco Polo used to live. The latter in particular looks much as it did when the great traveller lived there; 'Million', his nickname in Venice, referred to the million tall tales he brought back with him from China. Nearby, Codussi's **San Giovanni Grisostomo** (1504) was his last work, a seminal piece of Renaissance architecture that contains Giovanni Bellini's last altar painting (*SS. Jerome, Christopher and Augustine*), as well as a beautiful high altarpiece by Sebastiano del Piombo.

Further towards the railway station up the Grand Canal, signposted off the Strada Nuova (Via 28 Aprile), stands the enchanting Gothic **Ca' d'Oro**, finished in 1440 and now housing the **Galleria Franchetti** (*open Mon 8.15–2, Tues–Sun 8.15am–9.15pm; adm*). In its collection are Mantegna's stern *St Sebastian*, Guardi's series of Venetian views, an excellent collection of Renaissance bronzes and medallions by Pisanello and Il Riccio, Tullio Lombardo's charming *Double Portrait*, and now sadly faded fragments of the famous frescoes by Giorgione and Titian from the Fóndaco dei Tedeschi. Also present are minor works by Titian, including a voluptuous *Venus*. The building itself is famous for the intricate traceries of its façade, best appreciated from the Grand Canal, and the courtyard, with a beautifully carved well-head by Bartolomeo Bon.

Due north, near the Fondamenta Nuove, stands the church of the **Gesuiti** (*open daily 10–12 and 5–7; currently covered in scaffolding, undergoing some sorely needed restoration work*), built by the Jesuits when the Republic relaxed its restrictions against them, in 1714–29: a Baroque extravaganza, full of *trompe l'œil* of white and green-grey marble draperies that would make a fitting memorial for Liberace. A previous church on this same site was the parish church of Titian, to which he contributed the *Martyrdom of St Lawrence* – the saint on a grill revered by Titian's patron, Philip II of Spain.

Cannaregio

Crumbling, piquant Cannaregio is the least visited *sestiere* in Venice, and here, perhaps, more than anywhere else in the city, you can begin to feel what everyday life is like behind the tourist glitz – children playing tag on the bridges, old men in shorts messing around in unglamorous, unpainted boats on murky canals, neighbourhood greasy spoons and bars, banners of laundry waving gaily overhead.

Northern Cannaregio was Tintoretto's home base, and he is buried in the beautiful Venetian Gothic **Madonna dell'Orto** (*open Mon–Sat 10–7, Sun 1–5; adm*). It also contains several of his jumbo masterpieces, such as the *Sacrifice of the Golden Calf*, in which Tintoretto painted himself bearing the idol – though he refrained from predicting his place in the *Last Judgement*, which hangs opposite it. He also painted the highly original *Presentation of the Virgin* in the south aisle, near one of Cima da Conegliano's greatest works, *St John the Baptist*. The first chapel by the door has a *Madonna* by Giovanni Bellini.

From the Campo Madonna dell'Orto, take a short walk down the Fondamenta Contarini, where, across the canal, in the wall of the eccentric **Palazzo Mastelli** you can see one of Venice's curiosities: an old, stone relief of a Moor confronting a camel. There are three more 'Moors' in the **Campo dei Mori**, just in front of the Madonna dell'Orto. The original identities of these mysterious figures have long been forgotten, although a fourth one, embedded in one corner of the square and with a metal nose like Tycho Brahe, is named Signor Antonio Rioba. He featured in many Venetian pranks of yore: anonymous satires or denunciations would be signed in his name, and new arrivals in the city would be sent off to meet him.

Also in the area is another little church, **Sant'Alvise** (*open Mon–Sat 10–5, Sun 1–5; adm*), which must be the loneliest church in Venice. Its main features are a forceful *Calvary* by Giambattista Tiepolo and a set of charming tempera paintings that Ruskin called the 'Baby Carpaccios', but which are now attributed to Carpaccio's master, Lazzaro Bastiani, as Carpaccio would only have been about eight years old when they were painted.

Three *rii* to the south of Sant'Alvise is the **Ghetto** – THE Ghetto, that is, for, like '*Arsenal*', the Venetians invented it: *ghetto* derives from the word '*getto*' meaning 'casting in metals', and there was an iron foundry here which preceded the establishment of a special quarter to which all Jews were ordered to move in 1516. The name is poignantly, coincidentally apt, for in Hebrew '*ghetto*' comes from the root for 'cut off'. And cut off its residents were in Venice, for the Ghetto is an island, surrounded by a moat-like canal, and at night all Jews had to be within its windowless walls. Cramped for space, the houses are tall, with very low ceilings, which, as many people have noted, eerily presages ghetto tenements of centuries to come. But the Venetians did not invent the mentality behind the Ghetto; Spanish Jews in the Middle Ages were segregated, as were the Jews of ancient Rome. In fact, Venetian law specifically protected Jewish citizens and forbade preachers from inciting mobs against them – a common enough practice in the 16th century. Jewish refugees came to Venice from all over Europe; here they were relatively safe, even if they had to pay for it with high taxes and rents. When Napoleon threw open the gates of the Ghetto in 1797, it is said that the impoverished residents who remained were too weak to leave. The island of the **Ghetto Nuovo**, the oldest section, is a melancholy place, its small *campo* often empty and forlorn. The **Scuola Grande Tedesca** is the oldest of Venice's five synagogues, built by German Jews in 1528, and is in the same building as the small **Museo Comunità Israelitica/Ebraica** (*open June–Sept Sun–Fri 10–7; Oct–May Sun–Fri 10–4.30; guided visits on the half-hour summer 10.30–5.30; winter 10.30–3.30; closed Sat and*

Jewish hols; adm). The informative tours (in English) organized by the museum visit this synagogue and two others, the **Scuola Spagnola** – an opulent building by Longhena – and the **Scuola Levantina**.

Light years from the Ghetto in temperament, but only three minutes away on foot, the **Palazzo Labia** (next to the 1580 **Ponte delle Guglie**), has a ballroom with Giambattista Tiepolo's lavish, sensuous frescoes on the *Life of Cleopatra*. The *palazzo* is now owned by RAI, the Italian state broadcaster, and the ballroom is open for concerts (*call* **t** *041 781 277 well in advance to arrange for free tickets or to make an appointment to visit between 3 and 4pm on Wed, Thurs and Fri*). Away from the *palazzo* towards the railway station runs the garish, lively **Lista di Spagna**, Venice's tourist highway, lined with restaurants, bars, hotels and souvenir stands that are not always as cheap as they should be.

San Giorgio Maggiore and the Giudecca

The little islet of San Giorgio Maggiore, crowned by Palladio's church of **San Giorgio Maggiore** (*open daily 9.30–12.30 and 2.30–6.30; adm to campanile*), dominates the view of the Lagoon from the Piazzetta San Marco (*vaporetto* Line 82). Built according to his theories on harmony, with a temple front, it seems to hang between the water and the sky, bathed by light with as many variations as Monet's series on the Cathedral of Rouen. The austere white interior is relieved by Tintoretto's *Fall of Manna* and his celebrated *Last Supper* on the main altar, which is also notable for the fine carving on the Baroque choir stalls. A lift can whisk you to the top of the **Campanile** for a remarkable view over Venice and the Lagoon. The old monastery, partly designed by Palladio, is now the headquarters of the Giorgio Cini Foundation, dedicated to the arts and the sciences of the sea, and venue for frequent exhibitions and conferences.

La Giudecca (Line 82) actually consists of eight islands that curve gracefully like a Spanish *tilde* just south of Venice. Prominent among its buildings is a string of empty mills and factories – the product of a brief 19th-century flirtation with industry – and for the most part the atmosphere is relatively quiet and homely. Like Cannaregio, it's seldom visited, though a few people wander over to see Palladio's best church, **Il Redentore** (*open Mon–Sat 10–5, Sun 1–5; adm*). In 1576, during a plague that killed 46,000 Venetians, the Doge and the senate vowed that if the catastrophe ended they would build a church and visit it once a year until the end of time. Palladio completed the Redentore in 1592, and on the third Sunday of each July a bridge of boats was constructed to take the authorities across from the Zattere. This event, the *Festa del Redentore*, is still one of the most exciting events on the Venetian calendar. The Redentore itself provides a fitting backdrop; Palladio's temple front, with its interlocking pediments, matches its basilican interior, with curving transepts and dome. The shadowy semi-circle of columns behind the altar adds a striking, mystical effect, all that survives of Palladio's desire to built a circular church, which he deemed most perfect to worship the essence of God.

The Lagoon and its Islands

Pearly and melting into the bright sky, iridescent blue or murky green, a sheet of glass yellow and pink in the dawn, or leaden, opaque grey, Venice's Lagoon is one of its wonders, a desolate, often melancholy and strange, often beautiful and seductive 'landscape' with a hundred personalities. It is 56km long and averages 8km across; half of it, the Laguna Morta ('Dead Lagoon'), where the tides never reach, consists of mud flats except in the spring, while the shallows of the Laguna Viva are always submerged, and cleansed by tides twice a day. To navigate this treacherous sea, the Venetians have developed an intricate network of channels, marked by *bricole* – wooden posts topped by orange lamps – that keep their craft from running aground. When threatened, the Venetians only had to pull out the *bricole* to confound their enemies; and as such the Lagoon was always known as 'the sacred walls of the nation'. Keeping the Brenta and other rivers from silting it up kept engineers busy for centuries.

The city of the Venetians, by divine providence founded in the waters and protected by their environment, is defended by a wall of water. Therefore should anybody in any manner dare to infer damage to the public waters he shall be considered as an enemy of our country and shall be punished by no less pain than that committed to whomever violates the sacred border of the country. This act will be enforced forever.
16th-century edict of the Maistrato alle Acque

'Forever' unfortunately ended in the 20th century. New islands were made of landfill dredged up to deepen the shipping canals, upsetting the delicate balance of lagoon life; outboards and *vaporetti* churn up the gook from the Lagoon and canal beds, and send corroding waves against Venice's fragile buildings. These affect the tide, and increase both the number of *acque alte* and unnaturally low tides that embarrassingly expose Venice's underthings – and let air in where it was never supposed to go, accelerating the rot and the subsidence of its wooden piles and substructures.

Then there are the ingredients in the water itself. The Lagoon is a messy stew of 60 years' worth of organic waste, phosphates, agricultural and industrial by-products and sediments – a lethal mixture that ecologists warn will take a century to purify, even if by some miracle pollution is stopped now. It's a sobering thought, especially when many Venetians in their 50s remember when even the Grand Canal was clean enough to swim in.

And in recent years the Lagoon has been sprouting the kind of blooms that break a girl's heart – algae, 'green pastures' of it, stinking and choking its fish. No one is sure if the algae epidemic isn't just part of a natural cycle; after all, there's an old church on one Lagoon island called San Giorgio in Alga (St George in Algae). Crops of algae are on record in the 1700s and 1800s and at the beginning of the 20th century, at times when water temperatures were abnormally high because of the weather. But other statistics are harder to reconcile with climatic cycles: since 1932, 78 species of algae have disappeared from the Lagoon, while 24 new ones have blossomed, these mostly microaglae thriving off the surplus of phosphates. These chemicals have now been banned in the Lagoon communities, leading to a noticeable fall in recent algae counts.

Once the largest of the 39 Lagoon islands were densely inhabited, each occupied by a town or at least a monastery. Now all but a few have been abandoned, many tiny ones with only a forlorn, vandalized shell of a building, overgrown with weeds. Occasionally one hears of plans to bring them back to life, only to wither on the vine of Italian bureaucracy. If you think you have a good idea for one, take it up with the Revenue Office (Intendenza di Finanza).

The Lido and South Lagoon

The Lido, one of the long spits of land that form the protective outer edge of the Lagoon, is by far the most glamorous of the islands, one that has given its name to countless bathing establishments, bars, amusement arcades and cinemas all over the world. On its 12 kilometres of beach, poets, potentates and plutocrats at the turn of the last century spent their holidays in palatial hotels and villas, making the Lido the pinnacle of Belle Epoque fashion, so brilliantly evoked in Thomas Mann's *Death in Venice*, and Visconti's subsequent film. The story was set and filmed in the **Grand Hotel des Bains**, just north of the **Palazzo del Cinema**, where Venice now hosts its Film Festival.

The Lido is still the playground of the Venetians and their visitors, with its bathing concessions, riding clubs, tennis courts, golf courses and shooting ranges. The free beach, the **Spiaggia Comunale**, is on the north part of the island, a 15-minute walk from the *vaporetto* stop at San Nicolò (go down the Gran Viale, and turn left on the Lungomare d'Annunzio), where you can hire a changing hut and frolic in the sand and sea.

Further north, beyond the private airfield, the **Porto di Lido** is maritime Venice's front door, the most important of the three entrances into the Lagoon, where you can watch the ships of the world sail by. This is where the Doge would sail to toss his ring into the waves, in the annual 'Marriage of the Sea'. It is stoutly defended by the mighty **Forte di Sant'Andrea** on the island of Le Vignole, built in 1543 by Venice's fortifications genius Sanmicheli. In times of danger, a great chain was extended from the fort across the channel.

One of the smaller Lagoon islands just off the Lido, with its landmark onion-domed campanile, is **San Lazzaro degli Armeni** (*vaporetto no.20 from San Zaccharia at 3.10; tours begin daily at 3.25; adm*). It was Venice's leper colony in the Middle Ages, but in 1715 the then-deserted island was given to the Mechitarist Fathers of the Armenian Catholic Church after they were expelled from Greece by the Turks. Today their monastery is still one of the world's major centres of Armenian culture and its monks, always noted as linguists, run a famous polyglot press able to print in 32 languages, one of the last survivors in a city once renowned for its publishing. Tours of San Lazzaro include a museum filled with relics of the ancient Christian history of Armenia, as well as memorabilia of Lord Byron, who spent a winter visiting the fathers and bruising his brain with Armenian. The fathers offer inexpensive prints of Venice for sale; or else they would appreciate a donation.

Islands in the North Lagoon

Most Venetian itineraries take in the islands of Murano, Burano and Torcello, all easily reached by inexpensive *vaporetti*. Lines 41 and 42 from Fondamenta Nuove to Murano call at the cypress-studded cemetery island of **San Michele**, with its simple but elegant church of **San Michele in Isola** (*open daily 7.30–12 and 3–4*) by Mauro Codussi (1469), his first-known work and Venice's first taste of the Florentine Renaissance, albeit with a Venetian twist in the tri-lobed front. It contains the tomb of Fra Paolo Sarpi, who led the ideological battle against the Pope when the Republic was placed under the Great Interdict of 1607. Venice, considering St Mark the equal of St Peter, refused to be cowed and won the battle of will after two years, thanks mainly to Sarpi, whose *Treatise on the Interdict* proved it was illegal. In return, he was jumped and knifed by an assassin: '*Agnosco stylum romanae curiae,*' he quipped ('I recognize the method or the "dagger" of the Roman court.'). His major work, the critical *History of the Council of Trent*, didn't improve his standing in Rome, but made him a hero in Venice. Sarpi's main interest, however, was science; he supported Copernicus and shared notes with Galileo, then lecturing at Padua, and 'discovered' the contraction of the iris.

The **cemetery** itself is entered through the cloister next to the church (*open April–Sept daily 7.30–6; Oct–Mar daily 7.30–4*). The Protestant and Orthodox sections contain the tombs of some of the many foreigners who preferred to face eternity from Venice, among them Ezra Pound, Sergei Diaghilev, Frederick Rolfe (Baron Corvo) and Igor Stravinsky. The gate-keeper provides a basic map.

Murano

The island of Murano (*vaporetti lines 41 and 42 from San Zaccaria or Fondamenta Nuove, nos. 12, 13 or 14 from Fondamenta Nuove, or the DM, a fast route from Tronchetto, Piazzale Roma and Ferrovia*) is synonymous with glass, the most celebrated of Venice's industries. The Venetians were the first in the Middle Ages to rediscover the secret of making crystal glass, and especially mirrors, and it was a secret they kept a monopoly on for centuries by using the most drastic measures: if ever a glassmaker let himself be coaxed abroad, the Council of Ten sent their assassins after him in hot pursuit. However, those who remained in Venice were treated with kid gloves. Because of the danger of fire, all the forges in Venice were relocated to Murano in 1291, and the little island became a kind of republic within a republic – minting its own coins, policing itself, even developing its own list of NHs (*nobili homini* – noblemen) in its own *Golden Book* – aristocrats of glass, who built solid palaces along Murano's own Grand Canal.

But glass-making declined like everything else in Venice, and only towards the end of the 19th century were the forges once more stoked up on Murano. Can you visit them? You betcha! After watching the glass being made, there's the inevitable tour of the 'Museum Show Rooms' with their American funeral parlour atmosphere, all solicitude, carpets and hush-hush – not unfitting, as some of the blooming chandeliers, befruited mirrors and poison-coloured chalices begin to make Death look good. There is no admission charge, and there's not even too much pressure to buy. It wasn't always so kitschy. The **Museo Vetrario** or Glass Museum (*open April–Oct Thurs–Tues 10–5; Nov–Mar Thurs–Tues 10–4; adm included in San Marco museums admission*), in the 17th-century Palazzo Giustinian on Fondamenta Cavour, has some simple pieces from Roman times, and a choice collection of 15th-century Murano glass.

Nearby stands another good reason to visit this rather dowdy island, the Veneto-Byzantine **Santi Maria e Donato** (*open daily 9.30–12 and 4–7; adm*), a contemporary of St Mark's basilica, with a beautiful arcaded apse. The floor is paved with a marvellous 12th-century mosaic, incorporating coloured pieces of ancient Murano glass, and on the wall there's a fine Byzantine mosaic of the Virgin. The relics of Bishop Donato of Euboea were nabbed by Venetian body-snatchers, but in this case they outdid themselves, bringing home not only San Donato's bones but those of the dragon the good bishop slew with a gob of spit; you can see them hanging behind the altar.

Back on the Fondamenta dei Vetrai, the 15th-century **San Pietro Martire** (*open daily 9–12 and 3–6*) has one of Giovanni Bellini's best altarpieces, *Pala Barbarigo* (1484), a monumental *Sacra Conversazione* of the Madonna enthroned with Sts Mark and Augustine, and Doge Barbarigo, that achieves a rare serenity that perfectly suits the subject.

Burano

Burano (*vaporetto line 12 from Fondamenta Nuove*) is the Legoland of the Lagoon, where everything is in brightly coloured miniature – the canals, the bridges, the leaning tower, and the houses, painted with a Fauvist sensibility in the deepest of colours. Traditionally on Burano the men fish and the women make Venetian point, 'the most Italian of all lace work', beautiful, intricate and murder on the eyesight. All over Burano you can find samples on sale (of which a great deal are machine-made or imported), or you can watch it being made at the **Scuola dei Merletti** in Piazza Galuppi (*open April–Oct Wed–Mon 10–5; Nov–Mar Wed–Mon 10–4; adm*). 'Scuola' in this case is misleading; no young woman in Burano wants to learn such an excruciating art. The school itself was founded in 1872, when traditional lacemaking was already in decline. In the sacristy of the church of **San Martino** (with its tipsily leaning campanile) look for Giambattista Tiepolo's *Crucifixion*, which Mary McCarthy aptly described as 'a ghastly masquerade ball'.

From Burano you can hire a *sandola* (small gondola) to **San Francesco del Deserto**, some 20 minutes to the south. St Francis is said to have founded a chapel here in 1220, and the whole islet was subsequently given to his order for a **monastery** (*visitors welcome daily 9–11 and 3–5.30; donations appreciated*). In true Franciscan fashion, it's not the buildings you'll remember (though there's a fine 14th-century cloister), but the love of nature evident in the beautiful gardens.

Torcello

Though fewer than 100 people remain on Torcello (*vaporetto line 12 from Fondamenta Nuove*), this small island was once a serious rival to Venice herself. According to legend, its history began when God ordered the bishop of Roman

Altinum, north of Mestre, to take his flock away from the heretical Lombards into the Lagoon. From a tower the bishop saw a star rise over Torcello, and so led the people of Altinum to this lonely island to set up their new home. It grew quickly, and for the first few centuries it seems to have been the real metropolis of the Lagoon, with 20,000 inhabitants, palaces, a mercantile fleet and five townships; but malaria decimated the population, the *Sile* silted up Torcello's corner of the Lagoon, and the bigger rising star of Venice drew its citizens to the Rialto.

Torcello is now a ghost island overgrown with weeds, its palaces either sunk into the marsh or quarried for their stone; narrow paths are all that remain of once bustling thoroughfares. One of these follows a canal from the landing stage past the picturesque Ponte del Diavolo to the grass-grown piazza in front of the magnificent Veneto-Byzantine **Cathedral of Santa Maria Assunta** with its lofty campanile, founded in 639 and rebuilt in the same Ravenna basilica-style in 1008. The interior (*no longer a cathedral, although mass is celebrated every Sunday during the summer; open April–Oct daily 10.30–5.30; Nov–Mar daily 10–5; adm*) has the finest mosaics in Venice, all done by 11th- and 12th-century Greek artists, from the wonderful floor to the spectacular *Last Judgement* on the west wall and the unsettling, heart-rending *Teotoco*, the stark, gold-ground mosaic of the thin, weeping Virgin portrayed as the 'bearer of God'.

Next to the cathedral is the restored 11th-century octagonal church of **Santa Fosca**, surrounded by an attractive portico, a beautiful and rare late-Byzantine work. Near here stands an ancient stone throne called the **Chair of Attila**, though its connection with the Hunnish supremo is nebulous. Across the square, the two surviving secular buildings of Torcello, the Palazzo del Consiglio and Palazzo dell'Archivio, contain the small **Museo dell'Estuario** (*open Tues–Sun 10–12.30 and 2–5; adm*), with an interesting collection of archaeological finds and artefacts from Torcello's former churches.

Florence

09

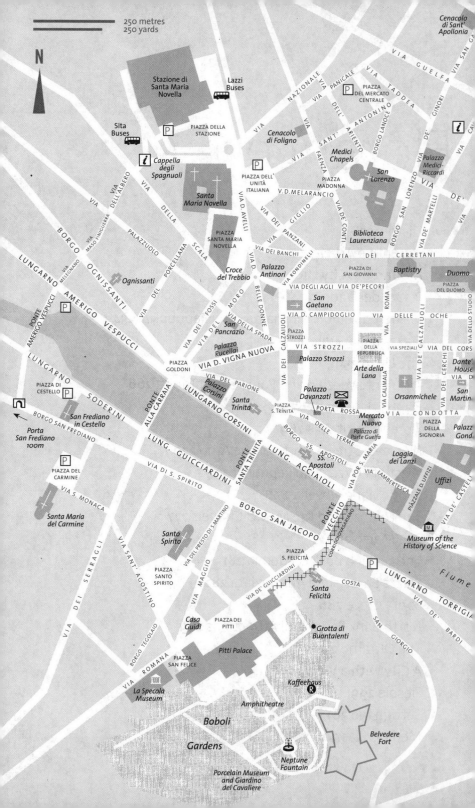

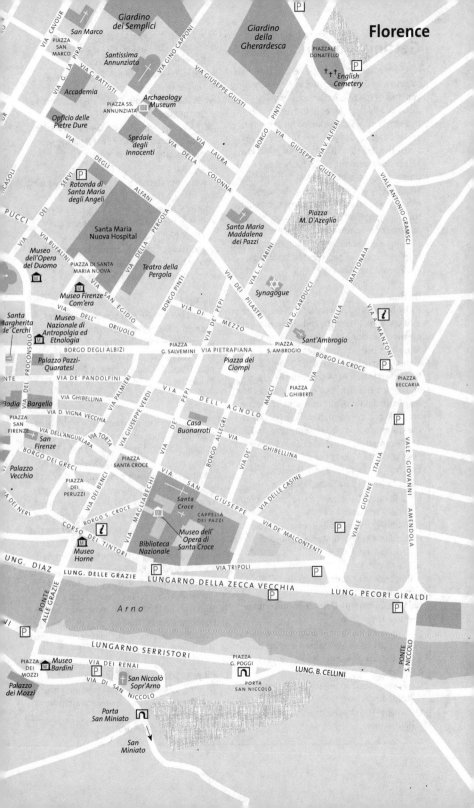

Florence

VIA CAVOUR

PIAZZA SAN MARCO

San Marco

VIA G. LA PIRA

Giardino dei Semplici

VIA C. BATTISTI

Santissima Annunziata

VIA GINO CAPPONI

VIA GIUSEPPE GIUSTI

Giardino della Gherardesca

PIAZZALE DONATELLO

English Cemetery

P

P

Accademia

PIAZZA SS. ANNUNZIATA

Archaeology Museum

VIA DELLA COLONNA

VIA LAURA

VIA GINO CAPPONI

BORGO PINTI

VIA GIUSEPPE GIUSTI

VIA V. ALFIERI

VIALE ANTONIO GRAMSCI

Opficio delle Pietre Dure

Spedale degli Innocenti

PUCCI

VIA DEI SERVI

P

ALFANI

DEGLI

Rotonda di Santa Maria degli Angeli

Santa Maria Nuova Hospital

VIA DELLA PERGOLA

VIA SAN EGIDIO

Santa Maria Maddalena dei Pazzi

VIA L. C. FARINI

Piazza M. D'Azeglio

VIA G. CARDUCCI

MATTONAIA

VIA A. MANZONI

VIA BUFALINI

Museo dell'Opera del Duomo

M

PIAZZA DI SANTA MARIA NUOVA

Teatro della Pergola

BORGO PINTI

VIA DI PEPI

VIA DEI PILASTRI

Synagogue

i

M Museo Firenze Com'era

VIA DELL' ORIUOLO

BORGO DEGLI ALBIZI

PIAZZA G. SALVEMINI

VIA PIETRAPIANA

PIAZZA S. AMBROGIO

Sant'Ambrogio

BORGO LA CROCE

Santa Margherita de' Cerchi

M Museo Nazionale di Antropolgia ed Etnologia

Palazzo Pazzi-Quaratesi

VIA DE' PANDOLFINI

VIA DEL PROCONSOLO

VIA DE' MEZZO

Piazza dei Ciompi

VIA MACCI

PIAZZA L. GHIBERTI

P

PIAZZA BECCARIA

Badia

Bargello

VIA GHIBELLINA

VIA D. VIGNA VECCHIA

VIA PALMIERI

VIA GIUSEPPE VERDI

VIA DE' PEPI

DELL' AGNOLO

Casa Buonarroti

VIA GHIBELLINA

P

PIAZZA SAN FIRENZE

San Firenze

VIA DELL'ANGUILLARA

BORGO DEI GRECI

VIA TORTA

PIAZZA SANTA CROCE

BORGO ALLEGRI

VIA DE'

VIA DELLE CASINE

VIALE GIOVINE ITALIA

VIALE GIOVANNI AMENDOLA

Palazzo Vecchio

PIAZZA DEI PERUZZI

VIA DE' BENCI

VIA SAN GIUSEPPE

Santa Croce

CAPPELLA DEI PAZZI

VIA DE' MALCONTENTI

VIA DEI NERI

CORSO DEI TINTORI

i

VIA MAGLIABECHI

BORGO S. CROCE

Museo dell' Opera di Santa Croce

P

M Museo Horne

Biblioteca Nazionale

P

VIA TRIPOLI

P

P

UNG. DIAZ

LUNG. DELLE GRAZIE

LUNGARNO DELLA ZECCA VECCHIA

LUNG. PECORI GIRALDI

PONTE ALLE GRAZIE

Arno

P

P

LUNGARNO SERRISTORI

PONTE S. NICCOLÒ

P

PIAZZA DEI MOZZI

M Museo Bardini

VIA DEI RENAI

PIAZZA G. POGGI

LUNG. B. CELLINI

Palazzo dei Mozzi

VIA DI SAN NICCOLÒ

San Niccolò Sopr'Arno

PORTA SAN NICCOLÒ

Porta San Miniato

San Miniato

Getting Around

Florence is now one of the best Italian cities to get around; best, because nearly everything you'll want to see is within easy walking distance and large areas in the centre are pedestrian zones; there are no hills to climb, and it's hard to lose your way for very long.

Just to make life difficult, Florence has two sets of **address numbers** on every street – red ones for business, blue or black for residences; your hotel might be either one. However, recent years have seen some improvement in the signage department: every major piazza, landmark or monument now has a plaque offering relevant background information, and helpful maps have been posted in strategic positions throughout the city.

By Bus

City buses (ATAF; *www.ataf.net*) can whizz or inch you across Florence, and are an excellent means of reaching sights on the periphery. Most lines begin at Santa Maria Novella station, and pass by Piazza del Duomo or Piazza San Marco. ATAF supply an excellent and comprehensive booklet, including a clear map, with details of all bus routes. These are available at the information/ticket booth at the station, tourist offices, some bars, and at ATAF's central office in Piazza della Stazione, **t** 055 565 0222. Ticket prices: €1.03 for 6omins, €1.81 for 3hrs, €4.13 for 24hrs. The most useful buses for visitors are listed below.

6 Via Rondinella–Piazza San Marco– Duomo–Station–Soffiano

7 Station–Duomo–San Domenico–Fiesole

10 Station–Duomo–S. Marco–Ponte a Mensola–Settignano

11 Viale Calatafimi–S. Marco–Piazza Indipendenza–Station–Porta Romana–Poggio Imperiale

11a Viale Calatafimi–Duomo–Porta Romana–Poggio Imperiale

13 Station–Ponte Rosso–Parterre (car park)–Piazza Libertà–Viale Mazzini–Campo di Marte–Piazzale Michelangelo–Porta Romana

14c Rovezzano–Duomo–Station–Careggi (hospital)

17 Cascine–station–Duomo–Via Lamarmora–Salviatino

25 Station–S. Marco–Piazza Libertà–Via Bolognese–Pratolino

28 Station–Via R Giuliani–Castello–Sesto Fiorentino

37 Station–Ponte alla Carraia–Porta Romana–Certosa del Galluzzo

38 Porta Romana–Pian del Giullari (you need to book this one from the telephone near the bus stop at Porta Romana, **t** 0167 019794)

As part of the continuing campaign against city smog, a fleet of Lilliputian electric buses, routes A, B and D, have recently been introduced in the city. These mainly serve the centre, often taking circuitous routes, and are a good way of seeing some of the sights if you've had enough walking. Details of routes can be found on the ATAF maps.

By Taxi

Taxis in Florence don't cruise; you'll find them in ranks at the station and in the major piazzas, or else ring for a radio taxi: **t** 055 4798 or **t** 055 4390. Taxi meters will start at €2.21 plus extras, adding 74¢ per km. There is a minimum charge of €3.65.

By Car

Just a few years ago the traffic problem in Florence was one of the grimmest in Italy. But in 1988, Florence greatly enlarged the limited access zone, the *zona di traffico limitato*.

Within the ZTL only buses, taxis, and cars belonging to residents are permitted; otherwise, you are required to pay to park in one of the city's **car parks** (there's the underground car park at the station, or the cheaper, big park at the Parterre, near Piazza Libertà) or take your chances on a side street or on metered parking around the Fortezza.

This new regulation was then followed by whole areas, especially around Piazza della Signoria and the Duomo, becoming totally traffic-free zones. The only danger is the odd ambulance or police car, the speeding mopeds and the deadly silent bicycle.

Bicycle, Scooter and Car Hire

Hiring a bike can save you tramping time and angst but it's not risk-free. Watch out for cars and pedestrians.

You can hire a motorbike at:

Alinari, Via Guelfa 85r, **t** 055 280500 or Via dei Bardi 35, **t** 055 234 6436.

Motorent, Via San Zanobi 9r, **t** 055 490113.

Florence by Bike, Via San Zanobi 120/122r, **t** 055 488992.

Promoturist, Via Baccio Bandinelli 43, **t** 055 701863. For mountain bikes only.

Between 8am and 7.30pm, visitors can now take advantage of one of the (almost) free bicycles supplied by the *comune* of Florence. There are various pick-up points around town, the most central being the Fortezza, the Parterre (for the car parks), Piazza Strozzi, Piazza Stazione, Piazza San Marco, the central market and Porta Romana. They cost about 50¢ for the day.

When you can't take any more art, hire a car and escape into the ravishing countryside. Most rental firms are within easy walking distance of the station.

Avis, Borgo Ognissanti 128r, **t** 199 100133.

Europcar, Borgo Ognissanti 53r, **t** 800 014410.

Hertz, Via M. Finiguerra 33, **t** 199 112211.

Italy by Car, Borgo Ognissanti 134r, **t** 055 287161.

Maggiore-Budget, Via M. Finiguerra 31r, **t** 055 210238.

Program, Borgo Ognissanti 135, **t** 055 282916.

Tourist Information

APT tourist service: *www.firenze.turismo. toscana.it, info@firenze.turismo.toscana.it*

There are two **guides for the disabled**, both of which can be picked up at the tourist office. The more comprehensive is only available in Italian, but it covers access to sites and restaurants, etc. in great detail and has a good map. (For further information on travel and specialist organizations, *see* p.87.)

Florence

The main tourist office is a bit out of the way, near Piazza Beccaria on **Via Manzoni 16**, **t** 055 23320 (*open Mon–Fri 8–6, Sat 8–2*).

There is a branch at Via Camilla Cavour 1r, **t** 055 290832, *infoturismo@provincia.fi.it* (*open Mon–Sat 8.15–7.15, Sun 8.30–1.30*).

There is also an office at Borgo Santa Croce 29r, **t** 055 234 0444, **f** 055 226 4524 (*open Mon–Sat 9–7, Sun and hols 9–2*).

A new office has opened on the south side of the station in Piazza della Stazione, **t** 055 212245, **f** 055 238 1226, *turismo3@comune.fi.it, www.comune.firenze.it* (*open Mon–Sat 8.30–7, Sun 8.30–1.30*).

During the summer, look out for the temporary mobile 'Tourist Help Points' run by the Vigili Urbani (the traffic police), set up in the centre of town.

Fiesole

Via Portigiani 3, **t** 055 598720/055 597 8373, **f** 055 598822 (*open year-round Mon–Sat 8.30–7.30, Sun 10–7, hols 10–4*).

Practical A–Z

American Express: Via Dante Alighieri 22r, **t** 055 50981, just off Piazza della Repubblica.

Central post office: Via Pellicceria, near Piazza della Repubblica, **t** 055 27631 (*open Mon–Fri 8.15–7, Sat 8.15–12.30; telegram office open Mon–Sat 8.15–7; call **t** 160 for information*).

E-mail services: you can send e-mail, use the Internet or fax from all over the city nowadays; one such service is **Internet Train**, Via Zannoni 1r, **t** 055 211103, *www.internettrain.it*, or Via Guelfa 24a, **t/f** 055 214794 (*opening hours differ from branch to branch*); they are also agents for the Swiss Post International if you want to avoid the bureaucratic slow-pokes in the Posta Italiana. Mac users might try **Intotheweb**, Via de' Conti 23r, **t** 055 264 5628 (*open daily 10am–midnight*).

Lost property in Italian is *Oggetti smarriti* or *Oggetti ritrovati*. The office is in Via Circondaria 17b, **t** 055 328 3942.

Medical: for an ambulance or first aid, call Misericordia, Piazza del Duomo 20, **t** 055 212222. Doctor's night service, **t** 055 287788. For general medical **emergencies** call **t** 118. The general **hospital** Santa Maria Nuova, in Piazza S. M. Nuova, **t** 055 27581, is the most convenient. **Tourist Medical Service** (24hrs a day) is staffed by English- and French-speaking doctors at Via Lorenzo il Magnifico 59; ring first on **t** 055 475411. If you find yourself hospitalized while in Florence, the **AVO** (Association of Hospital Volunteers) provides volunteer interpreters, **t** 055 425 0126/055 234 4567.

Pharmacies: open 24 hours every day in **Santa Maria Novella station**, also **Molteni**, Via Calzaiuoli 7r and **Taverna**, Piazza San Giovanni 20r, by the baptistry.

Police: emergency **t** 113. The *Ufficio Stranieri*, in the *Questura*, Via Zara 2, **t** 055 49771 (*open Mon–Fri 8.30–12.30*), handles most foreigners' problems, and usually has someone around who speaks English. Go here for residents' permits, etc.

Tourist aid police: Via Pietrapiana 50, **t** 055 203911 (*open Mon–Fri 8.30–7.30, Sat 8.30–1.30*). Interpreters available to help you report thefts or resolve other problems.

Shopping

Fashion

Although central Florence sometimes seems like one solid boutique, the city is no longer the queen of Italian fashion – the long lack of a central airport, more than anything else, sent most of the big designers to Milan. Nevertheless, the big fashion names of the 1960s and 70s, and the international chain stores, are well represented in smart Via Tornabuoni, Via Calzaiuoli and around the Duomo, and the new overhaul of Gucci and the arrival of Prada has updated the city's slightly fusty image.

Leather

Via della Vigna Nuova. Leather is something Florence is still known for, and you'll see plenty of it in this central street.

The Leather School, entrance at Piazza Santa Croce 16 or Via San Giuseppe 5r. An unusual institution, occupying part of Santa Croce's cloister, with less expensive goods.

Piazza Santa Croce and surrounding streets.

Jewellery

Ponte Vecchio. Florence is also famous for its jewellery. The shops on and around the bridge are forced by the nature of their location into wide-open competition, and good prices for Florentine brushed gold (although much of it is made in Arezzo these days) and antique jewellery are more common than you may think. Elsewhere, there are two other stores worth seeking out.

Il Gatto Bianco, Borgo SS. Apostoli 12r. Contemporary designs (earrings, rings, necklaces, etc.) are crafted on the premises in silver, gold and other metals with pearls and precious stones.

Pepita Studio, Borgo degli Albizi 23r. Fun, chunky, young designs in plexiglass, wood and glass. Prices are very reasonable.

Marbled Paper

Florence is one of the few places in the world to make marbled paper, an art brought over from the Orient by Venice in the 12th century. Each sheet is hand-dipped in a bath of colours to create a delicate, lightly coloured clouded design; no two sheets are alike. Marbled-paper-covered stationery items or just sheets of marbled paper are available at many places, including:

Giulio Giannini e Figlio, Piazza Pitti 36r. The oldest manufacturer in Florence.

Il Papiro, with three shops at: Via Cavour 55r; Piazza del Duomo 24r; Lung. Acciaiuoli 42r.

La Bottega Artigiana del Libro, Lungarno Corsini 40r.

Il Torchio, Via dei Bardi 17, **t** 055 234 2862. Here the workbench is in the shop so you can see the artisans in action. These shops (and many others) also carry Florentine paper with its colourful Gothic patterns.

Books

Bookworms do better in Florence than most Italian cities, and prices of books in English seem to have come down in recent years, so there are a fair number of places to browse for holiday reading.

The Paperback Exchange, Via Fiesolana 31r. A wide selection in English, with many books about Florence.

Seeber, Via Tornabuoni 70r. An alternative to the Exchange, also has a good selection.

Feltrinelli, Via Cavour 12–20r. Books in English and an excellent range of art books.

BM Bookshop, Borgo Ognissanti 4r. Ditto here.

Franco Maria Ricci, Via delle Belle Donne 41r. A fabulous collection of art books.

Il Viaggio, Borgo degli Albizi 41r. Florence's best travel bookshop, stocking a wide selection of travel guides and maps, including walking maps, covering both Italy and the rest of the world, in English and Italian.

The big English-stocking bookshops like Seeber and Feltrinelli also have a wide selection of books in Italian.

Antiques and Art Galleries

Borgo Ognissanti and the various Lungarni are the place to look.

P. Bazzanti e Figli, Lungarno Corsini 44. Here you can pick up an exact replica of the bronze boar in the Mercato Nuovo.

Atelier Alice, Via Faenza 72r. Much easier to carry is an Italian carnival mask.

Via Maggio. This street is full of upmarket antiques shops.

Serious collectors may want to check Florence's busy auction houses:

Casa d'Aste Pandolfini, Borgo degli Albizi 26, **t** 055 234 0888.

Casa d'Aste Pitti, Via Maggio 15, **t** 055 239 6382.

Sotheby's Italia, Via G Capponi 26, **t** 055 247 9021 (*call for appointment*).

Cloth

Casa dei Tessuti, Via de' Pecori 20–24r, **t** 055 215961. Keeps Florence's ancient cloth trade alive with lovely linens, silks and woollens. During the lunch break, you might catch a lecture on the history of Florence with special reference to the textile industry.

Silver, Crystal and Porcelain

A Poggi, Via Calzaiuoli 105r and 116r. One of the city's widest selections (including Florence's own Richard-Ginori).

Children's Toys and Clothes

Città del Sole, Via Cimatori 21r. The best toy shop in Florence.

Cirri, Via Por Santa Maria 38–40r. A fairytale selection of dresses.

Food

Mercato Centrale. Good for a number of speciality food shops.

Allrientar Gastronomia, Borgo SS. Apostoli. Pick up items such as truffle cream here.

La Porta del Tartufo, Borgo Ognissanti 133r. Virtually confines itself to different types of truffles or 'truffled' foods ranging from *grappa* to salmon paste.

Il Procacci, Via Tornabuoni 64r. A high-quality *alimentari* (food shop) selling regional specialities as well as foreign foods. It's most famous as the venue for a lunchtime *prosecco* and *panino tartufato*. Also a bar.

Gola e Cantina, Piazza Pitti 16. Offers a good selection of wines, oils and vinegars, and cookery books (in both English and Italian).

La Bottega del Brunello, Via Ricasoli 81r. Divided in two parts, one for display and one for tasting the wine and specialities on sale.

Casa del Vino, Via dell'Ariento 16r. With wine-tastings plus snacks in the San Lorenzo street market.

Enoteca dei Giraldi, Via Giraldi. Exclusively in Tuscan wines from lesser-known producers, with over 140 labels (you can also eat there).

Le Volpi e L'Uva, Piazza de' Rossi 1. Situated behind the Ponte Vecchio on the square, this also stocks lesser-known labels.

Enoteca Murgia, Via dei Banchi 57, off Piazza Santa Maria Novella. Good for wines and spirits in general.

Marchesi de' Frescobaldi, Via di Santo Spirito 11. One of the largest wine suppliers in Italy; visit their ancient cellars.

Farmaceutica di Santa Maria Novella, Via della Scala 16. Selling medieval cures and Dominican remedies since 1612.

Markets

Florence's lively street markets offer good bargains, fake designer glad rags and even some authentic labels.

San Lorenzo market. Easily the largest and most boisterous.

Sant'Ambrogio. A bustling food market.

Mercato Nuovo (Straw Market). The most touristic, but not flagrantly so.

Piazza Santo Spirito. Home to different markets on different days:

Food, clothes and shoes (small). *Open daily exc Sun.*

Craft and flea market (big). *Open every 2nd Sun of month.*

Organic food market. *Open every 3rd Sun.*

Cascinc, along the river. A weekly market where many Florentines buy their clothes. Here you may easily find designer clothes off the back of a lorry, shoes and lots more besides. *Open Tues am.*

Mercato delle Pulci (Flea Market), Piazza dei Ciompi. Perhaps the most fun market, offering all kinds of desirable junk. *Open Sun.*

Sports and Activities

On the Water

The one activity most summertime visitors begin to crave after tramping through the sights is a dip in a pool.

Piscina le Pavoniere, Cascine. The prettiest in Florence. *Open June–Sept 10–6.30.*

Bellariva, up the Arno at Lungarno Colombo 2. *Open June–Sept 11–5.*

Amici del Nuoto, Via del Romito 38, **t** 055 483951. *Open all year.*

Costoli, Via Paoli, near Campo di Marte, **t** 055 623 6027. *Open all year.*

If there's enough water in the Arno, you can try rowing or canoeing:

Società Canottieri Comunali, Lungarno Ferrucci 6, **t** 055 681 2151.

Società Canottieri Firenze, Lungarno dei Medici 8, **t** 055 238 1010 (membership only).

Horse-racing and Riding

Ippodromo Il Visarno, Cascine, **t** 055 422 6076. Florence's flat race course.

Ippodromo della Mulina, Cascine, **t** 055 411107. Also at the Cascine, Florence's trotting course.

Maneggio Mirinelle, Via di Macia 21, **t/f** 055 887 8066. The nearest place to go riding in the Tuscan hills.

Centro Ippico Ugolino, Via Oliveta 12, **t** 055 230 1289. You can also ride here, near the golf course.

Golf

Golf Club Ugolino, on the Chiantigiana, **t** 055 230 1009. The nearest 18-hole golf course to Florence is in Gràssina, 7km southeast of the city; a lovely course.

Where to Stay

Florence ✉ 50100

Florence has some lovely hotels, and not all of them at Grand Ducal prices, although base rates are the highest in Tuscany. As in any city, the higher cost of living means you won't find much inexpensive accommodation.

Historic old palace-hotels are the rule rather than the exception; those listed below are some of the more atmospheric and charming, but to be honest, few are secrets, so reserve as far in advance as possible. Also note that nearly every hotel in Florence with a restaurant will require half-board, and many will also try to lay down a heavy breakfast charge as well that is supposed to be optional.

There are almost 400 hotels in Florence but not enough for anyone who arrives in June and September without a reservation (Easter is even more busy). But don't despair; there are several hotel consortia that can help you find a room in nearly any price range for a small commission. If you're arriving by car or train, the most useful will be ITA.

ITA: in Santa Maria Novella station, **t** 055 282893, *open 9–9*; or in the AGIP service station at Peretola, to the west of Florence on A11, **t** 055 421 1800. Between March and November there's an office in the Chianti-Est service plaza on the A1, **t** 055 621349. No bookings can be made over the telephone and a booking fee of between €2.32 and €7.75 is charged, according to the category of hotel.

Florence Promhotels: Viale A. Volta 72, **t** 055 570481, **f** 055 587189. Free booking service.

Luxury

*****Excelsior**, Piazza Ognissanti 3, **t** 055 2715, **f** 055 210278, *www.westin.com/ excelsiorflorence*. In the city the luxury leader is former Florentine address of Napoleon's sister Caroline. Lots of marble, neoclassically plush, lush and green with plants, immaculately staffed, with decadently luxurious bedrooms, many of which have river views (for a price).

*****Helvetia & Bristol**, Via dei Pescioni 2, **t** 055 287814, **f** 055 288353, *www.charming hotels.it*. If you prefer luxury on a smaller scale, this has 52 exquisitely furnished bedrooms, each one different, all with rich fabrics adorning windows, walls and beds; Stravinsky, Bertrand Russell and Pirandello stayed here; added pluses are the restaurant and the winter garden.

*****Regency**, Piazza d'Azeglio 3, **t** 055 245247, **f** 055 234 6735, *www.regency-hotel.com*. In Florence's plane-tree-shaded 'London Square', there's an even smaller gem, charming and intimate with only 33 air-conditioned rooms; between the two wings there's an elegant town garden. The public rooms are beautifully panelled, and the fare in the dining room superb.

★★★★★The Savoy, Piazza della Repubblica 7, **t** 055 283313, **f** 055 284840, *www.rfhotels. com*. The old, crumbling Savoy reopened in spring 2000 under the Forte Group, now striking a minimalist tone with décor in shades of cream, beige and grey; it has a bar and restaurant where you can sit out on the piazza.

★★★★Lungarno, Borgo San Jacopo 14, **t** 055 27261, **f** 055 268437, *www.lungarnohotels. com*. A discreet hotel enjoying a marvellous location on the river, only two minutes' walk from the Ponte Vecchio. The ground floor sitting/breakfast room and bar, and the new restaurant, which specializes in fish, take full advantage of this, with picture windows looking on to the water. The building is modern, but incorporates a medieval tower. The best rooms have balconies with 'The View'. Book ahead for these.

★★★★Monna Lisa, Borgo Pinti 27, **t** 055 247 9751, **f** 055 247 9755, *www.monnalisa.it*. A Renaissance palace, now owned by the descendants of sculptor Giovanni Dupre, which has a stern façade and, it is said, staff to match, but behind them hides one of the loveliest small hotels in Florence. The *palazzo* is well preserved and the furnishings are family heirlooms, as are the many works of art. Rooms vary wildly; try to reserve one of the tranquil rooms that overlook the garden. Breakfast is available, and it has private parking.

★★★★Grand Hotel Baglioni, Piazza Unità Italiana 6, **t** 055 23580, **f** 055 235 8895, *www.hotelbaglioni.it*. A reliable and reasonably priced (for its category) choice right next to the train station, the Baglioni is popular with tour groups and business clients but has managed to retain a pleasant, old-fashioned feel. Rooms are comfortable, but its biggest plus is the top-floor restaurant, which offers close-up views of the Duomo and Medici chapels from huge picture windows. In the summer, the bar and restaurant move outside to the extensive terrace.

★★★★Gallery, Vicolo del'Oro 2, **t** 055 27263, **f** 055 268557, *galleryhotel@lungarnohotels.it*. Florence's most exciting hotel is a shrine to contemporary interior design. It is by no means stark, however, and the position (a mere two minutes from the Ponte Vecchio) is superb. It has a comfortable library, a smart bar and a restaurant.

★★★★Astoria, Via del Giglio 9, **t** 055 239 8095, **f** 055 214632, *www.boscolo.com*. Recently refurbished, in a grand 16th-century palazzo near San Lorenzo market, this has more character than many of those located near the station. Public rooms are suitably impressive and some of the bedrooms likewise; avoid those on the lower floors.

★★★★Kraft, Via Solferino 2, **t** 055 284273, **f** 055 239 8267, *www.krafthotel.it*. Frequently used by upmarket tour groups, this is handy for the opera season (it is two minutes' walk from the Teatro del Maggio Musicale Fiorentino), and has the added advantage of a small rooftop pool. Bedrooms are light and sunny, and comfortably furnished with cheerful fabrics. The suites on the top floor have great views. There is a restaurant.

★★★★Principe, Lungarno Vespucci 34, **t** 055 284848, **f** 055 283458, *www.hotelprincipe. com*. This is one of the most pleasant among the many hotels along the Arno – a small, comfortable hotel, centrally air-conditioned and soundproofed, with a little garden at the back; the nicer rooms have terraces over the river.

Very Expensive

★★★★Calzaiuoli, Via Calzaiuoli 6, **t** 055 212456, **f** 055 268310, *www.calzaiuoli.it*. Just a few steps from Piazza Signoria and on a traffic-free street is a comfortable hotel with modern, nicely decorated rooms and wonderful views from the top floor.

★★★★Villa Carlotta, Via Michele di Lando 3, **t** 055 233 6134, **f** 055 233 6147, *www. venere.it/firenze/villacarlotta*. Located in a quiet residential district in the upper Oltrarno, close to the Porta Romana, this Tuscan-Edwardian building has 26 sophisticated rooms which have been tastefully refurnished and have every mod con. There's a garden and glassed-in veranda, where the large breakfasts are served; a private garage offers safe parking.

★★★Hermitage, Vicolo Marzio 1, **t** 055 287216, **f** 055 212208, *www.hermitagehotel.com*.

You have to look hard to find this little hotel tucked away behind the Ponte Vecchio on the north side of the river. It is built upside-down; the lift takes you to the fifth floor with its ravishing roof garden, reception and elegant blue and yellow sitting room. The bedrooms below are on the small side, but you will find them charmingly furnished with antiques and tasteful fabrics.

***Beacci Tornabuoni**, Via Tornabuoni 3, **t** 055 212645, **f** 055 283594, *www.bthotel.it*. Another excellent small hotel which puts you in the centre of Florence, on the top three floors of an elegant palace. Rooms are comfortable, air-conditioned and equipped with minibars, though it's more fun to sit over your drink on the roof terrace.

***Loggiato dei Serviti**, Piazza SS. Annunziata 3, **t** 055 289592, **f** 055 289595, *www.loggiato deiservitihotel.it*. Located on Florence's most beautiful square (now traffic-free), the front rooms of this delightful hotel overlook Brunelleschi's famous portico. The 16th-century building was originally a convent, and many of the architectural features remain. Recommended.

Relais Uffizi, Chiasso de' Baroncelli/Chiasso del Buco 16, **t** 055 267 6239, **f** 055 265 7909, *www.relaisuffizi.it*. The only hotel which overlooks Piazza della Signoria, the Relais Uffizi is hidden down a series of narrow lanes. The 13 rooms of varying shapes and sizes are decorated and furnished with style while the atmosphere is informal. You can relax in the sitting room and watch the ever-changing piazza below.

Expensive

****Villa Belvedere**, Via Benedetto Castelli 3, **t** 055 222501, **f** 055 223163, *www.villa belvedere.com*. Not one of the more interesting buildings to be found in this part of peripheral Florence (1km above Porta Romana), but a very pleasant alternative to central accommodation nevertheless, with a beautiful garden, tennis court, a nice little pool and good views. Rooms are modern and comfortable. For trips into town, you can leave your car and catch a nearby bus. Light meals are served in the restaurant.

***Morandi alla Crocetta**, Via Laura 50, **t** 055 234 4747, **f** 055 248 0954, *www.welcome hotelmorandi.it*. Small but popular, with 10 rooms in the university area northeast of Piazza San Marco. Run by an Irishwoman and her family, the building was a convent in the 16th century, and some of the comfortable and pleasant rooms still have the odd fresco. Two rooms have private terraces.

***Torre Guelfa**, Borgo SS. Apostoli 8, **t** 055 239 6338, **f** 055 239 8577, *www.torre guelfa.3000.it*. Boasting the tallest privately owned tower in Florence, bang in the middle of the *centro storico*. There's a grand double salon, a sunny breakfast room, and stylish bedrooms in pastel shades with wrought iron and hand-painted furniture, as well as the chance to sip an *aperitivo* while contemplating a 360° view.

***Mario's**, Via Faenza 89, **t** 055 216801, **f** 055 212039, *www.hotelmarios.com*. A haven in a street with more than its fair share of hotels, many of them of dubious quality. Convenient for the station and a block or two from the central market, the atmosphere is friendly and the décor rustic Florentine. A generous breakfast is served and guests are pampered with fresh flowers and fruit on arrival. If you don't want to sleep with the windows closed, ask for a room at the back; the street can be noisy.

***Aprile**, Via della Scala 6, **t** 055 216237, **f** 055 280947, *www.hotelaprile.it*. Convenient for the station, this was once a Medici palace and appropriately has a bust of Cosimo I above the door. Vaulted ceilings and frescoes remain intact, and the bedrooms all have period furniture although some are on the gloomy side; there's a shady courtyard.

***Orto de' Medici**, Via San Gallo 30, **t** 055 483427, **f** 055 461276, *www.orto deimedici.it*. A little 19th-century *palazzo* near Piazza San Marco in the university district, this has grand public rooms with frescoed ceilings and chandeliers. The bedrooms, not all with private bath, are plain in comparison. There is a pretty terrace.

***Silla**, Via dei Renai 5, **t** 055 234 2888, **f** 055 234 1437, *www.hotelsilla.it*. Ten minutes' walk east of the Ponte Vecchio on the south bank of the river, this manages to be central, yet in a quiet and relatively green neighbourhood. The old-fashioned *pensione* is on the first floor of a 16th-century *palazzo* and the spacious breakfast terrace has great views over the Arno and beyond.

★★★**Delle Tele**, Via Panzani 10, t 055 290797, f 055 238 2419. Recently renovated rooms with double-glazed windows, on the busy street from the station to the Duomo.

★★**Casci**, Via Cavour 13, t 055 211686, f 055 239 6461, *www.hotelcasci.com*. The Lombardis, owners of this 15th-century palazzo (once home to Rossini), run a relaxed and cheerful ship. The breakfast room has a frescoed ceiling while the recently refurbished bedrooms are bright and modern. The choice few look on to a garden at the back.

★★**Alessandra**, Borgo SS. Apostoli 17, t 055 283438, f 055 210619, *www.hotelalessandra. com*. A modest hotel in a *palazzo* designed by Michelangelo's pupil, Baccio d'Agnolo, on a central but quiet back street; there are 25 rooms. Not all have private baths; the best have waxed parquet floors and antiques.

Moderate

★★**La Scaletta**, Via Guicciardini 13, t 055 283028, f 055 289562, *www.lascaletta.com*. Between the Ponte Vecchio and the Pitti Palace is a friendly *pensione* with a roof garden and great views into Boboli. The 12 bedrooms (not all with bathrooms and some of which sleep up to four) are decently furnished, the nicest with some antique pieces. Very moderately priced dinner available.

★★**Belletini**, Via de' Conti 7, t 055 213561, f 055 28355, *www.firenze.net/hotelbelletini*. A friendly place near the Medici chapels, decorated in traditional Florentine style; a couple of rooms have stunning views of the nearby domes. There's a good, generous breakfast. A newly opened annexe around the corner houses an additional six stylishly furnished rooms, which are slightly more expensive. TV, air-conditioning, cots, and parking nearby.

★★**Boboli**, Via Romana 63, t 055 229 8645, f 055 233 7169, *hotelboboli@hotelboboli.com*. Near the back entrance of the Boboli gardens. The brightest rooms are right at the top of the four-storey building, but there is no lift. Or if you want quiet (Via Romana is quite noisy), go for a room on the inner courtyard. Breakfast on a terrace in summer.

★**Maxim**, Via dei Medici 4, t 055 217474, f 055 283729, *www.firenzealbergo.it/home/ hotelmaxim*. This centrally located budget hotel has had a facelift. The reception area is bright and elegant, and the bedrooms are well furnished and modern. All are ensuite and one even has a jacuzzi. Air-conditioning, and parking nearby.

★**Bellavista**, Largo Alinari 15, t 055 284528, f 055 284874, *bellavistahotel@iol.it*. A simple and clean choice. Situated in west Florence, it is convenient for both train and bus stations. A couple of the rooms have views of the Duomo; a few have private bathrooms.

★**Sorelle Bandini**, Piazza Santo Spirito 9, t 055 215308, f 055 282761. Remains popular, in spite of its state of disrepair and relatively high prices. This is partly due to the romantic loggia along one side of the fourth-storey hotel, but also to its location on fascinating Piazza Santo Spirito, bustling by day and lively (and noisy) at night. Expect uncomfortable beds, cavernous rooms, heavy Florentine furniture and a certain shabby charm.

★**Bavaria**, Borgo degli Albizi 26, t/f 055 234 0313, *www.eidnet.com/hotelbavaria*. The 16th-century façade is said to be frescoed by Vasari, but don't get your hopes up. The furniture is spartan minimalist formica, though the rooms (some of them vast) are clean and cheap. Some have splendid views of the city.

★**Firenze**, Piazza dei Donati 4, t 055 214203, f 055 212370. Newly renovated in an excellent location, between Piazza Signoria and the Duomo; the rather unimaginative rooms now all have bathrooms.

Residenza Johlea Uno, Via San Gallo 80, t 055 463 3292, f 055 463 4552, *www.johanna.it*. A remarkable bargain in terms of what it offers for the price, the Johlea is under the same ownership as the two Johannas (*see* below). Situated 10mins' walk north of the central market, the rooms are comfortable and well furnished with taste and style and all have excellent bathrooms. Breakfast is supplied on trays in the rooms. On the top floor is a small sitting room and a roof terrace affording 360° views of the city.

★★**Residenza Johanna Cinque Giornate**, Via Cinque Giornate 12, t/f 055 473377, *www.*

johanna.it. Good value for money in a city where bargains are few and far between, located some way from the centre (near the Fortezza da Basso). The villa stands in its own garden and there are six comfortable rooms, each equipped with a breakfast tray and kettle, as well as a sitting room with plenty of reading material. Guests are left to themselves, but other facilities are of a three-star standard; parking available nearby at extra cost.

***Classic Hotel**, Viale Machiavelli 25, **t** 055 229351, **f** 055 229353, *www.classichotel.it*. A good alternative in a very pleasant location just above Porta Romana on the way to Piazzale Michelangelo, a five-minute walk to a bus stop. The pink-washed villa stands in a shady garden (a welcome respite from the heat of the city), and breakfast is served in the conservatory in summer.

Azzi, Via Faenza 56, **t/f** 055 213806, *hotelazzi@hotmail.com*. This friendly, clean, simple *pensione* is near the market. It has had a recent facelift, and has the added bonus of a terrace for summer.

Inexpensive

Residenza Johanna, Via Bonifacio Lupi 14, **t** 055 481896, **f** 055 482721. Only a tiny brass plaque over the bell identifies this building, just north of Piazza San Marco. There are no TVs or phones in the rooms, no doorman, and not all rooms have private baths, but the furnishings are comfortable, the bedrooms are prettily decorated and there's lots of reading material to hand. Breakfast is on a do-it-yourself tray in each room, and there are kettles in the corridor.

***Scoti**, Via de' Tornabuoni 7, **t** 055 292128, *www.hotelscoti@hotmail.com*. A simple and cheap *pensione* with a surprisingly upmarket address, which could be ideal if you would rather splurge on the wonderful clothes in the surrounding shops. It has basic, large rooms with up to four beds each and no private bathrooms, but bags of atmosphere, starting with the floor-to-ceiling frescoes in the sitting room.

***Orchidea**, Borgo degli Albizi 11, **t/f** 055 248 0346, *hotelorchidea@yahoo.it*. Run by an Anglo-Italian family in a 12th-century building where Dante's in-laws once lived. One of

the seven cheerful rooms has a private shower; the best of the rest look on to a garden at the back.

Istituto Gould, Via dei Serragli 49, **t** 055 12576, **f** 055 280274, *gould.reception@dada.it*. An excellent budget choice near Santo Spirito, the Isitituo Gould is run by the Valdese church. Rooms vary in size from singles (a couple) to quads and not all have their own bathrooms; book early to secure singles or doubles. No smoking, and you have to check in during office hours.

Fiesole ✉ 50014

Many frequent visitors to Florence wouldn't stay anywhere else: it's cooler, quieter, and at night the city far below twinkles as if made of fairy lights.

*****Villa San Michele**, Via Doccia 4, **t** 055 567 8200, **f** 055 567 8250, *www.villasan michele_orient_express.com* (*luxury*). Built as a monastery in the 14th century, this hotel is the superb choice if money happens to be no object, set in a breathtaking location just below Fiesole with a façade and loggia reputedly designed by Michelangelo himself. After suffering bomb damage during the Second World War, it was carefully reconstructed to create one of the most beautiful hotels in Italy, set in a lovely Tuscan garden, complete with a pool. Each of its 29 rooms is richly and elegantly furnished and air-conditioned; the more plush suites have jacuzzis. The food is delicious, and the reasons to go down to Florence begin to seem insignificant.

***Villa Fiesole**, Via Beato Angelico 35, **t** 055 597252, **f** 055 599133, *www.villafiesole.it* (*luxury*). This new hotel was once part of the San Michele convent, and shares part of its driveway with the hotel of the same name. The smart, neoclassical-style interiors are variations on a fresh blue and yellow colour scheme. Light meals are served in a sunny dining room or on the adjacent terrace, and there is a pool. The whole is wheelchair-accessible. The facilities (and prices) here are decidedly four-star.

****Villa Aurora**, Piazza Mino 38, **t** 055 59100, **f** 055 59587, *www.logica.net/aurora* (*very expensive*). An agreeable 19th-century villa, located right on Fiesole's famous piazza from where the no.7 bus will whisk you down to central Florence in 20mins. The 25 bedrooms have rustic antiques and splendid views over the city. Some of the bathrooms are poky. There is a restaurant – on a terrace overlooking Florence in the summer – and the bar next door (which can be noisy at times) is under the same ownership.

Le Cannelle, Via Gramsci 52–6, **t** 055 597 8336, **f** 055 597 8292, *www.lecannelle.com* (*expensive–moderate*). A new, friendly B&B run by two sisters on the main street. Rooms are comfortably rustic and there is a pretty breakfast room.

★★★**Pensione Bencistà**, Via Benedetto di Maiano 4, **t/f** 055 59163, *pensione bencista@iol.it* (*moderate*). Another former monastery with views from its flower-decked terrace which are every bit as good as those at Villa San Michele, and the welcome will be more friendly. Bedrooms are all comfortably furnished with solid antique pieces. The three little sitting rooms are particularly inviting in cooler weather when fires are lit. Half-board – breakfast and either lunch or dinner – is obligatory here, but prices are reasonable.

★**Villa Sorriso**, Via Gramsci 21, **t** 055 59027, **f** 055 597 8075, *www.paginegialle.it/albergosorriso.01* (*inexpensive*). An unpretentious, comfortable hotel in the centre of Fiesole, with a terrace overlooking Florence.

★**Villa Baccano**, Via Bosconi 4, **t/f** 055 59341, *www.villabaccano.it* (*inexpensive*). In the hills 2km out of the centre of Fiesole, in a lovely garden setting.

Villa Hotels in the Florentine Hills

If you're driving, you may consider lodging outside the city where parking is hassle-free and the summer heat is less intense.

Very Expensive

★★★**Villa Villoresi**, Via Campi 2, Colonnata di Sesto Fiorentino, **t** 055 443692, **f** 055 442063, *www.ila-chateau.com/villores*. Contessa Cristina Villoresi's family home is a lovely oasis in the middle of one of Florence's more un-lovely suburbs, which hasn't been too pristinely restored, retaining much of its slightly faded appeal as well

as its frescoed ceilings, antiques and chandeliers. The villa boasts the longest loggia in Tuscany, to which five of the best, and grandest, bedrooms have direct access. Other rooms are a good deal plainer and somewhat cheaper.

★★★**Villa le Rondini**, Via Vecchia Bolognese 224, **t** 055 400081, **f** 055 268212, *www.villa lerondini.it*. Occupying several buildings in a pleasant setting 7km north of Florence, surrounded by olive and cypress trees. The most interesting rooms are in the 16th-century villa. There is a very pleasant pool.

Villa Poggio San Felice, Via San Matteo Arcetri 24, **t** 055 220016, **f** 055 233 5388, *www.wel.it*. A delightful alternative to city hotels, this is a 15th-century villa on a hill just south of Porta Romana, near the observatory. It was once owned by a Swiss hotel magnate, whose descendants have restored the house and gardens (designed by Porcinaie) and opened them up to guests. There are five double bedrooms, all furnished with family antiques, and all with stunning views. *Bed and breakfast only, closed Dec–Feb.*

Moderate

★★★**Hermitage**, Via Gineparia 112, Bonistallo, **t** 055 877040, **f** 055 879 7057, *www.hotel hermitageprato.it*. Near Poggio a Caiano is a fine, affordable choice for families; there's a pool and air-conditioning, not to mention gallons of fresh air and quiet.

★★**Villa Natalia**, Via Bolognese 106, **t** 055 490773, **f** 055 470773. A rather faded villa, with bedrooms filled with antiques; the atmosphere in the public rooms is a little institutional, but there's a bus stop nearby for the short trip to Florence. Book ahead.

Eating Out

Florence has plenty of fine restaurants; even in the cheaper places standards are high, and if you don't care for anything fancier there will be lots of good red Chianti to wash down your meal. By popular demand, the city centre is full of *tavole calde*, pizzerias and snack bars (one of the best pizza-by-the-slice places is just across from the Medici Chapels).

Please note that many of the best places are likely to close for all or part of August; you would also be wise to call ahead and reserve, even a day or two in advance.

Florence's Most Ephemeral Art

Florentine food is on the whole extremely simple, with the emphasis on the individual flavours and fresh ingredients. A typical *primo* could be *pappardelle*, a type of wide tagliatelle egg-pasta, served usually with a meat sauce, or game such as wild boar, rabbit and duck. Soups are also popular: try the *ribollita*, a thick, hearty soup unique to the region, made with yesterday's bread, beans, black cabbage and other vegetables; or *pappa al pomodoro*, another bread-based soup flavoured with tomatoes, basil and sludgy local olive oil.

The most famous main course in Florence is the *bistecca alla fiorentina*, a large steak on the bone, two inches thick, cut from loin of beef and cooked on charcoal simply seasoned with salt and pepper. As for the vegetables, you could try *piselli alla fiorentina*, peas cooked with oil, parsley and diced bacon; or *tortino di carciofi*, a delicious omelette with fried artichokes; *fagioli all'uccelletto*, cannellini beans stewed with tomatoes, garlic and sage; and *spinaci saltati* – fresh spinach sauteed with garlic and olive oil. Florentine desserts tend to be sweet and fattening: *bomboloni alla crema* are vanilla-filled doughnuts and *le fritelle di San Giuseppe* are bits of deep-fried batter covered in sugar. If you prefer cheese, try the sturdy *pecorino toscano*.

Very Expensive

Enoteca Pinchiorri, Via Ghibellina 87, near the Casa Buonarroti, **t** 055 242777. One of the finest gourmet restaurants in Italy, boasting two Michelin stars. The owners inherited the wine shop and converted it into a beautifully appointed restaurant, with meals served in a garden court in the summer; the cellars contain some 80,000 bottles of the best Italy and France have to offer. The cooking, a mixture of *nouvelle cuisine* and traditional Tuscan recipes, wins prizes every year. Italians tend to complain about the minute portions. Prices are reckoned to be €100 excluding wine, but the sky's the limit if you go for a more interesting bottle. *Open Mon and Wed 7.30–10, Tues, Thurs–Sat 12.30–2 and 7.30–10, closed Aug.*

Cibreo, Via dei Macci 118r, **t** 055 234 1100. One of the most Florentine of Florentine restaurants is close to the market of Sant' Ambrogio. The décor is simple – food is the main concern, and all of it is market-fresh. You can go native and order tripe *antipasto*, cockscombs and kidneys, or play it safe with prosciutto from the Casentino, a fragrant soup (no pasta here) of tomatoes, mussels and bell pepper, leg of lamb stuffed with artichokes, topped off with a delicious lemon *crostata*, cheesecake, or a chocolate cake to answer every chocaholic's dream. Booking is essential. *Open Tues–Sat 12.50–2.30 and 7.30–11.15, closed Aug.*

Da Stefano, Via Senese 271, Galuzzo, **t** 055 204 9105. Generally acknowledged to be the best seafood restaurant in the town, this is worth the 10-minute drive it takes to get there. *Eves only, closed Sun.*

Alle Murate, Via Ghibellina 52r, **t** 055 240618, *www.florence-gourmet.it*. By the Bargello, this 'creative traditional' restaurant is elegant but relaxed, serving two set menus, one Tuscan and one different – spaghetti with sea bass, or pigeon stuffed with peppers and potatoes, or ducks' livers with ceps and rosemary. *Dinner only, closed Mon.*

Don Chisciotte, Via C Ridolfi 4r, **t** 055 475430. A small place between the Fortezza Basso and Piazza dell'Indipendenza, serving inventive Italian food with a particular emphasis on fish and vegetables. Let yourself be tempted by baked baby squid, delicate warm vegetable and fish salad, or green tagliatelle with scampi and courgettes. *Closed Aug, and Sun and Mon lunch.*

Expensive

Buca Lapi, Via del Trebbio 1r, **t** 055 213768. Located since 1800 in the old wine cellar of the lovely Palazzo Antinori, serving traditional favourites, from *pappardelle al cinghiale* (wide pasta with boar) and a *bistecca fiorentina con fagioli* that is hard to beat, downed with many different Tuscan wines. *Closed Sun and Mon lunch.*

Beccofino, Piazza degli Scarlatti, **t** 055 290076. On the river under the British Institute, you could almost be in London or New York once inside this new, trendy restaurant, but the food is decidedly Italian. Dishes are enhanced by a creative touch and are elegantly presented. Both fish and meat dishes are excellent and change with the seasons: octopus salad, pasta flavoured with courgettes and saffron, sea bass on a bed of truffle-flavoured mash, and a fabulous *bistecca alla Fiorentina*. You can also eat a light meal in the wine bar where prices are considerably lower. *Closed Mon.*

Caffé Concerto, Lungarno C. Colombo 7, **t** 055 677377. This has a lovely setting on the north bank of the Arno, east of the city centre, and a warm wood and glass interior with lots of greenery. Creative cuisine. *Open Mon–Sat noon–2.30 and 8–11, closed three weeks in Aug.*

Pane e Vino, Via San Niccolò 70r (in the Oltrarno, just in from Ponte alla Grazie), **t** 055 247 6956. This pleasant and informal place has a superb wine list, and very knowledgeable staff to go with it. The *menu degustazione* changes daily, and offers seven small courses; with any luck, the superb porcini mushroom flan will be available. *Mon–Sat 7.30–midnight.*

Coco Lezzone, Via del Parioncino 26r (off Lungarno Corsini), **t** 055 287178. In old Florentine dialect this means big, smelly cook, but don't let the name put you off. The atmosphere is informal and the food – Tuscan classics using the highest quality fresh ingredients – is truly excellent. *Open Mon–Sat 12.30–2 and 8–10.30.*

Taverna del Bronzino, Via delle Route 25–27r, **t** 055 495220. An elegant, traditional restaurant north of the Duomo, featuring plenty of Tuscan dishes – the *bistecca alla fiorentina* is succulent and tender – and delights like truffle-flavoured tortellini; there are several seafood choices for each course. *Open Mon–Sat 12.30–2.30 and 7.30–10.30, closed three weeks in Aug.*

Ristorante Ricchi, Piazza S. Spirito 8r, **t** 055 215864, *www.caffericchi.it*. This new fish restaurant has tables on magical Piazza Santo Spirito. Inside, the décor is contemporary and elegant, with tables lined up against the walls. The generous plate of *antipasto* is good and main courses include the catch of the day roasted on a bed of potatoes and tomatoes. There are a few meat dishes too. *Open Mon–Sat 8–10.30.*

Moderate

Antico Fattore, Via Lambertesca 1/3r, **t** 055 288975, *www.anticofattore.it*. This traditional Florentine *trattoria*, popular with locals and tourists alike, suffered serious damage in the 1993 Uffizi bomb, but it is back in business now and serving excellent and reasonably-priced local dishes. Try pasta with wild boar or deer sauce and *involtini* with artichoke hearts. *Open Mon–Sat 12.15–2.45 and 7.15–10.30, closed 2 weeks in Aug.*

Il Latini, Via dei Palchetti 6r (by Palazzo Rucellai), **t** 055 210916, *www.illatini.com*. Something of an institution in Florence, crowded (prepare to queue; they don't accept bookings) and noisy but fun, where you eat huge portions of Florentine classics at long tables. The *primi* aren't great; so go for the *bistecca* or, more unusual, the *gran pezzo* – a vast rib-roast of beef. The house wine is good. *Closed Mon and all of Aug.*

Angiolino, Via Santo Spirito 57r, **t** 055 239 8976. It has lost some of its genuinely 'characteristic' qualities after renovation, but it's still a reliable place to eat Tuscan standards. *Closed Mon.*

Baldovino, Via Giuseppe 22r (Piazza Santa Croce), **t** 055 241773. An excellent *trattoria/pizzeria* run by a young Scotsman, where you can eat anything from a big salad, filled foccaccia or pizza to a full menu of pasta, fish and steaks from the Val di Chiana. *Open Tues–Sun 11.30–2.30 and 7–11.30.*

Buca Mario, Piazza degli Ottaviani 16r, **t** 055 214179. Steep stairs take you down into one of Florence's traditional 'cellar restaurants', a place full of Florentine atmosphere with a menu to match. The soups here are superb – *pappa al pomodoro* and *ribollita*, or you could try the tagliatelle with porcini. *Ossobuco* is also excellent (in tomato sauce, Florentine-style). *Open Thurs–Tues 12.30–2.30 and 7.30–10.30.*

Cavolo Nero, Via dell'Ardiglione 22, **t** 055 294744. This little restaurant, tucked away in a side street near Piazza del Carmine, has quite a following among Florentine trendies. The interior is white on yellow with as many tables as possible crowded into the attractive room and there is a pretty garden at the back. The food is mainly Mediterranean with a twist (curried monkfish, rabbit with wild fennel), but there are also plenty of local standards such as spaghetti with clams. *Open Mon–Sat noon–2.30 and 8–11, closed 2 weeks mid Aug.*

Coquinarius, Via della Oche 15r, **t** 055 230 2153. You can eat or drink just about anything at this café/wine bar/restaurant. It is a useful stop off for a light meal or snack in the centre of tourist land. Snacks include a series of hot *crostone* (toasted Tuscan bread with various toppings) and salads. Wines by the bottle or the glass. *Open Sept–April daily 9am–11pm; May–Aug Mon–Sat 9am–11pm.*

The Fusion Bar, Gallery Hotel Art, Vicolo dell'Oro 5, **t** 055 27263, *www.lungarno hotels.com.* Go for something completely different in the ultra-cool, East-meets-West atmosphere of the Gallery hotel's (*see* p.225) bar and restaurant. Their version of 'Fusion Food' is not completely convincing, but the setting makes up for this. They also serve light lunches and brunch at the weekends. *Open Tues–Sun 7.30pm–10.30pm, Sat, Sun brunch 11.30am–2.30pm.*

Antico Ristoro di Cambi, Via Sant' Onofrio 1r, **t** 055 217134. In the Oltrarno, some way to the west of the centre, is a place very popular with the Florentine *intellighenzia*. The food is genuinely Florentine, the classic soups – *ribollita* and *pappa al pomodoro* – are tasty and warming, and the *bistecca alla Fiorentina* impressive. *Open Mon–Sat noon–2.30 and 7.30–10.30.*

La Vecchia Bettola, Viale Ariosto 32–34r, **t** 055 224158. A noisy *trattoria*, west of the Carmine, with great food; the menu changes daily, but you can usually find their classic *tagliolini con funghi porcini*. The grilled meats are tasty, and the ice cream is from Vivoli. *Closed Sun and Mon.*

Osteria Santo Spirito, Piazza Santo Spirito 16r, **t** 055 238 2383. If there is no room at Borgo Antico, this is just a walk across the piazza. Sit outside and enjoy a choice of cold dishes, pastas (try the gnocchi with melted cheese infused with truffle oil), vegetarian dishes and more. The décor inside is unusual for Florence – warm red paintwork with contemporary lighting. *Open daily 12.30–2.30 and 7.30–11.30.*

Ottorino, Via delle Oche 12/16r, **t** 055 21515. An elegant restaurant just south of the Duomo which serves typically Tuscan food including a mixed platter of deep-fried brains, tiny lamb cutlets and vegetables. *Open Mon–Sat 12.15–2.30, 7.15–10.30. Closed 2nd half of Aug.*

Sostanza, Via della Porcellana 25r, **t** 055 212691. Just west of Santa Maria Novella is one of the last authentic Florentine trattorias, a good place to eat *bistecca*. One of their most famous dishes is the simple but delectable *petto di pollo al burro*, chicken breast sautéed in butter. *Open Mon–Fri 12.30–2 and 7.30–9.30.*

Zibibbo, Via di Terzollina 3r, **t** 055 433383. A wonderful restaurant serving traditional Tuscan fare but in a stylish, un-Tuscan setting (pink-varnished floorboards, contemporary furniture). Plenty of choice between meat and fish dishes. Worth the trip up to the northernmost extremes of town. *Open Mon–Sat 1–3 and 8–11.*

Cheap

Trattoria Cibreo, Via de' Macci 114, **t** 055 234 1100. A little annexe to smart Cibreo (*see* p.230), this is one of the best deals in town; the food is the same, but served in a rustic setting on cheaper porcelain – and your bill will be a third of that of those dining next door. *Open Tues–Sat 12.50–2.30 and 7.30–11.15.*

Aquacotta, Via dei Pilastri 51r, **t** 055 242907. This restaurant, north of Piazza Sant' Ambrogio, is named after the simple but delicious bread soup, one of the specialities; you could follow that by deep-fried rabbit accompanied by crisply fried courgette flowers. *Open Mon–Sat 7.30–10.*

Borgo Antico, Piazza Santo Spirito 6, **t** 055 210437. Popular with a young trendy crowd, so you may have to wait for a table, especially in summer. Inside, the music can be unbearably loud, but the pizza is decent, and there are plenty of other choices. *Open daily 12.30–2.30 and 7.30–11.30.*

La Casalinga, Via Michelozzi 9r, **t** 055 218624. A family-run *trattoria*, also near Piazza Santo Spirito, and always busy, which is not surprising given the quality of the simple home cooking and the low prices. The *ribollita* is excellent. *Open Mon–Sat noon–2.30 and 7–9.45.*

Trattoria del Carmine, Piazza del Carmine 18r, t 055 218601. A traditional, bustling *trattoria* in the San Frediano district, often full. The long menu includes such staples as *ribollita*, *pasta e fagioli* and roast pork, but also features seasonal dishes such as risotto with asparagus or mushrooms, pasta with wild boar sauce and *ossobuco*. *Closed Sun and 3 weeks in Aug.*

Al Tranvai, near the Carmine in Piazza Torquato Tasso 14r, t 055 225197. The two rows of tables in this cheerful little place are always full, and you may not get much elbow room. The menu changes daily, but the *crostini misti* are always on offer, and there's lots of offal: tripe, *lampredotto* (intestines), chicken gizzards, etc. *Open Mon–Fri 7.30–10.30.*

Il Pizzaiuolo, near the Sant'Ambrogio market at Via dei Macci 113r, t 055 241171. One of the best, boasting a real Neapolitan pizza maker, whose creations are puffy and light. There's lots more to choose from, but long queues. *Open Mon–Sat 12.30–3.30 and 7.30–1am, closed Aug.*

Da Mario, Via della Rosina 2r, t 055 218550. Mario's *trattoria*, located at the back of the central market, is always buzzing, and there is usually a queue for the few rather cramped tables; don't expect a table to yourself. The food is pure Tuscan, excellent and cheap. *Open Mon–Sat noon–2pm, cash only.*

Da Ruggero, Via Senese 89r, t 055 220542. A tiny, family-run *trattoria* a little way from the centre of town; it's always full, so book. The traditional food is home cooked; try the excellent *pappardelle alla lepre* (with hare sauce) and good puddings. *Closed Tues and Wed, and 3 weeks July–Aug.*

Santa Lucia, Via Ponte alle Mosse 102r, t 055 353255. North of the Cascine there is a genuine Neapolitan pizzeria. It's a noisy, steamy and unromantic place but it makes up for its lack of glamour by serving what is possibly the best pizza in Florence. *Open 7.30–1am, closed Wed and Aug; cash only.*

There aren't many **vegetarian** restaurants as such in Florence, though non-meat eaters will find plenty of choice (pastas, risotto, etc.) to tempt them. Specifically **vegetarian** restaurants include:

Ruth's, Via Farini 2/A, t 055 248 0888. A new, bright and modern kosher vegetarian restaurant next to the synagogue, serving fish and Middle Eastern dishes. *Open 12.30–2.30 and 8–10.30, closed Fri dinner and Sat lunch.*

Il Vegetariano, Via delle Ruote 30r, t 055 47030. Located to the west of San Marco; self-service with excellent fresh food. *Closed Sun lunch and Mon.*

Cafés and *Gelaterie*

Caffè Italiano, Via Condotta 56r, t 055 291082. Right in the centre of town, a popular lunch time stop for locals who crowd in for the excellent hot and cold dishes. On two levels: downstairs for standing at the bar, upstairs for a longer sit. The atmosphere is old-fashioned, particularly in the tearoom upstairs. Newspapers are on offer for browsing. *Cash only.*

Caffè Ricchi, Piazza Santo Spirito. A local institution. It continues to serve excellent light lunches and wonderful ice cream. The outside tables enjoy the benefit of one of the most beautiful piazzas in Florence.

Gilli, Piazza della Repubblica 13–14r. Many of Florence's grand old cafés were born in the last century, though this one, the oldest, dates back to 1733, when the Mercato Vecchio still occupied this area; its two panelled back rooms are especially pleasant in the winter. *Open Wed–Mon.*

Dolci e Dolcezze, Piazza Cesare Beccaria 8r, t 055 234 5438. East of Sant' Ambrogio market, this has the most delicious cakes, pastries and marmalades in the city. It now has another shop at Via del Corso 41r. *Closed Mon.*

Dolce Vita, Piazza del Carmine. This is the place where fashionable young Florentines model their latest togs – a favourite pastime since the 14th century. *Closed Sun and 2 weeks in Aug.*

Giubbe Rosse, Piazza della Repubblica. Famous as the rendezvous of Florence's literati at the turn of the century; the chandelier-lit interior has changed little since.

Hemingway, Piazza Piattellina 9r, t 055 284781 (*booking advised*). A beautifully appointed bar done out in pale blues with rattan furniture. You can enjoy teas and coffees, as well as cocktails, interesting light meals and an excellent brunch on Sundays. The owner is a chocaholic, so the chocolates and puddings are a dream. *Open weekdays 4.30–late, Sun 11–8.*

Il **Granduca**, Via dei Calzaiuoli 57r. Creamy concoctions that challenge those of nearby rival Perché No. *Closed Wed.*

Il **Triangulo delle Bermude**, Via Nazionale 61r. Has a superb choice.

La Via del' Té, Piazza Ghiberti 22r. Looking on to the Sant' Ambrogio food market, this offers a huge range of teas to choose from plus sweet and savoury snacks.

L'Oasi, Via dell'Oriuolo 5, near the Duomo. Sophisticated ice cream flavours, and a good choice of cakes.

Vivoli, Via Isola delle Stinche 7r, between the Bargello and Santa Croce. Florence lays some claim to being the ice cream capital of the world, a reputation that owes much to the decadently delicious confections and rich *semifreddi* served here. *Closed Mon.*

Perché No, Via Tavolini 194. Arctic heaven near Via Calzaiuoli, with wonderful ice cream in 1940s surroundings.

Festa del Gelato, Via del Corso 75r. Boasts over 100 variations of ice cream.

Baby Yoghurt, Via Michelozzo 13r. This frozen yoghurt claims to be healthy, though it tastes so creamy that it's hard to believe.

Gelateria de' Ciompi, Via dell'Agnolo 121r. This traditional Florentine ice cream parlour, tucked around the corner from Santa Croce, prides itself on its authentic home-made recipes, some of which are over 50 years old.

Ricchi, Piazza Santo Spirito. The Oltrarno champ, with a huge choice and a scrumptious *tiramisú*. *Closed Sun and early Aug.*

Rivoire, Piazza della Signoria 5r. Florence's most elegant and classy watering hole, with a marble-detailed interior as lovely as the Piazza della Signoria itself.

Wine Bars

Florence is full of wine bars, from new-generation places to simple 'holes in the wall'.

Cantinetta dei Verazzano, Via dei Tavolini 18–20r. Part bakery (selling delicious bread and cakes), part wine bar, this centrally located place belongs to the Verazzano wine estate and serves its own very good wine exclusively; sip it with a plate of mixed *crostini* at hand.

Fuori Porta, Via Monte alle Croci 10r, t 055 234 2483, *www.fuoriporta.it*. Possibly the most famous of all, where there are some 600 labels on the wine list and dozens of whiskeys and grappas. Among the snacks and hot dishes on offer, try one of the *crostoni*, a huge slab of local bread topped with something delicious and heated under the grill. *Closed Sun.*

Le Volpi e L'Uva, Piazza dei Rossi, t 055 239 8132. The knowledgeable and helpful owners specialize in relatively unknown labels, and snacks include a marvellous selection of French and Italian cheeses.

Enoteca Baldovino, Via San Giuseppe 18r, t 055 234 7220. A bright, cheerful wine bar down the northern side of Santa Croce with snacks and pasta. *Open daily noon–midnight, closed 4–6pm, and Mon in winter.*

Pitti Gola e Cantina, Piazza Pitti 16, t 055 212704. A delightful little place situated bang opposite the Pitti palace, with a good choice of wines from Tuscany and beyond, snacks and other more substantial dishes. *Closed Mon.*

Enoteca dei Giraldi, Via dei Giraldi. Near the Bargello, this hosts art exhibitions and runs wine-tasting courses as well as supplying excellent food and drink.

The bar on the corner of Via de' Neri and Via de' Benci, traditional and full of office workers at lunchtime and locals in the early evenings, all of whom appreciate the range of tasty nibbles and hot dishes at reasonable prices. *Closed Sun.*

Vini, Via dei Cimatori 38r. One of the last of its kind in Florence, where you can join the locals standing on the street, glass and *crostino* in hand. *Closed Sun.*

Entertainment and Nightlife

Nightlife with Great Aunt Florence is still awaiting its Renaissance; she's conservative, somewhat deaf and retires early – 1am is late in this city. However, there are plenty of people who wish it weren't so, and slowly, slowly, Florence by night is beginning to mean more than the old *passeggiata* over the Ponte Vecchio and an ice cream.

Look for listings of concerts and events in Florence's daily, *La Nazione*. The tourist office's free *Florence Today* contains bilingual monthly information and a calendar, as does a booklet called *Florence Concierge Information*, available in hotels and tourist offices. The monthly *Firenze Spettacolo*, sold at newsstands, contains a brief section on events in English, but the comprehensive listings are easy to understand even in Italian. The annual guide *Guida locali di Firenze* also gives listings. For all current films being shown in Florence, look in the local paper.

Performance Arts

The opera and ballet season runs from September to Christmas and concerts from January to April at the **Teatro del Maggio Musicale Fiorentino**, and in the **Maggio Musicale** festival, which features all three, from mid-April until the end of June. There is usually more opera in July.

Classical Concerts

Teatro del Maggio Musicale Fiorentino, Via del Corso 16, **t** 055 211158, *www.maggiofiorentino.com*. Symphony concerts, recitals, opera and ballet are all held at Florence's municipal opera house.

Teatro della Pergola, Via della Pergola 12–32, **t** 055 226 4316, *www.amicimusica.fi.it*. The excellent chamber music series held in the stunning 18th-century Teatro della Pergola is promoted by the Amici della Musica.

Teatro Verdi, Via Ghibellina 99, **t** 055 212320, *www.teatroverdifirenze.it*. The red and gold Teatro Verdi is home to Tuscany's regional orchestra, who perform there regularly from late Nov–May.

Scuola di Musica di Fiesole, Villa la Torraccia, San Domenico, Fiesole, **t** 055 597851, *www.scuolamusica.fiesole.fi.it*. One of Italy's best known music schools promotes a series of chamber music concerts.

Many smaller events take place year-round in churches, cloisters and villas.

Rock and Jazz Concert Venues

Auditorium Flog, Via M Mercati 24b, **t** 055 490437. One of the best places in Florence to hear live music year-round, often hosting ethnic music events. Look out for the Musica dei Popoli festival in November.

Teatro Puccini, Via delle Cascine 41, **t** 055 362067.

Teatro Verdi, Via Ghibellina 99, **t** 055 212320.

Tenax, Via Pratese 46, **t** 055 308160, *www.tenax.org*. A spacious venue on the outskirts of town, which is very popular and so usually crowded. Stages lots of live rock concerts, with bands ranging from international names to local groups.

Palasport, Viale Paoli, **t** 055 678841. Big-name rock and jazz bands nearly always play at this venue in Campo di Marte, which seats several thousand.

Saschall, Lungarno Aldo Moro 3, **t** 055 650 4112, *www.saschall.it*. Risen from the ashes (not literally) of the old Teatro Tenda, the brand new 3,000-seat venue plays host to all kinds of music (including musicals). See local press for details.

In the summer, there are lots of live music venues all over the city, many of them free.

Musicus Concentus, Piazza del Carmine 14, **t** 055 287347. Brings in big-name jazz performers, classical artists and others to Florence.

Box office, Via Alamanni 39, **t** 055 210804. A central ticket agency for all the major events in Tuscany and beyond, including classical, rock, jazz, etc.

Cinemas

English-language films are shown throughout the summer two evenings a week at the Odeon in Piazza Strozzi and open-air screens are erected in several venues in Florence with two different films in Italian each evening from mid-June until mid-Sept. Details appear in the local newspapers.

The following show original language (*v.o.*, usually English) films:

Odeon Cinehall, Piazza Strozzi, **t** 055 214068, *www.cinehall.it*. Shows latest releases on Mon and Tues.

Fulgor, Via Masi Finiguerra, **t** 055 238 1881, *www.cinemafulgor.it*. Showings in English on Thurs.

Cinema Astro, Piazza di San Simeone, opposite Vivoli's, no tel. The films they show here have usually been around for a while. *Closed Mon and May–Sept.*

Spazio Uno, Via del Sole 10, **t** 055 215634. Occasionally has original language films.

Clubs

Universale, Via Pisana 77r. A vast ex-cinema, newly opened with designer décor, a restaurant, several bars and a pizzeria, all accompanied by live music and a giant cinema screen. Chic, sleek surroundings for a sleek, chic crowd. *Open 8.30pm–2am, closed Mon.*

Rex Caffé, Via Fiesolana 25r, **t** 055 248 0331. The number one winter hotspot until Universale opened its doors, featuring an unusual décor, tapas, music and dancing. *Closed June–Aug.*

Central Park, Parco delle Cascine. In summer, possibly the trendiest place in Florence, full of serious clubbers dancing to live music on three dance floors. *Open Tues–Sat 11pm–4am.*

Parterre, Piazza della Libertà. Another outdoor club; two bars, concerts and video screens.

Lido, Lungarno Pecori Giraldi 1. A small place in a pretty setting on the Arno. *Closed Mon.*

Full-Up, Via della Vigna Vechhia 25r. Mirrored walls, disco lighting, and dated music. *Open Tues–Sat 11pm–4am.*

Mago Merlino, Via dei Pilastri 31r. A relaxed tearoom/bar with live music, theatre, shows and games.

Du Monde, Via San Niccolò 103r. End up at this cocktail bar offering food, drink and music until five in the morning.

Caffedecò, Piazza della Libertà 45–46r. There's often live jazz here, in elegant Art Deco surroundings, where Florence's swells put on the dog. *Closed Mon.*

Caffè La Torre, Lungarno Cellini 65r, **t** 055 680643. A small club with jazz concerts.

Jazz Club, Via Nuova de' Caccini 3, **t** 055 247 9700. A small club, with regular jazz.

Riflessi d'Epoca, Via dei Renai 13r. Frequently has live jazz in a smoky ambience. It also stays open later than the average club.

Maracanà, Via Faenza 4. Try this for live music with a Latin feel – samba, mambo and bossanova. *Closed June–Aug.*

Maramao, Via dei Macci 79r. Slick and cool; music is often Latin-American. *Closed Mon.*

Ex-Mood, Corso dei Tintori 4. The old Mood club, still a cool venue, located in a cavernous basement with bar and decent dance space. *Open Wed–Sun 10pm–4am.*

Yab, Via Sassetti 5r, **t** 055 215168, *www.yab.it*. Yab has been around for a long time, and so have some of the punters who hang out there – it is favoured by a decidedly older crowd. It has recently been completely redesigned and has a vast dance space and a great sound system. *Closed May–Sept.*

Soulciety, Via San Zanobi 114b, **t** 055 830 3513. Popular with Florence's Senegalese community but otherwise a relatively little-known dance venue. *Open Tues–Sun 11.30pm–4am, closed June–Sept.*

Girasol, Via del Romito 1, **t** 055 474948. If it's Latin sounds you are into, head north of the city to Girasol for live bands and DJs. The space is small, so be sure to arrive early. *Open Tues–Sun 8pm–2.30am.*

Pubs

Irish pubs are big in Florence, and you will also find the odd English and Scottish version.

The Fiddler's Elbow, Piazza Santa Maria Novella 7r, **t** 055 215056. One of the original pubs in Florence, with some live music and an ex-pat atmosphere. A bit grim.

James Joyce, Lungarno B. Cellini 1r, **t** 055 658 0856. An Irish pub with literary pretensions, the James Joyce enjoys a pleasant location with a big garden near the river. Books and magazines are on hand for browsing.

Robin Hood, Via dell'Oriuolo. Similar to the above.

The Lion's Fountain, Borgo degli Albizi 34r, **t** 055 234 4412. A nice place which also serves food until late.

Il Rifrullo, Via San Niccolò 55r, **t** 055 234 2621. Year-round, an older pub/wine bar; probably the most popular of all and one of the first to attract people to the Oltrarno.

Gay Clubs

Tabasco, Piazza Santa Cecilia 3r, **t** 055 213000. Italy's first gay bar, opened in the 1970s.

Crisco, Via Santi Egidio 43r, **t** 055 248 0580. Another one to try. *Closed Tues.*

Il Piccolo Café, Borgo Santa Croce 23, **t** 055 200 1057. A tiny, friendly, arty bar. *Open daily from 5pm.*

Flamingo, Via Pandolfini 26r. Offers a cocktail bar and disco. *Closed Tues.*

Fine balm let Arno be;
The walls of Florence all of silver rear'd,
And crystal pavements in the public way...
14th-century madrigal by Lapo Gianni

Magari! – if only! – the modern Florentine would add to this vision, to this city of art and birthplace of the Renaissance, built by bankers and merchants whose sole preoccupation was making more florins. The precocious capital of Tuscany began to slip into legend back in the 14th century, during the lifetime of Dante; it was noted as

Tuscany

No region could be more essentially Italian. Its Renaissance culture and art became Italy's in common, and its dialect, as refined by Dante, cast a hundred others into the shadows to become the Italian language. Nevertheless, Tuscany seems to stand a bit aloof from the rest of the nation; it keeps its own counsel, never changes its ways, and faces the world with a Mona Lisa smile that has proved irresistible to northerners since the days of Shelley and Browning. Today Britons, Dutchmen, Germans and Americans jostle each year for the privilege of paying hundreds of euros for a month in a classic Tuscan farmhouse; in Florence, they stand in queues like refugees, waiting to enter churches and museums that are the shrines of Tuscan art.

For a province that has contributed so much to Western civilization since the Middle Ages, Tuscany's career remains slightly mysterious. Some have attempted to credit its cultural prominence to an inheritance from the ancient Etruscans, but most of modern Tuscany was never more than provincial throughout Etruscan and Roman times. Out of the Dark Ages, inexplicably, new centres of learning and art appeared, first in Pisa and Florence, and then in a dozen other towns, inaugurating a cultural renaissance that really began as early as the 1100s.

As abruptly as it began, this brilliant age was extinguished in the 16th century, but it left behind a new province of Europe, finished, solid, and well-formed. Tuscany can be excused a little complacency. Though prosperous and enlightened, fully a part of modern Italy today, the region for centuries has seemed perfectly content to let the currents of culture and innovation flow elsewhere. There's no sense in painting when anything new would have to hang next to Da Vincis and Botticellis, no incentive to build in a city full of churches and palaces by the medieval masters. After the surprising wave of bad taste that brought the Renaissance to a close, Tuscany was shamed into an introspectiveness and cultural conservatism of almost Chinese proportions. Of course these centuries, during which Tuscany has quietly cultivated its own garden, have not been without some advantages. Its cities and their art treasures have been preserved with loving care. So has the countryside; if anything the last few hundred years have emphasized the frugal, hard-working side of the Tuscan character, the side that longs for the rural life, counts its pennies, and finds tripe with chickpeas a perfectly satisfying repast. All this at times makes a striking contrast with the motorways, the new industry around the cities, and the hordes of tourists descending on Florence, Pisa and Siena.

different even before the Renaissance, before Boccaccio, Masaccio, Brunelleschi, Donatello, Leonardo da Vinci, Botticelli, Michelangelo, Machiavelli, the Medici...

> *This city of Florence is well populated, its good air a healthy tonic; its citizens are well dressed, and its women lovely and fashionable, its buildings are very beautiful, and every sort of useful craft is carried on in them, more so than any other Italian city. For this many come from distant lands to see her, not out of necessity, but for the quality of its manufactures and arts, and for the beauty and ornament of the city.*
>
> Dino Compagni in his *Chronicle* of 1312

According to the tourist office, in 1997, 685 years after Dino, a grand total of over seven million tourists (Americans, Germans, French and Britons are still the top four groups) spent at least one night in a Florentine hotel. Some, perhaps, had orthodontist appointments. A large percentage of the others came to inhale the rarefied air of the cradle of Western civilization, to gaze at some of the loveliest things made by mortal hands and minds, to walk the streets of new Athens, the great humanist 'city built to the measure of man'. Calling Florence's visitors 'tourists', however, doesn't seem quite right; 'tourism' implies pleasure, a principle alien to this dour, intellectual, measured town. 'Pilgrims' is perhaps the better word, cultural pilgrims who throng the Uffizi, the Accademia, the Bargello to gaze upon the holy mysteries of our secular society, to buy postcards and replicas, the holy cards of our day.

Someone wrote a warning on a wall near Brunelleschi's Santo Spirito, in the Oltrarno: *'Turista con mappa/alla caccia del tesoro/per finire davanti ad un piatto/di spaghetti al pomodoro'* ('Tourist with a map, on a treasure hunt, only to end up in front of a plate of spaghetti with tomato sauce'). Unless you come with the right attitude, Florence can be as disenchanting as cold spaghetti. It only blossoms if you apply your mind as well as your vision, if you go slowly and do not let the art bedazzle until your eyes glaze over in dizzy excess (a common complaint, known in medical circles as the Stendhal syndrome). Realize that loving and hating Florence at the same time may be the only rational response. It is the capital of contradiction; you begin to like it because it goes out of its way to annoy.

History

The Etruscans, who founded Florence perhaps as early as 1000 BC, were coy about providing any further details; the city's early history remains a puzzle. Like so many cities, however, Florence seems to begin with a bridge. Dante and many other writers commonly invoke the *marzocco*, the battered ancient icon that sat in the middle of the Ponte Vecchio and any number of bridges that preceded it until a flood swept it away in the 14th century. Often pictured as a lion (like the replacement for the original made by Donatello, now on display in the Bargello Museum), the *marzocco* may really have been a mounted cult image of the god Mars. Nothing could be more fitting, for in the centuries of its greatness Florence was a town full of trouble.

The city's apprenticeship in strife came during the endless Italian wars of the 4th–2nd centuries BC, when Rome was consolidating its hold on the peninsula. Florence seems usually to have chosen the wrong side. Sulla razed it to the ground

Florentine Duality

Dante's *Vita Nuova*, the autobiography of his young soul, was only the beginning of Florentine analysis; Petrarch, the introspective 'first modern man', was a Florentine born in exile; Ghiberti was the first artist to write an autobiography, Cellini wrote one of the most readable; Alberti invented art criticism; Vasari invented art history; Michelangelo's personality, in his letters and sonnets, looms as large as his art. In many ways Florence broke away from the medieval idea of community and invented the modern concept of the individual, most famously expressed by Lorenzo de' Medici's friend, Pico della Mirandola, whose *Oration on the Dignity of Man* tells us what the God on the Sistine Chapel ceiling was saying when he created Adam: '...And I have created you neither celestial nor terrestrial, neither mortal nor immortal, so that, like a free and able sculptor and painter of yourself, you may mould yourself entirely in the form of your choice.'

To attempt to understand Florence, remember one historical constant: no matter what the issue, the city always takes both sides, vehemently and often violently, especially in the Punch and Judy days of Guelphs and Ghibellines. In the 1300s this was explained by the fact that the city was founded under the sign of Mars, the war god; but in medieval astronomy Mars is also connected with Aries, another Florentine symbol and the sign of the time of spring blossoms. (The Annunciation, at the beginning of spring, was Florence's most important festival.) One of the city's oldest symbols is the lily (or iris), flying on its oldest gonfalons. Perhaps even older is its *marzocco*, originally an equestrian statue of Mars on the Ponte Vecchio, later replaced by Donatello's grim lion.

Whatever dispute rocked the streets, Great Aunt Florence often expressed her schizophrenia in art, floral Florence versus stone Florence, epitomized by the irreconcilable differences between the two most famous works of art: Botticelli's graceful *Primavera* and Michelangelo's cold, perfect *David*. The 'city of flowers' seems a joke; it has nary a real flower, nor even a tree, in its stone streets; indeed, all effort has gone into keeping nature at bay, surpassing it with geometry and art. And yet the Florentines were perhaps the first since the Romans to discover the joys of the countryside. The rusticated stone palaces, like fortresses or prisons, hide charms as delightful as Gozzoli's frescoes in the Palazzo Medici-Riccordi. Luca della Robbia's dancing children and floral wreaths are contemporary with the naked, violent warriors of the Pollaiuolo brothers; the writhing, quarrelsome statuary in the Piazza della Signoria is sheltered by one of the most delicate *loggie* imaginable.

After 1500, all the good, bad and ugly symptoms of the Renaissance peaked in the mass fever of Mannerism. Then, drifting into a debilitating twilight, Florence gave birth to the artistic phenomenon known as kitsch – the Medici Princes' chapel is an early kitsch classic. Since then, worn out perhaps, or embarrassed, this city built by merchants has kept its own counsel, expressing its argumentative soul in overblown controversies about traffic, art restoration and the undesirability of fast-food counters and cheap *pensioni*. We who find her fascinating hope she some day comes to remember her proper role, bearing the torch of culture instead of merely collecting tickets for the culture torture.

during the Social Wars, and the town seems to have struggled back only gradually. Julius Caesar helped it along by planting a colony of veterans here in 59 BC. Roman Florence prospered, trading throughout the whole Empire. Its street plan survives in the neat rectangle of straight streets at the city's core. The town had an impressive forum right in the middle, at what is now Piazza della Repubblica.

If almost nothing remains from Roman times, it is only because Florence has been continuously occupied ever since, its centre constantly replanned and rebuilt. There were some hard times, especially during the Greek–Gothic wars of the 6th century and the Lombard occupation, but the city regained importance in the time of Charlemagne, becoming for a while the seat of the 'march' of Tuscany. Here, in what must have been one of the most fascinating eras of the city's history, once again we are left without much information. Florence, for whatever reason, was one of the first inland cities to regain its balance after the fall of the Empire. During the Dark Ages the city was already beginning to develop the free institutions of the later republic, and establishing the trading connections that were later to make it the merchant capital of Europe. About 1115, on the death of the famous **Countess Matilda of Tuscany**, Florence became a self-governing *comune*.

The Florentine Republic

From the beginning, circumstances forced the city into an aggressive posture against enemies within and outside its walls. Florence waged constant war against the extortionist petty nobles of the hinterlands, razing their castles and forcing them to live in the city. As an important **Guelph** stronghold, Florence constantly got itself into trouble with the emperors, as well as with **Ghibelline** Pisa, Pistoia, and Siena, towns that were to become its sworn enemies. In its darkest hour, after the crushing defeat at Monteaperti in 1260, the Sienese almost succeeded in convincing their allies to bury Florence. A good sack would have been fun; Florence by the mid-13th century was possibly the richest banking and trading centre anywhere, and its gold florin had become a recognized currency across Europe.

In truth, Florence had no need of outside enemies. All through its history, the city did its level best to destroy itself. Guelph fought Ghibelline with impressive rancour, and when there were no Ghibellines left the Guelphs split into factions called the **Blacks and Whites** and began murdering each other. In a different dimension, the city found different causes of civil strife in the class struggles between the *popolo grosso* – the 'fat commons' or wealthy merchant class – and the members of the poorer guilds. Playing one side against the other was the newly urbanized nobility. They brought their gangster habits to town with them, turning Florence into a forest of tall brick tower-fortresses and carrying on bloody feuds in the streets that the city officials were helpless to stop. No historian has ever been able to explain how medieval Florence avoided committing suicide altogether. But despite all the troubles, this was the era of **Dante** (d. 1321, in political exile in Ravenna) and **Giotto** (d. 1337), the beginning of Florence's cultural golden age. Banking and the manufacture of wool (the leading commodity in the pre-industrial economy) were booming, and the florins kept rolling in no matter which faction was on top.

In 1282, and again in 1293, Florence tried to clean up its violent and corrupt government by a series of reforms; the Ordinamenti della Giustizia finally excluded the nobles from politics. It didn't work for long. Political strife continued throughout the 14th century, along with eternal wars with Lucca, Pisa and Siena, and some novel catastrophes. In 1339 Edward III of England repudiated his enormous foreign debt and Florence's two largest banks, the Bardi and Peruzzi, went bust. Plagues and famines dominated the 1340s; the plague of 1348, the Black Death, killed three-fifths of the population (and provided the frame story for Boccaccio's *Decameron*). The nobles and merchants then took advantage of the situation to establish tight boss rule. Their Guelph Party building is on Via Porta Rossa, where the spoils were divided – the original Tammany Hall. A genuine revolution in 1378 among the *ciompi*, the wool trade proletariat, might have succeeded if its leaders had been half as devious and ruthless as their opponents.

Florence's continuing good luck again saw it through, however, and prosperity gradually returned after 1400. In 1406 Pisa was finally conquered, giving Florence a seaport. Florentine armies bested the Visconti of Milan twice, and once (1410) even occupied Rome. At the dawn of the Renaissance not only Florence's artists, scholars and scientists were making innovations – the city government in the 1420s and '30s invented the progressive income tax and the national debt.

The Rise of the Medici

Although they are said to have begun as pharmacists (*medici*), by 1400 the House of Medici was the biggest merchant concern in Florence. With the resources of the Medici Bank behind him, **Cosimo de' Medici** installed himself as the city's political godfather, coercing or buying off the various interests and factions. In 1469 his grandson Lorenzo inherited the job, presiding over the greatest days of the Renaissance and a sustained stretch of peace and prosperity. Opposition, squashed originally by Cosimo, stayed squashed under Lorenzo. His military campaigns proved successful on the whole, and his impressive propaganda machine gave him an exaggerated reputation as a philosopher-king and patron of the arts. Lorenzo almost ruined the Medici Bank through neglect, but then made up his losses from public funds. His personal tastes in art seem to have been limited to knick-knacks, big jewels and antique bronzes, but his real hobby was nepotism. His son Giovanni, later to be made **Pope Leo X** at the age of 38, became a cardinal at 14.

Two years after Lorenzo's death, the wealthy classes of Florence finally succeeded in ending Medici rule when they exiled Lorenzo's weak son and successor, Piero in 1494. The republic was restored, but soon came under the influence of a remarkable Dominican demagogue, **Girolamo Savonarola**. Thundering out a fierce fundamentalist line, his preaching resulted in the famous 1497 'Bonfire of Vanities' on the Piazza della Signoria, when the people collected their paintings, fancy clothes, carnival masks and books and put them to the flame (a Venetian merchant offered instead to buy the whole lot from them, but the Florentines hurriedly sketched a portrait of him too, and threw it on the pyre). But Savonarola was more than a ridiculous prude. His idealistic republicanism resulted in some real democratic reforms for the new government, and his emphasis on morals provided a much needed purgative after the reigning depravity of the last 200 years. The friar reserved his strongest blasts, however, for the corruption of the Church; not a bad idea in the time of Alexander VI, the Borgia pope. When Savonarola's opponents, the **Arrabbiati** ('Infuriated'), beat his supporters, the **Piagnoni** ('snivellers'), in the 1498 elections, the way was clear for Alexander to order the friar's execution. Savonarola burned on 22 May 1498, on the same spot where the 'Bonfire of Vanities' had been held.

The Medici returned in 1512, thanks to Pope Julius II and his Spanish troops. The Spaniards' exemplary sack of Prato, with remarkable atrocities, was intended as a lesson to the Florentines. It had the desired effect, and Lorenzo's nephew Giuliano de' Medici was able to re-enter the city. When Giuliano was elected **Pope Clement VII** in 1523 he attempted to continue running the city at a distance, but yet another Medici expulsion would take place after his humiliation in the sack of Rome in 1527, followed by the founding of the last Florentine republic.

By now Florentine politics had become a death struggle between an entire city and a single family; in the end the Medici would prove to have the stronger will. The last republic lived nervously in an atmosphere of revolutionary apocalypse; meanwhile Clement intrigued with the Spaniards for his return. An imperial army arrived in 1530 to besiege the city and, despite heroic last-ditch resistance, Florence had to capitulate when its commander sold out to the Pope and turned his guns on the city itself. In 1532 the Medici broke the terms of the surrender agreement by abolishing all self-government, obtaining the title of Grand Dukes of Tuscany from Emperor Charles V.

To all intents and purposes Florentine history ends here. **Cosimo I Medici** (d. 1574) ruled over a state that declined rapidly into a provincial backwater. When the last Medici, fat Gian Gastone, died in 1737, the powers of Europe gave the duchy to the House of Lorraine. With the rest of Tuscany, Florence was annexed to Piedmont-Sardinia in 1859, and from 1865 to 1870 it served as the capital of united Italy.

Today, despite repeated attempts to diversify the local economy through the creation of new industrial areas on the outskirts, Florence largely lives on the sheer weight of its past creativity. It suffered badly in the **Second World War**, when the retreating German army blew up all the bridges over the Arno except the Ponte Vecchio, and destroyed many medieval buildings along the river's edge. Still worse damage was caused by the great floods of November 1966. The most recent damage to be inflicted on the city came in May 1993, when a bomb – planted by the Mafia – exploded near the Uffizi. The building of the new airport extension, which the Florentines hope will help make up some of the economic ground they've lost to Milan, includes the building of a whole new satellite city, a new Florence ('Firenze Nuova'). The buildings on the marshland (northwest of the city) have been demolished, the land flattened, and the project for a new city to include housing, shops, leisure facilities, a new law court and a new Fiat factory is already under way. Meanwhile Florence works hard to preserve what it already has. Pollution from nearby industry continues to eat away at monuments. Private companies, banks and even individuals finance 90 per cent of the art restoration in Florence, with techniques invented by the city's innovative Institute of Restoration.

Florentine Art

Under the assault of historians and critics over the last two centuries 'Renaissance' has become such a vague and controversial word as to be nearly useless. Nevertheless, however you choose to interpret this rebirth of the arts, and whatever dates you assign it, Florence inescapably takes the credit for initiating it. This is no small claim. Combining art, science and humanist scholarship into a visual revolution that often seemed pure sorcery to their contemporaries, a handful of Florentine geniuses taught the Western eye a new way of seeing. Perspective seems a simple enough trick to us now, but its discovery determined everything that followed, not only in art but in science and philosophy as well.

Florence in its centuries of brilliance accomplished more than any city, ever – far more than Athens in its classical age. The city's talents showed early, with the construction of the famous Baptistry, perhaps as early as 700. From the start Florence showed a remarkable adherence to the traditions of antiquity. New directions in architecture – the Romanesque after the year 1000 – had little effect; what passed for Romanesque in Florence was a unique style, evolved by a self-confident city that probably believed it was accurately restoring the grand manner of the Roman world. This new architecture (see the Baptistry, San Miniato, Santa Maria Novella), based on elegantly simple geometry with richly inlaid marble façades and pavements, was utterly unlike even the creations of nearby Pisa and Siena, and began a continuity of style that would reach its climax with the work of **Brunelleschi** and **Alberti** in the 1400s.

Likewise in painting and sculpture, Florentines made an early departure from Byzantine-influenced forms, and avoided the International Gothic style that thrived so well in Siena. Vasari's famous *Lives of the Artists* (1547) lays down the canon of Florentine artists, the foundation of all subsequent art criticism. It begins with **Cimabue** (c. 1240–1302), who according to Vasari first began to draw away from Byzantine stylization towards a more 'natural' way of painting. Cimabue found his greatest pupil **Giotto** (1266–1337) as a young shepherd boy, chalk-sketching sheep on a piece of slate. Brought to Florence, Giotto soon eclipsed his master's fame (artistic celebrity being another recent Florentine invention) and achieved the greatest advances on the road to the new painting, a plain, idiosyncratic approach that avoided Gothic prettiness while exploring new ideas in composition and expressing psychological depth in his subjects. Even more importantly Giotto, through his intuitive grasp of perspective, was able to go further than any previous artist in representing his subjects as actual figures in space. In a sense Giotto invented space; it was this, despite his often awkward and graceless draughtsmanship, that so astounded his contemporaries.

Vasari, for reasons of his own, neglected the artists of the Florentine trecento, and many critics have tended to follow slavishly – a great affront to the master artist and architect **Andrea Orcagna** (d. 1368; works include the Loggia dei Lanzi and the Orsanmichele tabernacle) and others including **Taddeo** and **Agnolo Gaddi** (d. 1366 and 1396), whose frescoes can be compared to Giotto's at Santa Croce.

The Quattrocento

The next turn in the story, what scholars self-assuredly used to call the 'Early Renaissance', comes with the careers of two geniuses who happened to be good friends. **Donatello** (1386–1466), the greatest sculptor since the ancient Greeks, inspired a new generation of not only sculptors but painters to explore new horizons in portraiture and three-dimensional representation. **Brunelleschi** (1377–1446), neglecting his considerable talents in sculpture for architecture and science, not only built the majestic cathedral dome, but threw the Pandora's box of perspective wide open by mathematically codifying the principles of foreshortening.

The new science of painting occasioned an explosion of talent unequalled before or since, as a score of masters, most of them Florentine by birth, each followed the dictates of his own genius to create a range of themes and styles hardly believable for one single city in a few short decades of its life. To mention only the most prominent:

Lorenzo Ghiberti (d. 1455), famous for the bronze doors of the Baptistry; **Masaccio** (d. 1428), the eccentric prodigy much copied by later artists, best represented by his naturalistic frescoes in Santa Maria del Carmine and Santa Maria Novella; **Domenico Ghirlandaio** (d. 1494), Michelangelo's teacher and another master of detailed frescoes; **Fra Angelico** (d. 1455), the most spiritual, and most visionary of them all, the painter of the Annunciation at San Marco; **Paolo Uccello** (d. 1475), one of the most provocative of all artists, who according to Vasari drove himself bats with too-long contemplation of perspective and the newly discovered vacuum of empty space; **Benozzo Gozzoli** (d. 1497), a happier soul, best known for the springtime Procession of the Magi in the Medici Palace; **Luca Della Robbia** (d. 1482), greatest of a family of sculptors, famous for the cantoria of the Cathedral Museum and exquisite blue and white terracottas all over Tuscany; **Antonio Pollaiuolo** (d. 1498), an engraver and sculptor with a nervously perfect line; **Fra Filippo Lippi** (d. 1469), who ran off with a brown-eyed nun to produce **Filippino Lippi** (d. 1504) – both of them exceptional painters and sticklers for detail; and finally **Sandro Botticelli** (d. 1510); his progress from the secret garden of pure art, expressed in his astounding early mythological pictures, to conventional holy pictures, done after the artist fell under the sway of Savonarola, marks the first signs of trouble and the first failure of nerve in the Florentine imagination.

Leonardo, Michelangelo and the Cinquecento

With equal self-assurance the critics used to refer to the early 1500s as the beginning of the 'High Renaissance'. **Leonardo da Vinci**, perhaps the incarnation of Florentine achievement in both painting and scientific speculation, lived until 1519, but spent much of his time in Milan and France. **Michelangelo Buonarroti** (d. 1564) liked to identify himself with Florentine republicanism, but finally abandoned the city during the siege of 1530 (even though he was a member of the committee overseeing Florence's defence). His departure left Florence with no important artists except the surpassingly strange **Jacopo Pontormo** (d. 1556) and **Rosso Fiorentino** (d. 1540). These two, along with Michelangelo, were key figures in the bold, neurotic, avant-garde art that has come to be known as Mannerism. This first conscious 'movement' in Western art can be seen as a last fling amid the growing intellectual and spiritual exhaustion of 1530s Florence, conquered once and for all by the Medici. The Mannerists' calculated exoticism and exaggerated, tortured poses, together with the brooding self-absorption of Michelangelo and many others, are the prelude to Florentine art's remarkably abrupt downturn into decadence, and prophesy its final extinction.

There was another strain to Mannerism in Florence, following the cold classicism of Raphael of Urbino, less disturbed, less intense and challenging than Michelangelo or Pontormo. With artists like Agnolo Bronzino (d. 1572), the sculptor **Bartolomeo Ammannati** (d. 1592), **Andrea del Sarto** (d. 1531), and **Giorgio Vasari** himself (d. 1574), Florentine art loses almost all imaginative and intellectual content, becoming a virtuoso style of interior decoration perfectly adaptable to saccharine holy pictures, portraits of newly enthroned dukes, or absurd mythological fountains and ballroom ceilings. In the cinquecento, with plenty of money to spend and a long Medici tradition of patronage to uphold, this tendency soon got out of hand. Under the reign of Cosimo I, indefatigable collector of pietra dura tables, silver and gold gimcracks, and exotic stuffed animals, Florence gave birth to the artistic phenomenon modern critics call kitsch.

In the cinquecento, Florence taught vulgarity to the Romans, degeneracy to the Venetians, and preciosity to the French. Oddly enough the city had as great an influence in its age of decay as in its age of greatness. The cute, well-educated Florentine pranced across Europe, finding himself praised as the paragon of culture and refinement. Even in England – though that honest nation soon found him out:

A little Apish hatte, couched fast to the Pate, like an Oyster,
French Camarick Ruffes, deepe with a witnesse, starched to the purpose,
Delicate in speach, queynte in arraye: conceited in all poyntes:
In Courtly guyles, a passing singular odde man...
          Mirror of Tuscanism, Gabriel Harvey, 1580

It's almost disconcerting to learn that Florence gave us not only much of the best of our civilization, but even a lot of the worst. Somehow the later world of powdered wigs and chubby winged putti is unthinkable without 1500s Florence. Then again, so is all the last 500 years of art unthinkable without Florence, not to mention modern medicine (the careful anatomical studies of the artists did much to help set it on its way) or technology (from the endless speculations and gadgets of Leonardo) or political science (from Machiavelli). The Florentines of course found the time to invent opera too, and give music a poke into the modern world. And without that little discovery of the painters, so simple though perhaps so very hard for us in the 20th century to comprehend – the invention of space – Copernicus, Newton, Descartes and all who followed them would never have discovered anything.

But Florence soon tired of the whole business. The city withdrew into itself, made a modest living, polished its manners and its conceit, and generally avoided trouble. Not a peep has been heard out of it since 1600.

Around the City

Piazza del Duomo

Tour groups circle like sharks around the three great spiritual monuments of medieval Florence. Postcard-vendors prey, and sax players play to a human carnival from a hundred nations that mills about the cathedral good-naturedly while ambulances of a medieval brotherhood dedicated to first aid stand at the ready in case anyone swoons from ecstasy or art-glut.

The Baptistry

Open Mon–Sat 12–7, Sun 8.30–2; adm.

To begin to understand what magic made the Renaissance first bloom by the Arno, look here; this ancient, mysterious building is the egg from which Florence's golden age was hatched. By the quattrocento, Florentines firmly believed their baptistry was originally a Roman temple to Mars, a touchstone linking them to a legendary past. Scholarship sets its date of construction between the 6th and 9th centuries, in the darkest Dark Ages, which makes it even more remarkable; it may as well have dropped from heaven. Its distinctive dark green and white marble facing, the tidily classical pattern of arches and rectangles that deceived Brunelleschi and Alberti, was probably

Highlights of Florence

Florence's museums, palaces and churches contain more good art than perhaps any city in Europe, and to see it all without hardship to your eyes, feet and sensibilities would take at least three weeks and a small fortune in admission charges. If you have only a few days to spend, and if you might never come back again, the highlights will easily take up all of your time – the **Cathedral** and **Baptistry**, the paintings in the **Uffizi** (preferably not all in the same day) and the sculptures in the **Bargello**, which is more worthy of your brief time than the **Accademia**, where the rubbernecks pile in to see Michelangelo's *David*. Stop in for a look at the eccentric **Orsanmichele**, and see the Arno from the **Ponte Vecchio**, taking in some of the oldest streets.

If your heart leans towards the graceful lyricism of the 1400s, don't miss the **Cathedral Museum** and the Fra Angelicos in **San Marco**; if the lush virtuosity of the 1500s is your cup of tea, visit the Pitti Palace's **Galleria Palatina**. Two churches on the edges of the centre, **Santa Maria Novella** and **Santa Croce**, are galleries in themselves, containing some of the greatest Florentine art; **Santa Maria del Carmine** has the restored frescoes of Masaccio and company. Devotees of the Michelangelo cult won't want to miss the Medici Chapels and library at **San Lorenzo**. When the stones begin to weary you, head for the green oasis of the **Boboli Gardens**. Finally, climb up to **San Miniato**, for the beautiful medieval church and the enchanting view over the city.

Most of the important museums, excluding the Palazzo Vecchio, are state-run and can be pre-booked. Call **t** 055 294 883.

added around the 11th century. The masters who built it remain unknown, but their strikingly original exercise in geometry provided the model for all of Florence's great church façades. When it was new, there was nothing remotely like it in Europe; to visitors from outside the city it must have seemed almost miraculous.

Every 21 March, New Year's Day on the old Florentine calendar, all the children that had been born over the last 12 months would be brought here for a great communal baptism, a habit that helped make the baptistry not merely a religious monument but a civic symbol, in fact the oldest and fondest symbol of the republic. As such the Florentines never tired of embellishing it. Under the octagonal cupola, the glittering 13th- and 14th-century gold-ground mosaics show a strong Byzantine influence, perhaps laid by mosaicists from Venice. The decoration is divided into concentric strips: over the apse, dominated by a 28ft figure of Christ, is a *Last Judgement*, while the other bands, from the inside out, portray the *Hierarchy of Heaven*, *Story of Genesis*, *Life of Joseph*, *Life of Christ* and the *Life of St John the Baptist*, the last band believed to be the work of Cimabue. The equally beautiful mosaics over the altar and in the vault are the earliest, signed by a monk named Iacopo in the early 1200s. New lighting installed in 1999 has vastly improved visitors' view of the ceiling.

To match the mosaics, there is an intricate tessellated marble floor, decorated with signs of the Zodiac; the octagonal space in the centre was formerly occupied by the huge font. The green and white patterned walls of the interior are remarkable, combining influences from the ancient world and modern inspiration for something new, the perfect source that architects of the Middle Ages and Renaissance would strive to match. Much of the best design work is in the **galleries**, partially visible from the floor.

The baptistry is hardly cluttered; besides a 13th-century Pisan-style baptismal font, only the **Tomb of Anti-Pope John XXIII** by Donatello and Michelozzo stands out. This funerary monument, with marble draperies softening its classical lines, is one of the prototypes of the Early Renaissance. But how did Anti-Pope John, deposed by the Council of Constance in 1415, earn the privilege of a tomb here? Why, it was thanks to him that Giovanni di Bicci de' Medici made a fortune as head banker to the Curia.

The Gates of Paradise

Historians used to pinpoint the beginning of the 'Renaissance' as the year 1401, when the merchants' guild, the Arte di Calimala, sponsored a competition for the baptistry's north doors. The **South Doors** (the main entrance) had already been completed by Andrea Pisano in 1330 in the style of the day. Their 28 panels in quatrefoil frames depict scenes from the life of St John the Baptist and the seven Cardinal and Theological Virtues – formal and elegant works in the best Gothic manner.

The celebrated competition of 1401 – perhaps the first ever held in the annals of art – pitted the seven greatest sculptors of the day against one another. Judgement was based on trial panels of the Sacrifice of Isaac, and in a dead heat at the end of the day were the two by Brunelleschi and Lorenzo Ghiberti, now displayed in the Bargello. Ghiberti's more classical-style figures were eventually judged the better, and it was a serendipitous choice; he devoted nearly the rest of his life to creating the most beautiful bronze doors in the world while Brunelleschi, disgusted by his defeat, went on to build the most perfect dome. Ghiberti's first efforts, the **North Doors** (1403–24), are contained, like Pisano's, in 28 quatrefoil frames. In their scenes on the Life of Christ, the Evangelists, and the Doctors of the Church, you can trace Ghiberti's progress over the 20 years he worked in the increased depth of his compositions, not only visually but dramatically; classical backgrounds begin to fill the frames, ready to break out of their Gothic confines. Ghiberti also designed the floral frame of the doors; the three statues, of John the Baptist, the Levite and the Pharisee, by Francesco Rustici, were based on a design by Leonardo da Vinci and added in 1511.

Ghiberti's work pleased the Arte di Calimala, and they set him loose on another pair of portals, the **East Doors** (1425–52), his masterpiece and one of the most awesome achievements of the age. Here Ghiberti (perhaps under the guidance of Donatello) dispensed with the small Gothic frames and instead cast 10 large panels that depict the Old Testament in Renaissance high gear, reinterpreting the forms of antiquity with a depth and drama that have never been surpassed. Michelangelo declared them 'worthy to be the Gates of Paradise'. The doors (they're actually copies – some of the original panels, restored after flood damage, are on display in the Museo dell'Opera del Duomo) have been cleaned recently, and stand in gleaming contrast to the others. In 1996 copies of Andrea Sansovino's marble statues of Christ and John the Baptist (1502) and an 18th-century angel were installed over the doors. The originals had begun to fall to bits in 1974; they too are now in the Museo dell'Opera.

Ghiberti wasn't exactly slow to toot his own horn; according to himself, he planned and designed the Renaissance on his own. His unabashedly conceited *Commentarii* were the first attempt at art history and autobiography by an artist, and a work as revolutionary as his doors in its presentation of the creative God-like powers of the artist. In a typical exhibition of Florentine pride he also put busts of his friends among the prophets and sibyls that adorn the frames of the East Doors. Near the centre, the balding figure with arched eyebrows and a little smile is Ghiberti himself.

The Duomo

Open Mon–Wed and Fri 10–5, Thurs 10–3.30, Sat 10–4.45, Sun 1.30–4.45.

For all its importance and prosperity, Florence was one of the last cities to plan a great cathedral. Work began in the 1290s, with the sculptor Arnolfo di Cambio in charge, and from the beginning the Florentines attempted to make up for their delay with sheer audacity. 'It will be so magnificent in size and beauty,' according to a decree of 1296, 'as to surpass anything built by the Greeks and Romans.' In response Arnolfo planned what in its day was the largest church in Catholicism; he confidently laid the foundations for an enormous octagonal crossing 146ft in diameter, then died before working out a way to cover it, leaving future architects the job of designing the biggest dome in the world.

Beyond its presumptuous size, the cathedral of Santa Maria del Fiore shows little interest in contemporary innovations and styles; a visitor from France or England in the 1400s would certainly have found it somewhat drab and architecturally primitive. Visitors today often circle confusedly around its grimy, ponderous bulk. Instead of the striped bravura of Siena or the elegant colonnades of Pisa, they behold an astonishingly eccentric green, white and red pattern of marble rectangles and flowers – like Victorian wallpaper, or as one critic expressed it, 'a cathedral wearing pyjamas'. In the sun, the cathedral under its sublime dome sports festively above the dullish dun and ochre sea of Florence; in dismal weather it sprawls morosely across its piazza like a beached whale tarted up with a lace doily front.

The fondly foolish **façade** cannot be blamed on Arnolfo. His original design, only one-quarter completed, was taken down in a late 16th-century Medici rebuilding programme that never got off the ground. The Duomo turned a blank face to the world until the present neo-Gothic extravaganza was added in 1888. Walk around to the north side to see what many consider a more fitting door, the **Porta della Mandorla** crowned with an Assumption of the Virgin in an almond-shaped frame (hence 'Mandorla'), made by Nanni di Banco in 1420.

Brunelleschi's Dome

Open Mon–Fri 8.30–7, Sat 8.30–5.40; adm.

Brunelleschi's dome, more than any landmark, makes Florence Florence. Many have noted how the dome repeats the rhythm of the surrounding hills, echoing them with its height and beauty; from those city streets fortunate enough to have a clear view, it rises among the clouds with all the confident mastery, proportions and perfect form that characterize the highest aspirations of the Renaissance. But if it seems miraculous, it certainly isn't divine; unlike the dome of the Hagia Sophia, suspended from heaven by a golden chain, Florence's was made by man.

Losing the competition for the baptistry doors was a bitter disappointment to Filippo Brunelleschi. His reaction was typically Florentine: not content with being the second-best sculptor, he turned his talents to a field where he thought no one could beat him, launching himself into a study of architecture and engineering, visiting Rome and probably Ravenna to snatch secrets from the ancients. When proposals were solicited for the cathedral's dome in 1418, he was ready with a brilliant *tour de force*. Not only would he build the biggest, most beautiful dome of the time, but he would do it without any expensive supports while work was in progress, making use of a cantilevered system of bricks that could support itself while it ascended.

Brunelleschi studied, then surpassed the technique of the ancients. To the Florentines, who could have invented the slogan 'form follows function' for their own tastes in building, it must have come as a revelation: the most logical way of covering the space was a work of perfect beauty. Brunelleschi's dome put a crown on the achievements of Florence. After 500 years it is still the city's pride and symbol.

The best way to appreciate Brunelleschi's genius is by touring inside the two concentric shells of the dome (*see* over), but before entering, note the eight marble ribs that define its octagonal shape; hidden inside are the three huge stone chains that bind them together. Work on the balcony around the base of the dome, designed by Giuliano da Sangallo, was halted in 1515 after Michelangelo commented that it resembled a cricket's cage. As for the lantern, the Florentines were famous for their fondness and admiration for Doubting Thomas, and here they showed why. Even though they marvelled at the dome, they still doubted that Brunelleschi could construct a proper lantern, and forced him to submit to yet another competition. He died before it was begun, and it was completed to his design by Michelozzo.

The Interior

After the façade, the austerity of the Duomo interior is startling. There is plenty of room – contemporary writers mention 10,000 souls packed inside to hear Savonarola's sermons. But, the Duomo hardly seems a religious building – more a *Florentine* building, with simple arches and counterpoint of grey stone and white plaster, full of old familiar Florentine things. Near the entrance, on the right-hand side, are busts of Brunelleschi and Giotto. On the left wall, posed inconspicuously, are the two most conspicuous monuments to private individuals ever erected by the Florentine Republic. The one on the right, is to **Sir John Hawkwood**, the English *condottiere* whose name the Italians mangled to Giovanni Acuto, a commander who served Florence for many years and is perhaps best known to English speakers as the hero of *The White Company* by Sir Arthur Conan Doyle. Hawkwood had the Florentines' promise to build him an equestrian statue after his death; it was a typical Florentine trick to pinch pennies and cheat a dead man, but they hired the greatest master of perspective, Paolo Uccello, to make a fresco that looked like a statue (1436). Twenty years later, they pulled the same trick again, commissioning Andrea del Castagno to paint the non-existent equestrian statue of another *condottiere*, Niccolò da Tolentino. A little further down, Florence commemorates its own secular scripture with Michelino's well-known fresco of Dante, a vision of the poet and his *Paradiso* outside the walls of Florence. Two singular icons of Florence's fascination with science stand at opposite ends of the building: behind the west front, a bizarre clock painted by Uccello and, in the pavement of the left apse, a gnomon fixed by the astronomer Toscanelli in 1475. A beam of sunlight strikes it every year at the summer solstice.

For building the great dome, Brunelleschi was accorded a special honour – he is one of the few Florentines to be buried in the cathedral. His tomb may be seen in the **Excavations of Santa Reparata** (*the stairway descending on the right of the nave; open Mon–Sat 10–5; adm*). Arnolfo di Cambio's cathedral was constructed on the ruins of the ancient church of Santa Reparata, which lay forgotten until 1965. Excavations have revealed not only the palaeo-Christian church and its several reconstructions, but also the remains of its Roman predecessor – a rather confusing muddle of walls that have been tidied up in an ambience that resembles an archaeological shopping centre. A coloured model helps explain what is what, and glass cases display items found in the dig, including the spurs of Giovanni de' Medici, who was buried here in 1351. In the ancient crypt of Santa Reparata are 13th-century tomb slabs, and in another section there's a fine pre-Romanesque mosaic pavement.

There is surprisingly little religious art – the Florentines for reasons of their own have carted most of it off into the Cathedral Museum (*see* p.252). Under the dome are the entrances to the two sacristies, with terracotta lunettes over the doors by Luca della Robbia; the scene of the Resurrection over the north sacristy is one of his earliest and best works. He also did the bronze doors beneath it, with tiny portraits on the handles of Lorenzo il Magnifico and his brother Giuliano de' Medici, targets of the Pazzi conspiracy in 1478. In the middle apse, there is a beautiful bronze urn by Ghiberti containing relics of the Florentine St Zenobius. The only conventional religious decorations are the frescoes some 200ft up in the dome, mostly by Vasari. As you stand squinting at them, try not to think that the cupola weighs around 25,000 tons.

A door on the left aisle near the Dante fresco leads up into the **dome** (*open Mon–Fri 8.30–7 and Sat 8.30–5.40; adm*). The complicated network of stairs and walks between the inner and outer domes (not too difficult, if occasionally claustrophobic and vertiginous) was designed by Brunelleschi, and offers an insight on how thoroughly the architect thought out the problems of the dome's construction, even inserting hooks to hold up scaffolding for future cleaning or repairs; Brunelleschi installed restaurants to save workers the trouble of descending for meals. There is also no better place to get an idea of the dome's scale; the walls of the inner dome are 13ft thick, and those of the outer dome 6ft. These give the dome enough strength and support to preclude the need for further buttressing.

From the gallery of the dome you can get a good look at the lovely **stained glass** by Uccello, Donatello, Ghiberti and Castagno in the seven circular windows, or *occhi*, made during the construction of the dome, which are being restored one by one. Further up, the views through the small windows offer tantalizing hints of the breathtaking panorama from the marble lantern at the top. The bronze ball at the very top was added by Verrocchio, and can hold almost a dozen people when open.

Giotto's Campanile

The dome steals the show, putting one of Italy's most beautiful bell towers in the shade both figuratively and literally. The dome's great size – 366ft to the bronze ball – makes the campanile look small, though 280ft is not exactly tiny. Giotto was made director of the cathedral works in 1334, and his basic design was completed after his death (1337) by Andrea Pisano and Francesco Talenti. It is difficult to say whether they were entirely faithful to the plan. Giotto was an artist, not an engineer. After he died, his successors realized the thing, then only 40ft high, was about to tumble over, a problem they overcame by doubling the thickness of the walls.

Besides its lovely form, the green, pink and white campanile's major fame rests with Pisano and Talenti's **sculptural reliefs** – a veritable encyclopaedia of the medieval world view with prophets, saints and sibyls, allegories of the planets, virtues and sacraments, the liberal arts and industries (the artist's craft is fittingly symbolized by a winged figure of Daedalus). All of these are copies of the originals now in the Cathedral Museum. If you can take another 400 steps or so, the **terrace** on top (*open daily 8.30–7.30; adm*) offers a slightly different view of Florence and of the cathedral itself.

Loggia del Bigallo

The most striking secular building on the Piazza del Duomo is the Loggia del Bigallo, south of the baptistry near the beginning of Via de' Calzaiuoli. This 14th-century porch was built for one of Florence's great charitable confraternities, the Misericordia, which still has its headquarters across the street and operates the ambulances parked in front; in the 13th and 14th centuries members courageously nursed and buried victims of the plague. The Loggia itself originally served as a lost and found office for children; if unclaimed after three days they were sent to foster homes.

East of the Loggia del Bigallo is a stone bench labelled the 'Sasso di Dante' – **Dante's Stone** – where the poet would sit and take the air, observing his fellow citizens and watching the construction of the cathedral.

Museo dell'Opera del Duomo

Open Mon–Sat 9–7.30, Sun 9–1.40; adm.

The Cathedral Museum (Piazza del Duomo 9, near the central apse) is one of Florence's finest, and houses both relics from the construction of the cathedral and the masterpieces that once adorned it. It reopened in early 2000 after major restructuring to improve the layout and make it more visitor-friendly: there is now full disabled access, better information, a more logical layout, in a more or less chronological order, and greatly increased floor space. The courtyard has been covered by a glass roof and turned into an exhibition room; and there are long-term plans to incorporate two neighbouring buildings into the museum, doubling its size.

The entrance leads into the new ticket hall – pristine in marble and stone, the same materials used in the Duomo's construction – and past the bookshop. Just after the entrance are several fragments of Roman reliefs, then two anterooms which contain restored statues or bits of statues that once adorned the façade of the Duomo.

The first hall is devoted to the cathedral's sculptor-architect Arnolfo di Cambio and contains the statues he made to adorn it: the unusual Madonna with the glass eyes, Florence's old patron saints, Reparata and Zenobius, and nasty old Boniface VIII, who sits stiffly on his throne like an Egyptian god. There are the four Evangelists, including a St John by Donatello, and a small collection of ancient works – Roman sarcophagi and an Etruscan cippus carved with dancers. Note the 16th-century 'Libretto', a fold-out display case of saintly odds and ends. The Florentines were never enthusiastic about the worship of relics, and long ago they shipped San Girolamo's jawbone, John the Baptist's index finger and St Philip's arm across the street.

A nearby room contains a collection of altarpieces, triptychs and paintings of saints including Giovanni del Biondo's *Saint Sebastian*. Also here are a series of marble relief panels by Baccio Bandinelli from the altarpiece of the cathedral. A small room adjacent to this contains a section (several fragments pieced together) of the door known as the 'Porta della Mandorla' on the north side of the Duomo. This is an intricately carved marble relief including a small figure of Hercules with his stick, significant in that it was the first representation of the adult male nude and a taste of things to come, more of a statue than a relief. Also in this room are two statues known as *The Profetini*, which once stood over the door and are attributed to the young Donatello.

On the landing of the stairs stands the *Pietà* that Michelangelo intended for his own tomb. The artist, increasingly cantankerous in his old age, became exasperated with this complex work and took a hammer to the arm of the Christ – the first known instance of an artist vandalizing his own creation. His assistant repaired the damage and finished part of the figures of Mary Magdalene and Christ. According to Vasari, the hooded figure of Nicodemus is Michelangelo's self-portrait.

Upstairs, the first room is dominated by the two **Cantorie**, two marble choir balconies with exquisite bas-reliefs, made in the 1430s by Luca della Robbia and Donatello. Both works rank among the Renaissance's greatest productions. Della Robbia's delightful horde of laughing children dancing, singing and playing instruments is a truly angelic choir, Apollonian in its calm and beauty. It is perhaps the most charming work ever to have been inspired by the forms of antiquity. Donatello's *putti*, by contrast, dance, or rather race, through their quattrocento decorative motifs with fiendish Dionysian frenzy. Grey and weathered prophets by Donatello and others stand along the white walls. These originally adorned the façade of the campanile. According to Vasari, while carving the most famous of these, *Habbakuk* (better known as *lo Zuccone*, or 'baldy'), Donatello would mutter under his breath 'Speak, damn you. Speak!' The next room contains the original panels on the Spiritual Progress of Man from Giotto's campanile, made by Andrea Pisano.

The first thing you see as you enter the last room is Donatello's statue *Mary Magdalene*, surely one of the most jarring figures ever sculpted, ravaged by her own piety and penance, her sunken eyes fixed on a point beyond this vale of tears. This room is dedicated to works removed from the baptistry, especially the lavish silver altar (14th–15th-century), made by Florentine goldsmiths, portraying scenes from the life of the Baptist. Antonio Pollaiuolo used the same subject to design the 27 needlework panels that once were part of the priest's vestments. There are two 12th-century Byzantine mosaic miniature masterpieces, and a St Sebastian triptych by Giovanni del Biondo that may well be the record for arrows; the poor saint looks like a hedgehog.

A ramp leads into the new part of the museum from the room containing the panels from the campanile. Cases either side display the collection of pulleys and other instruments used in the construction of the cathedral. At the bottom of the ramp on the left is Brunelleschi's death mask, facing a model of the lantern, which he was never to see. A window behind this model cleverly gives a close up view of the cupola itself, which is topped by that self-same lantern.

A series of rooms off a long corridor contain bits and pieces brought out of storage, including the four carved façades, artists' models for the design of the cricket's-cage pattern round the base of the cupola. The corridor leads into a room whose walls are filled with drawings of the Duomo from the 1875 competition to design the façade.

From here, a staircase leads down into the courtyard where eight of Ghiberti's panels from the *Gates of Paradise* are on display. The plan was to reconstruct the doors in their entirety, including the surrounds, and then to display them on the huge marble wall which has been constructed in the courtyard. However the restoration of the final panels is far from finished, and the doors won't be ready for another two years or so; the blank marble wall sits there, bare but for the three statues at its foot.

Via de' Calzaiuoli and Piazza della Repubblica

Of all the streets that radiate from the Piazza del Duomo, most people almost intuitively turn down the straight, pedestrian-only Via de' Calzaiuoli, the Roman street that became the main thoroughfare of medieval Florence, linking the city's religious centre with the Piazza della Signoria. Widening of this 'Street of the Shoemakers' in the 1840s has destroyed much of its medieval character, and the only shoe shops to be seen are designer-label. Its fate seems benign, though, compared with what happened to the Mercato Vecchio, in the fit of post-Risorgimento 'progress' that converted it into the **Piazza della Repubblica**, a block to the right along Via Speziali.

On the map, it's easy to pick out the small rectangle of narrow, straight streets around Piazza della Repubblica; these remain unchanged from the little *castrum* of Roman days. At its centre, the old forum deteriorated through the Dark Ages into a shabby market square and the Jewish ghetto, a densely populated quarter known as the Mercato Vecchio, the epitome of the picturesque for 19th-century tourists but an eyesore for the movers and shakers of the new Italy, who tore it down. They erected a triumphal arch to themselves and proudly blazoned it with the inscription 'THE ANCIENT CITY CENTRE RESTORED TO NEW LIFE FROM THE SQUALOR OF CENTURIES'. The sad result, the Piazza della Repubblica, is one of the most ghastly squares in Italy, a brash intrusion of ponderous 19th-century buildings. Just the same, it is popular with locals and tourists alike, closed to traffic and full of outdoor cafés, something of an oasis among the narrow, stern streets of medieval Florence.

From Piazza della Repubblica the natural flow of street life will sweep you down to the **Mercato Nuovo**, the old Straw Market, bustling under a beautiful loggia built by Grand Duke Cosimo in the 1500s. Nowadays vendors hawk purses, stationery, toys, clothes, umbrellas and knick-knacks. In medieval times this was the merchants' exchange, where any merchant who committed the crime of bankruptcy was publicly spanked before being carted off to prison; in times of peace it sheltered Florence's battle-stained *carroccio*. Florentines often call the market the 'Porcellino' (piglet) after the large bronze boar erected in 1612. The current boar was put in place in 1999, a copy of a copy of the ancient statue in the Uffizi. The drool spilling from the side of its mouth reminds us that Florence is no splashy city of springs and fountains. Rub the piglet's snout, and supposedly destiny will one day bring you back to Florence. The pungent aroma of the tripe sandwiches sold nearby may give you second thoughts.

Orsanmichele

Open Mon–Fri 9–12 and 4–6, Sat and Sun 9–1 and 4–6.

There is a wonderfully eccentric church on Via de' Calzaiuoli that looks like no other in the world: Orsanmichele rises up in a tall, neat three-storey rectangle. It was built on the site of ancient San Michele ad Hortum (popularly reduced to 'Orsanmichele'), a 9th-century church located near a vegetable garden, which the *comune* destroyed in 1240 to erect a grain market; after a fire in 1337 the current market building (by Francesco Talenti and others) was erected, with a loggia on the ground floor and emergency storehouses on top where grain was kept against a siege.

The original market had a pilaster with a painting of the Virgin that became increasingly celebrated for performing miracles. The area around the Virgin became known as the Oratory, and when Talenti reconstructed the market, his intention was to combine both its secular and religious functions; each pilaster of the loggia was assigned to a guild to adorn with an image of its patron saint. In 1380, when the market was relocated, the entire ground floor was given over to the functions of the church, and Francesco Talenti's son Simone was given the task of closing in the arcades with lovely Gothic windows, later bricked in.

The church is most famous as a showcase of 15th-century Florentine sculpture, displaying the stylistic innovations through the decades. Each guild sought to outdo the others by commissioning the finest artists of the day to carve their patron saints and create elaborate canopied niches to hold them. The first statue to the left of the door is one of the oldest: Ghiberti's bronze *St John the Baptist*, erected in 1416 for the Arte di Calimala, the first life-sized Renaissance statue cast in bronze. Continuing to the left on Via de' Lamberti you can compare it with Donatello's *St Mark*, patron of the linen dealers and used-cloth merchants. Finished in 1411, it is considered the first free-standing marble statue of the Renaissance.

The niches continue around Via dell'Arte della Lana, named after the Wool Merchants' Guild, the richest after that of the Bankers. Their headquarters, the **Palazzo dell'Arte della Lana**, is linked by an overhead arch with Orsanmichele; built in 1308, it was restored in 1905 in a William Morris style of medieval picturesque. The first statue on this façade of Orsanmichele is *St Eligio*, patron of smiths, by Nanni di Banco (1415), with a niche embellished with the guild's emblem (black pincers) and a bas-relief below showing one of this rather obscure saint's miracles – apparently he shod a horse by cutting off its hoof, shoeing it, then sticking it back on the leg. The other two statues on this street are bronzes by Ghiberti, the Wool Guild's *St Stephen* (1426) and the Exchange Guild's *St Matthew* (1422), the latter an especially fine work.

On the Via Orsanmichele façade stands a copy of Donatello's famous *St George* (the original now in the Bargello) done in 1417 for the Armourers' Guild, with a dramatic predella of the saint slaying the dragon, also by Donatello, that is one of the first known works to make use of perspective; next are the Stonecutters' and Carpenters' Guild's *Four Crowned Saints* (1415, by Nanni di Banco), inspired by Roman statues. Nanni also contributed the Shoemakers' *St Philip* (1415), while the next figure, *St Peter*, is commonly attributed to Donatello (1413). Around the corner on Via Calzaiuoli stands the bronze *St Luke*, patron of the Judges and Notaries, by Giambologna, a work of 1602 in a 15th-century niche, and the *Doubting of St Thomas* by Andrea del Verrocchio (1484), made not for a guild but the Tribunal of Merchandise, who like St Thomas wanted to be certain before making a judgement. In the rondels above some of the niches are terracottas of the guilds' symbols by Luca della Robbia.

Orsanmichele's dark **interior** (*open Mon–Fri 9–12 and 4–6, Sat and Sun 9–1 and 4–6; closed first and last Mon of month*) is ornate and cosy, with more of the air of a guild-hall than a church. It makes a picturebook medieval setting for one of the masterpieces of the trecento: Andrea Orcagna's beautiful Gothic **tabernacle** (*open 9–12 and 4–6*), a large, exquisite work in marble, bronze and coloured glass framing a contemporary painting of the Madonna (either by Bernardo Daddi or Orcagna himself), replacing the miraculous one, lost in a fire. The Tabernacle was commissioned by survivors of the 1348 Black Death. On the walls and pilasters are faded 14th-century frescoes of saints, placed as if members of the congregation; if you look at the pilasters on the left as you enter and along the right wall you can see the old chutes used to transfer grain.

Piazza della Signoria

Now that this big medieval piazza is car-free, it serves as a great corral for tourists, endlessly snapping pictures of the Palazzo Vecchio or strutting in circles like pigeons. In the old days it would be full of Florentines, the stage set for the tempestuous life of their republic. The public assemblies met here, and at times of danger the bells would ring and the piazza fill with citizen militias, assembling under the banners of the quarters and guilds. Savonarola held his Bonfire of Vanities here, and only a few years later the disenchanted Florentines ignited their Bonfire of Savonarola on the same spot. (You can see a painting of the event at San Marco.) Today the piazza is still the favoured spot for political rallies.

The three graceful arches of the **Loggia dei Lanzi**, next to the Palazzo Vecchio, were the reviewing stand for city officials during assemblies and celebrations. Florentines often call it the Loggia dell'Orcagna, after the architect who designed it in the 1370s. In its simple classicism the Loggia anticipates the architecture of Brunelleschi and all those who came after him. The city has made it an outdoor sculpture gallery, with some of the best known works in Florence: Cellini's triumphant *Perseus* (*currently being restored*) and Giambologna's *Rape of the Sabines*, other works by Giambologna, and a chorus of Roman-era Vestal Virgins along the back wall. Cosimo himself stands imperiously at the centre of the piazza, a bronze equestrian statue also by Giambologna.

All the statues in the piazza are dear to the Florentines. Some are fine works of art; others have only historical associations. Michelangelo's *David*, a copy of which stands in front of the *palazzo* near the spot the artist intended for it, was meant as a symbol of republican virtue and Florentine excellence. At the opposite extreme, locals are taught almost from birth to ridicule the **Neptune Fountain**, a pompous monstrosity with a giant marble figure of the god. The sculptor, Ammannati, thought he would upstage Michelangelo, though the result is derisively known to all Florence as Il Biancone ('Big Whitey'). Bandinelli's statue of *Hercules and Cacus* is almost as big and just as awful; according to Cellini, it looks like a 'sack of melons'.

Palazzo Vecchio

Open Mon–Wed and Fri–Sun 9–7; Thurs 9–2; adm. The Piazza Signoria façade is currently under restoration. Entrance in Via della Ninna.

When Goethe made his blitz-tour of Florence, the Palazzo Vecchio (also called the Palazzo della Signoria) helped pull the wool over his eyes. 'Obviously,' thought the great poet, 'the people...enjoyed a lucky succession of good governments' – a remark which, as Mary McCarthy wrote, could make the angels in heaven weep. But none of Florence's chronic factionalism mars Arnolfo di Cambio's temple of civic aspirations, part council hall and part fortress. In many ways, the Palazzo Vecchio is the ideal of 'stone Florence' (see p.239): rugged and imposing, with a rusticated façade that was to inspire so many of the city's private palaces, yet designed according to the proportions of the Golden Section of the ancient Greeks. Its dominant feature, the 308ft tower, is a typical piece of Florentine bravado, long the highest point in the city.

The Palazzo Vecchio occupies the site of the old Roman theatre and the medieval Palazzo dei Priori. In the 13th century this earlier palace was flattened along with the Ghibelline quarter interred under the piazza, and in 1299 the now ascendant Guelphs called upon Arnolfo di Cambio, master builder of the cathedral, to design the most impressive 'Palazzo del Popolo' (as the building was originally called) possible. The palace's unusual trapezoidal shape is often, but rather dubiously, explained as Guelph care not to have any of the building touch land once owned by Ghibellines. One doubts that even in the 13th century property realities allowed such delicacy of sentiments; nor does the theory explain why the tower has swallowtail Ghibelline crenellations, as opposed to the square Guelph ones on the palace itself. Later additions to the rear of the palace have obscured its shape even more, although the façade is essentially as Arnolfo built it, except for the bet-hedging monogram over the door hailing Christ the King of Florence, put up in the nervous days of 1529, when the Imperial army of Charles V was on its way to destroy the last Florentine republic. The inscription replaces an earlier one left by Savonarola. The room at the top of the tower was used as prison for celebrities and dubbed the *alberghetto*; inmates in 'the little hotel' included Cosimo il Vecchio before his brief exile, and Savonarola, who spent his last months, between torture sessions, enjoying a superb view of the city before his execution in the piazza below.

Inside the Palazzo Vecchio

Today the Palazzo Vecchio serves as Florence's city hall, but nearly all its historical rooms are open to the public. With few exceptions, the interior decorations date from the time of Cosimo I, when he moved his Grand Ducal self from the Medici palace in 1540. To politically 'correct' its acres of walls and ceilings in the shortest amount of time, he turned to his court artist Giorgio Vasari, famed more for the speed at which he could execute a commission than for its quality. On the ground floor of the *palazzo*, before you buy your ticket, you can take a look at some of Vasari's more elaborate handiwork in the **courtyard**, redone for the occasion of Francesco I's unhappy marriage to the plain and stupid Habsburg Joanna of Austria in 1565.

Vasari's suitably grand staircase ascends to the vast **Salone dei Cinquecento**, added by Savonarola for meetings of the 500-strong Consiglio Maggiore, the reformed republic's democratic assembly. Leonardo da Vinci and Michelangelo were commissioned in 1503 to paint the two long walls of the *salone* in a kind of Battle of the Brushes. Unfortunately, neither came near to completing the project; Leonardo managed to fresco a section of the wall, using the experimental techniques that were to prove the undoing of his *Last Supper* in Milan, while Michelangelo only completed the cartoons before being summoned to Rome by Julius II, who required the sculptor of the *David* to pander to his own personal megalomania.

In the 1560s Vasari removed what was left of Leonardo's efforts and refrescoed the room as a celebration of Cosimo's military triumphs over Pisa and Siena, complete with an apotheosis of the Grand Duke on the ceiling. These wall scenes are inane: big, busy, crowded with men and horses who appear to have all the substance of overcooked pasta. The sculptural groups lining the walls of this large room (the Italian parliament sat here from 1865 to 1870 when Florence was the capital) are only slightly more stimulating; even Michelangelo's *Victory*, on the wall opposite the entrance, is more virtuosity than vision: a vacuous young idiot posing with one knee atop a defeated old man still half-submerged in stone, said to be a self-portrait of the sculptor. Its neighbour, a muscle-bound *Hercules and Diomedes* by Vicenzo de' Rossi, probably was inevitable in this city obsessed by the possibilities of the male nude.

Beyond the *salone*, behind a modern glass door, is a much more intriguing room the size of a closet. This is the **Studiolo of Francesco I**, designed by Vasari in 1572 for Cosimo's melancholic and reclusive son, where he would escape to brood over his real interests in natural curiosities and alchemy. The little study, windowless and more than a little claustrophobic, has been restored to its original appearance, lined with allegorical paintings by Vasari, Bronzino and Allori, and bronze statuettes by Giambologna and Ammannati, their refined, polished, and erotic mythological subjects part of a carefully thought-out 16th-century programme on Man and Nature. The lower row of paintings conceals Francesco's secret cupboards where he kept his most precious belongings, his pearls and crystals and gold.

After the *salone* a certain fuzziness begins to set in. Cosimo I's propaganda machine in league with Vasari's fresco factory produced room after room of self-glorifying Medicean puffery. The first series of rooms, known as the **Quartiere di Leone X**, carry ancestor-worship to extremes, each chamber dedicated to a different Medici: in the first Cosimo il Vecchio returns from exile amid tumultuous acclaim; in the second Lorenzo il Magnifico receives the ambassadors in the company of a dignified giraffe; the third and fourth are dedicated to the Medici popes, while the fifth, naturally, is for Cosimo I, who gets the most elaborate treatment of all.

Upstairs the next series of rooms is known as the **Quartiere degli Elementi**, with more works of Vasari and his studio, depicting allegories of the elements. In a small room, called **Terrazzo di Giunone**, is the original of Verrocchio's boy with the dolphin, from the courtyard fountain. A balcony across the Salone dei Cinquecento leads to the **Quartiere di Eleonora di Toledo**, Mrs Cosimo I's private apartments. Her chapel is one of the masterpieces of Bronzino, who seemed to relish the opportunity to paint something besides Medici portraits. The **Sala dell'Udienza**, beyond the second chapel, has a magnificent quattrocento coffered ceiling by Benedetto and Giuliano da Maiano, and walls painted by Mannerist Francesco Salviati (1550–60).

The last room, the **Sala dei Gigli** ('of the lilies') boasts another fine ceiling by the da Maiano brothers; it contains Donatello's restored bronze *Judith and Holofernes*, a late and rather gruesome work of 1455; the warning to tyrants inscribed on its base was added when the statue was abducted from the Medici palace and placed in the Piazza della Signoria. Off the Sala dei Gigli are two small rooms of interest: the **Guardaroba**, or unique 'wardrobe' adorned with 57 maps painted by Fra Egnazio Danti in 1563, depicting all the world known at the time. The **Cancelleria** was Machiavelli's office from 1498 to 1512, when he served the republic as a secretary and diplomat. He is commemorated with a bust and a portrait. Poor Machiavelli would probably be amazed to learn that his very name had become synonymous with cunning, amoral intrigue. After losing his job upon the return of the Medici, and at one point being tortured and imprisoned on false suspicion of conspiracy, Machiavelli was forced to live in idleness in the country, where he wrote his political works and two fine plays, feverishly trying to return to favour. His concern throughout had been to advise realistically, without mincing words, the fractious and increasingly weak Italians on how to create a strong state. His evil reputation came from his openly stating what rulers do, rather than what they would like other people to think they do.

The **Collezione Loeser**, a fine assortment of Renaissance art left to the city in 1928 by Charles Loeser, the Macy's department-store heir, is also housed in the Palazzo Vecchio, in the mezzanine before you exit the museum.

The Uffizi

Queues in the summer are very common; try to arrive early. Open Tues–Sun 8.15–6.50; adm exp. Pre-book by phone, t 055 294883: pay at the door when you pick up your ticket.

Florence has the most fabulous art museum in Italy, and as usual we have the Medici to thank; for the building that holds these treasures, however, credit goes to Grand Duke Cosimo's much maligned court painter. Poor Giorgio Vasari! His roosterish boastfulness and the conviction that his was the best of all possible artistic worlds, set next to his very modest talents, have made him a comic figure in most art criticism. On one of the rare occasions when he tried his hand as an architect, though, he gave Florence something to be proud of. The Uffizi ('offices') were built as Cosimo's secretariat, incorporating the old mint (producer of the first gold florins in 1252), the archives and the large church of San Pier Scheraggio, with plenty of room for the bureaucrats needed to run Cosimo's efficient, modern state. The matched pair of arcaded buildings have coldly elegant façades that conceal Vasari's surprising innovation: iron reinforcements that make the huge amount of window area possible and keep the building stable on the soft sandy ground. It was a trick that would be almost forgotten until the Crystal Palace and the first American skyscrapers. Almost from the start the Medici began to store some of their huge collection in parts of the building. There are galleries in the world with more works of art – the Uffizi counts some 1,800 – but the Uffizi overwhelms by the fact that everything in it is worth looking at.

The Uffizi has undergone major reorganization in the last couple of years. Some of this involved the restoration of remaining damage after the bomb of 1993 (all but a very few paintings are now back on display), but improvements have also been made on a practical level. Major restoration of the vaulted rooms on the ground floor has resulted in a vastly improved space; there are now three entrances (for individuals, for groups and for pre-paid tickets), bookshops, cloakrooms, video and computer facilities and information desks.

If you are particularly keen on seeing a certain painting, note that rooms may be temporarily closed when you visit; this often seems to depend on staff availability. There is a list of these closures at the ticket counters. Some works are still hung out of chronological order, and the rooms containing work by Caravaggio and Rubens are closed until further notice (although two of the Caravaggios are at present hung in Room 16 – *see* p.263).

From the ticket counter you can take the lift or sweeping grand staircase up to the second floor, where the Medici once had a huge theatre, now home to the **Cabinet of Drawings and Prints**. Although the bulk of this extensive and renowned collection is only open to scholars with special permission, a roomful of tempting samples gives a hint at what they have a chance to see.

Nowadays one thinks of the Uffizi as primarily a gallery of paintings, but when it first opened visitors came for the fine collection of Hellenistic and Roman marbles. Most of these were collected in Rome by Medici cardinals, and not a few were sources of Renaissance inspiration. The **vestibule** at the top of the stairs contains some of the best, together with Flemish and Tuscan tapestries made for Cosimo I and his successors. **Room 1**, usually shut, contains excellent early Roman sculpture.

Rooms 2–6: 13th and 14th Centuries

The Uffizi's paintings are arranged in chronological order, the better to educate its visitors on trends in Italian art. The roots of the Early Renaissance are most strikingly revealed in **Room 2**, dedicated to the three great **Maestà** altarpieces by the masters of the 13th century. All portray the same subject of the Madonna and Child enthroned with angels. The one on the right, by Cimabue, was painted around the year 1285 and represents a breaking away from the flat, stylized Byzantine tradition. To the left is the so-called *Rucellai Madonna*, painted around the same period by the Sienese Duccio di Buoninsegna for Santa Maria Novella. It resembles Cimabue's in many ways, but with a more advanced technique for creating depth, and the bright colouring that characterizes the Sienese school. Giotto's altarpiece, painted some 25 years later, takes a great leap forward, not only in his use of perspective, but in the arrangement of the angels, standing naturally, and in the portrayal of the Virgin, gently smiling, with real fingers and breasts.

To the left, **Room 3** contains representative Sienese works of the 14th century, with a beautiful Gothic *Annunciation* (1333) by Simone Martini and the brothers Pietro and Ambrogio Lorenzetti. **Room 4** is dedicated to 14th-century Florentines: Bernardo Daddi, Nardo di Cione, and the delicately coloured *San Remigio Pietà* by Giottino. **Rooms 5 and 6** portray Italian contributions to the International Gothic school, most dazzlingly Gentile da Fabriano's *Adoration of the Magi* (1423), two good works by Lorenzo Monaco, and the *Thebaid* of Gherardo Starnina, depicting the rather unusual activities of the 4th-century monks of St Pancratius of Thebes, in Egypt.

Rooms 7–9: Early Renaissance

In the Uffizi, at least, it's but a few short steps from the superbly decorative International Gothic to the masters of the Early Renaissance. **Room 7** contains minor works by Fra Angelico, Masaccio and Masolino, and three masterpieces. Domenico Veneziano's pastel *Madonna and Child with Saints* (1448) is one of the rare pictures by this Venetian master who died a pauper in Florence. It is a new departure not only for its soft colours but for the subject matter, unifying the enthroned Virgin and saints in one panel, in what is known as a *Sacra Conversazione*. Piero della Francesca's famous *Double Portrait of the Duke Federigo da Montefeltro and his Duchess Battista Sforza of Urbino* (1465) depicts one of Italy's noblest Renaissance princes – and surely the one with the most distinctive nose. Piero's ability to create perfectly still, timeless worlds is even more evident in the allegorical 'Triumphs' of the Duke and Duchess painted on the back of their portraits. A similar stillness and fascination floats over into the surreal in Uccello's *Rout of San Romano* (1456), or at least the third of it still present (the other two panels are in the Louvre and London's National Gallery; all three once decorated the bedroom of Lorenzo il Magnifico in the Medici palace). Both Piero and Uccello were deep students of perspective, but Uccello went half-crazy; applying his principles to a violent battle scene has left us one of the most provocative works of all time – a vision of warfare in suspended animation, with pink, white and blue toy horses, robot-like knights, and rabbits bouncing in the background.

Room 8 is devoted to the works of the rascally romantic Fra Filippo Lippi, whose ethereally lovely Madonnas were modelled after his brown-eyed nun. In his *Coronation of the Virgin* (1447) she kneels in the foreground with two children, while the artist, dressed in a brown habit, looks dreamily towards her; in his celebrated *Madonna and Child with Two Angels* (1445) she plays the lead before the kind of mysterious landscape Leonardo would later perfect. Lippi taught the art of enchanting Madonnas to his student Botticelli, who has some lovely works in this room and the next; Alesso Baldovinetti, a pupil of the far more holy Fra Angelico, painted the room's beautiful *Annunciation* (1447).

Room 9 has two small scenes from the *Labours of Hercules* (1470) by Antonio Pollaiuolo, whose interest in anatomy, muscular expressiveness and violence presages a strain in Florentine art that culminated in the great Mannerists. He worked with his younger brother Piero on the refined, elegant *SS. Vincent, James and Eustace*, trans-ferred here from San Miniato. This room also contains the Uffizi's best-known forgery: *The Young Man in a Red Hat* or self-portrait of Filippino Lippi, believed to have been the work of an 18th-century English art dealer who palmed it off on the Grand Dukes.

Botticelli: Rooms 10–14

To accommodate the bewitching art of 'Little Barrels' and his 20th-century admirers, the Uffizi converted four small rooms into one great Botticellian shrine. Although his masterpieces displayed here have become almost synonymous with the Florentine Renaissance at its most spring-like and charming, they were not publicly displayed until the beginning of the 19th century, nor given much consideration outside Florence until the early 20th century. Botticelli's best works date from his days as a darling of the Medici – family members crop up most noticeably in the *Adoration of the Magi* (1476), where you can pick out Cosimo il Vecchio, Lorenzo il Magnifico and Botticelli himself (in the right foreground, in a yellow robe, gazing at the spectator). His *Annunciation* is a graceful, cosmic dance between the Virgin and the Angel Gabriel. In the *Tondo of the Virgin of the Pomegranate* the lovely melancholy goddess who was to become his Venus makes her first appearance.

Botticelli is best known for his sublime mythological allegories, nearly all painted for the Medici and inspired by the Neoplatonic, humanistic and hermetic currents that pervaded the intelligentsia of the late 15th century. Perhaps no painting has been debated so fervently as *La Primavera* (1478). This hung for years in the Medici Villa at Castello, and it is believed that the subject of the Allegory of Spring was suggested by Marsilio Ficino, one of the great natural magicians of the Renaissance, and that the figures represent the 'beneficial' planets able to dispel sadness. *Pallas and the Centaur* has been called another subtle allegory of Medici triumph – the rings of Athena's gown are supposedly a family symbol. Other interpretations see the taming of the sorrowful centaur as a melancholy comment on reason and civilization.

Botticelli's last great mythological painting, *The Birth of Venus*, was commissioned by Lorenzo di Pierfrancesco and inspired by a poem by Poliziano, Lorenzo il Magnifico's Latin and Greek scholar, who described how Zephyr and Chloris blew the newborn goddess to shore on a scallop shell, while Hora hastened to robe her, a scene Botticelli portrays once again with dance-like rhythm and delicacy of line. Yet the goddess of love floats towards the spectator with an expression of wistfulness – perhaps reflecting the artist's own feelings of regret. For artistically, the poetic, decorative style he perfected in this painting would be disdained and forgotten in his own lifetime. Spiritually, Botticelli also turned a corner after creating this haunting, uncanny beauty – his and Florence's farewell to a road not taken. Although Vasari's biography of Botticelli portrays a prankster rather than a sensitive soul, the painter absorbed more than any other artist the *fin-de-siècle* neuroticism that beset the city with the rise of Savonarola. So thoroughly did he reject his Neoplatonism that he would only accept commissions of sacred subjects or supposedly edifying allegories like his *Calumny*, a small but rather disturbing work, and a fitting introduction to the dark side of the quattrocento psyche.

This large room also contains works by Botticelli's contemporaries. There are two paintings of the *Adoration of the Magi*, one by Ghirlandaio and one by Filippino Lippi, which show the influence of Leonardo's unfinished but radical work in pyramidal composition (in the next room); Leonardo himself got the idea from the large *Portinari Altarpiece* (1471), at the end of the room, a work by Hugo van der Goes, brought back from Bruges by Medici agent Tommaso Portinari.

Rooms 15–24: More Renaissance

Room 15 is dedicated to the Florentine works of Leonardo da Vinci's early career. Here are works by his master Andrea Verrocchio, including the *Baptism of Christ*, in which Leonardo painted the angel on the left. Art critics believe the *Annunciation* (1475) is almost entirely by Leonardo – the soft faces, botanical details and misty, watery background would become his trademarks. Most influential was his unfinished *Adoration of the Magi* (1481), an unconventional composition that Leonardo abandoned when he left Florence for Milan. Although at first glance it's hard to make out much more than a mass of reddish chiaroscuro, the longer you stare, the better you'll see the serene Madonna and Child surrounded by anxious, troubled humanity, with an exotic background of ruins, trees and horsemen.

Other artists in Room 15 include Leonardo's peers: Lorenzo di Credi, whose religious works have eerie garden-like backgrounds, and the nutty Piero di Cosimo, whose dreamy *Perseus Liberating Andromeda* includes an endearing mongrel of a dragon that gives even the most reserved Japanese tourist fits of giggles. Tuscan maps adorn **Room 16**, as well as scenes by Hans Memling. Temporarily housed here, away from their normal home in Room 43, are Caravaggio's *Bacchus* and *The Head of Medusa*, believed to be self-portraits. In its day the fleshy, heavy-eyed *Bacchus*, half portrait and half still life, was considered highly iconoclastic.

The octagonal **Tribuna** (Room 18) with its mother-of-pearl dome and *pietra dura* floor and table was built by Buontalenti in 1584 for Francesco I and, like the Studiolo in the Palazzo Vecchio, was designed to hold Medici treasures. For centuries the best-known of these was the *Venus de' Medici*, a 2nd-century BC Greek sculpture, farcically claimed as a copy of Praxiteles' celebrated *Aphrodite of Cnidos*, the most erotic statue in antiquity. In the 18th century, amazingly, this rather ordinary girl was considered the greatest sculpture in Florence; today most visitors walk right by without a second glance. Other antique works include the *Wrestlers* and the *Knife Grinder*, both copies of Pergamese originals, the *Dancing Faun*, the *Young Apollo*, and the *Sleeping Hermaphrodite* in the adjacent room, which is usually curtained off.

The real stars of the Tribuna are the Medici court portraits, many of them by Bronzino, who was not only able to catch the likeness of Cosimo I, Eleanor of Toledo and their children, but could also aptly portray the spirit of the day – these are people who took themselves very seriously indeed. They have for company Vasari's posthumous portrait of *Lorenzo il Magnifico* and Pontormo's *Cosimo il Vecchio*, Andrea del Sarto's *Girl with a Book by Petrarch*, and Rosso Fiorentino's *Angel Musician*, an enchanting work entirely out of place in this stodgy temple.

Two followers of Piero della Francesca, Perugino and Luca Signorelli, hold pride of place in **Room 19**; Perugino's *Portrait of a Young Man* is believed to be modelled on his pupil Raphael. Signorelli's *Tondo of the Holy Family* was to become the inspiration for Michelangelo's (*see* below). The room also contains Lorenzo di Credi's *Venus*, inspired by Botticelli. The Germans appear in **Room 20**: Dürer's earliest known work, the *Portrait of his Father* (1490), done at age 19, and *The Adoration of the Magi* (1504). Also here are Lucas Cranach's Teutonic *Adam and Eve* and his *Portrait of Martin Luther* (1543), not someone you'd necessarily expect to see in Florence. **Room 21** is dedicated to the great Venetians, most famously Bellini and his uncanny *Sacred Allegory* (1490s), the meaning of which has never been satisfactorily explained. There are two minor works by the elusive Giorgione, and a typically weird *St Dominic* by Cosmè Tura.

Later Flemish and German artists appear in **Room 22**, works by Gerard David and proto-Romantic Albrecht Altdorfer, and a portrait attributed to Hans Holbein of

Sir Thomas More. **Room 23** is dedicated to non-Tuscans Correggio of Parma and Mantegna of the Veneto, as well as Boltraffio's strange *Narcissus.*

Rooms 25–27: Mannerism

The window-filled South Corridor, with its views over the city and its fine display of antique sculpture, marks only the halfway point in the Uffizi but nearly the end of Florence's contribution. In the first three rooms, however, local talent rallies to produce a brilliantly coloured twilight in Florentine Mannerism. By most accounts, Michelangelo's only completed oil painting, the *Tondo Doni* (1506), was the spark that ignited Mannerism's flaming orange and turquoise hues. Michelangelo was 30 when he painted this unconventional work, in a medium he disliked (sculpture and fresco being the only fit occupations for a man, he believed). It's a typical Michelangelo story that when the purchaser complained the artist was asking too much for it, Michelangelo promptly doubled the price. As shocking as the colours are the spiralling poses of the Holy Family, sharply delineated against a background of five nude, slightly out-of-focus young men of uncertain purpose (are they pagans? angels? boyfriends? or just fillers?) – an ambiguity that was to become a hallmark of Mannerism; as the *Ignudi* they later appear on the Sistine Chapel ceiling. In itself, the *Tondo Doni* is more provocative than immediately appealing; the violent canvas in Room 27, Rosso Fiorentino's *Moses Defending the Children of Jethro,* was painted some 20 years later and at least in its intention to shock the viewer puts a cap on what Michelangelo began.

Room 26 is dedicated mainly to Raphael, who was in and out of Florence in 1504–8. Raphael was the sweetheart of the High Renaissance. His Madonnas, like *The Madonna of the Goldfinch,* have a tenderness that was soon to be over-popularized by others and turned into holy cards, a cloying sentimentality added over the centuries. It's easier, perhaps, to see Raphael's genius in non-sacred subjects, like *Leo X with Two Cardinals,* a perceptive portrait study of the first Medici pope with his nephew Giulio de' Medici, later Clement VII.

The same room contains Andrea del Sarto's most original work, the fluorescent *Madonna of the Harpies* (1517), named after the figures on the Virgin's pedestal. Of the works by Pontormo, the best is in **Room 27**, *Supper at Emmaus* (1525), a strange canvas with the Masonic symbol of the Eye of God hovering over Christ's head.

Rooms 28–45

The Uffizi fairly bristles with masterpieces from other parts of Italy and abroad. Titian's delicious nudes, especially the voluptuous *Venus of Urbino,* raise the temperature in **Room 28**; Parmigianino's hyper-elegant *Madonna with the Long Neck* (1536) in **Room 29** is a fascinating Mannerist evolutionary dead-end. **Room 31** holds Paolo Veronese's *Holy Family with St Barbara,* bathed in a golden Venetian light, with a gorgeously opulent Barbara. Sebastiano del Piombo's *Death of Adonis,* in **Room 32**, is notable for its melancholy, autumn atmosphere, and Venus's annoyed look. Tintoretto's shadowy *Leda* languidly pretends to restrain the lusty swan.

Room 41 is Flemish domain, with brand-name art by Rubens and Van Dyck; the former's *Baccanale* may be the most grotesque canvas in Florence. **Room 42**, the *Sala della Niobe*, was reopened in December 1998 after the bomb damage was repaired. A series of statues, *Niobe and her Sons* (18th-century copies of Hellenic works), are housed in the high, arched-ceilinged room, which is covered in pristine plaster and gold leaf. **Room 43** houses some striking Caravaggios.

Struggle on gamely to **Room 44**, where there are three portraits by Rembrandt including two self-portraits, and landscapes by Ruysdael. **Room 45** has some fine 18th-century works, including portraits by Chardin, Goya and Longhi, and Venetian landscapes by Guardi and Canaletto. Even more welcome by this time is the **bar**, with a summer terrace and in a superb position overlooking Piazza della Signoria.

The **Contini Bonacossi** collection, once housed in the Meridiana Pavilion at Palazzo Pitti, was moved to the Uffizi in 1999. Visits are by appointment only (**t** *055 265 4321*), and there is a separate entrance in Via Lambertesca. The Uffizi ticket is also valid for this. This recent bequest includes works of Cimabue, Duccio and Giovanni Bellini, some sculpture and china, and also paintings by El Greco, Goya and Velazquez – the last represented by an exceptional work, *The Water Carrier of Seville*.

Corridoio Vasariano

Open for limited periods during the year. It is now open to individuals, not just groups. Hours are also very limited. Call t 055 265 4321 for info and bookings (obligatory); adm exp.

In 1565, when Francesco I married Joanna of Austria, the Medici commissioned Vasari to link their new digs in the Pitti Palace with the Uffizi and the Palazzo Vecchio in such a manner that the Archdukes could make their rounds without rubbing elbows with their subjects. With a patina of 400 years, it seems that Florence wouldn't look quite right without this covered catwalk, leapfrogging on rounded arches from the back of the Uffizi, over the Ponte Vecchio, daintily skirting a medieval tower, and darting past the façade of Santa Felicità to the Pitti Palace.

The Corridoio does not only offer interesting views of Florence: it has been hung with a celebrated collection of artists' self-portraits, beginning, reasonably, with Vasari himself before continuing in chronological order, past the Gaddis and Raphael to Rembrandt, Van Dyck, Velazquez, Hogarth, Reynolds, Delacroix and Corot.

The Museum of the History of Science (Museo di Storia della Scienza)

Open summer 9.30–5, Tues and Sat 9.30–1, closed Sun; winter 9.30–5, Tues 9.30–1, 2nd Sun of month 10–1; adm exp.

For all that Florence and Tuscany contributed to the birth of science, it is only fitting to have this museum in the centre of the city, behind the Uffizi in Piazza Giudici. Much of the first floor is devoted to instruments measuring time and distance: Arabian astrolabes and pocket sundials, Tuscan sundials in the shape of Platonic solids, enormous elaborate armillary spheres and a small reliquary holding the bone of Galileo's finger, erect, like a final gesture to the city that until 1737 denied him a Christian burial. Here, too, are two of his original telescopes and the lens with which he discovered the four moons of Jupiter. Other scientific instruments come from the Accademia del Cimento (of 'trial' or 'experiment'), founded in 1657 by Cardinal Leopoldo de' Medici, the world's first scientific organization, dedicated to Galileo's principle of enquiry and proof by experimentation. 'Try and try again' was its motto.

Upstairs, there's a large room filled with machines used to demonstrate principles of physics, which the women who run the museum will operate if you ask. Two unusual ones are the 18th-century automatic writer and the instrument of perpetual motion. The rooms devoted to medicine contain a collection of 18th-century wax anatomical models, designed to teach budding obstetricians about unfortunate foetal positions, as well as a fine display of surgical instruments from the period.

The Ponte Vecchio and Ponte Santa Trínita

Bent bridges seeming to strain like bows
And tremble with arrowy undertide...
Elizabeth Barrett Browning, 'Casa Guidi Windows'

Often at sunset the Arno becomes a stream of molten gold, that is, during those months when it has a respectable flow of water. But even in the torrid days of August, when the Arno shrivels into muck and spittle, its two famous bridges retain their distinctive beauty. The most famous of these, the **Ponte Vecchio** or 'Old Bridge', crosses the Arno at its narrowest point; the present bridge, with its three stone arches, was built in 1345, and replaces a wooden construction from the 970s, which in turn was the successor to a span that may well have dated back to the Romans. On this wooden bridge, at the foot of the *Marzocco*, or statue of Mars, Buondelmonte dei Buondelmonti was murdered in 1215, setting off the wars of the Guelphs and Ghibellines. The original *Marzocco* was washed away in a 14th-century flood, and Donatello's later version has been carted off to the Bargello.

Like old London Bridge, the Ponte Vecchio is covered with shops and houses. By the 1500s it had become the street of hog butchers, although, after Vasari built Cosimo's secret passage on top, the Grand Duke evicted the butchers and replaced them with goldsmiths. They have been there ever since, and shoppers from around the world descend on it each year to scrutinize the traditional Florentine talent for jewellery – not a few of the city's great artists began their careers as goldsmiths, beginning with Ghiberti and Donatello, and ending with Cellini, whose bust adorns the middle of the bridge. In the 1966 flood the shops did not prove as resilient as the Ponte Vecchio itself, and a fortune of gold was washed down the Arno.

In the summer of 1944, the river briefly became a German defensive line during the slow painful retreat across Italy. Before leaving Florence, the Nazis blew up every one of the city's bridges, saving only, on Hitler's special orders, the Ponte Vecchio, though they blasted a large number of ancient buildings on each side of the span to create piles of rubble to block the approaches. Florence's most beautiful span, the **Ponte**

Santa Trínita, was the most tragic victim. Immediately after the war the Florentines set about replacing the bridges exactly as they were: for Santa Trínita, old quarries had to be reopened to duplicate the stone, and old methods revived to cut it (modern power saws would have done it too cleanly). The graceful curve of the three arches was a problem; they could not be constructed geometrically, and considerable speculation went on over how the architect (Ammannati, in 1567) did it. Finally, recalling that Michelangelo had advised Ammannati on the project, someone noticed that the same form of arch could be seen on the decoration of the tombs in Michelangelo's Medici Chapel, constructed most likely by pure artistic imagination. Fortune lent a hand in the reconstruction; of the original statues of the 'Four Seasons', almost all the pieces were fished out of the Arno and rebuilt. Spring's head was eventually found by divers completely by accident in 1961.

Dante's Florence

Dante would contemplate his Beatrice, the story goes, at Mass in the **Badia Fiorentina** (*entrance on Via Dante Alighieri; open Mon only 3–6*), a Benedictine church on Via del Proconsolo across from the Bargello, with a lovely Gothic spire to grace this corner of the Florentine skyline. The church has undergone many rebuildings since Willa, widow of a Margrave of Tuscany, began it in around 990, but there is still a monument to Ugo, the 'Good Margrave' mentioned in Dante, and a painting of the Madonna appearing to St Bernard by Filippo Lippi.

Between the Badia and Via del Calzaiuoli, a little corner of medieval Florence has survived the changes of centuries. In these quiet, narrow streets you can visit the **Casa di Dante** (*open Mar–Oct Mon–Tues and Thurs–Sat 10–6, Sun 10–2; Nov–Feb Mon–Tues and Thurs–Sat 10–4, Sun 10–2; adm*), which was actually built in 1911 over the ruins of an amputated tower house, although scholars all agree that the Alighieri lived somewhere in the vicinity. Near the entrance is an edition of *The Divine Comedy*, printed in tiny letters on a poster. Upstairs are copies of Botticelli's line illustrations.

Nearby, the stoutly medieval **Torre del Castagna** is all that remains of the original Palazzo del Popolo, the residence of the *priori*, the governors of the city, before the construction of the Palazzo Vecchio. Dante himself was a *priore* once, and he would have spent his two-month term of office living here, as the law required. After giving up on Beatrice, Dante married Gemma Donati, in the **Santa Margherita** church on the same block. Another church nearby, **San Martino del Vescovo** (*open Mon–Sat 10–12 and 3–5, closed Sun*), has a fine set of frescoes from the workshop of Ghirlandaio.

Museo Nazionale del Bargello

Open daily 8.15–1.50; closed 1st and 3rd Sun, and 2nd and 4th Mon of month; adm.

Across from the Badia Fiorentina looms the Bargello, a battlemented urban fortress, well proportioned yet of forbidding grace; for centuries it saw duty as Florence's prison. Today its only inmates are men of marble, gathered together to form Italy's finest collection of sculpture, a fitting complement to the paintings in the Uffizi. The Bargello is 'stone Florence' (*see* p.239) squared to the sixth degree, rugged and austere *pietra forte*, the model for the even grander Palazzo Vecchio. Even the treasures it houses are hard, definite, certain – and almost unremittingly masculine. The Bargello offers the best insight available into Florence's golden age, and it was a man's world indeed.

Completed in 1255, the Bargello was intended as Florence's Palazzo del Popolo, though by 1271 it served instead as the residence of the foreign *podestà*, or chief magistrate, installed by Guelph leader Charles of Anjou. The Medici made it the headquarters of the captain of police (the *Bargello*), the city jail and torture chamber, a function it served until 1859. In the Renaissance it was the peculiar custom to paint portraits of the condemned on the exterior walls of the fortress; Andrea del Castagno was so good at it that he was nicknamed Andrea of the Hanged Men. All of these ghoulish souvenirs have long since disappeared, as have the torture instruments – burned in 1786, when Grand Duke Peter Leopold abolished torture and the death sentence in Tuscany, only a few months after the Venetians led the way. Today the **Gothic courtyard**, former site of the gallows and chopping block, is a delightful place, owing much to an imaginative restoration in the 1860s. The encrustation of centuries of *podestà* armorial devices and plaques in a wild vocabulary of symbols, the shadowy arcades and stately stairs combine to create one of Florence's most romantic corners.

The main ground-floor gallery is dedicated to Michelangelo and his century, although it must be said that the Michelangelo of the Bargello somewhat lacks the accustomed angst and ecstasy. The real star of the room is **Benvenuto Cellini**, who was, besides many other things, an exquisite craftsman and daring innovator.

The stairway from the courtyard leads up to the shady **loggia**, now converted into an aviary for Giambologna's charming bronze birds, made for the animal grotto at the Medici's Villa di Castello.

The **Salone del Consiglio Generale**, formerly the courtroom of the *podestà*, contains the greatest masterpieces of Early Renaissance sculpture. And when Michelangelo's maudlin self-absorption and the Mannerists' empty virtuosity begin to seem tiresome, a visit to this room will prove a welcome antidote. Donatello's originality and vision are strikingly modern – and mysterious. On the wall hang the two famous trial reliefs for the second set of baptistry doors, by Ghiberti and Brunelleschi, both depicting the Sacrifice of Isaac. The remainder of the first floor houses fascinating collections of decorative arts donated to the Bargello in the last century.

Some of the most interesting items are in the next rooms, especially the works in the **ivory collection** – Carolingian and Byzantine diptychs, an 8th-century whalebone coffer from Northumbria adorned with runes, medieval French miniatures chronicling 'The Assault on the Castle of Love', 11th-century chess pieces, and more.

A stairway from the ivory collection leads up to the **Second Floor**. It houses some of the finest enamelled terracottas of the della Robbia family workshop, a room of portrait busts, works by Antonio Pollaiuolo and Verrocchio, including his *David* and lovely *Young Lady with a Nosegay*. There is also a collection of armour, and the most important collection of small Renaissance bronzes in Italy.

Piazza San Firenze to the Duomo

The strangely shaped square that both the Badia and the Bargello call home is named after the large church of **San Firenze**, now partially used as Florence's law courts. At the corner of the square and Via Gondi, the **Palazzo Gondi** is a fine Renaissance palace built for a merchant by Giuliano da Sangallo in 1489 but completed only in 1884; it's not easy to pick out the discreet 19th-century additions. A block from the square on Via Ghibellina, the **Palazzo Borghese** (No.110) is one of the finest neoclassical buildings in the city, erected in 1822 for a party in honour of Habsburg Grand Duke Ferdinand III. The host was one of the wealthiest men of his day, the Roman prince Camillo Borghese, husband of Pauline Bonaparte and the man responsible for shipping many of Italy's art treasures off to the Louvre.

From Piazza San Firenze, Via del Proconsolo leads straight to the Piazza del Duomo, passing by way of the **Palazzo Pazzi-Quaratesi** (No.10), the 15th-century headquarters of the banking family that organized the conspiracy against Lorenzo and Giuliano de' Medici. No.12, the Palazzo Nonfinito – begun in 1593 but, as its name suggests, never completed – is now the home of the **Museo Nazionale di Antropologia ed Etnologia** (*open Wed–Mon 9–1; adm*), founded in 1869, the first ethnological museum in Italy, with an interesting collection of Peruvian mummies, musical instruments collected by Galileo Chini (who decorated the Liberty-style extravaganzas at Viareggio), some lovely and unusual items of Japan's Ainu and Pakistan's Kafiri, and a large number of skulls from all over the world.

Florence As It Was

Borgo degli Albizi, the fine old street passing in front of the Palazzo Nonfinito, was in ancient times the Via Cassia, linking Rome with Bologna, and it deserves a leisurely stroll for its palaces (especially No.18, the cinquecento Palazzo Valori, nicknamed 'Funny Face Palace' for its surreal, semi-relief herm-busts of Florentine immortals on three floors of the façade). If Borgo degli Albizi, too, fails to answer to the Florence you've been seeking, take Via dell'Oriuolo (just to the left at Piazza G. Salvemini) for the **Museo di Firenze Com'Era** (Museum of Florence As It Was), located at the big garden at No.24 (*open Fri–Wed 9–2; adm*). The jewel of this museum is right out in front, the nearly room-sized *Pianta della Catena*, most beautiful of the early views of Florence. It is a copy; the original, made in 1490 by an unknown artist – that handsome fellow pictured in the lower right-hand corner – was lost during the last war in a Berlin museum. This fascinating painting captures Florence at the height of the Renaissance, a city of buildings in bright white, pink and tan; the great churches are without their façades, the Uffizi and Medici chapels have not yet appeared, and the Medici and Pitti palaces are without their later extensions.

The museum is not large. At present it contains only a number of plans and maps, as well as a collection of amateurish watercolours of Florence's sights from the last century, and paintings of Florence's surroundings by Ottone Rosai, a local favourite who died in 1957. For some further evidence, look around the corner of Via Sant'Egidio, where some recent remodelling has uncovered posters over the street from 1925, announcing plans for paying the war debt and a coming visit of the *Folies Bergère*. The Florentines have restored them and put them under glass.

From Via dell'Oriuolo, Via Folco Portinari takes you to Florence's main hospital, **Santa Maria Nuova**, founded in 1286 by the father of Dante's Beatrice, Folco Portinari. A tomb in the hospital's church, Sant'Egidio, is all that remains of the family. Readers of Iris Origo's *The Merchant of Prato* will recognize it as the workplace of the good notary, Ser Lapo Mazzei. The portico, by Buontalenti, was finished in 1612.

Collezione A Della Ragione

Complesso delle Oblate, Via Sant'Egidio 21. Due to open late 2003, visits by appt; call t 055 262 5961 for information.

After the trip down Florence's Memory Lane, you may be in the mood to reconsider the 20th century in Florence's only museum of modern art. There are typical still lifes by De Pisis; equally still landscapes by Carlo Carra; mysterious baths by De Chirico; Tuscan landscapes by Mario Mafai, Antonio Donghi and Ottone Rosai; a speedy Futurist horse by Fortunato Depero and a window with doves by Gino Severini; a number of richly coloured canvases by Renato Guttuso, paintings after Tintoretto by Emilio Vedova, and many others.

Medieval Streets North of the Arno

Just west of Via Por Santa Maria, the main street leading down to the Ponte Vecchio, you'll find some of the oldest and best-preserved lanes in Florence. Near the Mercato Nuovo at the top of the street (*see* p.154) stands the **Palazzo di Parte Guelfa**, the 13th-century headquarters of the Guelph party, and often the real seat of power in the city, paid for by property confiscated from the Ghibellines; in the 15th century Brunelleschi added a hall on the top floor and an extension. Next door is the guildhall of the silk-makers, the 14th-century **Palazzo dell'Arte della Seta** still bearing its bas-relief emblem, or *stemma*, of a closed door, the age-old guild symbol. It's worth continuing around the Guelph Palace to Via Pellicceria to see the medieval buildings on the tiny square near Via delle Terme, named after the old Roman baths.

Palazzo Davanzati

Closed for restoration since 1994. You can see an exhibition on the palace on the ground floor, 8.30–1.50; closed alternate Sundays and Mondays.

To get an idea of what life was like inside these sombre palaces some 600 years ago, stroll over to nearby Via Porta Rossa, site of the elegant Palazzo Davanzati, now arranged as the **Museo della Casa Fiorentina Antica**, one of the city's most delightful museums, offering a chance to step back into domestic life of yore. Originally built in the mid-14th century for the Davizzi family, the house was purchased by merchant Bernardo Davanzati in 1578 and stayed in the family until the 1900s. Restored by an antique collector in 1904, it is the best-preserved medieval-Renaissance house in Florence.

Piazza Santa Trínita

Three old Roman roads – Via Porta Rossa, Via delle Terme and Borgo SS. Apostoli – lead into the irregularly shaped Piazza Santa Trínita. Borgo SS. Apostoli is named after one of Florence's oldest churches, the little Romanesque **Santi Apostoli** (11th century), which is located in the sunken Piazzetta del Limbo, former cemetery of unbaptized babies.

Piazza Santa Trínita itself boasts an exceptionally fine architectural ensemble, grouped around the 'Column of Justice' from the Roman Baths of Caracalla, given by Pius IV to Cosimo I, and later topped with a red statue of Justice by Francesco del Tadda. Its pale granite is set off by the palaces of the piazza: the High Renaissance-Roman **Palazzo Bartolini-Salimbeni** by Baccio d'Agnolo (1520) on the corner of Via Porta Rossa, formerly the fashionable Hôtel du Nord where Herman Melville stayed; the medieval **Palazzo Buondelmonti**, with a 1530 façade by Baccio d'Agnolo, once home to the reading room and favourite haunt of such literati in the 19th century as Dumas, Browning, Manzoni and Stendhal; and the magnificent curving **Palazzo Spini-Ferroni**, the largest medieval palace in Florence, built in 1289 and still retaining its original battlements. This is now home to the heirs of the Florentine designer Ferragamo and houses a retail outlet and a fascinating small **museum** of Ferragamo's life and work, including some of the most beautiful shoes in the world (*open Mon–Fri 9–1 and 2–6 by appt only, t 055 336 0456; free*).

Santa Trínita

Open Mon–Sat 8–12 and 4–6, Sun 4–6 only.

The church of Santa Trínita has stood here, in one form or another, since the 12th century; its unusual accent on the first syllable (from the Latin *Trinitas*) is considered proof of its ancient foundation. Although the pedestrian façade added by Buontalenti in 1593 isn't especially welcoming, step into its shadowy 14th-century interior for several artistic treats, beginning with the **Bartolini-Salimbeni Chapel** (fourth on the right), frescoed in 1422 by the Sienese Lorenzo Monaco; his marriage of the Virgin takes place in a Tuscan fantasy backdrop of pink towers. He also painted the chapel's graceful, ethereally coloured altarpiece, the *Annunciation*.

In the choir, the **Sassetti Chapel** is one of the masterpieces of Domenico Ghirlandaio, completed in 1495 for wealthy merchant Francesco Sassetti and dedicated to the Life of St Francis, but also to the life of Francesco Sassetti, the city and his Medici circle: the scene above the altar, of Francis receiving the Rule of the Order, is transferred to the Piazza della Signoria, watched by Sassetti (to the right, with the fat purse) and Lorenzo il Magnifico; on the steps stands the great Latinist Poliziano with Lorenzo's three sons. The *Death of St Francis* pays homage to Giotto's similar composition in Santa Croce. The altarpiece, the *Adoration of the Shepherds* (1485), is one of Ghirlandaio's best-known works, often described as the archetypal Renaissance painting, a contrived but charming classical treatment; the Magi arrive through a triumphal arch, a Roman sarcophagus is used as manger and a ruined temple for a stable – all matched by the sibyls on the vault; the sibyl on the outer arch is the one who supposedly announced the birth of Christ to Augustus.

Santa Trínita is a Vallombrosan church and the first chapel to the right of the altar holds the Order's holy of holies, a painted crucifix formerly in San Miniato. The story goes that on a Good Friday, a young noble named Giovanni Gualberto was on his way to Mass when he met the man who had recently murdered his brother. Rather than take his revenge, Gualberto pardoned the assassin in honour of the holy day. When he arrived at church to pray, this crucifix nodded in approval of his mercy. Giovanni was so impressed that he went on to found the Vallombrosan order in the Casentino.

The **sanctuary** was frescoed by Alesso Baldovinetti, though only four Old Testament figures survive. In the second chapel to the left the marble *Tomb of Bishop Benozzo Federighi* (1454) is by Luca della Robbia. In the fourth chapel, a detached fresco by Neri di Bicci portrays San Giovanni Gualberto and his fellow Vallombrosan saints.

West of Piazza della Repubblica

The streets west of Piazza della Repubblica have always been the choicest district of Florence, and **Via de' Tornabuoni** the city's smartest shopping street. These days you won't find many innovations: Milan's current status as headquarters of Italy's fashion industry is a sore point with Florence.

In the bright and ambitious 1400s, however, when Florence was the centre of European high finance, Via de' Tornabuoni and its environs was the area the new merchant élite chose for their palaces. Today's bankers build great skyscrapers for the firm and settle for modest mansions for themselves; in Florence's heyday, things were reversed. Bankers and wool tycoons really owned their businesses. While their places of work were quite simple, their homes were imposing city palaces, all built in the same conservative style and competing with each other in size like some Millionaires' Row in 19th-century America.

The champion was the **Palazzo Strozzi**, a long block up Via de' Tornabuoni from Piazza Trínita. This rusticated stone cube of fearful dimensions squats in its piazza, radiating almost visible waves of megalomania. There are few architectural innovations in the Palazzo Strozzi, but here the typical Florentine palace is blown up to the level of the absurd: although three storeys like other palaces, each floor is as tall as three or four normal ones, and the rings to tie up horses could hold elephants. Like Michelangelo's *David*, Florence's other beautiful monster, it emits the unpleasant sensation of what Mary McCarthy called the 'giganticism of the human ego', the will to surpass not only antiquity but nature herself. Nowadays, at least, the Strozzi palace is moderately useful as a space to hold temporary exhibitions.

Palazzo Rucellai

There are two other exceptional palaces in the quarter. At the north end of Via de' Tornabuoni stands the beautiful golden **Palazzo Antinori** (1465, architect unknown), which has Florence's grandest Baroque façade, **San Gaetano** (1648, by Gherardo Silvani), as its equally golden companion, despite being decorated with statues that would look right at home in Rome but look like bad actors in Florence.

The second important palace, Florence's most celebrated example of domestic architecture, is the **Palazzo Rucellai**, in Via della Vigna Nuova. Its original owner, Giovanni Rucellai, was a quattrocento tycoon like Filippo Strozzi, but an intellectual as well, whose *Zibaldone*, or 'commonplace book' is one of the best sources available on the life and tastes of the educated Renaissance merchant. In 1446 Rucellai chose Leon Battista Alberti to design his palace. Actually built by Bernardo Rossellino, it follows Alberti's precepts and theories in its use of the three classical orders; instead of the usual rusticated stone, the façade has a far more delicate decoration of incised irregular blocks and a frieze, elements influential in subsequent Italian architecture – though far more noticeably in Rome than Florence itself. Originally the palace was only five bays wide, and when another two bays were added later the edge was left ragged, unfinished, a nice touch, as if the builders could return at any moment and pick up where they left off. The frieze, like that on Santa Maria Novella, portrays the devices of the Medici and the Rucellai families (Giovanni's son married a daughter of Piero de' Medici), a wedding fêted in the **Loggia dei Rucellai** across the street, also designed by Alberti.

Piazza Goldoni and Ognissanti

Before taking leave of old Florence's west end, head back to the Arno and **Piazza Goldoni**, named after the great comic playwright from Venice. The bridge here, the **Ponte alla Carraia**, is new and nondescript, but its 1304 version played a leading role in that year's most memorable disaster: a company staging a water pageant of the *Inferno*, complete with monsters, devils and tortured souls, attracted such a large crowd that the bridge collapsed under the weight, and all were drowned.

The most important building on the piazza, the **Palazzo Ricasoli**, was built in the 15th century but bears the name of one of unified Italy's first Prime Ministers, Bettino 'Iron Baron' Ricasoli. Just to the east on Lungarno Corsini looms the enormous **Palazzo Corsini**, the city's most prominent piece of Roman Baroque extravagance, begun in 1650 and crowned with a bevy of statues. The Corsini, the most prominent family of 17th- and 18th-century Florence, were reputedly so wealthy that they could ride from Florence to Rome entirely on their own property. The **Galleria Corsini** (*adm by appt only, t 055 218994; Mon, Wed and Fri between 9 and 12, enter from Via Parione*), houses paintings by Giovanni Bellini, Signorelli, Filippino Lippi and Pontormo, and *Muses* from the ducal palace of Urbino, painted by Raphael's first master, Timoteo Viti. It also has the rarest of Florentine amenities: a garden, a 17th-century oasis of box hedges, Roman statues, lemon trees and tortoises. Further east on Lungarno Corsini stood the Libreria Orioli, which caused a scandal when it published the first edition of *Lady Chatterley's Lover* in 1927.

To the west of Piazza Goldoni lies the old neighbourhood of the only Florentine to have a continent named after him. Amerigo Vespucci (1451–1512) was a Medici agent in Seville, and made two voyages from there to America on the heels of Columbus. His parish church, **Ognissanti** (All Saints; *open 8–12.30 and 5–7.30*), is set back from the river behind a Baroque façade, on property donated in 1256 by the Umiliati, a religious order that specialized in wool-working. The Vespucci family tomb is below the second altar to the right, and Amerigo himself is said to be pictured next to the Madonna in the fresco of the Madonna della Misericordia. Also buried in Ognissanti was the Filipepi family, one of whom was Botticelli. The best art is to be found in the **convent**, just to the left of the church at No.42 (*open Sat, Mon and Tues 9–12; you may have to ring*). Frescoed in the refectory is the great *Last Supper*, or *Cenacolo*, painted by Domenico Ghirlandaio in 1480. It's hard to think of a more serene and elegant Last Supper, alike to a garden party with its background of fruit trees and exotic birds; a peacock sits in the window, cherries and peaches litter the lovely tablecloth. On either side of the fresco are two scholarly saints moved from the church itself; Ghirlandaio's *St Jerome* and, on the right, young Botticelli's *St Augustine*.

Santa Maria Novella

Open Mon–Thurs and Sat 9.30–5; Fri, Sun and hols 1–5; adm.

As in so many other Italian cities, the two churches of the preaching orders – the Dominicans' Santa Maria Novella and the Franciscans' Santa Croce – became the largest and most prestigious in the city, where wealthy families vied to create the most beautiful chapels and tombs. In Florence, by some twitch of city planning, both of these sacred art galleries dominate broad, stale squares that do not invite you to linger; in the irregular **Piazza Santa Maria Novella** you may find yourself looking over your shoulder for the ghosts of the carriages that once raced madly around the two stout obelisks set on turtles, just as in a Roman circus, in the fashionable carriage races of the 1700s. The arcade on the south side, the **Loggia di San Paolo**, is very much like Brunelleschi's *Spedale degli Innocenti*, although it suffers somewhat from its use as a busy bus shelter; the lunette over the door, by Andrea della Robbia, is the *Meeting of SS. Francis and Dominic*. Santa Maria Novella redeems the anomie of its square with its stupendous black and white marble **façade**, the finest in Florence. The lower part, with its looping arcades, is Romanesque work in the typical Tuscan mode, finished before 1360. In 1456 Giovanni Rucellai commissioned Alberti to complete it, a remarkably fortunate choice. Alberti's half not only perfectly harmonizes with the original, but perfects it with geometrical harmonies to create what appears to be a kind of Renaissance Sun Temple. The original builders started it off by orientating the church to the south instead of west, so that at noon the sun streams through the 14th-century rose window. The only symbol Alberti put on the façade is a blazing sun; the

Santa Maria Novella

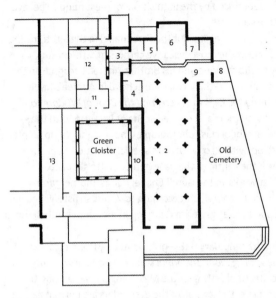

1 Masaccio's *Trinità*
2 Brunelleschi's Pulpit
3 Cappella Strozzi
4 Sacristy
5 Cappella Gondi
6 Sanctuary
7 Fillippo Strozzi Chapel
8 Rucellai Chapel
9 Gothic Tombs
10 *Universal Deluge*
11 Spanish Chapel
12 Chiostrino dei Morte
13 Refectory

unusual sundials, over the arches on the extreme right and left, were added by Cosimo I's court astronomer Egnazio Danti. The base of the façade is also the base of an equilateral triangle, with Alberti's sun at the apex. The beautiful frieze depicts the Rucellai emblem (a billowing sail), as on the Palazzo Rucellai. The wall of Gothic recesses to the right, enclosing the old cemetery, are *avelli*, or family tombs.

The **interior** is vast, lofty and more 'Gothic' in feel than any other church in Florence – no thanks to Vasari, who was set loose to remodel the church to 16th-century taste, painting over the original frescoes, removing the rood screen and Dominicans' choir from the nave, and remodelling the altars; in the 1800s restorers did their best to de-Vasari Santa Maria with neo-Gothic details. Neither party, however, could touch two of the interior's most distinctive features – the striking stone vaulting of the nave and the perspective created by the columns marching down the aisles, each pair placed a little closer together as they approach the altar.

Over the portal at the entrance is a fresco lunette by Botticelli that has recently been restored. One of Santa Maria Novella's best-known pictures has also recently been restored and is at the second altar on the left: Masaccio's *Trinità*, painted around 1425, one of the revolutionary works of the Renaissance. Masaccio's use of architectural elements and perspective gives his composition both physical and intellectual depth. The flat wall becomes a deeply recessed Brunelleschian chapel, calm and classical, enclosed in a coffered barrel vault; at the foot of the fresco a bleak skeleton decays in its tomb, bearing a favourite Tuscan reminder: 'I was that which you are, you will be that which I am.'

Above this morbid suggestion of physical death kneel the two donors; within the celestially rational inner sanctum the Virgin and St John stand at the foot of the

Cross, humanity's link with the mystery of the Trinity. In the nearby pulpit, designed by Brunelleschi, Galileo was first denounced by the Inquisition for presuming to believe that the earth went around the sun.

There is little else to detain you in the aisles, but the first chapel in the left transept, the raised **Cappella Strozzi**, is one of the most evocative corners of 14th-century Florence, frescoed entirely by Nardo di Cione and his brother, Andrea Orcagna; on the vault pictures of St Thomas Aquinas and the Virtues are echoed in Andrea's lovely altarpiece *The Redeemer Donating the Keys to St Peter and the Book of Wisdom to St Thomas Aquinas*; on the left wall there's a crowded scene of Paradise, with the righteous lined up in a medieval school class photograph. On the right, Nardo painted a striking view of Dante's *Inferno*, with all of a Tuscan's special attention to precise map-like detail. Dramatically in the centre of the **nave** hangs Giotto's *Crucifix* (c.1300), one of the artist's first works. In the **Gondi Chapel** hangs another famous *Crucifix*, carved in wood by Brunelleschi, which, according to Vasari, so astonished his friend Donatello that he dropped the eggs he was carrying in his apron for their lunch when he first saw it.

The charming fresco cycle in the **sanctuary** (1485–90), painted by Domenico Ghirlandaio, is the *Lives of the Virgin, St John the Baptist and the Dominican Saints* portrayed in magnificent architectural settings; little Michelangelo was among the students who helped him complete it. Nearly all of the bystanders are portraits of Florentine quattrocento VIPs, including the artist himself (in the red hat, in the *Expulsion of St Joachim from the Temple*), but most prominent are the ladies and gentlemen of the Tornabuoni house. More excellent frescoes adorn the **Filippo Strozzi Chapel**, the finest work ever to come from the brush of Filippino Lippi, painted in 1502 near the end of his life; the exaggerated, dark and violent scenes portray the lives of St Philip (his crucifixion and his subduing of the dragon before the Temple of Mars, which creates such a stench that it kills the heathen prince) and of St John the Evangelist (raising Drusiana from the dead and being martyred in boiling oil). The chapel's beautifully carved tomb of Filippo Strozzi is by Benedetto da Maiano. The **Rucellai Chapel** contains a marble statue of the Madonna and Bambino by Nino Pisano and a fine bronze tomb by Ghiberti, which makes an interesting comparison with the three Gothic tombs nearby in the right transept. One of these contains the remains of the Patriarch of Constantinople, who died in here after the failure of the Council of Florence in 1439 to reunite the Western and Eastern Churches.

The Green Cloister and Spanish Chapel

More great frescoes, restored after the flood, await the visitor in Santa Maria Novella's Cloisters, open as a city museum (*entrance just to the left of the church; open Sat–Thurs 9–2; adm*). The first cloister, the so-called **Green Cloister**, one of the masterpieces of Paolo Uccello and his assistants, is named for the *terraverde* or green earth pigment used by the artist, which lends the scenes from Genesis their eerie, ghostly quality. Much damaged by time and neglect, they are nevertheless striking for their two Uccellian obsessions – perspective and animals. Best known, and in better condition than the others, is Uccello's surreal *Universal Deluge*, a composition framed by the steep walls of two arks, before and after views, which have the uncanny effect of making the scene appear to come racing out of its own vanishing point, a vanishing point touched by divine wrath in a searing bolt of lightning. In between the claustrophobic walls the flood rises, tossing up a desperate ensemble of humanity, waterlogged bodies, naked men bearing clubs, crowded in a jam of flotsam and jetsam in the dark waters. In the right foreground, amidst all the panic, stands a tall robed man, seemingly a visionary, perhaps even Noah himself, looking heavenward while a flood victim seizes him by the ankles.

The **Spanish Chapel** at the far end of the cloisters takes its name from the Spanish court followers of Eleonora di Toledo who worshipped here; the Inquisition had earlier made the chapel its headquarters in Florence. The chapel is, again, famous for its frescoes, the masterpiece of a little-known 14th-century artist named Andrea di Buonaiuto, whose subject was the Dominican cosmology, beautifully portrayed so that even the 'Hounds of the Lord' (a pun on the Order's name, the 'Domini canes') on the right wall seem more like pets than militant bloodhounds sniffing out unorthodox beliefs. The church behind the scene with the hounds is a fairy-pink confection of what Buonaiuto imagined the Duomo would look like when finished; it may well be Arnolfo di Cambio's original conception. Famous Florentines, including Giotto, Dante, Boccaccio and Petrarch, stand to the right of the dais supporting the pope, emperor and various sour-faced hierophants. Off to the right the artist has portrayed four rather urbane Vices with dancing girls, while the Dominicans lead stray sheep back to the fold. On the left wall, St Thomas Aquinas dominates the portrayal of the Contemplative Life, surrounded by Virtues and Doctors of the Church.

The oldest part of the monastery, the **Chiostrino dei Morti** (1270s), contains some 14th-century frescoes, while the **Great Cloister** beyond is now off limits, the property of the Carabinieri, the new men in black charged with keeping the Italians orthodox. Off the Green Cloister, the **Refectory** is a striking hall with cross vaulting and frescoes by Alessandro Allori, now serving as a museum.

Around Santa Maria Novella: Stazione Centrale

Just behind, but a world apart from Santa Maria Novella, another large, amorphous square detracts from one of Italy's finest modern buildings – the **Stazione Centrale**, designed by the architect Michelucci in 1935. Adorned by only a glass block canopy at the entrance (and an early model of that great Italian invention, the digital clock), the station is nevertheless remarkable for its clean lines and impeccable practicality.

San Lorenzo and the Medici Chapels

The lively quarter just east of Santa Maria Novella has been associated with the Medici ever since Giovanni di Bicci de' Medici commissioned Brunelleschi to rebuild the ancient church of San Lorenzo in 1420; subsequent members of the dynasty lavished bushels of florins on its decoration and Medici pantheon, and on several projects commissioned from Michelangelo. The mixed result of all their efforts could be held up as an archetype of the Renaissance, described by Walter Pater as 'great rather by what it designed or aspired to do, than by what it actually achieved'. San Lorenzo's façade of corrugated brick, was the most *nonfinito* of all of Michelangelo's unfinished projects; commissioned by Medici Pope Leo X in 1516, the project never got further than Michelangelo's scale model, which may be seen in the Casa Buonarroti. To complete the church's dingy aspect, the piazza in front contains a universally detested 19th-century statue of Cosimo I's dashing father, Giovanni delle Bande Nere, who died at the age of 28 of wounds received fighting against Emperor Charles V.

The **interior** was completed after Brunelleschi's death to his design, classically calm in good grey *pietra serena*. Of the artistic treasures it contains, most riveting are **Donatello's pulpits**, the sculptor's last works, completed by his pupils after his death in 1466. Cast in bronze, the pulpits were commissioned by Donatello's friend and patron Cosimo il Vecchio. Little in Donatello's previous work prepares the viewer for these scenes of Christ's passion and Resurrection with their rough and impression-istic details, their unbalanced, emotional and overcrowded compositions, more reminiscent of Rodin than anything Florentine. Off the left transept the **old sacristy** is a beautiful vaulted chamber with calmer sculptural decoration by Donatello. Just beyond the Bronzino a door leads into the 15th-century **cloister**, and from there a stair leads up to Michelangelo's **Biblioteca Laurenziana** (*open Mon–Sat 8.30–1.30*).

The Medici Chapels

Open daily 8.15–5; closed 2nd and 4th Sun and 1st, 3rd and 5th Mon of month.

San Lorenzo is most famous, however, for the Medici Chapels, which lie outside and behind the church. The entrance leads through the crypt, a dark and austere place where many of the Medici are actually buried.

Their main monument, the family obsession, is just up the steps, and has long been known as the **Chapel of the Princes** (*currently under restoration*), a stupefying, costly octagon of death that, as much as the Grand Dukes fussed over it, lends their memory an unpleasant aftertaste of bric-a-brac that grew and grew. Perhaps only a genuine Medici could love its trashy opulence; all of Grand Duke Cosimo's descen-dants worked like beavers to finish it according to the plans left by Cosimo's illegitimate son, Giovanni de' Medici. Yet even today it is only partially completed, the *pietre dure* extending only part of the way up the walls. The 19th-century frescoes in the cupola are a poor substitute for the originally planned 'Apotheosis of the Medici' in lapis lazuli, and the two statues in gilded bronze in the niches over the sarcophagi are nothing like the intended figures to be carved in semi-precious stone. The most interesting feature is the inlaid *pietra dura* arms of Tuscan towns and the large Medici arms above, with their familiar six red boluses. (The balls probably derive from the family's origins as pharmacists (*medici*), and opponents called them 'the pills'. Medici supporters, however, made them their battle cry in street fights: 'Balls! Balls!')

A passageway leads to Michelangelo's **New Sacristy**, commissioned by Leo X to occupy an unfinished room originally built to balance Brunelleschi's Old Sacristy.

Michelangelo's first idea was to turn it into a new version of his unfinished, overly ambitious Pope Julius Tomb, an idea quickly quashed by his Medici patrons, who requested instead four wall tombs. Michelangelo only worked on two of the monuments, but managed to finish the New Sacristy itself, creating a silent and gloomy mausoleum, closed in and grey, a chilly, introspective cocoon calculated to depress even the most chatty tour groups.

Nor are the famous tombs guaranteed to cheer. Both honour nonentities: that of *Night and Day* belongs to Lorenzo il Magnifico's son, the Duke of Nemours, and symbolizes the Active Life, while the *Dawn and Dusk* is of Guiliano's nephew, Lorenzo, Duke of Urbino, who symbolizes the Contemplative Life (true to life in one respect – Lorenzo was a disappointment to Machiavelli and everyone else, passively obeying his uncle Pope Leo X). Idealized statues of the two men, in Roman patrician gear, represent these states of mind, while draped on their sarcophagi are Michelangelo's four allegorical figures of the Times of Day, so heavy with weariness and grief they seem ready to slide off on to the floor. The most finished figure, *Night*, has always impressed the critics; she is almost a personification of despair, the mouthpiece of Michelangelo's most bitter verse:

Sweet to me is sleep, and even more to be like stone
While wrong and shame endure;
Not to see, nor to feel, is my good fortune.
Therefore, do not wake me; speak softly here.

Both statues of the dukes look towards the back wall, where a large double tomb for Lorenzo il Magnifico and his brother Giuliano was originally planned, to be decorated with river gods. The only part of this tomb ever completed is the statue of the *Madonna and Child* now in place, accompanied by the Medici patron saints, the doctors Cosmas and Damian.

In 1975, charcoal drawings were discovered on the walls of the little room off the altar (*ask at the cash desk for a permit, as only 12 people can enter at one time*). They were attributed to Michelangelo, who may have hidden here in 1530, when the Medici had regained Florence and apparently would only forgive the artist for aiding the republican defence if he would finish their tombs. But Michelangelo had had enough of their ducal pretences and went off to Rome, never to return to Florence.

Mercato Centrale and Perugino

What makes the neighbourhood around San Lorenzo so lively is its street market (*open Tues–Sat, also open Mon in summer*), which the Florentines run with an almost Neapolitan flamboyance. Stalls selling clothes and leather extend from the square up Via dell'Ariento and vicinity (nicknamed 'Shanghai') towards the **Mercato Centrale** (*open Mon–Fri 7–2; some stalls also open Sat afternoon*), Florence's main food market, a cast-iron and glass confection of the 1870s, brimful of fresh fruit and vegetables, leering boars' heads and mounds of tripe.

Beyond the market, at Via Faenza 42, is the entrance to Perugino's **Cenacolo di Foligno** fresco, housed in the ex-convent of the Tertiary Franciscans of Foligno (*open *daily 9–12; ring the bell*). This 1490s Umbrian version of the Last Supper was discovered in the 1850s and has recently been restored.

Palazzo Medici-Riccardi

San Lorenzo became the Medici's church because it stood just round the corner from the family palace – a huge, stately building on Via Cavour constructed by Alberti and Michelozzo about the same time as the Rucellai Palace. The family's coat-of-arms, which you've probably already noticed everywhere in Florence, is prominently displayed in the corners.

The main reason for visiting is one of Florence's hidden delights: Benozzo Gozzoli's 1459 fresco *Procession of the Magi*, located in the **Cappella dei Magi** upstairs (*open Thurs–Tues 9–7; adm. Only a few people allowed in at a time; in summer you can reserve, t 055 276 0340*). Painting in a delightful, decorative manner more reminiscent of International Gothic than the awakening Renaissance style of his contemporaries, Gozzoli took a religious subject and turned it into a merry, brilliantly coloured pageant of beautifully dressed kings, knights and pages, accompanied by greyhounds and a giraffe, who travel through a springtime landscape of jewel-like trees and castles. This is a largely secular painting, representing less the original Three Kings than the annual pageant of the *Compagnia dei Magi*, Florence's richest confraternity. The scene is wrapped around three walls of the small chapel – you feel as if you had walked straight into a glowing fairytale world. Most of the faces are those of the Medici and other local celebrities; Gozzoli certainly had no qualms about putting himself among the crowd of figures on the right wall, with his name written on his red cap. In the foreground, note the black man carrying a bow. Blacks, as well as Turks, Circassians, Tartars and others, were common enough in Renaissance Florence, originally brought as slaves. By the 1400s, however, contemporary writers mention them as artisans, fencing masters, soldiers and one famous archery instructor, who may be the man pictured here. For an extraordinary contrast, pop into the **gallery** (up the second set of stairs) with its 17th-century ceiling by Neapolitan Luca Giordano, showing the last, unspeakable Medici floating around in marshmallow clouds.

San Marco

Convent open daily 8.15–1.50, Sat 8.15–6.50; closed 1st and 3rd Sun of month and 2nd and 4th Mon of month; adm. Church open 7–12 and 4–7 daily.

Despite all the others who contributed to this Dominican monastery and church, it has always been best known for the work of its most famous resident. Fra Angelico lived here from 1436 until his death in 1455, spending the time turning Michelozzo's simple **cloister** into a complete exposition of his own deep faith, expressed in bright playroom colours and angelic pastels. Fra Angelico painted the frescoes in the corners of the cloister, and on the first floor there is a small museum of his work, collected from various Florentine churches, as well as a number of early 15th-century portraits by Fra Bartolomeo, capturing some of the most sincere spirituality of the age. The *Last Supper* in the refectory is by Ghirlandaio. Other Fra Angelico works include the *Life of Christ* series, in which all the saved are well-dressed Italians holding hands. They get to keep their clothes in heaven, while the bad (mostly princes and prelates) are stripped to receive their interesting tortures.

Right at the top of the stairs to the monks' dormitory, your eyes meet the Angelic Friar's masterpiece, a miraculous *Annunciation* that offers an intriguing comparison with Leonardo's *Annunciation* in the Uffizi. The subject was a favourite with Florentine artists, not only because it was a severe test – expressing a divine revelation with a composition of strict economy – but because the Annunciation, falling near the spring equinox, was New Year's Day for Florence until the Medici adopted the pope's calendar in the 17th century. In each of the monks' cells, Fra Angelico and students painted the *Crucifixion*, all the same but for some slight differences in pose; glancing in the cells down the corridor in turn gives the impression of a cartoon. One of the cells belonged to Savonarola, who was the prior here during his period of dominance in Florence; it has the simple furniture of the period and a portrait of Savonarola by Fra Bartolomeo. In a nearby corridor, you can see an anonymous painting of the monk and two of his followers being led to the stake on Piazza della Signoria. Michelozzo's Library, off the main corridor, is as light and airy as the cloisters below; in it is displayed a collection of choir books, one illuminated by Fra Angelico.

On Via La Pira is the entrance to the **Giardino dei Semplici**, the botanical garden created for Cosimo I. The garden maintains its original layout, with medicinal herbs, Tuscan plants, flowers and tropical plants in its greenhouses (*open Mon–Fri 9–1; adm*).

Galleria dell'Accademia

Open Tues–Sun 8.15–6.50; adm exp.

From Piazza San Marco, Via Ricasoli makes a beeline for the Duomo, but on most days the view is obstructed by the crowds milling around No.60; in the summer the queues are as long as those at the Uffizi, everyone anxious to get a look at Michelangelo's *David*. Just over a hundred years ago Florence decided to take this precocious symbol of republican liberty out of the rain and install it, with much pomp, in a specially built classical exedra in this gallery. David is currently being cleaned up; work should last until the summer of 2003, but in the meantime they are working on him bit by bit, so he is partially visible.

Michelangelo completed the *David* for the city in 1504, when he was 29, and it was the work that established the overwhelming reputation he had in his own time. The monstrous block of marble – 16ft high but unusually shallow – had been quarried 40 years earlier by the Cathedral Works and spoiled by other hands. The block was offered around to several other artists, including Leonardo da Vinci, before young Michelangelo decided to take up the challenge of carving the largest statue created since Roman times. And it is the dimensions of the *David* that remain the biggest surprise in these days of endless reproductions. Certainly as a political symbol of the

Republic, he is excessive – the irony of a David the size of a Goliath is disconcerting – but as a symbol of the artistic and intellectual aspirations of the Renaissance period he is unsurpassed.

And it's hard to deny, after gazing at this enormous nude, that these same Renaissance aspirations by the 1500s began snuggling uncomfortably close to the frontiers of kitsch. Disproportionate size is one symptom; the calculated intention to excite a strong emotional response is another. In the *David*, virtuosity eclipses vision, and commits the even deadlier kitsch sin of seeking the sterile empyrean of perfect beauty – most would argue that Michelangelo here achieves it, perhaps capturing his own feelings about the work in the *David*'s chillingly vain, self-satisfied expression. This is also one of the few statues to have actually injured someone. During a political disturbance in the Piazza della Signoria, its arm broke off and fell on a farmer's toe. In 1991 it was David's toe that fell victim when a madman chopped it off. Since then, the rest of his anatomy has been shielded by glass.

In the Galleria next to the *David* are Michelangelo's famous *nonfiniti*, the four *Prisoners* or *Slaves*, worked on between 1519 and 1536, sculpted for Pope Julius' tomb and left in various stages of completion, although it is endlessly argued whether this is by design or through lack of time. Whatever the case, they illustrate Michelangelo's view of sculpture as a prisoner in stone just as the soul is a prisoner of the body. When Michelangelo left them, the Medici snapped them up to decorate Buontalenti's Grotta fountain in the Boboli gardens.

The gallery was founded by Grand Duke Pietro Leopold in 1784 to provide Academy students with examples of art from every period. The big busy Mannerist paintings around the *David* are by Michelangelo's contemporaries, among them Pontormo's *Venus and Cupid*, with a Michelangelesque Venus among theatre masks. Other rooms contain a good selection of quattrocento painting, including the *Madonna del Mare* by Botticelli, a damaged Baldovinetti, the *Thebaid* by a follower of Uccello, and Perugino's *Deposition*. The painted frontal of the **Adimari chest** shows a delightful wedding scene of the 1450s with the baptistry in the background that has been reproduced in half the books ever written about the Renaissance.

The hall off to the left of the *David* was formerly the women's ward of a hospital, depicted in a greenish painting by Pontormo. Now it is used as a gallery of plaster models by 19th-century members of the Accademia.

The excellent **Collection of Old Musical Instruments** once housed in the Palazzo Vecchio has moved to the Accademia. The collection of some 150 exhibits, including several violins and cellos by Cremona greats like Stradivarius and Guarneri, are on display in a room on the ground floor, properly organized and labelled.

Piazza Santissima Annunziata

This lovely square, really the only Renaissance attempt at a unified ensemble in Florence, is surrounded on three sides by arcades. In its centre, gazing down the splendid vista of Via dei Servi towards the Duomo, stands the equestrian statue of

Ferdinand I (1607) by Giambologna and his pupil Pietro Tacca, made of bronze from Turkish cannons captured during the Battle of Lepanto. More fascinating than Ferdinand are the pair of bizarre Baroque fountains, also by Tacca, that share the square. Though of a nominally marine theme, they resemble tureens of bouillabaisse that any ogre would be proud to serve, topped by grinning winged monkeys.

In the 1420s Filippo Brunelleschi struck the first blow for classical calm in this piazza when he built the celebrated **Spedale degli Innocenti** (*open Thurs–Tues 8.30–2, closed Wed; adm*) and its famous portico – an architectural landmark, but also a monument to Renaissance Italy's long, hard and ultimately unsuccessful struggle towards some kind of social consciousness. Even in the best of times, Florence's poor were treated like dirt; if any enlightened soul had been so bold as to propose even a modern conservative 'trickle down' theory to the Medici and the banking élite, their first thought would have been how to stop the leaks. Babies, at least, were treated a little better. The Spedale degli Innocenti was the first hospital for foundlings in Italy and the world (at the left end of the loggia you can still see the original window-wheel where babies were anonymously abandoned until 1875). Today it is a nursery school. The Spedale was Brunelleschi's first completed work and demonstrates his use of geometrical proportions adapted to traditional Tuscan Romanesque architecture. His lovely portico is adorned with the famous blue and white tondi of infants in swaddling clothes by Andrea della Robbia, added as an appeal to charity in the 1480s after several children died of malnutrition. Brunelleschi also designed the two beautiful cloisters of the convent; the **Chiostro delle Donne**, reserved for the hospital's nurses (located up the ramp on the right at No.13), is especially fine. Upstairs, the **Museo dello Spedale** (*open Thurs–Tues 8.30–2; adm*) contains a number of detached frescoes from Ognissanti and other churches, among them an unusual series of red and orange prophets by Alessandro Allori; other works include a *Madonna and Saints* by Piero di Cosimo, a *Madonna and Child* by Luca della Robbia, and the brilliant *Adoration of the Magi* (1488) painted by Domenico Ghirlandaio for the hospital's church, a crowded, colourful composition featuring portraits of members of the Arte della Lana, who funded the Spedale.

Santissima Annunziata

To complement Brunelleschi's arches, the old church of Santissima Annunziata was rebuilt and given a broad arcaded portico by Michelozzo facing the street. Behind the portico the architect added the **Chiostrino dei Voti**, a porch decorated with a collection of early 16th-century frescoes, including two by Andrea del Sarto. The best of these, faded as it is, is a finely detailed *Nativity* by Alessio Baldovinetti, one of the quattrocento's under-appreciated masters.

The church itself is the gaudiest in Florence; its freshly gilded elliptical dome, its unusual polygonal tribune around the sanctuary and megatons of *pietra dura* have helped it become the city's high-society parish, where even funerals are major social events. The huge candlelit chapel in the rear is the Tempietta, also by Michelozzo, sheltering a miraculous painting of *The Annunciation*.

Archaeological Museum

Open Mon 2–7, Tues and Thurs 8.30–7, Wed and Fri–Sun 8.30–2; adm.

From Piazza SS. Annunziata, Via della Colonna leads to Florence's **Museo Archeologico**, housed in the 17th-century Palazzo della Crocetta, originally built for Grand Duchess Maria Maddalena of Austria. Like nearly every other museum in Florence, this impressive collection was begun by the Medici, beginning with Cosimo il Vecchio and accelerating with the insatiable Cosimo I and his heirs. The Medici were especially fond of Etruscan things, while the impressive Egyptian collection was begun by Leopold II in the 1830s.

The **Etruscan collection** is on the first floor, including the famous bronze *Chimera*, a remarkable beast with the three heads of a lion, goat and snake. This 5th-century BC work, dug up near Arezzo in 1555 and immediately snatched by Cosimo I, had a great influence on Mannerist artists. There is no Mannerist fancy about its origins, though; like all such composite monsters, it is a religious icon, a calendar beast symbolizing the three seasons of the ancient Mediterranean agricultural year. In the same corridor stands the *Arringatore*, or Orator, a monumental bronze of the Hellenistic period, a civic-minded and civilized-looking gentleman, dedicated to Aulus Metellus, and the statue of *Minerva*. Also to be found in this section are other Etruscan bronzes, big and small. The cases here are full of wonderful objects, anything from tiny animals to jewellery, carved mirrors and household objects such as plates – there's even a strainer. All these show just how skilled the Etruscans were in casting bronze.

The beautifully lit **Egyptian collection**, also on the first floor, has been expanded and modernized. It includes some interesting small statuettes, mummies, canopic vases, and a unique wood-and-bone chariot, nearly completely preserved, found in a 14th-century BC tomb in Thebes.

On the second floor there is plenty of Greek art; Etruscan noble families were wont to buy up all they could afford. The beautiful Hellenistic horse's head once adorned the Palazzo Medici-Riccardi. The *Idolino*, a bronze of a young athlete, is believed to be a Roman copy of a 5th-century BC Greek original. There is an excellent *Kouros*, a young man in the archaic style from 6th-century BC Sicily. An unusual, recent find, the silver *Baratti Amphora*, was made in the 4th century BC in Antioch and covered with scores of small medallions showing mythological figures. Scholars believe that the images and their arrangement may encode an entire system of belief, the secret teaching of one of the mystic-philosophical cults common in Hellenistic times, and they hope some day to decipher it. There's a vast collection of Greek pottery (including the massive *François vase* in Room 2), and large Greek, Roman and Renaissance bronzes, recently brought out of storage. There are also several fabulous Greek marble sculptures dating from *c.* 500 BC.

There is virtually nothing displayed on the ground floor now although temporary exhibitions are held there. In the garden are several reconstructed Etruscan tombs (*open to visitors on Sat 8.30–2*). The fabulous collection of precious stones, coins and, most notably, cameos (amassed by the Medici) is now permanently on display in the corridor which runs between the museum and the church of Santissima Annunziata.

Santa Maria Maddalena dei Pazzi and the Synagogue

East of the Archaeological Museum, Via della Colonna becomes one of Florence's typical straight, boring Renaissance streets. It's well worth taking a detour down Borgo Pinti, to No.58, to visit one of the city's least known but most intriguing churches, **Santa Maria Maddalena dei Pazzi** (*open daily 9–12 and 5–7; voluntary donation*), a fine example of architectural syncretism. The church itself was founded in the 13th century, rebuilt in classically Renaissance style by Giuliano da Sangallo, then given a full dose of Baroque when the church was rededicated to the Counter-Reformation saint of the Pazzi family. Inside it's all high theatre, with a gaudy *trompe l'œil* ceiling, paintings by Luca Giordano, florid chapels, and a wild marble chancel. From the sacristy a door leads down into a crypt to the chapterhouse, which contains a frescoed *Crucifixion* (1496), one of Perugino's masterpieces. Despite the symmetry and quiet, contemplative grief of the five figures at the foot of the Cross and the stillness of the luminous Tuscan-Umbrian landscape, the fresco has a powerful impact. It has never been restored; in the 1966 flood, the water came within four inches of it, and stopped.

Florence's Jewish community, although today a mere 1,200 strong, has long been one of the most important in Italy, invited to Florence by the Republic in 1430, but repeatedly exiled and readmitted until Cosimo I founded Florence's Ghetto in 1551. When the Ghetto was opened up in 1848 and demolished soon after, a new **synagogue** (1874–82) was built in Via L C Farini: a tall, charming, Mozarabic Pre-Raphaelite hybrid inspired by the Hagia Sophia and the Transito Synagogue of Toledo (*open April, May, Sept and Oct Sun–Thurs 10–5 and Fri 10–2; June–Aug Sun–Thurs 10–6 and Fri 10–3; Nov–Feb Sun–Thurs 10–2; adm*). Although seriously damaged by the Nazis in August 1944, as well as by the Arno in 1966, it has since been lovingly restored. There's a small **Jewish Museum** upstairs (*opening hours as for synagogue; call t 055 245252/3 for info*), which has a documentary history of Florentine Jews.

Sant'Ambrogio and the Flea Market

The streets of Sant'Ambrogio are among the most dusty and piquant in the city centre, a neighbourhood where tourists seldom tread. Life revolves around **Sant'Ambrogio** and its neighbouring food market made of cast iron in 1873; the church (rebuilt in the 13th century, 19th-century façade) is of interest for its artwork: the second chapel on the right has a lovely fresco of the *Madonna Enthroned with Saints* by Orcagna (or his school) and the **Cappella del Miracolo**, just left of the high altar, contains Mino da Fiesole's celebrated marble *Tabernacle* (1481) and his own tomb. The chapel has a fresco of a procession by Cosimo Rosselli, especially interesting for its depiction of 15th-century celebrities, including Pico della Mirandola and Rosselli himself (in a black hat, in the group on the left). Andrea Verrocchio is buried in the fourth chapel on the left; on the wall by the second altar, there's a *Nativity* by Baldovinetti. The fresco of an atypical *St Sebastian* in the first chapel of the left is by Agnolo Gaddi.

From Sant'Ambrogio take Via Pietrapiana to the bustling **Piazza dei Ciompi**, named after the wool-workers' revolt of 1378. In the morning, Florence's flea market or

Mercatino takes place here, the best place in town to buy that 1940s radio or outdated ball gown you've always wanted. One side of the square is graced with the **Loggia del Pesce**, built by Vasari in 1568 for the fishmongers of the Mercato Vecchio; when that was demolished the loggia was salvaged and re-erected here.

Casa Buonarroti

Open Wed–Mon 9.30–2; adm exp; look out for their temporary exhibitions.

Michelangelo never lived in this house at Via Ghibellina 70, although he purchased it in 1508. That wasn't the point, especially to an artist who had no thought for his own personal comfort, or anyone else's – he never washed, and never took off his boots, even in bed. Real estate was an obsession of his, as he struggled to restore the status of the semi-noble but impoverished Buonarroti family. His nephew Leonardo inherited the house and several works of art in 1564; later he bought the two houses next door to create a memorial to his uncle, hiring artists to paint scenes from Michelangelo's life. In the mid-19th century, the house was opened to the public as a Michelangelo museum.

The ground floor is dedicated to mostly imaginary portraits of the artist, and works of art collected by his nephew's descendants, including an eclectic Etruscan and Roman collection. The main attractions, however, are upstairs, beginning with Michelangelo's earliest known work, the beautiful bas-relief *The Madonna of the Steps* (1490–1), the precocious work of a 16-year-old influenced by Donatello and studying in the household of Lorenzo il Magnifico; the relief of a battle scene, inspired by classical models, dates from the same period. Small models and drawings of potential projects line the walls; there's the wooden model for the façade of San Lorenzo, with designs for some of the statuary Michelangelo intended to fill in its austere blank spaces – as was often the case, his ideas were far too grand for his patron's purse and patience. The next four rooms were painted in the 17th century to illustrate Michelangelo's life, virtues and apotheosis, depicting a polite, deferential and pleasant Michelangelo hobnobbing with popes. Those who know the artist best from *The Agony and the Ecstasy* may think they painted the wrong man by mistake. One of the best sections is a frieze of famous Florentines in the library. Other exhibits include a painted wooden *Crucifix* discovered in Santo Spirito in 1963 and believed by most scholars to be a documented one by Michelangelo, long thought to be lost; the contrapposto position of the slender body, and the fact that only Michelangelo would carve a nude Christ, weigh in favour of the attribution.

Santa Croce

Open Mon–Sat 9.30–5.30, Sun 1–5.30; adm.

Santa Maria Novella was the Dominicans' church, and so naturally the Franciscans had to have one just as big and grand. The original church, said to have been founded by St Francis himself, went by the board in Florence's colossal building programme of the 1290s. Arnolfo di Cambio planned its successor, largely completed by the 1450s,

Santa Croce

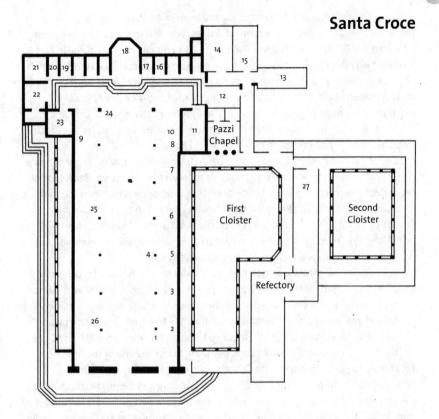

1 Madonna del Latte
2 Tomb of Michaelangelo
3 Monument to Dante
4 Benedetto da Maiano's Pulpit
5 Vittorio Alfieri's Tomb
6 Tomb of Machiavelli
7 Donatello's *Annuniciation*
8 Tomb of Leonardo Bruni
9 Tomb of Carlo Malaspini
10 Tomb of Rossini
11 Castellani Chapel
12 Baroncelli Chapel
13 Medici Chapel
14 Sacristy

15 Rinuccini Chapel
16 Peruzzi Chapel
17 Bardi Chapel
18 Sanctuary
19 Bardi di Libertà Chapel
20 Bardi di Vernio Chapel
21 Niccolini Chapel
22 Bardi Chapel
23 Salviati Chapel
24 Monument to Alberti
25 Tomb of Lorenzo Ghiberti
26 Galileo's Tomb
27 Museo dell'Opera di Santa Croce

but a job of 'restoration' by Vasari in the 1560s ruined much of the original interior. The façade, in the accustomed Florentine black and white marble, nevertheless has something of the Victorian Gothic about it – just as it should, since it was only added in the 1850s, a gift from Sir Francis Sloane. Of all the modern façades on Italy's churches, built to atone finally for the chronic Renaissance inability ever to finish anything, this one may be the best.

Like Santa Maria Novella the interior is a museum in itself. Starting clockwise from the left side: near the door is the **tomb of Galileo**, whose remains were moved here only after the Church grudgingly consented to allow him a Christian burial in 1737. For a while it was the custom to bury great Italians here, as a sort of Tuscan Westminster Abbey, and you'll see plenty of tombs along both sides, mostly of thoroughly forgotten men of the 19th century. Two chapels down, the *Monument to Carlo Marsuppini* is a mine of good quattrocento sculpture, mostly by Verrocchio and Desiderio da Settignano. Look in the Bardi Chapel in the left transept for the Crucifix by Donatello (the one Brunelleschi said looked like a peasant).

Many of the small vaulted chapels that flank the high altar contain important late (1330s) works by Giotto, his assistants and his followers. In the second **Bardi Chapel** is a series of frescoes on the Life of St Francis that can be compared with the more famous ones at Assisi. The **Peruzzi Chapel** frescoes detail the *Lives of St John the Evangelist and St John the Baptist*. These works had a tremendous influence on all the later Florentine artists, but by the 18th century they were considered eyesores and whitewashed for 150 years – hence their fragmentary state.

Two of Giotto's immediate artistic heirs, the Gaddi, also contributed much to Santa Croce. Agnolo Gaddi did the stained glass around the high altar, as well as the fascinating series of frescoes on the *Legend of the Cross* – how Seth received a branch from St Michael and planted it over Adam's grave, how the tree that grew from it was shaped into a beam for a bridge, then buried by Solomon when his guest the Queen of Sheba prophesied that it would someday bring about the end of the Jews. The beam was dug up and shaped into Christ's cross, later found by St Helena, Constantine's mother, and then stolen by a Persian king and eventually recovered by the Emperor Heraclius. In the **sacristy**, off to the right, there are more fine frescoes by Agnolo Gaddi's father Taddeo, and yet more Gaddis in the Castellani Chapel (Agnolo) and Baroncelli Chapel (Taddeo).

Back down the right side of the church, Donatello's **tabernacle** has a beautiful relief of the *Annunciation*. Then some more **tombs**: Rossini, Machiavelli, Michelangelo, and Dante. Michelangelo's is the work of Vasari, who thought himself just the fellow for the job. Vasari's vandalism ruined most of the chapels on this side, once embellished with frescoes by Orcagna and other great trecento painters. His replacements, like his tomb for Michelangelo, are misfortunes. Dante isn't buried here at all. The Florentines always thought they would eventually get his body back from Ravenna; once they even bribed a pope to order the Ravennese to give it up, whereupon the body mysteriously disappeared for a decade or two until the affair was forgotten.

The Pazzi Chapel

Open Mon–Sat 9.30–5.30, Sun 1–5.30; entrance through Santa Croce; adm.

This chapel is well worth a visit. Brunelleschi, who could excel on the monumental scale of the cathedral dome, saved some of his best work for small places. Without knowing the architect, and something about the austere religious tendencies of the Florentines, the Pazzi Chapel is inexplicable, a Protestant reformation in architecture unlike anything ever built before. The 'vocabulary' is essential Brunelleschi, the geometric forms emphasized by the simplicity of the decoration: *pietra serena* pilasters and rosettes on white walls, arches, 12 terracotta *tondi* of the Apostles by Luca della Robbia, coloured rondels of the Evangelists in the pendentives by Donatello, and a small, stained-glass window by Baldovinetti. Even so, that is enough. The contemplative repetition of elements makes for an aesthetic that posed a direct challenge to the International Gothic of the time.

Leaving the Pazzi Chapel (notice Luca della Robbia's terracotta decorations on the portico), a doorway on the left of the cloister leads to Brunelleschi's **Second Cloister**, designed with the same subtlety and one of the quietest spots in Florence.

The old monastic buildings off the first cloister now house the **Museo dell'Opera di Santa Croce** (*open Mon–Sat 9.30–5.30, Sun 1–5.30; adm*), where you can see Cimabue's celebrated *Crucifix*, devastated by the flood, and partly restored after one of Florence's perennial restoration controversies. The refectory wall has another fine fresco by Taddeo Gaddi, of the *Tree of the Cross and the Last Supper*; fragments of Orcagna's frescoes salvaged from Vasari's obliteration offer powerful, nightmarish vignettes of The Triumph of Death and Hell. Donatello's huge, gilded bronze statue *St Louis of Toulouse* (1423) – a flawed work representing a flawed character, according to Donatello – was made for the façade of Orsanmichele. The museum also contains works by Andrea della Robbia, and a painting of Mayor Bargellini with a melancholy Santa Croce submerged in the 1966 flood for a backdrop; under the colonnade there's a statue of Florence Nightingale, born in and named after the city in 1820.

Around Santa Croce: the Horne Museum

The east end of Florence, a rambling district packed with artisans and small manufacturers, traditionally served as the artists' quarter in Renaissance times. It's still one of the livelier neighbourhoods today, with a few lingering artists lodged in the upper storeys, hoping to breathe inspiration from the very stones where Michelangelo walked. It is a good place to observe the workaday Florence behind the glossy façade.

From Santa Croce, the pretty Borgo Santa Croce leads towards the Arno and the delightful **Horne Museum**, housed in a Renaissance palace, at Via de' Benci 6 (*open Mon–Sat 9–1; closed Sun and hols; adm*). Herbert Percy Horne (1844–1916) was an English art historian, biographer of Botticelli, and Florentinophile, who bequeathed his collection to the nation.

North Bank Peripheral Attractions

The Cascine

The newer sections of the city are, by and large, irredeemably dull. Much of Florence's traffic problem is channelled through its ring of avenues, or *viali*, laid out in the 1860s by Giuseppe Poggi to replace the demolished walls. On and along them are scattered points of interest, including some of the old city gates.

Bus 17C from the station or Duomo will take you through the congestion to the **Cascine**, the long (3.5km), narrow public park lining this bank of the Arno, originally used as the Medici's dairy farm, or *cascina*, and later as a Grand Ducal hunting park and theatre for public spectacles. A windy autumn day here in 1819 inspired Shelley to compose the 'Ode to the West Wind'. Florentines come to the Cascine by day to play; it contains a riding school, race tracks, a small amusement park and zoo for the children, tennis courts, and a swimming pool. At night they come to ogle the transvestites strutting their stuff on the *viale*.

Beyond the train station, cars and buses hurtle around and around the **Fortezza da Basso**, an enormous bulk built by Antonio da Sangallo on orders from Alessandro de' Medici in 1534. It immediately became the most hated symbol of Medici tyranny. Ironically, the duke who built the Fortezza da Basso was one of very few to meet his end within its ramparts – stabbed by his relative and bosom companion 'Lorenzaccio' de' Medici. As a fortress, the place never saw any action as thrilling or vicious as the Pitti fashion shows that take place behind the walls in its 1978 aluminium exhibition hall.

Just east of the Fortezza, at the corner of Via Leone X and Viale Milton, there's an unexpected sight rising above the sleepy residential neighbourhood – the five graceful onion domes of the **Russian Church**, made even more exotic by the palm tree tickling its side. In the 19th century, Florence was a popular winter retreat for Russians who could afford it, among them Dostoevsky and Gorky. Completed by Russian architects in 1904, it is a pretty jewel box of brick and majolica decoration, open on the third Sunday of the month, when the priest comes from Nice to hold a morning service in Russian.

The Stibbert Museum

Open in summer Mon–Wed 10–2, Fri–Sun 10–6; adm.

From Piazza della Libertà, the dull Via Vittorio Emanuele heads 1km north to Via Stibbert and the Stibbert Museum (alternatively, take bus 31 or 32 from the station). Those who make the journey to see the lifetime's accumulations of Frederick Stibbert (1838–1906), who fought with Garibaldi and hobnobbed with Queen Victoria, can savour Florence's most bizarre museum, and one of the city's most pleasant small parks, laid out by Stibbert with a mouldering Egyptian temple sinking in a pond – and just make sure that you obey the sign on the door: 'Comply with the Forbidden Admittances!'.

Stibbert's Italian mother left him a 14th-century house, which he joined to another house to create a Victorian's sumptuous version of what a medieval Florentine house should have looked like – 64 rooms to contain a pack-rat's treasure hoard of all things brilliant and useless, from an attributed Botticelli, to snuff boxes, to what a local guide intriguingly describes as 'brass and silver basins, used daily by Stibbert'.

Stibbert's serious passion, however, was armour, and he amassed a magnificent collection from all times and places. The best pieces are not arranged in dusty cases, but with a touch of Hollywood, on grim knightly mannequins ranked ready for battle.

The Oltrarno

Once over the Ponte Vecchio, a different Florence reveals itself: greener, quieter, and less burdened with traffic. The Oltrarno is not a large district: a chain of hills squeezes it against the river, and their summits afford some of the best views over the city.

Once across the Arno, the Medici's catwalk becomes part of the upper façade of **Santa Felicità**, one of Florence's most ancient churches, believed to have been founded by the Syrian Greek traders who introduced Christianity to the city, and established the first Christian cemetery in the small square in front of the church.

Rebuilt in the 18th century, there is one compelling reason to enter, for here, in the first chapel on the right, is the *ne plus ultra* of Mannerism: Pontormo's weirdly luminous *Deposition* (1528), painted in jarring pinks, oranges and blues that cut through the darkness of the little chapel. The composition itself is highly unconventional, with an effect that derives entirely from the use of figures in unusual, exaggerated poses; there is no sign of a cross, the only background is a single cloud. Sharing the chapel is Pontormo's *Annunciation* fresco, a less idiosyncratic work, as well as four tondi of the Evangelists in the cupola, partly the work of Pontormo's pupil and adopted son, Bronzino.

The Pitti Palace

As the Medici consolidated their power in Florence, they made a point of buying up the most important properties of their former rivals, especially their proud family palaces. The most spectacular example of this was Cosimo I's acquisition of the Pitti Palace, built in 1457 by a powerful banker named Luca Pitti who seems to have had vague ambitions of toppling the Medici and becoming the big boss himself. The palace, with its extensive grounds, now the Boboli Gardens, was much more pleasant than the medieval Palazzo Vecchio, and in the 1540s Cosimo I and his wife Eleanor of Toledo moved in for good. The palace remained the residence of the Medici, and later the House of Lorraine, until 1868. The original building, said to have been designed by Brunelleschi, was only as wide as the seven central windows of the façade. Succeeding generations found it too small for their burgeoning hoards of bric-a-brac, and added several stages of symmetrical additions, resulting in a long, bulky profile, resembling a rusticated Stalinist ministry, but a landscaped one.

There are eight separate **museums** in the Pitti; the ticket office for them all is in the far right corner of the forecourt.

Galleria Palatina

Open Tues–Sun 8.15–6.50; adm.

This is the Pitti museum most people see, containing the Grand Dukes' famous collection of 16th–18th-century paintings, stacked on the walls in enormous gilt frames under the berserk opulence of frescoed ceilings celebrating planets, mythology and, of course, the ubiquitous Medici. The gallery is on the first floor of the right half of the palace; the ticket office is on the ground floor, off Ammannati's exaggerated rustic courtyard, a Mannerist masterpiece.

After the entrance to the Galleria is the neoclassical **Sala Castagnoli**, with the *Tavola delle Muse* in its centre, itself an excellent introduction to the Florentine 'decorative arts'; the table, a paragon of the intricate art of *pietra dura*, was made in the 1870s. The Galleria's best paintings are in the five former reception rooms off to the left. However, the set route takes you through the other part of the palace first, starting with the adjacent **Sala di Prometeo** containing Filippo Lippi's lovely *Tondo of the Madonna and Child* and Baldassare Peruzzi's unusual *Dance of Apollo*. Next you can peek into the **Sala di Bagni**, the Empire bathroom of Elisa Baciocchi, Napoleon's sister, who ruled the Département de l'Arno between 1809 and 1814, and seemingly spent much of those years redecorating the Pitti. Caravaggio's *Sleeping Cupid* is a couple of rooms up, in the **Sala dell'Educazione di Giove**. The next room to this is the pretty **Sala della Stufa**, frescoed with the *Four Ages of the World* by Pietro da Cortona.

The first of the reception rooms, the **Sala dell'Iliade** (frescoed in the 19th century), has some fine portraits by the Medici court painter and Rubens' friend, Justus Sustermans. Two *Assumptions* by Andrea del Sarto, *Philip II* by Titian and a Velazquez equestrian portrait of Philip IV share the room with one of the most unusual residents of the gallery, *Queen Elizabeth*, who seems uncomfortable in such company.

The **Sala di Giove**, used as the Medici throne room, contains one of Raphael's best-known portraits, the lovely and serene *Donna Velata* (1516). The small painting *The Three Ages of Man* is usually attributed to Giorgione. The **Sala di Marte** has two works by Rubens, *The Four Philosophers* and *The Consequences of War*, as well as excellent portraits by Tintoretto and Van Dyck. The restored *Annunciation of San Godenzo*, by Andrea del Sarto, is now back in place after a long absence, and there is also Titian's rather dashing *Cardinal Ippolito de' Medici* in Hungarian costume.

In the **Sala di Apollo** there's more Titian – his *Portrait of a Grey-eyed Gentleman*, evoking the perfect 16th-century English gentleman, and his more sensuous than penitent *Mary Magdalene* – as well as works by Andrea del Sarto and Van Dyck. The last reception room is the **Sala di Venere**, with several works by Titian, including his early *Concert*, believed to have been partly painted by Giorgione and a powerful *Portrait of Pietro Aretino*, Titian's close and caustic friend, who complained to the artist that it was all too accurate and gave it to Cosimo I. There are two beautiful landscapes by Rubens, painted at the end of his life, and an uncanny self-portrait, *La Menzogna* ('The Falsehood') by Neapolitan Salvator Rosa. The centrepiece statue, the *Venus Italica*, was commissioned by Napoleon from neoclassical master Antonio Canova in 1812 to replace the *Venus de' Medici* which he 'centralized' off to Paris.

Next to the Sala di Venere is the **Sala delle Nicchie**, currently home to several paintings from Raphael's Florence days as long as work continues on the frescoes in the **Sala di Saturno**. These include the *Maddalena and Agnolo Doni* (1506) and the *Madonna 'del Granduca'*, influenced by the paintings of Leonardo. Some 10 years later, Raphael had found his own style, beautifully evident in his famous *Madonna della Seggiola* ('of the chair'), perhaps the most popular work he ever painted.

The right half of the Pitti also contains the **State Apartments** (*included as part of the visit to the Galleria Palatina*). These were last redone in the 19th century by the Dukes of Lorraine, with touches by the Kings of Savoy.

Galleria d'Arte Moderna

Open 8.30–1.50, closed 2nd and 4th Sun and 1st, 3rd and 5th Mon of month; adm exp; tickets from main ticket office on ground floor.

On the second floor above the Galleria Palatina has been installed Florence's modern – read late 18th- to 20th-century – art museum, with over 30 rooms. Though the monumental stair may leave you breathless (the Medici negotiated it with sedan chairs and strong-shouldered servants), consider a visit for some sunny painting of the Italy of your great-grandparents. The 'Splatterers' or *Macchiaioli* (Tuscan Impressionists) illuminate **Room 16** and the rest of the museum, with an interval of enormous Risorgimento battle scenes. What comes as a shock, especially if you've been touring Florence for a while now, is that the marriage between painting and sculpture that characterizes most of Italian art history seems to have resulted in a nasty divorce in the late 1800s: while the canvases radiate light, statuary becomes disturbingly kitsch, obsessed with death and beauty.

Museo degli Argenti

Open daily 8.30–1.50; afternoon visits by appt only, t 055 238 8709; closed 1st and last Mon of month.

The ground floor on the left side of the Pitti was used as the Medici summer apartments and now contains the family's remarkable collection of jewellery, vases, trinkets and pricey curiosities. The Grand Duke's guests would be received in four of the most delightfully frescoed rooms to be found anywhere in Florence, beginning with the **Sala di Giovanni di San Giovanni**, named after the artist who painted it in the 1630s. The three **reception rooms** were painted in shadowy blue *trompe l'œil* by two masterful Bolognese illusionists, Agostino Michele and Angelo Colonna.

More Pitti Museums

The **Museum of Costumes** (*open daily 8.15–1.50; closed 2nd and 4th Sun and 1st, 3rd and 5th Mon of month*) is housed on the second floor of the palace, near to the Galleria d'Arte Moderna; which has the reconstructed dress Eleanor of Toledo was buried in – the same one that she wears in Bronzino's famous portrait. The **Porcelain Museum** (*open Jan–Feb, Nov–Dec 8.15–4.30; Mar 8.15–5.30; April–May, Sept–Oct 8.15–6.30; June–Aug 8.15–7.30; closed 1st and last Mon of month; adm inc with Boboli ticket*) is housed in the casino of Cosimo III, out in the Giardino del Cavaliere in the Boboli Gardens (*follow the signs*).

Boboli Gardens

Open from 9am until one hour before sunset; adm; t 055 265 1838.

Stretching back invitingly from the Pitti, the shady green of the Boboli Gardens, Florence's largest (and only) central public garden, is an irresistible oasis in the middle of a stone-hard city. Originally laid out by Buontalenti, the Boboli reigns as queen of all formal Tuscan gardens, the most elaborate and theatrical, a Mannerist-Baroque co-production of Nature and Artifice laid out over a steep hill, full of shady nooks and pretty walks and beautifully kept. The park is populated by a platoon of statuary, many of them Roman works, others absurd Mannerist pieces.

There are three entrances and exits: through the main courtyard of the Pitti Palace, from Via Romana and in Porta Romana. The main, route, from the Pitti Palace, starts at the **Amphitheatre**, which ascends in regular tiers from the palace, and was designed like a small Roman circus to hold Medici court spectacles. It has a genuine obelisk, of Rameses II from Heliopolis, snatched by the ancient Romans and shipped here by the Medici branch in Rome. The granite basin, large enough to submerge an elephant, came from the Roman Baths of Caracalla. Straight up the terrace is the **Neptune Fountain**; a signposted path leads from there to the pretty **Kaffeehaus**, a boat-like pavilion with a prow and deck offering a fine view of Florence and drinks in the summer. From here the path continues up to the **Belvedere Fort** (*currently under restoration*). Other signs from the Neptune Fountain point the way up to the secluded **Giardino del Cavaliere**, located on a bastion on Michelangelo's fortifications. Cosimo III built the casino here to escape the heat in the Pitti Palace; the view over the ancient villas, vineyards and olives is pure Tuscan enchantment. The **Porcelain Museum** here (*see* p.293) contains 18th- and 19th-century examples of chinawork from Sèvres, Meissen and Vienna.

At the bottom right-hand corner of the garden lies the remarkable **Grotta di Buontalenti**, one of the architect's most imaginative works, anticipating Gaudí with his dripping, stalactite-like stone, from which fantastic limestone animals struggle to emerge. Casts of Michelangelo's *nonfiniti* slaves stand in the corners, replacing the originals put there by the Medici, while back in the shadowy depths stands a luscious statue of Venus coming from her bath by Giambologna. Once restoration is complete, after a drought of centuries, the Grotta should soon gush again.

Casa Guidi

Piazza San Felice 8; open April–Nov Mon, Wed and Fri 3–6; closed Dec–Mar; donations expected.

In the old days the neighbourhood around the Pitti was a fashionable address, but during the 19th century rents for a furnished palace were incredibly low. Shortly after their secret marriage, the Brownings found one of these, the Casa Guidi at the perfect place to settle; during their 13 years here they wrote their most famous poetry. The house is now owned by the Browning Institute. Dostoevsky wrote *The Idiot* while living nearby, at No.21 Piazza Pitti.

Stuffed Animals and Wax Cadavers

Past the Pitti on Via Romana 17, is one of Florence's great oddball attractions, the **La Specola** museum (*open Thurs–Tues 9–1; adm*). The **Zoological Section** has a charmingly old-fashioned collection of nearly everything that walks, flies or swims, from the humble sea worm to the rare Madagascar Aye-Aye or the swordfish, with an accessory case of different blades. The real horror show stuff, however, is kept hidden away in the **Museum of Waxes**; dotty, prudish old Cosimo III was a hypochondriac and morbidly obsessed with diseases, which his favourite artist, a Sicilian priest named Gaetano Zumbo, was able to portray with revolting realism.

Santo Spirito

Open Mon–Fri 8.30–12 and 4–6, Sat and Sun 4–6; closed Wed pm.

Piazza Santo Spirito, the centre of the Oltrarno, usually has a few market stalls in the morning under the plane trees as well as a quiet café or two. In the evening it changes face and the bars fill with people, who meet and chat in the piazza and on the church steps until the early hours. On one side, a plain 18th-century façade hides Brunelleschi's last, and perhaps greatest church. He designed Santo Spirito in 1440 and lived to see only one column erected, but subsequent architects were faithful to his elegant plan for the interior. This is done in the architect's favourite pale grey and *pietra serena* articulation; a rhythmic forest of columns with semicircular chapels is gracefully recessed into the transepts and the three arms of the crossing. The effect is somewhat spoiled by the ornate 17th-century *baldacchino*, which sits in this enchanted garden of architecture like a 19th-century bandstand.

The art in the chapels is meagre, as most of the good paintings were sold off over the years. The best include Filippino Lippi's beautiful, restored *Madonna and Saints* in the right transept and Verrocchio's jewel-like *St Monica and Nuns* in the opposite transept. To the left of the church, in the **refectory** (*open Tues–Sat 10–1.30, Sun and hols 10–12.30; adm*) of the vanished 14th-century convent, are the scanty remains of a *Last Supper* and a well-preserved, highly dramatic *Crucifixion* by Andrea Orcagna.

Santa Maria del Carmine and the Cappella Brancacci

Open 10–5 (last adm 4.45), Sun and hols 1–5; closed Tues; adm; only 30 people are admitted at a time, for 15 minutes; you can usually avoid waiting if you go at lunchtime.

There is little to say about the surroundings, the piazza-cum-car park, the rough stone façade, or the interior of the Oltrarno's other great church, Santa Maria del Carmine, which burned in 1771 and was reconstructed shortly after. Miraculously, the **Cappella Brancacci**, one of the landmarks in Florentine art, survived both the flames and attempts by the authorities to replace it with something more fashionable. Three artists worked on the Brancacci's frescoes: Masolino, who began them in 1425, and who designed the cycle; his pupil Masaccio, who worked on them alone for a year before following his master to Rome, where he died at the age of 27; and Filippino Lippi, who finished them 50 years later. Filippino took care to imitate Masaccio as closely as possible, and the frescoes have an appearance of stylistic unity. Between 1981 and 1988 they were subject to one of Italy's most publicized restorations, cleansed of 550 years of dirt and overpainting, enabling us to see what so thrilled the painters of the Renaissance.

Masaccio in his day was a revolution and a revelation in his solid, convincing naturalism; his figures stand in space, without any fussy ornamentation or Gothic grace, very much inspired by Donatello's sculptures. Masaccio conveyed emotion with broad, quick brushstrokes and with his use of light, most obvious in the *Expulsion of Adam and Eve*, one of the most memorable and harrowing images created in the Renaissance. In the *Tribute Money*, the young artist displays his mastery of artificial perspective and light effects. The three episodes in the fresco show an official demanding tribute from the city, St Peter fetching it on Christ's direction from the mouth of a fish, and lastly, his handing over of the money to the official.

Other works by 'Shabby Tom' include *St Peter Baptizing* on the upper register, and *St Peter Healing with his Shadow* and *St Peter Enthroned and Resurrecting the Son of the King of Antioch*, the right half of which was finished by Filippino Lippi. The elegant Masolino is responsible for the remainder, except for the lower register's *Release of St Peter from Prison*, *St Peter Crucified* and *St Paul Visiting St Peter in Prison*, all by Filippino Lippi, based on Masaccio's sketches.

Among the detached frescoes displayed in the cloister and refectory is a good one by Filippino's dad, Fra Filippo Lippi, who was born nearby in Via dell'Ardiglione.

A City with a View

Great Aunt Florence, with her dour complexion and severe, lined face, never was much of a looker from street level, but she improves with a bit of distance, either mental or from one of her hilltop balconies: the Belvedere Fort, San Miniato, Piazzale Michelangelo, Bellosguardo, Fiesole or Settignano.

Belvedere Fort and Arcetri

One of Florence's best and closest balconies is the rather run-down **Belvedere Fort** (*currently closed for what looks to be a long bout of restoration*), a graceful, six-point star designed by Buontalenti and built in 1590–5, not so much for the sake of defence but to remind any remaining Florentine republicans who was boss. Since 1958, it has been used for special exhibitions, but you can usually enjoy unforgettable views of Florence and the surrounding countryside from its ramparts. Leading up to it is one of Florence's prettiest streets, **Costa San Giorgio**, which begins in Piazza Santa Felicità, just beyond the Ponte Vecchio.

In this part of Florence, the countryside begins right at the city wall, a rolling landscape of villas and gardens, olives and cypresses. Via San Leonardo winds its way out towards Arcetri; a 10-minute walk will take you to the 11th-century **San Leonardo in Arcetri** (*usually open Sun am*). There is a wonderful 13th-century pulpit, originally built for San Pier Scheraggio, and a small rose window, made according to legend from a wheel of Fiesole's *carroccio*, captured by Florence in 1125.

San Miniato

Open summer daily 8–7.30, winter daily 8–12.30 and 2.30–7.30.

From Porta San Miniato you can walk up to San Miniato church on the stepped Via di San Salvatore al Monte, complete with the Stations of the Cross, or take the less

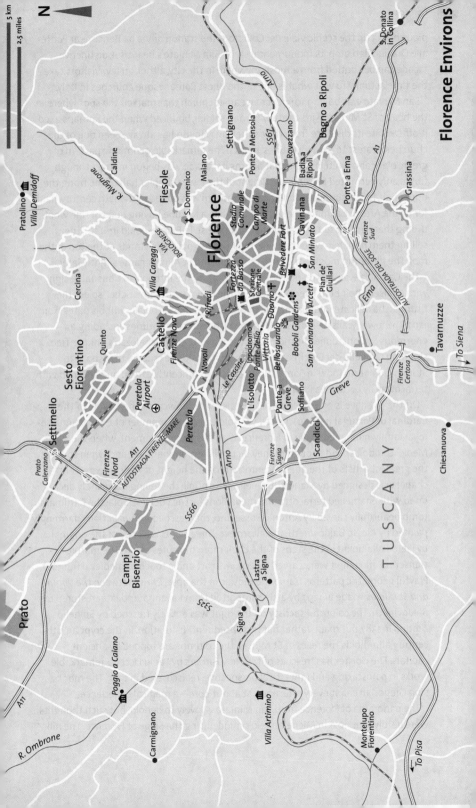

Florence Environs

N
5 km
2.5 miles

Florence

TUSCANY

Prato
Settimello
Prato Calenzano
Campi Bisenzio
Sesto Fiorentino
Settignano
Quinto
Cercina
Caldine
Fiesole
S. Domenico
Maiano
Settignano
Ponte a Mensola
Rovezzano
Bagno a Ripoli
S. Donato in Collina
Pratolino
Villa Demidoff
R. Mugnone
Via Careggi
Villa Careggi
Via Bolognese
Castello
Firenze Nova
Rifredi
Novoli
Peretola Airport
Peretola
Firenze Nord
Firenze Mare
Autostrada Firenze-Mare
A11
A11
Le Cascine
L'Isolotto
Ponte della Vittoria
Ippodromo
Ponte a Greve
Soffiano
Scandicci
Arno
Firenze Signa
Lastra a Signa
Signa
SS66
SS35
Poggio a Caiano
Carmignano
R. Ombrone
Montelupo Fiorentino
Villa Artimino
To Pisa
Stadio Comunale
Campo di Marte
Fortezza da Basso
Stazione Centrale
Duomo
Belvedere Fort
Boboli Gardens
Bellosguardo
San Miniato
San Leonardo in Arcetri
Pian de' Giullari
Gavinana
Badia a Ripoli
Ponte a Ema
Grassina
Firenze Sud
A1
Autostrada del Sole
Greve
Ema
Firenze Certosa
Tavarnuzze
Chiesanuova
To Siena
Arno
SS67

pious bus 13 up the scenic Viale dei Colli from the station or Via de Benci, near Ponte alle Grazie. High atop its monumental steps, San Miniato's beautiful, distinctive façade can be spotted from almost anywhere in the city, although few visitors take the time actually to visit what is one of the finest Romanesque churches in Italy.

San Miniato was built in 1015, over an earlier church that marked the spot where the head of St Minias, a 3rd-century Roman soldier, bounced when the Romans axed it off. Despite its distance from the centre San Miniato has always been one of the churches dearest to the Florentines' hearts. The remarkable geometric pattern of green, black and white marble that adorns its façade was begun in 1090, though funds only permitted the embellishment of the lower, simpler half of the front; the upper half, full of curious astrological symbolism was added in the 12th century, paid for by the Arte di Calimala, the guild that made a fortune buying bolts of fine wool, dyeing them a deep red or scarlet that no one else in Europe could imitate, then selling them back for twice the price; their proud gold eagle stands at the top of the roof. The glittering mosaic of Christ, the Virgin and St Minias, came slightly later.

The Calimala was also responsible for decorating the interior, an unusual design with a raised choir built over the crypt. As the Calimala became richer, so did the fittings; the delicate intarsia **marble floor** of animals and zodiac symbols dates from 1207. The lower walls were frescoed in the 14th and 15th centuries, including an enormous St Christopher. At the end of the nave stands Michelozzo's unique, free-standing **Cappella del Crocifisso**, built in 1448 to hold the crucifix that spoke to St John Gualberto (now in Santa Trínita); it is magnificently carved and adorned with terracottas by Luca della Robbia.

Off the left nave is one of Florence's Renaissance showcases, the **Chapel of the Cardinal of Portugal** (1461–6). The 25-year-old cardinal, a member of the Portuguese royal family, happened to die in Florence at an auspicious moment, when the Medici couldn't spend enough money on publicly prominent art, and when some of the greatest artists of the quattrocento were at the height of their careers. The chapel was designed by Manetti, Brunelleschi's pupil; the ceiling exquisitely decorated with enamelled terracotta and medallions by Luca della Robbia; the Cardinal's tomb beautifully carved by Antonio Rossellino; the frescoed *Annunciation* charmingly painted by Alesso Baldovinetti; the altarpiece *Three Saints* is a copy of the original by Piero Pollaiuolo. Up the steps of the choir more treasures await. The marble transenna and pulpit were carved in 1207, with art and a touch of medieval humour. Playful geometric patterns frame the mosaic in the apse, *Christ between the Virgin and St Minias*, made in 1297 by artists imported from Ravenna, and later restored by Baldovinetti. The colourful **sacristy** on the right was entirely frescoed by Spinello Aretino in 1387, but made rather flat by subsequent restoration. In the **crypt** an 11th-century altar holds the relics of St Minias; the columns are topped by ancient capitals. The **cloister** has frescoes of the Holy Fathers by Paolo Uccello, remarkable works in painstaking and fantastical perspective, rediscovered in 1925. The monks sing Gregorian chant every afternoon at about 4pm – a magical experience.

The panorama of Florence from San Miniato is lovely to behold, but such thoughts were hardly foremost in Michelangelo's mind during the Siege of Florence. The hill was vulnerable, and to defend it he hastily erected the fortress (now surrounding the cemetery to the left of the church), placed cannons in the unfinished 16th-century campanile (built to replace one that fell over), and shielded the tower from artillery with mattresses. He grew fond of the small church below San Miniato, **San Salvatore al Monte**, built by Cronaca in the late 1400s, which he called his 'pretty country lass'.

With these associations in mind, the city named the vast, square terrace car park below **Piazzale Michelangelo**, the most popular viewpoint only because it is the only one capable of accommodating an unlimited number of tour buses (though now there are restrictions on the length of time buses are allowed to stop, the situation has improved a bit). On Sunday afternoons, crowds of Florentines habitually make a stop here during their afternoon *passeggiata*. Besides another copy of the *David* and a fun, tacky carnival atmosphere rampant with souvenirs, balloons and ice cream, the Piazzale offers views that can reach as far as Pistoia on a clear day.

Bellosguardo

Many would argue that the finest view over Florence is from Bellosguardo, located almost straight up from Porta Romana at the end of the Boboli Gardens or Piazza Torquato Tasso. Non-mountaineers may want to take a taxi; the famous viewpoint, from where you can see every church façade in the city, is just before Piazza Bellosguardo. The area is a peaceful little oasis of superb villas and houses gathered round a square – there are no shops, bars or indeed anything commercial.

Fiesole

Florence liked to regard herself as the daughter of Rome, and in her fractious heyday explained her quarrelsome nature by the fact that her population from the beginning was of mixed race, of Romans and 'that ungrateful and malignant people who of old came down from Fiesole', according to Dante.

First settled in the 2nd millennium BC, Fiesole became the most important Etruscan city in the region. Yet from the start Etruscan *Faesulae*'s relationship with Rome was rocky, especially after sheltering Catiline and his conspirators in 65 BC. Its lofty position made Fiesole too difficult to capture, so the Romans built a camp below on the Arno to cut off its supplies. Fiesole was eventually taken, and dwindled as the camp below grew into the city of Florence, growth the Romans encouraged to spite the old Etruscans on their hill. This easily defended hill, however, ensured Fiesole's survival in the Dark Ages. When times became safer, families began to move back down to the Arno to rebuild Florence. They returned to smash up most of Fiesole after defeating it in 1125; since then the little town has remained aloof, letting Florence dominate and choke in its own juices far, far below.

But ever since the days of the *Decameron*, whose storytellers retreated to its garden villas to escape the plague, Fiesole has played the role of Florence's aristocratic suburb; its cool breezes, beautiful landscapes and belvedere views make it the perfect refuge from the torrid Florentine summers. There's no escaping the tourists, however;

we foreigners have been tramping up and down Fiesole's hill since the days of Shelley. A day trip has become an obligatory part of a stay in Florence, and although Fiesole has proudly retained its status as an independent *comune*, you can make the 20-minute trip up on Florence city bus 7 from the station or Piazza San Marco. If you have the time, walk up (or perhaps better, down) the old lanes bordered with villas and gardens to absorb some of the world's most civilized scenery.

Around Piazza Mino

The long sloping stage of Piazza Mino is Fiesole's centre, with the bus stop, the local tourist office, the cafés and the **Palazzo Pretorio**, its loggia and façade emblazoned with coats of arms. The square is named after a favourite son, the quattrocento sculptor Mino da Fiesole, whom Ruskin preferred to all others. An example of his work may be seen in the **Duomo**, whose plain façade dominates the north side of the piazza. Built in 1028, it was the only building spared by the vindictive Florentines in 1125. It was subsequently enlarged and given a scouring 19th-century restoration, leaving the tall, crenellated campanile as its sole distinguishing feature. Still, the interior has an austere charm, with a raised choir over the crypt that is similar to that of San Miniato.

Up the steps to the right are two works by Mino da Fiesole: the *Tomb of Bishop Leonardo Salutati* and an altar front. The main altarpiece in the choir, of the Madonna and saints, is by Lorenzo di Bicci, from 1440. Note the two saints frescoed on the columns; it was a north Italian custom to paint holy people as if they were members of the congregation. The crypt, holding the remains of Fiesole's patron, St Romulus, is supported by columns bearing doves, spirals and other early Christian symbols.

Located on Via Dupré, the **Bandini Museum** (*open summer daily 10–7, winter Wed–Mon 10–5; adm*) contains sacred works, including della Robbia terracottas and trecento paintings by Lorenzo Monaco, Neri di Bicci and Taddeo Gaddi.

Archaeological Zone

Behind the cathedral and museum is the entrance to what remains of *Faesulae*. Because Fiesole avoided trouble in the Dark Ages, its Roman monuments have survived in much better shape than those of Florence; although hardly spectacular, the ruins are charmingly set amid olive groves and cypresses.

The small **Roman theatre** (*open summer Wed–Mon 9.30–7, winter Wed–Mon 9.30–5; adm*) has survived well enough to host plays and concerts in the summer; Fiesole would like to remind you that in ancient times it had the theatre and plays while Florence had the amphitheatre and wild beast shows. Close by are the rather confusing remains of two superimposed temples, the baths and an impressive stretch of Etruscan walls (best seen from Via delle Mure Etrusche, below) that proved their worth against Hannibal's siege.

The **Archaeology Museum** (*opening hours as for Roman Theatre*), in a small 20th-century Ionic temple, displays early bronze figurines with flapper wing arms, Etruscan urns and stelae, including the interesting 'stele Fiesolana' with a banquet scene.

Walking around Fiesole

From Piazza Mino, Via San Francesco ascends steeply (at first) to the hill that served as the Etruscan and Roman acropolis. Halfway up is a terrace with extraordinary views of Florence and the Arno sprawl. The church nearby, the **Basilica di Sant'Alessandro**, was constructed over an Etruscan/Roman temple in the 6th century. At the top of the hill, square on the ancient acropolis, stands the monastery of **San Francesco**, its church containing a famous early cinquecento *Annunciation* by Raffaellino del Garbo and an *Immaculate Conception* by Piero di Cosimo.

There are much longer walks to be had along the hill behind the Palazzo Pretorio. The panoramic Via Belvedere leads back to Via Adriano Mari, and in a couple of kilometres to the bucolic **Montecéceri**, a wooded park where Leonardo da Vinci performed his flight experiments, and where Florentine architects once quarried their dark *pietra serena* from quarries now abandoned but open for exploration.

San Domenico di Fiesole

San Domenico is a pleasant walk from Fiesole towards Florence down Via Vecchia Fiesolana, a steep, narrow road that passes the **Villa Medici** (*Via Beato Angelico 2, privately owned, open Mon–Fri 9–1, ring the bell*), built by Michelozzo for Cosimo il Vecchio; Lorenzo and his friends of the Platonic Academy would come to escape the world within its lovely gardens; it was also Iris Origo's childhood home.

San Domenico, at the bottom of the lane, is where Fra Angelico first entered his monkish world. The church of **San Domenico** (15th century) contains his *Madonna with Angels and Saints*, in a chapel on the left, and a photograph of his *Coronation of the Virgin*, which the French snapped up in 1809 and sent to the Louvre. Across the nave there's a *Crucifixion* by the school of Botticelli, an unusual composition of verticals highlighted by the cypresses in the background. In the chapterhouse of the monastery (*ring the bell at No.4*) Fra Angelico left a fine fresco *Crucifixion* and a *Madonna and Child*, which is shown with its sinopia, before moving down to Florence and San Marco.

Badia Fiesolana

The lane in front of San Domenico leads to the Badia Fiesolana (*open Mon–Fri 9–5, Sat 9–12*), Fiesole's cathedral, built in the 9th century by Fiesole's bishop, an Irishman named Donatus, with a fine view over the countryside and Florence. Later enlarged, it preserves its original elegant façade, a charming example of the geometric black and white marble inlay decoration that characterizes Tuscan Romanesque churches, while the interior is adorned with *pietra serena* in the style of Brunelleschi.

Settignano

The least touristic hill above Florence is under the village of Settignano (bus 10 from the station or Piazza San Marco). The road passes **Ponte a Mensola**, Boccaccio's childhood home; he set scenes of the *Decameron* at the Villa Poggio Gherardo. A

Scottish Benedictine named Andrew founded its church of **San Martino a Mensola** in the 9th century and was later canonized. The church was rebuilt in the 1400s, it has three trecento works: Taddeo Gaddi's *Triptych*, his son Agnolo's paintings on Andrew's casket, and a high altar triptych by the school of Orcagna. Quattrocento works include Neri di Bicci's *Madonna and Saints* and an *Annunciation*.

Settignano is one of Tuscany's great cradles of sculptors, producing Desiderio da Settignano and Antonio and Bernardo Rossellino; Michelangelo spent his childhood here, at Villa Buonarroti. Strangely, they left behind no work as a reminder; the good art in **Santa Maria** church is by Andrea della Robbia (an enamelled terracotta *Madonna and Child*) and Buontalenti (the pulpit). However, there are more splendid views from Piazza Desiderio, and a couple of places to quaff a glass of Chianti.

Medici Villas

Like their Bourbon cousins in France, the Medici dukes liked to while their time away acquiring new palaces for themselves. In their case, however, the reason was less self-exaltation than simple property speculation; the Medici always thought generations ahead. As a result the countryside around Florence is littered with Medici villas, most now privately owned, though some are partly open to the public.

Villa Careggi

Open Mon–Fri 9–6, Sat 9–12; but you can stroll through the grounds for free.

Perhaps the best-known is Careggi (Viale Pieraccini 17, bus 14C from the station), originally a fortified farmhouse, but enlarged for Cosimo il Vecchio by Michelozzo in 1434. In the 1460s this villa became synonymous with the birth of humanism.

The greatest Latin and Greek scholars of the day, Ficino, Poliziano, Pico della Mirandola and Argyropoulos, would sometimes meet here with Lorenzo il Magnifico and hold philosophical discussions in imitation of a Platonic symposium, calling their informal society the Platonic Academy. It fizzled out when Lorenzo died. Cosimo il Vecchio and Piero had both died at Careggi and, when he felt the end was near, Lorenzo had himself carried out to the villa, with Poliziano and Pico della Mirandola to bear him company. After Lorenzo died, the villa was burned by Florentine republicans, though Cosimo I later had it rebuilt, and Francis Sloane had it restored.

Villa Demidoff at Pratolino

Open April–Sept Thurs–Sun 10–8; Mar and Oct Sun 10–6; closed Nov–Feb; adm. Take bus 25 which leaves about every 20mins from the station.

The village of Pratolino lies 12km north of Florence along Via Bolognese and it was here that Duke Francesco I bought a villa in the 1568 as a gift to his mistress, the Venetian Bianca Capello. Francesco commissioned Buontalenti – artist, architect, and hydraulics engineer – to design the enormous gardens. He made Pratolino the marvel of its day, full of water tricks, ingenious automata and a famous menagerie.

Sadly, none of Buontalenti's marvels has survived, but the largest ever example of this play between art and environment has – Giambologna's massive *Apennino*, a giant rising from stone, part stalactite, part fountain himself, conquering the dragon, said to be symbolic of the Medici's origins in the Mugello just north of here. The rest of the park, made into an English garden by the Lorena family and named for Prince Paolo Demidoff who bought it in 1872 and restored Francesco's servants' quarters as his villa, is an invitingly cool refuge from a Florentine summer afternoon.

Poggio a Caiano

Open Nov–Feb 8.15–3.30; April, May and Sept 8.15–5.30; Mar and Oct 8.15–4.30; June–Aug 8.15–6.30; adm. CAP buses, t 055 214637, go past every half-hour, departing from in front of McDonald's on the north side of the station.

Of all the Medici villas, Poggio a Caiano is the most evocative of the country idylls so delightfully described in the verses of Lorenzo il Magnifico; this was not only his favourite retreat, but is generally considered the very first Italian Renaissance villa. Lorenzo purchased a farmhouse here in 1480, and commissioned Giuliano da Sangallo to rebuild it in a classical style. It was Lorenzo's sole architectural commission, and its classicism matched the mythological nature poems he composed here, most famously 'L'Ambra', inspired by the stream Ombrone that flows nearby.

Sangallo designed the villa according to Alberti's description of the perfect country house in a style that presages Palladio, and added a classical frieze on the façade, sculpted with the assistance of Andrea Sansovino (now replaced with a copy). Some of the other features – the clock, the curved stair and central loggia – were later additions. In the **interior** Sangallo designed an airy, two-storey *salone*, which the two Medici popes had frescoed by 16th-century masters Pontormo, Andrea del Sarto, Franciabigio and Allori. The subject, as usual, is Medici self-glorification, and depicts family members dressed as Romans in historical scenes that parallel events in their lives. In the right lunette, around a large circular window, Pontormo painted the lovely *Vertumnus and Pomona* (1521), a languid summer scene under a willow tree, beautifully coloured. In another room, Francesco I and Bianca Cappello his wife died in 1587, only 11 hours apart; Francesco was always messing with poisons but in fact a nasty virus was the probable killer.

In the **grounds** (*open same hours as villa*) are fine old trees and a 19th-century statue celebrating Lorenzo's 'L'Ambra'.

Carmignano and Villa Artimino

A local bus continues 5km southwest of Poggio a Caiano to the village of **Carmignano**, which possesses, in its church of **San Michele** (*open daily 7.30–5, until 6 in summer*), Pontormo's uncanny painting *The Visitation* (1530s), a masterpiece of Florentine Mannerism. There are no concessions to naturalism here – the four soulful, ethereal women, draped in Pontormo's customary startling colours, barely touch the ground, standing before a scene as substantial as a stage backdrop. The result is one of the most unforgettable images produced in the 16th century.

Also to the south, at **Comeana** (3km, signposted), is the well-preserved Etruscan **Tomba di Montefortini**, a 7th-century BC burial mound, 35ft high and 260ft in diameter, covering two chambers. A long hall leads to the vestibule and tomb chamber, both covered with false vaulting; the latter preserves a shelf most probably used for gifts for the afterlife. Nearby, the equally impressive **Tomba dei Boschetti** was seriously damaged over centuries by local farmers (*both open Mon–Sat 8–2; closed Sun*).

The Etruscan city of Artimino, 4km to the west, was destroyed by the Romans and is now the site of a small town and another Medici property, the **Villa Artimino** ('La Ferdinanda'), built as hunting lodge for Ferdinando I by Buontalenti. Its semi-fortified air with buttresses was aimed to fit its sporting purpose, but the total effect is simple and charming, with the long roofline punctuated by innumerable chimneys and a graceful stair, added in the 19th century from a drawing by the architect in the Uffizi.

There is an **Etruscan Archaeological Museum** in the basement, containing findings from the tombs; among them a unique censer with two basins and a boat, bronze vases, and a red figured krater painted with initiation scenes, found in a 3rd-century tomb (*villa open for guided tours only on Tues, t 055 875 1427; museum open Thurs–Tues 9.30–12.30; adm*). There's a convenient place for lunch in the grounds. Also in Artimino is an attractive Romanesque church, **San Leonardo**, built of stones salvaged from earlier buildings.

Poggio Imperiale and the Certosa del Galluzzo

One last villa open for visits, the **Villa di Poggio Imperiale** (*open Wed 10–12 by request, t 055 220151*), lies south of Florence, at the summit of Viale del Poggio Imperiale, which leaves Porta Romana with a stately escort of cypress sentinels. Cosimo I grabbed this huge villa from the Salviati family in 1565, and it remained a ducal property until there were no longer any dukes to duke. Its neoclassical façade was added in 1808, and the audience chamber was decorated in the 17th century by the underrated Rutilio Manetti and others. Much of the villa is now used as a girls' school.

The **Certosa del Galluzzo** (also known as the Certosa di Firenze) lies further south, scenically located on a hill off the Siena road (*open Tues–Sun 9–12 and 3–6, 3–5 in winter; take bus 36 or 37 from the station*). Founded as a Carthusian monastery by 14th-century tycoon Niccolò Acciaiuoli, the monastery has been inhabited since 1958 by Cistercians; there are 12 now living there, one of whom takes visitors around.

The Certosa has a fine 16th-century courtyard and an uninteresting church, though the crypt-chapel of the lay choir contains some impressive tombs. The Chiostro Grande, surrounded by the monks' cells, is decorated with 66 majolica tondi of prophets and saints by Giovanni della Robbia and assistants; one cell is opened for visits, and it seems almost cosy. The Gothic Palazzo degli Studi, intended by the founder as a school, contains five lunettes by Pontormo, painted while he and his pupil Bronzino hid out here from the plague in 1522.

Language

The fathers of modern Italian were Dante, Manzoni, and television. Each did their part in creating a national language from an infinity of regional and local dialects; the Florentine Dante, the first 'immortal' to write in the vernacular, did much to put the Tuscan dialect into the foreground of Italian literature. Manzoni's revolutionary novel, *I Promessi Sposi* (The Betrothed), heightened national consciousness by using an everyday language all could understand in the 19th century. Television in the last few decades has been performing an even more spectacular linguistic unification; although the majority of Italians still speak a dialect at home, school and at work, their TV idols still insist on proper Italian.

Perhaps because they are so busy learning their own beautiful but grammatically complex language, Italians are not especially adept at learning others. English lessons, however, have been the rage for years, and at most hotels and restaurants there will be someone who speaks some English. In small towns and out of the way places, finding an Anglophone may prove more difficult. The words and phrases below should help you out in most situations, but the ideal way to come to Italy is with some Italian under your belt; your visit will be richer, and you're much more likely to make some Italian friends.

For a list of foods, *see* **Food and Drink**, p.72–4.

Pronunciation

Italian words are pronounced phonetically. Every vowel and consonant (except 'h') is sounded. Consonants are the same as in English, except the 'c' which, when followed by an 'e' or 'i', is pronounced like the English 'ch' (*cinque* thus becomes 'cheenquay'). Italian 'g' is also soft before 'i' or 'e' as in *gira*,

pronounced 'jee-ra'. 'H' is never sounded; 'z' is pronounced like 'ts'.

The consonants 'sc' before the vowels 'i' or 'e' become like the English 'sh' as in 'sci', pronounced 'shee'; 'ch' is pronouced like a 'k' as in Chianti, kee-an-tee; 'gn' as 'ny' in English (*bagno*, pronounced 'ban-yo'; while 'gli' is pronounced like the middle of the word 'million' (Castiglione, for example, is pronounced 'Ca-steel-yoh-nay').

Vowel pronunciation is: 'a' as in English father; 'e' when unstressed is pronounced like 'a' in 'fate' as in *mele*, when stressed can be the same or like the 'e' in 'pet' (*bello*); 'i' is like the 'i' in 'machine'; 'o' like 'e', has two sounds, 'o' as in 'hope' when unstressed (*tacchino*), and usually 'o' as in 'rock' when stressed (*morte*); 'u' is pronounced like the 'u' in 'June'.

The accent usually (but not always!) falls on the penultimate syllable. Also note that, in the big northern cities, the informal way of addressing someone as you, *tu*, is widely used; the more formal *lei* or *voi* is commonly used in provincial districts.

Useful Words and Phrases

yes/no/maybe *si/no/forse*
I don't know *Non lo so*
I don't understand (Italian) *Non capisco (italiano)*
Does someone here speak English? *C'è qualcuno qui che parla inglese?*
Speak slowly *Parla lentamente*
Could you assist me? *Potrebbe aiutarmi?*
Help! *Aiuto!*
Please/Thank you (very much) *Per favore/(Molte) grazie*
You're welcome *Prego*
It doesn't matter *Non importa*
All right *Va bene*
Excuse me *Mi scusi*
Be careful! *Attenzione!*

Nothing *Niente*
It is urgent! *È urgente!*
How are you? *Come sta?*
Well, and you? *Bene, e Lei?*
What is your name? *Come si chiama?*
Hello *Salve or ciao (both informal)*
Good morning *Buongiorno (formal hello)*
Good afternoon, evening *Buonasera (also formal hello)*
Good night *Buona notte*
Goodbye *ArrivederLa (formal), arrivederci, ciao (informal)*
What do you call this in Italian? *Come si chiama questo in italiano?*
What?/Who?/Where? *Che?/Chi?/Dove?*
When?/Why? *Quando?/Perché?*
How? *Come?*
How much? *Quanto?*
I am lost *Mi sono smarrito*
I am hungry/thirsty/sleepy *Ho fame/sete/sonno*
I am sorry *Mi dispiace*
I am tired *Sono stanco*
I am ill *Mi sento male*
Leave me alone *Lasciami in pace*
good/bad *buono; bravo / male; cattivo*
hot/cold *caldo/freddo*
slow/fast *lento/rapido*
up/down *su/giù*
big/small *grande/piccolo*
here/there *qui/lì*

Travel Directions

One (two) ticket(s) to Naples, please *Un biglietto (due biglietti) per Napoli, per favore*
one way *semplice/andata*
return *andata e ritorno*
first/second class *Prima/seconda classe*
I want to go to... *Desidero andare a...*
How can I get to...? *Come posso andare a...?*
Do you stop at...? *Ferma a...?*
Where is...? *Dov'è...?*
How far is it to...? *Quanto siamo lontani da...?*
What is the name of this station? *Come si chiama questa stazione?*
When does the next ... leave? *Quando parte il prossimo...?*
From where does it leave? *Da dove parte?*
How much is the fare? *Quant'è il biglietto?*
Have a good trip *Buon viaggio!*

Shopping, Services, Sightseeing

I would like... *Vorrei...*
Where is/are... *Dov'è/Dove sono...*
How much is it? *Quanto costa questo?*
open/closed *aperto/chiuso*
cheap/expensive *a buon prezzo/caro*
bank *banca*
beach *spiaggia*
bed *letto*
church *chiesa*
entrance/exit *entrata/uscita*
hospital *ospedale*
money *soldi*
newspaper (foreign) *giornale (straniero)*
pharmacy *farmacia*
police station *commissariato*
policeman *poliziotto*
post office *ufficio postale*
sea *mare*
shop *negozio*
room *camera*
tobacco shop *tabaccaio*
WC *toilette/bagno*
men *Signori/Uomini*
women *Signore/Donne*

Days

Monday *lunedì*
Tuesday *martedì*
Wednesday *mercoledì*
Thursday *giovedì*
Friday *venerdì*
Saturday *sabato*
Sunday *domenica*

Transport

airport *aeroporto*
bus stop *fermata*
bus/coach *autobus/pullman*
railway station *stazione ferroviaria*
train *treno*
platform *binario*
taxi *tassì*
ticket *biglietto*
customs *dogana*
seat (reserved) *posto (prenotato)*

Numbers

one *uno/una*
two/three/four *due/tre/quattro*
five/six/seven *cinque/sei/sette*
eight/nine/ten *otto/nove/dieci*
eleven/twelve *undici/dodici*
thirteen/fourteen *tredici/quattordici*
fifteen/sixteen *quindici/sedici*
seventeen/eighteen *diciassette/diciotto*
nineteen *diciannove*
twenty *venti*
twenty-one *ventuno*
thirty *trenta*
forty *quaranta*
fifty *cinquanta*
sixty *sessanta*
seventy *settanta*
eighty *ottanta*
ninety *novanta*
hundred *cento*
one hundred and one *centouno*
two hundred *duecento*
one thousand *mille*
two thousand *duemila*
million *milione*

Time

What time is it? *Che ore sono?*
day/week *giorno/settimana*
month *mese*
morning/afternoon *mattina/pomeriggio*
evening *sera*
yesterday *ieri*
today *oggi*
tomorrow *domani*
soon *fra poco*
later *dopo/più tardi*
It is too early/late *È troppo presto/tardi*

Driving

near/far *vicino/lontano*
left/right *sinistra/destra*
straight ahead *sempre diritto*
forward/backwards *avanti/indietro*
north/south *nord/sud*
east *est/oriente*
west *ovest/occidente*
crossroads *bivio*
street/road *strada/via*

square *piazza*
car hire *noleggio macchina*
motorbike/scooter *motocicletta/Vespa*
bicycle *bicicletta*
petrol/diesel *benzina/gasolio*
garage *garage*
This doesn't work *Questo non funziona*
mechanic *meccanico*
map/town plan *carta/pianta*
Where is the road to...? *Dov'è la strada per...?*
breakdown *guasto/panne*
driving licence *patente di guida*
driver *guidatore*
speed *velocità*
danger *pericolo*
parking *parcheggio*
no parking *sosta vietata*
narrow *stretto*
bridge *ponte*
toll *pedaggio*
slow down *rallentare*

Useful Hotel Vocabulary

I'd like a double room please *Vorrei una camera doppia, per favore*
I'd like a single room please *Vorrei una camera singola, per favore*
with bath, without bath *con bagno, senza bagno*
for two nights *per due notti*
We are leaving tomorrow morning *Partiamo domani mattina*
May I see the room, please? *Posso vedere la camera?*
Is there a room with a balcony? *C'è una camera con balcone?*
There isn't (aren't) any hot water, soap, *Manca/Mancano acqua calda, sapone,*
...light, toilet paper, towels *...luce, carta igienica, asciugamani*
May I pay by credit card? *Posso pagare con carta di credito?*
May I see another room please? *Per favore potrei vedere un'altra camera?*
Fine, I'll take it *Bene, la prendo*
Is breakfast included? *E' compresa la prima colazione?*
What time do you serve breakfast? *A che ora è la colazione?*
How do I get to the town centre? *Come posso raggiungere il centro città?*

Further Reading

General and Travel

Barzini, Luigi, *The Italians* (Hamish Hamilton, 1964). A perhaps too clever account of the Italians by an Italian journalist living in London, but one of the classics.

Goethe, J. W., *Italian Journey* (Penguin Classics, 1982). An excellent example of a genius turned to mush by Italy; brilliant insights and big, big mistakes.

Haycraft, John, *Italian Labyrinth* (Penguin, 1987). One of the latest attempts to unravel the Italian mess.

Hutton, Edward, *Florence, Assisi and Umbria Revisited*, *Venice and Venetia* and *Rome* (Hollis & Carter).

McCarthy, Mary, *The Stones of Florence* and *Venice Observed* (Penguin, 1986). Brilliant evocations of Italy's two great art cities, with an understanding that makes many other works on the subject seem sluggish and pedantic; don't visit them without it.

Morris, James, *Venice* (Faber & Faber, 1960). Another classic account of 'the world's most beautiful city'.

Morton, H. V., *A Traveller in Rome* and *A Traveller in Southern Italy* (Methuen, 1957, 1969). Among the most readable and delightful accounts of the region in print. Morton is a sincere scholar, and a true gentleman. Also a good friend to cats.

Nichols, Peter, *Italia, Italia* (Macmillan, 1973). Account of modern Italy by an old Italy hand.

History

Burckhardt, Jacob, *The Civilization of the Renaissance in Italy* (Harper & Row, 1975). The classic on the subject (first published 1860), the mark against which scholars still level their poison arrows of revisionism.

Carcopino, Jérome, *Daily Life in Ancient Rome* (Penguin, 1981). A thorough and lively account of Rome at the height of Empire – guaranteed to evoke empathy from modern city dwellers.

Ginsborg, Paul, *A History of Contemporary Italy: Society and Politics 1943–1988* (Penguin, 1990). A good modern account of events up to the fall of Rome.

Hale, J. R. (ed.), *A Concise Encyclopaedia of the Italian Renaissance* (Thames and Hudson, 1981). An excellent reference guide, with many concise, well-written essays.

Hibbert, Christopher, *Benito Mussolini, Rise and Fall of the House of Medici* and *Rome* (Penguin, 1965, 1979, 1985).

Joll, James, *Gramsci* (Fontana, 1977). A look at the father of modern Italian communism, someone we all should get to know better.

Morris, Jan, *The Venetian Empire* (Faber & Faber, 1980). A fascinating account of the Serenissima's glory days.

Procacci, Giuliano, *History of the Italian People* (Penguin, 1973). An in-depth view from the year 1000 to the present – also an introduction to the wit and subtlety of the best Italian scholarship.

Rand, Edward Kennard, *Founders of the Middle Ages* (Dover reprint, New York). A little-known but incandescently brilliant work that can explain Jerome, Augustine, Boethius and other intellectual currents of the decaying classical world.

Art and Literature

Boccaccio, Giovanni, *The Decameron* (Penguin, 1972). The ever-young classic by one of the fathers of Italian literature. Its irreverent worldliness still provides a salutary antidote to whatever dubious ideas persist in your mental baggage.

Calvino, Italo, *Invisible Cities, If Upon a Winter's Night a Traveller* (Picador). Provocative fantasies that could only have been written by an Italian. Even better is his compilation of *Italian Folktales*, a little bit Brothers Grimm and a little bit Fellini.

Cellini, *Autobiography of Benvenuto Cellini* (Penguin, trans. by George Bull). Fun reading by a swashbuckling braggart and world-class liar.

Clark, Kenneth, *Leonardo da Vinci* (Penguin).

Dante Alighieri, *The Divine Comedy* (plenty of good translations). Few poems have ever had such a mythical significance for a nation. Anyone serious about understanding Italy and the Italian world-view will need more than a passing acquaintance with Dante.

Gadda, Carlo Emilio, *That Awful Mess on Via Merulana* (Quartet Books, 1980). Italy during the Fascist era.

Gilbert/Linscott (ed.), *Complete Poems and Selected Letters of Michelangelo* (Princeton Press, 1984).

Henig, Martin (ed.), *A Handbook of Roman Art* (Phaidon, 1983). Essays on all aspects of ancient Roman art.

Levi, Carlo, *Christ Stopped at Eboli* (Penguin, 1982). Disturbing post-War realism.

Levy, Michael, *Early Renaissance* and *High Renaissance* (both Penguin, 1975). Old-fashioned accounts of the period, with a breathless reverence for the 1500s – but still full of intriguing interpretations.

Murray, Linda, *The High Renaissance* and *The Late Renaissance and Mannerism* (Thames and Hudson, both 1977). Excellent introduction to the period; also Peter and Linda Murray, *The Art of the Renaissance* (Thames and Hudson, 1963).

Petrarch, Francesco, *Canzoniere and Other Works* (Oxford, 1985). The most famous poems by the 'First Modern Man'.

Vasari, Giorgio, *Lives of the Artists* (Penguin, 1985). Readable, anecdotal accounts of the Renaissance greats by the father of art history, also the first professional philistine.

Wittkower, Rudolf, *Art and Architecture in Italy 1600–1750* (Pelican, 1986). The bible on Baroque, erudite and full of wit.

Index

Main page references are in **bold**. Page references to maps are in *italics*.
Sights in Rome, Venice and Florence are indexed under each city.